THE EPISTLE TO THE ROMANS

THE EPISTLE
TO THE ROMANS

A COMMENTARY

by

FRANZ J. LEENHARDT

*Professor of New Testament in the University
of Geneva, Switzerland*

LUTTERWORTH PRESS
LONDON

First published 1961
Second impression 1962
Third impression 1964

COPYRIGHT © 1957 DELACHAUX & NIESTLÉ S.A., NEUCHATEL
(SWITZERLAND)

ENGLISH TRANSLATION COPYRIGHT © 1961 LUTTERWORTH PRESS

This book originally appeared as L'Épître de Saint Paul aux Romains, *published in* 1957 *by Delachaux & Niestlé, Neuchâtel and Paris. The English translation has been made by Harold Knight, and the text used for the Epistle to the Romans is the Revised Standard Version, by permission of the Division of Christian Education, National Council of the Churches of Christ in the United States of America.*

Printed in Great Britain by
Latimer, Trend & Co. Ltd., Plymouth

SCHOLAE GENEVENSI

AD QUADRINGENTESIMUM ANNUM FELICITER PERDUCTAE

HOC OPUS DEDICO

QUO SCRIPTUM ILLUD PAULINUM MELIUS INTELLEGATUR

UNDE LARGISSIME HAUSIT

JOHANNES CALVINUS

CONDITOR

TO THE UNIVERSITY OF GENEVA

SAFELY BROUGHT TO ITS FOUR HUNDREDTH YEAR

I DEDICATE THIS WORK

FOR THE BETTER UNDERSTANDING OF THAT PAULINE TEXT

WHICH ABUNDANTLY INSPIRED

JOHN CALVIN

FOUNDER

CONTENTS

ABBREVIATIONS

A.Th.A.N.T.	*Abhandlungen zur Theologie des Alten und des Neuen Testaments*
B.Z.A.W.	*Beihefte zur Zeitschrift für die alttestamentliche Wissenschaft*
D.B.S.	*Dictionnaire de la Bible (Supplément)*
D.Th.C.	*Dictionnaire de théologie catholique*
J.B.L.	*Journal of Biblical Literature*
Jud.	*Judaica*
M.T.	*Massoretic Text*
R.A.C.	*Reallexicon für Antike und Christentum*
R.B.	*Revue biblique*
Rev. Sc. Rel.	*Revue des sciences religieuses*
R.H.P.R.	*Revue d'histoire et de philosophie religieuses* (Strasbourg)
R.Th.Ph.	*Revue de théologie et de philosophie* (Lausanne)
Th.Bl.	*Theologische Blätter*
Th.L.Z.	*Theologische Literaturzeitung*
Th.Wb.NT	*Theologisches Wörterbuch zum Neuen Testament*
Th.Z.	*Theologische Zeitschrift*
Z.N.W.	*Zeitschrift für die neutestamentliche Wissenschaft*
Z.Th.K.	*Zeitschrift für Theologie und Kirche*

GENERAL INTRODUCTION

AT THE CLOSE of the year A.D. 56, Paul arrived in Achaia, for a final stay, before taking to Jerusalem the fruit of the generosity of the Christian communities which he had founded among the Gentiles. He remained there three months and departed on the eve of the feast of unleavened bread (Acts 20: 3–6), that is, in the spring of 57. It would seem that it was during the course of this visit that he wrote the Epistle to the Romans.* The letter shows him to us as just on the point of leaving for Jerusalem (15: 25–26); he conveys to his readers greetings from Gaius his host, who might well have been the person whom he had baptized at Corinth (1 Cor. 1: 14);† he charges Phoebe, a deaconess of the church at Cenchreae, a Corinthian port, to take his letter to those to whom it is addressed.‡

* The date of the composition of the letter cannot be fixed with complete certainty. Different estimates are made of the time which would have been required for the events which took place after the appearance before Gallio, who was proconsul of Achaia from the spring of 51 to the spring of 52. The possible range of date extends from the end of 54 to the spring of 59. We ourselves adopt the chronology of Maurice Goguel (*Introduction au N.T.*, vol. IV. 2, pp. 201ff.). Similarly M.-J. Lagrange (*Épitre aux Romains*, 1931, p. xvii–xx). But W. Michaelis (*Einleitung in das Neue Testament*, 1954, 2nd ed., p. 165) dates the composition as Easter 56, at Philippi, perhaps at Troas. On the other hand, C. H. Dodd (*The Epistle of Paul to the Romans*, 1932, p. xxxvi) and Otto Michel (*Der Brief an die Römer*, 1955, p. i) date it later, and Ed. Meyer (*Ursprung und Anfänge des Christentums*, III, 1923, pp. 51–54) dates it as late as the winter of 58–59.

† No sure inference can be drawn from the mention of Erastus. In 2 Tim. 4: 20 an Erastus is also named, which proves only that at the time of the composition of 2 Tim. it was believed that there was an Erastus at Corinth.

‡ It has been disputed that the letter was written at Corinth; 15: 25 would seem to suggest that Paul is already on his way; 15: 30–31 shows that he already knows what Acts 20: 3 says he learnt only later. Since the authenticity of ch. 16 as a part of the letter is doubtful, the arguments for composition at Corinth become negligible (see T. M. Taylor: "The Place of Origin of Romans", *J.B.L.*, 1948, pp. 281–296).

9

The circumstances in which Paul was living at this period of his life do indeed fit in with the writing of a work such as this letter. In fact Paul's last stay in Greece is characterized by certain unique features. The work of the apostle in the eastern basin of the Mediterranean is completed. The main difficulties have been surmounted. The gospel of Jesus Christ has been preached and believed. The name of Christ has been proclaimed everywhere (15: 20). With relative calmness of mind, the apostle to the Gentiles can at this moment make a summary report, as it were, of the work of the preceding years. He is about to crown his activities by taking to the mother congregation the tangible evidence of the unity of Christ's church, the seal confirming the gratitude felt by Gentile believers towards the elect people of God. But he does not merely look backward. For some time now he has been entertaining a project which is no wild adventurer's whim. Christ has called him to be the apostle to the Gentiles, and if his task is completed in the area extending from Jerusalem to Illyria (15: 19) he is thus free to undertake new tasks. The name of Christ must be carried to spheres where it has not so far been proclaimed.

If the apostle imposed on himself the rule not to work where others had already worked, it was no doubt in order to save time. The plan of evangelizing Spain was the fruit of the apostolic conscience of a man whom Christ had set aside for the purpose of making manifest the power of gospel salvation, and that among the barbarians as well as among the Greeks (1: 1–17). Time was pressing; hence the watchword was "Forward!".* Hence there was added to the apostle's reflection about past achievements the thought of the continuation of his work, one might even say the undertaking of new work, for circumstances lent quite a new stamp to the projected mission to Spain.

* This note of urgency will be increased if we admit the influence on the apostle's thought of the eschatological motives which Johannes Munck (*Paulus und die Heilsgeschichte*, 1954) has emphasized, somewhat unilaterally, it is true (E. T. *Paul and the Salvation of Mankind*). The apostle believes that his work enters into God's plan and contributes to its realization, the second coming of Christ being the culmination of this plan. This theocentric or Christocentric motive of the mission is certainly an integral part of the apostle's thought and should never be neglected.

The origins of the Christian community in Rome are wrapped in obscurity. There is nothing to show that it was founded by the apostle Peter, which does not however exclude the idea that Peter went to Rome. But neither does it owe its existence to the apostle Paul, as is evident from Rom. 15: 20 and the almost diplomatic care which Paul took in addressing it (1: 5–6).* The capital of the empire saw the influx of so many people within its walls. Likewise the Jewish communities of the Diaspora maintained the closest relations with the mother country. It is no matter for surprise that faith in Jesus as Messiah was carried to Rome by travellers, and particularly by converted Jews.

The Jewish colony in Rome was moreover an important one (numbering about 40,000 souls, many of whom were descended from freedmen).† More than once it attracted the attention of the imperial police, and finally, by issuing a decree of expulsion against these Jews, Claudius terminated its legal existence.‡ This took place in 49. Suetonius links the troubles which arose at this time with the name of a certain Chrestus.§ It is probable that we should see here the name of

* Cf. M. Goguel, *op. cit.*, p. 292. Oscar Cullmann, *Saint Pierre, disciple apôtre, martyr*, 1952, p. 69. (E.T. *Peter: Disciple, Apostle, Martyr.*)

† Cf. J. Juster, *Les Juifs dans l'empire romain*, 1914, pp. 209ff. J. B. Frey, "Les communautés juives à Rome aux premiers temps de l'église", *Recherches de science religieuse*, 1930, pp. 275ff. Pompey had brought many Jews as slaves to Rome and they were to a great extent freed later. Some of them returned to Palestine; and it was probably to them that the so-called synagogue of the freedmen (Acts 6: 9) owed its name (cf. Strathmann, *Th.Wb.NT*, vol. IV, p. 269).

‡ Suetonius (*Vit. Caes.*, V, 524). "There was often trouble among the Jews. The emperors and the Romans in general entertained complicated feelings towards them, compounded of hatred for their religious particularism, which was regarded as absurd, scorn for their ritual practices, and a sort of respect for their tenacious originality. They were felt to be a puzzle. Several times the Jews had obtained special concessions towards their religious scruples, for example as regards the cult of imperial images; they were allowed to quarrel among themselves about the nomination of the high priest, or about questions of faith. But if their quarrels threatened to disturb public order, the police would intervene, and with a heavy hand." Eugène Albertini, *L'empire romain* (Peuples et Civilisations) 1929, pp. 95ff.

§ Suetonius (*Vit. Claud.*, 25): "*Judaeos impulsore Chresto assidue tumultuantes Roma expulit*". Cf. also Acts 18: 2. Dio Cassius (60: 6) indicates only an interdiction on meetings.

Christ, misspelt as a result of the identical pronunciation which was given at this period to the vowels e and i. If we are right in this supposition, then the disorders which caused the imperial authority to take drastic measures would have arisen in connexion with the development of the Messianic faith at the heart of the Jewish church in Rome. We do not know exactly how events developed. But it seems likely that the edict of Claudius had the result of bringing about a modification, perhaps a profound one, in the composition of the Christian community which was thus deprived of its Jewish-Christian elements. On the other hand, Gentile Christians cannot have been affected by the edict. Later the interdict against the Jews was toned down or revoked, for after the death of Claudius Judaism in Rome underwent a considerable extension, and, through Poppaea, even gained influence in the immediate circle of Nero.

It is easy to guess the complex problems which must have been raised, for the life of Christian groups in Rome, by this mass return of the Jews in general and of the Jewish Christians in particular. We have absolutely no idea what the proportion of this latter was in the total Christian community of the city. But whatever it may have been, it is essential to realize that, in the absence of the Jewish-Christian element, the young church evolved in a way which made difficult the task of reintegration when the Jewish Christians returned. Doctrine and practices had developed in a way which conflicted with the characteristic sentiments of the latter. There arose in consequence a situation of uneasiness and anxiety. It was perhaps such a situation which Paul had in mind when he wrote chapters 14 and 15: 1–13, although the very general terms which he uses do not allow us to draw any definite conclusions.

Since the useful work of F. C. Baur in referring literary problems to the historical situation by which they are governed, the Letter to the Romans has been subjected to a thorough scrutiny with a view to establishing the scope of the anti-Jewish polemic which is supposed to have inspired it.

A judgment on the letter as a whole has often been orientated by chs. 14 and 15, and the discussion which they develop has thus been assigned general importance. Critics have been confirmed in this method of approach by the short notice—unlike chs. 14 and 15 of a very violent character—which we read in ch. 16: 17–20. The whole of the last three chapters have been read in the light of this indignant outburst of the apostle. In fact this method is hardly correct. Ch. 16 raises difficult problems and it is doubtful whether it is an authentic part of the original letter. As for chs. 14 and 15, their theme, by contrast with the rest of the letter, is so novel, especially if it is considered above all as a practical problem, that it is surely unwise to make any generalizations on the basis of these chapters.

It is preferable to take as our point of departure the circumstances in which the letter was formulated and the data which it provides itself. Paul does not know the community to which he is writing, and apart from chs. 14–16 he does not in any way take into account what is going on there. The appeals whether direct or indirect which are to be found in the letter (2: 1, 17, 21; 6: 1, 11, 15, 20; 7: 1, 7) may not be considered as the signs of a debate with genuine partners; they are rather so much technical literary procedure, and reflect the style of the diatribe. On the other hand the situation of the apostle when he writes his letter, and which the letter itself discloses, turns our mind in a different direction. Paul has finished the work which he has undertaken; he himself tells us this. The countries he has visited form as it were an "ecclesiastical province" centring in Jerusalem, a homogeneous area of which the holy city is the focus.* The collection for the saints at Jerusalem is the concrete sign and evidence of this geographical and ecclesiastical homogeneity. But this action, the spiritual implications of which are so tremendous, also marks the end of an epoch and of a certain field of activity.

Paul considers that henceforth there is no longer scope for his missionary work in the east; in that area he has carried the preaching of the gospel to a point of perfection and to a fullness (πεπληρωκέναι, 15: 19) which obliges him to turn towards other horizons and to open a new chapter in the proclamation of the gospel to the Gentile world. He is now about to leave the "ecclesiastical province" of Jerusalem. We

* As is suggested by the difficult κύκλῳ of 15: 19.

13

should hardly be justified in supposing that his insistence on doing this deed of homage to Jerusalem is for him a way of taking leave of the mother church. Nevertheless his departure for the distant land of Spain will remove him by so great a distance from Jerusalem that he can no longer say that he is working concentrically from the latter city. Thus he writes to Rome in order to create a feeling of spiritual and material solidarity with the church of the capital without which his mission would be both false and impossible, since it would become a purely individual undertaking. When Paul writes to Rome his mind is full of his Spanish scheme.

If we feel that the letter is to be judged in the light of this close relation to a new evangelistic plan, we shall not wish to seek the motivation of its themes in the special situation of the church to which it is addressed. Not that we should be justified in discovering in these pages a dogmatic treatise clad in epistolary guise. It is with justice that both the Tübingen school and its recent antagonist, J. Munck, have reacted against this method of approach. Paul never wrote, so far as we know, except in regard to essential and immediate tasks; he always took up his pen under the pressure of the urgencies of his mission. There is nothing in him of the academic theologian. The letter written from Corinth to Rome is no exception to this rule.

However, in this particular case, Paul no longer has to deal with purely local questions. In the situation in which we now see him at Corinth, at the conclusion of his work in the east, Paul finds himself confronted by the problem implied in the enormous extension of the church. The pause which he now makes, in a tranquillity which he but rarely enjoys, enables him to view the development of the Christian mission with a gaze which takes in the whole sweep of the work already accomplished, while his meditation on the project of evangelizing the west brings to his survey of the past unlimited future prolongations foreseen by his missionary zeal. The letter to the Romans is the fruit of this meditation. While being a missionary document on the same basis as the other letters, it expresses, better than any other, certain fundamental aspects of missionary problematics.*

* Cf. J. Munck, *op. cit.* p. 297 and *passim*.

14

In fact the extension of the church raised a problem of fundamental importance which external conditions only made more vivid. In proportion as the church grew, it was threatened with the loss of its unity. The bonds between the various churches rested less and less on that natural and concrete support supplied by geographic proximity and the intercourse it facilitated. Do Christians still belong to the same "body" even when they never see each other and rarely hear news of each other? Just when he was taking to Jerusalem the sum of money collected by his efforts from the Gentile churches Paul might well have asked himself whether such a manifestation of church unity would still be possible had it been a question of distant communities in Spain or Gaul, evangelized during his travels. Jerusalem still remained, no doubt, the mother church, but for regions as distant as Spain, what specific role could this church still claim? The external framework of the church was undergoing such changes that ecclesiology itself ran the risk of becoming impaired; for as the concrete reality of the visible church was threatened, it was likely that Christians would begin to doubt its inner reality and essential being.

To this was added the problem raised by the adherence of numerous Gentiles whom the extension of the gospel would not fail to attract. Such people, by reason of their massive numbers and great distance from the localities which constituted the very cradle of the church, risked losing awareness of their unity with other Christians, and of their continuity with the root which bore them.

Paul might have answered such questions by elaborating a doctrine of the church which would have expressed the need for adaptation to the new conditions. He might have insisted on the organization of the communities into a unified church which would have secured inner unity and its outward manifestation. In that case we should have been able to read, from his pen, a sketch of the doctrine of the visible church, any solid lineaments of which one is always surprised to find missing in his writings. How natural it would have been to emphasize in these circumstances, and on the occasion of the successfully completed collection, the eminent role of Jerusalem, the authority of the college of the Twelve, the duty of remaining in communion with the seat of the apostles, and finally the benefits which such communion must bring to the church and the faithful. Or else, turning his attention to the capital of the empire and thinking of the future rather than the past, Paul might have developed his ideas to the advantage and honour of the church in Rome. If the apostle Peter had exercised his ministry there under the aegis of special hierarchical powers, Paul ought to have challenged the Christian Diaspora to close its ranks around the authority of Christ's Vicar.

But we find nothing of all this. We find even its opposite. The problem posed will be resolved from within, by an affirmation of the deepest reality and the inner mystery of the church. The object of his letter is to show that all believers benefit from the promises made to Abraham and that, by faith and baptism, they are thus incorporated into the people of God, thanks to the secret operation of the Holy Ghost. Paul writes to the young church which is growing up in the west in order to emphasize that the doctrine which is the very heart of the gospel, justification by faith, provides at the same time an affirmation of the unity and continuity of the "ecclesia" of God. In fact, contrary to what the Jews imagine, ancient Israel was not based on the law, but rather on faith, since the whole process of God's self-revelation and saving work is linked with the promise once made to Abraham. From its very beginning the people of God was recruited by faith; it is the reign of faith which constitutes the life of the church, the law and circumcision supervening only at a later date, and then applying to the people of Israel alone. Not only then are the Gentiles justified in sharing in the ancient promises which have found their realization in Jesus Christ; they must also clearly realize that they belong essentially to the trunk of the tree which has borne them, so as to be able to acknowledge the unity and continuity of the people of God through its changing historical destinies.

Hence Paul proposes to show what essentially constitutes the people of God, or the church. First of all he defines his point of view, which is that of the gospel, considered as the power of God working in the service of His love for men and their salvation, whoever they may be, whether Greeks or Jews, all being equally called to share in the promise. In order to benefit from this promise every man must strip himself of all those things to which he looks for self-justification, whether it be his religion, as is the case with the Gentiles, or good works to which the Jews are accustomed to point. Man is a being who is incapable of justifying himself: he is a paradox to himself, a distressing absurdity, a self-contradictory creature, for he is alienated from his true self and is blind to the real cause of torment. Hence the first essential is to reveal man to himself, so that he will give up the attempt to justify himself by means of the idols he creates or the works which he performs. Neither these gods nor these works have any true ontological foundation. All men are "sinners".

It is after pronouncing such a verdict that there rings out, like a clarion call summoning the dead to awake, the central proclamation of the gospel: Jesus Christ is ordained by God to deliver man from his errors and alienations, to restore him to the fulfilling of his true vocation by instituting a new charter for humanity; man's justification is not to be sought in himself, he receives it as a gift from God through faith in the Christ who died and rose again.

What does this mean? Paul will explain it by expounding first what faith is, then the work of Christ in the believer. His explanation of faith refers us to the promise, that is, the intervention by which God graciously prevents man and undertakes to restore to his life its true meaning and substance. Faith is the welcome which man, annihilated by the revelation of his sin, accords to God's merciful dealings, his accessibility to a transcendent initiative which can at last suspend the fatal process of his self-destruction.

The essential theme consists, it will be understood, in the exposition of the workings by which God accomplishes His promise. In His mercy God wishes to restore to communion with Himself the man who trusts in His grace, with the result that a new life is thus opened up to such a one, a life that is "just", the life of the man whom divine grace justifies.

The purpose of God is hence to found a new humanity, by bringing about a rupture with the past that is, up to the present, vitiated by the inheritance of sin. In this sense Jesus Christ is a new Adam undoing the maleficent work of the first Adam and furnishing humanity with new possibilities.

In order to undo the disastrous consequences of sin, Christ offered Himself in sacrifice so as to involve in His own death man corrupted by sin. Baptism is the sacrament which effects this association with the crucified Christ. But Christ overcame death. God raised Him from the dead so that He might associate with Himself in His eternal life those who accompanied Him in His humiliation. Jesus Christ is the fountain spring of a new life, life in the Spirit, who makes His presence felt in the heart of the believer.

It is thus that as a result of faith in Jesus Christ, men become children of Abraham. They are enabled to take advantage of the promise made to Israel from its very beginnings. There then arises, however, the problem of the destiny of historic Israel, the mass of whose members have rejected the fulfilment with which Jesus Christ crowned the promise made to Abraham. This problem demands attention in the perspective of Paul's thought, since his whole argument rests on the promises given to rebellious Israel. Does the unfaithfulness of the latter to its vocation annul the promise and in consequence the whole doctrine of salvation? The reply given to this question, by emphasizing the faithfulness of God and His freedom, develops the idea that the elect people are only momentarily outside the sphere of salvation, and that secretly God is preparing their reintegration and hence the ultimate demonstration of the excellence of His original promise.

But this reply leaves one question still open. Israel after the flesh formed a well-defined sociological unit: it was a distinct people and a theocracy. If the people of God is to be no longer recruited according to the ways of the flesh, but rather through baptism, then the ethnic form of the "ecclesia" of God has disappeared and at the same time the governing features of its political existence. The problem is how to define the sociological constitution of the new people whom Jesus Christ assembles. After laying down the fundamental principle that this people consists of men who by faith and baptism have become partakers in the sacrifice of Christ,

Paul shows how such a people lives. First it lives in the power of the gifts of the Spirit accorded to the measure of faith of its members; thus it grows and affirms itself in the world as the sphere of operation of the Spirit. Next it takes its place in the world by living within the framework of existing organisms without itself nourishing any theocratic pretensions, and in obedience to lawfully constituted authority, though without forgetting that no political authority can escape the judgment of God, in the light of which it must be assessed.

Such then is the people of God and such is to be its way of life in the world henceforth. In concrete reality it effects the mingling of two traditions whose peaceful co-existence must be assured by a charitable attitude. If some believers are attached to the customs of Israel after the flesh, their opinion must be respected even if one knows it to be unjustified. They are nevertheless part of Israel. Such questions of tradition and custom are secondary. What makes the church has nothing to do with questions of eating and drinking but the deep decision of a heart surrendered to the promise fulfilled in Jesus Christ.

Thus the young church is not a different church from the ancient church. The unity of the church is rooted in the divine plan which creates and sustains the church from the time of the initial promises up to that of their fulfilment, which is every day being renewed through the conversion of the heathen. Through the dramatic crises which have given to its historic form very diverse appearances, and in spite of the sociological rupture made inevitable by the decadence of the Israelite "ecclesia", the church of God, the elect people, the true Israel, persists because God is faithful to His promises.

It would seem paradoxical to present as the central theme of the Letter to the Romans the problem of the church, in view of the fact that this letter is the only one from the pen of Paul which nowhere contains the word $\dot{\epsilon}\kappa\kappa\lambda\eta\sigma\iota\alpha$.* The special expression $\sigma\hat{\omega}\mu\alpha \ X\rho\iota\sigma\tau o\hat{\upsilon}$ is found only in 12: 5, admittedly a passage where evidently the church is in question,

* Except in ch. 16 in a purely episodic way. The genuineness of this chapter as part of the letter is even subject to debate: see later.

but the local church is meant and the text is parenetic in character. However, there can be no doubt that chs. 9, 10 and 11, whose theme is Israel as the people of God, are speaking of the ἐκκλησία since this term translates קהל in the Septuagint. These chapters form one-third of the specifically theological part of the letter. It should be realized that the proportion is considerable. If these three chapters have not the same theme as the rest of the work, such a fault would have to be explained in the composition of a letter which in other respects develops its ideas with remarkable coherence. In point of fact, critics have been very ready to give up the attempt to grasp the letter in its totality and unity. Sanday and Headlam express a current opinion when they say that "with ch. 8 Paul finished his main argument; he has presented his conception of the gospel. But certain difficulties remain. . . ."* It is assumed that such secondary questions are cleared up in chs. 9, 10 and 11, which according to this thesis are of secondary importance like the themes which they treat. In short, if those chapters had not been written, the essential letter would remain. Let us admit it; to break up in this way the Letter to the Romans is an admission of defeat, a confession that one has not been able to find the key to the unity of the whole. What we do about these three chapters is the touchstone of our interpretation of the entire work.

Ought we to be surprised that the theme of the church, in spite of the absence of the word, should be as it were the horizon towards which all the main lines of the thought expounded in the letter tend? What ought to be a matter of surprise rather is that Paul should have been able to write at such length to the Romans without striking a theme which is apparently central to his other writings. Even the Letter to the Galatians furnished a contribution of capital importance to Pauline ecclesiology; the allegory of the two mothers and the idea of the Jerusalem above which is our mother, and the very characteristic expression to denote believers: the Israel of God (cf. 4: 21–23; 6: 16). Again, we ought rather to be surprised that the thought of the apostle, so firmly rooted in the notion of the church, so decidedly corporative in

* Sanday and Headlam, *Epistle to the Romans*, 5th ed. (I.C.C.) 1902, p. 225.

tendency, should have been able to conceive a doctrine of justification by faith in view of the individual alone, fixed in a splendid and distressing isolation. For Paul on the contrary, the believer belongs *ipso facto* to the people of God. If he does not speak of the "ecclesia" in the Letter to the Romans it is because he presupposes it everywhere; the idea of it inspires his thought on every page and he does more than speak of it in literal terms, he exhibits it in its concrete and living development from the original promise to the end of time.

Thus the Letter to the Romans must be recovered for the ecclesiological patrimony of Christianity. The way in which it has always been read, and especially since the Reformation, has suffered from a mistaken perspective. Justification by faith is not a doctrine designed to save individualism—taking the word in a pejorative sense. There is no such thing as Christian individualism, if this is intended to mean that the believer by a sort of spontaneous generation springs up in history without any sociological and mystical roots, a kind of perpetual creation *ex nihilo*.

It is true that in writing to the Romans the apostle had a very special problem in view. His thought envisages the church in its actual evolution rather than in its essential nature; what is in question is its historical unity, the unity of the generations, rather than the experienced unity of Christian brethren. Above all Paul is concerned to know by what paths God guides His church through the course of world history; how in the past He guided it from the moment when His first call to man engendered the seed of the church on the basis of the promise and the answer of faith; how in the future He will guide it after the distressing faithlessness of Israel has compelled Him to modify His plans. As for the present where the past and future join hands, it is a question of seeing how God recruits His church, how He brings it to birth and builds it up; in other words the centre of the perspective must be occupied by the notions of faith and baptism so as to throw into relief the process by which the church comes to be. He wishes to show how it emerges in history in order to see by what means it persists and how it safeguards its unity in spite of outward changes.

The genetic approach to the church presents the object in

a very different light from that in which it is viewed in the other letters. But it must be emphasized that the two points of view, both of them one-sided, are remarkably complementary. It is in this way that we can account for the fact that the sixteen chapters of the Letter to the Romans do not contain a single mention of, and not even an allusion to, the Lord's Supper; the idea of participation in His body nowhere occurs; on the other hand, baptism occupies a central position and it is well known that, for the apostle's thought, baptism had replaced circumcision (Col. 2: 11–12); it is indeed a question of the church in its growth. When one sees the importance of the Lord's Supper for the First Letter to the Corinthians, one is at first surprised by the silence of Romans; but on further thought it is explainable by the fact that here the apostle not only is not concerned with the concrete life of an actual church but also is envisaging the church in the moment of its genesis rather than in that of its existence. It was necessary to insist on baptism which "creates" the church, as did formerly circumcision.

On the other hand, the sixteen chapters of the First Letter to the Corinthians reserve no place for the notion of justification by faith; for the two allusions which may be found to this doctrine are without significance for the bearing of the argument (6: 11; 1: 30). On the other hand the doctrine of the unity and the holiness of the Body of Christ—a basic theme which the apostle many times applies to local circumstances—finds its root and its verification in communion with His one body. In writing to the Corinthians the apostle had to insist on the essence of church community, since here he was confronted by the problems arising from the existence of a church which was already built up.

Complementary truths—we cannot sufficiently insist on the point; but not exclusive nor in fact successive. Protestant theologians, without going so far as to call them incompatible, have failed to keep a balance between them in their eagerness to favour the teaching of the Letter to the Romans. Catholic theologians for their part have tended to overemphasize the teaching of the Epistle to the Corinthians. With regard to the former, we have already said that they should recognize that the Letter to the Romans does not

22

betray the consistently ecclesiastical thought of the apostle. With regard to the latter we must add that they should recognize unperturbed the ecclesiological significance of the idea of justification by faith. It is astonishing with what ease some critics have eliminated the central doctrine of the letter which Paul addressed to Rome; precisely to Rome as though he wished to forestall the danger that the Roman Christians might yield to the characteristically Roman temptation of building an ecclesiastical empire. It is a pity that catholic theologians have as a consequence come to agree with authors whose methods and conclusions they normally repudiate, and to declare with them that the doctrine of justification by faith is a polemical doctrine and somewhat episodic in character.* Albert Schweitzer was saying nothing else when he made of justification by faith a "secondary crater" in the lunar landscape which he traced of the apostle's mysticism.†

All these are so many ways of disturbing the balance of Paul's thought. It is true that his writings do not make things easy for us, seeing that they offer us the various aspects of his doctrine under the pressure of the circumstances which impelled him to write. The fact that we realize the conditions under which Paul wrote should however make us all the more vigilant. We must try to appreciate the organic unity of this scattered theology by weighing each element in view of the occasions which inspired the apostle to give it precise formulation. For this purpose above all we must probe deep enough into these formulations to catch, beyond the words, the throb of life, the faith, the hope and the love of this man who had only one thought, one basis of security and one joy; Jesus Christ, his Lord and his Saviour.

---

* This is so with J. Holzner, *Paulus*, 1937, pp. 334–335 (E.T. *Paul of Tarsus*), "a work which is an honour to catholic scholarship" says Fr. Benoit, *R.B.*, 1938, p. 453. (I have been able to consult only the 1st edition of Holzner.)

† A. Schweitzer, *Die Mystik des Apostels Paulus*, 1930, p. 220. (E.T. *The Mysticism of Paul the Apostle.*) Similarly already Wrede, *Paulus* (2nd ed.) 1907, p. 72. (E.T. *Paul.*)

The plan of the epistle is simple.* It should be noted that in the first eight chapters, the homogeneity of which has always been observed, Paul has two parallel structures of thought. In the first paragraph of the first section (1: 18—3: 20) he describes the condition of man as determined by sin; in the second paragraph he proclaims that Jesus Christ, who died for the justification of the believer, delivers the latter from his wretched state (3: 21–26); in a third paragraph, which is still shorter, he speaks of the charter which governs the new life of the liberated believer who is justified by faith alone, apart from the works of the law (3: 27–31); in the fourth paragraph he considers the power of faith which introduces us into such a new state of life (4: 1–25); finally, he evokes the horizons which faith opens up, speaking of the access of the believer to ultimate grace and his participation in divine life (5: 1–11).

Having arrived at this point one might suppose that the development of his thought is finished. On the contrary, it rebounds and we find again in this second part five paragraphs, corresponding exactly and in sequence to the five paragraphs of the first part; but what has just been said from the theological angle is now about to be resumed from the point of view of its anthropological implications.

First of all there is a new evocation of the condition of humanity under sin; but now the purpose is to illuminate man's condition by the light of justification through faith in Jesus Christ. The believer finds in Jesus Christ the possibility of a new condition of life; while the first Adam had introduced into the world sin and death (which was dramatically shown in ch. 1), the second Adam inaugurates the reign of true righteousness and life (5: 12–21). The second paragraph of the first part presented the death of Christ as the means

* This has however been much discussed and the arguments advanced on either side are often of great value. Two important contributions must be pointed out: A. Feuillet, "Le plan salvifique de Dieu d'après l'Épître aux Romains. Essai sur la structure littéraire de l'épître et sa signification théologique", *R.B.* 1950 (in this connexion, see S. Lyonnet, "Note sur le plan de l'Épître aux Romains." *Mélanges Lebreton, Rev. Sc. Rel.* 1951–1952); J. Dupont, "Le problème de la structure littéraire de l'Épître aux Romains", *R.B.* 1955; see also A. Brunot, *Le génie littéraire de saint Paul*, 1955.

which God had chosen for the salvation of believers; the corresponding paragraph of the second part treats of the death of Christ from the angle of the believer's participation in it through baptism (6: 1–23). The third point of the first part announced the reign of faith as opposed to the reign of the law; the third paragraph of the second part likewise discusses the law to show its function and its nature (7: 1–25). The fourth point of the first part defined faith by showing that it gave God the opportunity of manifesting His power to fulfil His promise; just so the fourth paragraph of the second part treats of the fulfilment of the promise, for there we read the section devoted to the life in the Spirit, which is the ultimate object of the promise and of prophecy (8: 1–17). Finally the fifth and last paragraph of the first part evoked the vistas of hope in the glory of God and supernatural peace, and it is these very themes which are treated in the last paragraph of the second part (8: 18–39); the kinship of these two sections is in fact so striking that it has been possible to draw up a synoptic sketch of them;* this kinship must be rooted in the very structure of the epistle and we have shown how these two periods occupy the same place in the two parallel parts.

The rest of the letter is easily divided up. Hence the analysis of the writing as a whole is as follows: *theme*; the gospel of justification preached by the apostle as far as Spain; its *theological* aspect (1: 18—5: 11); its *anthropological* aspect (5: 12—8: 39); its *historical* aspect (9: 1—11: 36); its *ethical* aspect (12: 1—15: 33). To all this are added the greetings and exordium of the beginning and finally the closing salutations of ch. 16.

SPECIAL QUESTIONS

The Letter to the Romans raises certain problems which have no exact parallel in the other letters of Paul.

The texual tradition of the closing chapters is rather confused. The final doxology (16: 25–27) has been variously placed. Although the principal manuscripts include it where

---

* N. A. Dahl, "Two Notes on Romans 5", *Studia Theologica*, V, 1951 (1952).

we normally read it, in some it is found elsewhere and not always in the same position. Some are unaware of it or suggest that their sources were so.*

These variations are certainly not unconnected with another fact, namely the existence of two versions of the letter of unequal length. Through Origen† we know that Marcion, among other cuts,‡ eliminated chs. 15 and 16. An abridged text was thus in circulation and it obviously influenced some Western testimonies. In the absence of chs. 15 and 16 a conclusion must have been given to the letter in certain cases by transferring the doxology to ch. 14. However, some copyists who knew the longer version have attempted a conflation by putting the doxology in both places. Or else they expressed their bewilderment in the face of these divergent traditions by leaving a space blank.

The case of Papyrus 46, the so-called Chester Beatty Papyrus, which is the most ancient testimony to the Pauline writings, does not fit into this scheme and calls for a more complicated explanation. P 46 places the doxology at the close of ch. 15. Why? The least that one can say is that there perhaps existed a tradition according to which the letter closed at ch. 15. In that case ch. 16 would be an addition.

Various considerations support this hypothesis. In fact ch. 16 surprises us in a letter addressed to a community which Paul had never visited. The names which compose this very long list of greetings are not for the most part specifically Roman; they are in point of fact found throughout the empire. Some of the personages mentioned have their chief connexions in Asia rather than in Italy. No doubt we cannot exclude the possibility that Prisca and Aquila had returned to Rome; but it is at Corinth and then at Ephesus that we in fact meet them.§ The mention of "the first convert in Asia"

* The doxology is found at the end of ch. 14 in L and the Antiochene recension; in AP etc., at the end of ch. 14 and at the end of ch. 16; in P 46 at the end of ch. 15. G F do not give the doxology at all, the first leaving a space blank after 14: 23. Finally D gives the doxology at the close of the letter, but the arrangement of the text at this point (accentuation, disposition of stiches) differs from what precedes.

† *Comm. Rom.* VII, 453, ed. Lommatzsch.

‡ He had also eliminated as a whole or in part ch. 4 and 9 to 11.

§ Acts 18: 18, 19, 26; 1 Cor. 16: 19; 2 Tim. 4: 19.

26

(16: 5) may be of interest to readers in Rome, but the person alluded to would more naturally reside in Ephesus. Among those named there is no mention of the authorities of the church at Rome, neither its founders, elders, nor bishops; this omission is surprising, especially when one remembers that Paul is writing to Rome to prepare the ground for his visit and in the hope of winning over to his missionary scheme this community which he has not founded. Diplomatic courtesy required that he should include a greeting to the local authorities.

For some time now it has been thought that ch. 16 might be part of a correspondence, now lost, between the apostle and the church at Ephesus. Paul had stayed for a long time at Ephesus and knew many people there. His allusion to the help received from Prisca and Aquila would recall one of the crises which Paul had undergone in Asia. It is the same with the mention that Andronicus and Junias were fellow prisoners of the apostle. The sharp warning given against those who cause divisions and scandals would harmonize with what we know of the special dangers threatening the church at Ephesus (cf. Acts 20: 29ff.) whilst it harmonizes ill with the serene tone which prevails in the rest of the letter; this note of vehemence is foreign even to chs. 14 and 15.

We realize of course that there are objections* to the hypothesis that these greetings were intended for Ephesus. The textual tradition is not favourable to it. This single chapter cannot of itself constitute a letter, and we know nothing of a more complete letter. How can we explain the adjunction of this fragment to a letter addressed to Rome? The very variety of the conjectures proposed on the matter seems to throw doubt on their solidity. But we must also admit that there are several difficulties to be surmounted if we wish to maintain that ch. 16 originally belonged to the Letter to the Romans. Goguel speaks of a post-scriptum added to the letter itself which he supposes concluded at 15: 33.† More precisely, we should have to admit a first adjunction in vv. 1-16, to which Paul would then have added a last warning written probably by his own hand (vv. 17-20);

* They may be consulted for example in M. Goguel, *op. cit.*
† *Op. cit.*, p. 259.

27

finally the salutations from his companions (vv. 21–23) which one might imagine to have been added later at their request, perhaps after the apostle had read his letter to them. This very laboured mode of composition would, certainly, easily explain the very heterogeneous character of this ch. 16. But what a host of conjectures!

Other conjectures again are permissible. Its composite character might be taken to show that its elements do in fact spring from various sources. When, at the end of the first century, a collection of the writings of the great apostle was made, what was found in the archives would have been collected and sorted, while circumstances would have reduced some texts to a fragmentary state. In this matter the function of the great church at Ephesus must have been of primary importance. The scrap of a letter which constitutes at least the main body of this ch. 16 would then have been joined to the apostle's letter, which, as it happened, was lacking in all personal notes. Let us observe in this connexion the opinion of some critics who think it right to detach from the chapter those verses concerning Phoebe. These lines authentically belong to the original letter to the Romans. Phoebe was probably entrusted with the task of bearing the letter and they were intended as commendatory words to the Roman Christians.* Also it is sometimes felt that the severe admonition of vv. 17–20 belongs to another document, of which these few lines are all that remains—a document penned by Paul but to whom we do not know.

Finally, T. W. Manson has suggested a compromise solution; the letter, he thinks, was sent to the Romans without ch. 16, but Paul also sent his letter to Ephesus together with ch. 16 which concerned only the Christian church there.†

* Thus P. Feine—J. Behm, *Einleitung in das Neue Testament*, 1950, p. 176. W. Michaelis, *op. cit.*, 1954 (2nd ed.) p. 163.

† T. W. Manson, "St. Paul's Letter to the Romans—and others" in *Bulletin of the John Rylands Library*, 1948, pp. 224–240. Manson reminds us that some MSS. do not carry in 1 : 7 and 15 the allusion to Rome; hence tradition is a little uncertain as to the addressees. J. Munck (*Paulus und die Heilsgeschichte*, 1954) has approved the thesis of Manson. Michaelis considers it interesting but improbable. The way in which we ourselves understand the general purpose of the letter makes the idea of a double destination seem unlikely to us also.

We cannot dogmatically say that it is impossible for the greetings of ch. 16 to have been sent to Rome. But we must recognize that it is at least possible, if not probable, that they were meant for the Christians at Ephesus.

The authenticity of both chs. 15 and 16 has been contested by several critics since Baur, but this thesis raises insurmountable difficulties and is no longer sustained. It is useless then to resurrect a false problem.

The doxology, in the judgment of some, is said to be foreign to the thought of the apostle. Its liturgical style is condemned as spurious; it is pointed out that Paul never qualifies God in this way ("the only wise" and "eternal"); the mention of the prophetic writings as disclosing the hidden mystery *after* the revelation in Christ has taken place is surprising as coming from the pen of Paul; we may explain it later. These real difficulties which aggravate the insecurity of the doxology in the textual tradition lead to the supposition that we may here be confronted by a conclusion which an old copyist has added.*

BIBLIOGRAPHICAL NOTE

It is both impossible and useless to give an exhaustive bibliography of critical writings devoted to the Letter to the Romans or principally referring to it. More complete indications will be found in works which it is in any case essential to consult for a profound study of the letter. From this special point of view the commentary of O. Michel, the last to appear in a list which begins with Origen, will give adequate information about the patristic and mediaeval commentaries. The sixteenth century witnessed the appearance of two works of capital importance which, as is well known, played a part of fundamental significance in the history of

* Thus recently Ernst Gaugler, *Der Brief an die Römer*, I, 1945, pp. 7–8. There is no reason to suspect for these verses a Marcionite origin, as M. Goguel suggests, *op. cit.*, pp. 250–253. J. Dupont (*MONΩI ΣOΦΩI ΘEΩI*, Rom. 16: 27, 1946) has stressed that the formula in question is rooted not in the Platonic tradition but in the literary tradition of Jewish doxologies. Similarly, "Pour l'histoire de la doxologie finale de l'Épître aux Romains", *Revue Bénédictine*, 1948; the author is favourable to the idea of the integrality of ch. 16.

the church: the Commentary on Romans by Luther (1515–1516)* and the *Loci theologici* of Melanchthon (1521). Calvin too commented on the Letter to the Romans along with the other books of the New Testament (with the well-known exception of the Book of Revelation). Since then, means of pursuing research and commentaries proper have gone on increasing. A list of dictionaries, grammars and textual editions will be found in the bibliography of J. Héring at the beginning of his commentary on the Letter to the Hebrews. Similarly with O. Michel's commentary.

Among commentaries we may mention those of: A. Tholuck (1824), C. Hodge (1835), H. Olshausen (1835), W. M. L. de Wette (1836–1848), J. Chr. Von Hofmann (1868), A. Bisping (1870), F. Godet (1879), H. Oltramare (1881), J. T. Beck (1884), A. Schlatter (1887, under the title *Erläuterungen* . . .), R. A. Lipsius (1891), A. Schäfer (1891), B. Weiss (1890), W. Sanday and A. C. Headlam (1895), R. Cornely (1896), H. Lietzmann (1906), A. Jülicher (1907), Th. Zahn (1910), E. Kühl (1913), M.-J. Lagrange (1914), K. Barth (1919), A. Pallis (1920), O. Bardenheuer (1926), C. H. Dodd (1932), J. Sickenberger (1932), A. Schlatter (1935, under the title *Gottesgerechtigkeit*), P. Althaus (1935), E. Brunner (1938), O. Kuss (1940), J. Huby (1940), A. Nygren (1944), E. Gaugler (1945, 1952), A. Viard (1948), H. Asmussen (1952), O. Michel (1955), K. Barth (1956).†

The study of P. Bonnard, "Où en est l'interprétation de l'Épître aux Romains", *Rev. Théol. Phil.* 1951, pp. 225–243 may be profitably studied as giving an exegetic and theological introduction to the general problems raised by our Letter. As for the critical problems suggested by the text, they will be shortly dealt with further on.

* ". . . a work flowing from a single powerful stream of inspiration, and characterized by remarkable clarity and vigour", writes H. Strohl in *L'Épanouissement de la pensée religieuse de Luther de* 1515 à 1520, p. 12. In the work of H. Strohl will be found a broad critical survey of Luther's commentary.

† English translations of these commentaries include: H. Olshausen, *Biblical Commentary on the New Testament*, containing the Epistle to the Romans, 1849; F. Godet, *Commentary on St. Paul's Epistle to the Romans*, 1895; A. Nygren, *Commentary on Romans*, 1952; E. Brunner, *The Letter to the Romans*, 1959; K. Barth, *Epistle to the Romans*, 1933, and *A Shorter Commentary on Romans*, 1959.

COMMENTARY

CHAPTER
I

Paul, a servant of Jesus Christ, called to be an apostle, set apart for the gospel of God ²which he promised beforehand through his prophets in the holy scriptures, ³the gospel concerning his Son, who was descended from David according to the flesh ⁴and designated Son of God in power according to the Spirit of holiness by his resurrection from the dead, Jesus Christ our Lord, ⁵through whom we have received grace and apostleship to bring about obedience to the faith for the sake of his name among all the nations, ⁶including yourselves who are called to belong to Jesus Christ;

⁷To all God's beloved in Rome, who are called to be saints: Grace to you and peace from God our Father and the Lord Jesus Christ.

(1) PAUL IS UNKNOWN to the church of Rome. In presenting himself to it he describes himself both as "a servant of Jesus Christ"* and as "an apostle". In his introductions, Paul described himself as "a servant" once only, namely in writing to the Philippians, where it is significant that he does not claim his title of apostle. On the other hand in writing to the Galatians, of whom he has to complain, he sharply and somewhat impatiently emphasizes this title. The first of these titles suggests humility; the second, authority. In addressing people whom he does not know, there would be a touch of arrogance in invoking only the second title, while to use only the first would savour of a displeasing astuteness.†

* The words are arranged thus in B.P.¹⁰, Origen, etc. Paul several times reversed the original order, Christ thus becoming a proper name (Rom. 8: 39; 2 Cor. 4: 5; Col. 2: 6). Χριστός already denoted "Messiah".

† Every Christian is a "servant of Christ" (1 Cor. 7: 23; Eph. 6: 6), but the word has here a very special meaning; cf. Phil. 2: 22. It is a question of being the servant of the Word; the prophets were already that, but every believer is too (see Lietzmann on 1: 1).

C

In the other letters Paul describes himself as an apostle "by the will of God". He expresses the same idea when he says here that he is "called to be an apostle", i.e. an apostle by vocation. He is exercising a divinely given mandate from which he draws both the justification of his missionary activities and the authority he claims in exercising them.*

In saying that he has been "set apart for the gospel", Paul refers to the special character of his apostolic vocation. In fact, Gal. 1: 15, 16, using the same terms, shows that the apostolic vocation of Paul means in fact his mission to the Gentile world. Hence "set aside for the gospel" certainly suggests the task peculiar to Paul as apostle of the Gentiles —that mission for the accomplishment of which he has renounced all things, and which he now wishes to pursue to its completion by carrying his missionary activity as far as Spain.†

From the very beginning the whole letter is placed within the perspective of the proclamation of the gospel to the heathen and of the latter's access to the knowledge of Jesus, the Messiah.

The expression "gospel of God"‡ suggests that the preaching with which the apostle has been entrusted springs from God as its ultimate author. It is God who sets aside His heralds and gives them their message. This message, though clad in human terms, is a Word of God, an action in which God is actively present, an event in which the thought of God

* In Jewish thought, the apostle (שָׁלִיחַ) is a delegate who enjoys the authority conferred on him by his mandate; he is legally a representative of the power which sends him. Not only envoys representing ecclesiastical authority were described thus, but also men who had fulfilled a specially important task which God had laid on them (whether priestly or otherwise; e.g. Moses, Elijah, etc.). The Christian apostolate, which probably goes back to Jesus Himself, has retained the same features: the apostle represents the power which sends him forth. On this point, cf. Strack-Billerbeck, III, pp. 2ff.; Rengstorf, *Th.Wb.NT*, I, pp. 406ff.

† Vocation, the sense of being set aside, makes the apostle akin to the prophets. Paul was certainly conscious of being, in the hands of God, an instrument for the realization of the divine plan of salvation. This is a point which Joh. Munck, *Paulus und die Heilsgeschichte*, 1954, stresses very forcibly though not without a certain exaggeration in order to deliver us from psychologizing theories of the Pauline apostolate.

‡ Cf. Rom. 15: 16; 2 Cor. 11: 7; 1 Th. 2: 2, 8, 9 (Mk. 1: 14; 1 Pet. 4: 17). Matt. 10: 20; Lk. 10: 16; 2 Cor. 5: 20.

is embodied and by which it enters into the course of human history. God is the real Subject of the apostolic gospel, it is He (i.e. the Holy Spirit, or Christ Himself) who speaks.*

(2) In speaking of the gospel of God, Paul already connects the proclamation of Jesus Christ with the plan of God which the prophets first disclosed. There is only one God, who speaks differently according to the diversity of times and seasons; but His message is eternally the same, for He is true; and He ever pursues the same work, for He is faithful. His veracity and His fidelity culminate in Jesus the Christ, who says "yes" to the promises, who is the utterly conclusive "Amen" (2 Cor. 1: 20; Rev. 3: 14); in Him all that God has said is verified and confirmed. In a sense there is nothing new about the gospel, as the whole letter will show; there is no rupture between the promises which appeared to be reserved to some only, and the reality which fulfilled them for all. The culmination which the prophetic oracles find in Jesus Christ elucidates them by showing the goal to which they tended. The end illuminates the meaning of the process which led up to it. Thus Holy Scripture in its totality arranges itself into a meaningful pattern. The Word of God to the elect people remains, for the hearers of the gospel message, the prophetic word announcing the coming of Jesus Christ. The Gentile Christian church inherits the most precious of all the treasures of Israel, namely the promise.

---

* In Paul's writings, "flesh" as opposed to "spirit" has always a pejorative sense. The formula "according to the spirit of holiness" is foreign to Paul; he would have written: "according to the Holy Spirit". It is surprising to find no allusion to the cross. The juxtaposition of his "Son" and "Son of God" shows that Paul is using a given formula. The Christology of this confession seems to distinguish two successive conditions of existence, separated by the resurrection which inaugurates the life of glory. In some ways it recalls that of Phil. 2: 5-11, though it cannot be identified with the latter; an adoptionist interpretation is not excluded (Michel). Cf. on the point C. H. Dodd, *Apostolic Preaching*, 1936, p. 14; *The Epistle of Paul to the Romans*, 1932, p. 4; R. Bultmann, *Theologie des Neuen Testaments*, 1948, p. 50 (E.T. *Theology of the New Testament*); O. Michel, pp. 30-1; Ed. Schweizer, *Erniedrigung und Erhöhung bei Jesus und seinen Nachfolgern*, 1955, pp. 55-56 (E.T. *Lordship and Discipleship*).

(3f.) Nothing expresses more clearly the continuity of God's plan and of His church than the historic roots of the gospel. For the essential function of the latter is to proclaim the good news of the fulfilment of God's plan at the very heart of the people which bears the promise. The gospel represents, not a break with the past, but a consummation of it. The Son of God is in the first place the Son of David.

To express his conviction on this point, Paul seems indeed to make use of a traditional formula, a confession probably of Palestinian origin, as is suggested by the concern to connect the Messiah with the lineage of David and the similarity with the preaching of Peter as reported in the Acts, 2: 22–36 (cf. 3: 13–15; 4: 10–12).* For the apostle himself the Son of God was pre-existent to His earthly birth, but the latter appeared as a historical event and doubtless also a natural one, for there is no allusion to any miraculous birth (neither here nor in Phil. 2 or Gal. 4: 4).† The Davidic origin of the Messiah was a postulate of faith; we must see here a theological affirmation: the name of David sums up the whole history of Israel and expresses the hope that one day it will find a glorious fulfilment.

To the human conditions of existence of the Son of God as the Son of David there succeed in contrast the conditions of existence to which He is introduced by His resurrection from the dead. He is "designated Son of God in power".‡ In accordance with the pattern of thought in Phil. 2, Paul has interpreted this formula as expressive of the glorification which followed the abasement of Christ. Of course the glorification of the Son is an act of power: hence the meaning is:

* Instead of γενομένου we read in 5161.441 and the Latin MSS. γεννωμένου (natus). Vulgate: *qui factus est ei.*

† Cf. Ps. Sol. 17: 21. The expression "Son of David" is found only there in the period before Christianity, but it had become a current expression among the contemporaries of Jesus; the rabbis will often use it (see Sanh. 97–98). Cf. Strack–Billerbeck, I, pp. 11, 525. E. Lohmeyer, *Gottesknecht und Davidssohn*, 2nd ed. 1953, pp. 64ff.

‡ ὁρίζειν: to limit or define, hence determine, constitute or establish (by deed or word), which comes to mean declare, manifest. Greek commentators adopted the latter sense. The parallelism with γενομένου suggests that we see in ὁρισθέντος the second phase of the career of the Son, and not an allusion to the divine predestination of which He is said to be the object (Vulg. *praedestinatus*).

36

"established as Son of God with power" (Godet). But the Pauline antithesis is concerned with the successive conditions experienced by the Son of God; the infirmity of His flesh has given place to the power of His Spirit. The resurrection has inaugurated, first for Him, and then for believers, a new era: the Christ has been designated "Son of God in power" by the fact that His resurrection has brought into being the age of the Spirit according to ancient prophecy.* The time foretold has come, in which God is to set up a personal communion between Himself and believers; it is the Son who accomplishes this work, thus manifesting that the power of God is at work in Him to inaugurate the promised new age. For the Son is at once the Bearer and the Dispenser of the Spirit.† Hence the expression "according to the Spirit of holiness" cannot be limited to the meaning that it is "the activity of the Holy Spirit manifested in Christ during His terrestrial existence" (Godet). The thought of Paul reaches out already to the post-resurrection ministry of Christ "designated Son of God in power"; henceforth the Holy Spirit which is also the Spirit of Christ will act with power.‡

Is the resurrection of Christ the cause of His exaltation or

* The relation between the Spirit and the "world to come", as inaugurated by the resurrection, is attested in Ez. 37: 14; Joel 2: 28. For Judaism, cf. W. Bousset, *Die Religion des Judentums*, 1926 (3rd ed.), p. 394 and *passim*. P. Volz, *Die Eschatologie der jüdischen Gemeinde*, 1934 (2nd ed.), p. 392. W. D. Davies, *Paul and Rabbinic Judaism*, 1948, p. 216. Strack-Billerbeck, III, pp. 192, 134, 615; IV, pp. 882, 915ff.

† Gal. 4: 6; cf. Acts 2:33. Paul says indifferently "Spirit of God" and "Spirit of Christ". It is well known that the idea of "power" is closely connected with the idea of the "Spirit" (Lk. 24: 48; Acts 1: 8; 1 Th. 1: 5; 1 Cor. 2: 1–5; Rom. 15: 19; 2 Tim. 1: 7). Our verse should be read in the light of the antithesis "weakness: power" (cf. 1 Cor. 5: 4; 2 Cor. 13: 4; 1 Cor. 1: 24). Note that these texts offer three possible combinations: "Spirit and power"; "power of the Spirit"; "spirit of power". Cf. W. Grundmann, *Der Begriff der Kraft in der neutestamentlichen Gedankenwelt*, 1932, and *Th.Wb.NT*, II, pp. 311–318.

‡ We should not try to be too subtle about the phrase "Spirit of holiness" (cf. Test. Lev. 18: 7). It is far-fetched to think with Lagrange that what is meant is "a very specially holy Spirit, different from the Holy Spirit". Πνεῦμα ἁγιωσύνης is the exact replica of "Holy Spirit" (Is. 63: 10; Ps. 51: 11); see O. Procksch, *Th.Wb.NT*, I, p. 116. See the wise remarks of W. Sanday and A. C. Headlam, *The Epistle to the Romans*, 1930 (5th ed.), p. 9.

37

does it merely disclose the latter? ἐξ can bear the two meanings: *in virtue of* and *since*. This ambiguity of the text is further accentuated by the absence of an article.*

It is probable that this confession of faith, just quoted by the apostle, was familiar to his Roman readers. Precision of phrase was less important for him than the hope of finding fellowship with his readers by a proclamation of the faith which he had in common with them.† This faith culminates in the confession of Christ as Lord, and it is with the sovereignty of Christ that Paul connects the mention of his apostolate about which he is anxious to give detailed information such as v. 1 could only have suggested.‡

(5) It is by the Lord Himself that Paul has been called to be an apostle. Now the name *Lord* (κύριος) evokes the One before whom every creature must bow the knee (Phil. 2: 10, 11). Jesus the Messiah, linked by His natural birth to the people of Israel alone, has become the Lord of all mankind. Hence the apostolate which He instituted concerns all men. The universal Israel is continuous with the limited Israel. The extension of the preaching of the gospel to include all men is based on the elevation of the Messiah Jesus to the rank of κύριος.§

* Whilst Godet considered the temporal sense abandoned, it is kept, for example, by Lietzmann, or J. Sickenberger, *Die Briefe des heiligen Paulus an die Korinther und Römer*, 1932 (4th ed.), p. 178. The ambiguity of the text is safeguarded by the translation: "following . . ." (A. Tricot, in *Bible Crampon;* S. Lyonnet, in *Bible de Jérusalem*). O. Michel adopts the causal sense: on the ground of the resurrection. Gaugler, still more explicit, completes: in the power of the resurrection.

† His formulae are pre-theological, as Dodd says in *Romans*, p. 5. He probably makes use of expressions which are current in Christianity, and this would explain the type of phrase found here, which is not usual with him, as also the phrasing of the Christological ideas which are out of harmony with the apostle's own Christological formulae. What is here suggested rather is the phraseology of Acts 2: 22–34.

‡ Father Boismard, *R.B.* 1953, makes an interesting comparison between our verse and Acts 13: 23–39 and Heb. 1 : 5, and insists that the thought of the verse should not be interpreted in terms of essences or natures; Paul could have said that the Son was *constituted* Son of God, "understanding this expression in a functional Messianic sense" (p. 17).

§ The plural "we have received" is probably a matter of style. Paul means himself, indirectly, modestly. Popular Greek and the style of

As far as Paul personally is concerned, the call of one who persecuted the first believers was the effect of a conspicuous grace; in the mind of Paul the notions of grace and of the apostolate were closely allied (1 Cor. 3: 10; 15: 10; Gal. 2: 9; cf. also Rom. 12: 3; 15: 15). But if the apostleship was, for Paul, the result of a peculiar grace, it is also clear that the first effect of grace which made him the slave of the Christ whom he was persecuting merged with his call to be an apostle. Conversion and vocation were for him one and the same event (Gal. 1: 15–16).*

The apostolic ministry to which Paul was called is intended to bring men into "obedience to the faith" (cf. 16: 26). This expression is not quite explicit; it may mean the obedience of the believer with regard to the objective content of the faith that is preached to him; or else an obedience which is called faith; or again obedience which leads to faith. The question of faith will be taken up again in ch. 4 where it will be seen that faith is always obedience, an act of inner submission to a word which is essentially a promise, an act which accepts as true the word or the person speaking and declaring what he is about to do. Faith is the response to a God who acts to open up new possibilities; it clings to a word which is also an action; it trusts in the "good news" which is always the ultimate content of what God says. The object of faith is not an abstract proposition, a static truth. Its object is a person and the word which renders that person actively present. Consequently in faith the objective and the subjective aspects are inseparably commingled; to isolate them from each other would be to distort them; faith arises only in an encounter, in a relation which concerns both God who speaks and man who listens, God who offers and man who receives, he who makes the promise by the preaching of the good news and the one to whom the promise is made.

The expression here used by Paul defines admirably the

diatribe passed very easily from the singular to the plural. Cf. K. Dieck, *Der schriftstellerische Plural bei Paulus*, 1900, and Von Dobschütz on 1 Th. 1: 3. See, in Paul, 2 Cor. 1: 12–13; 1 Cor. 9: 11, 12; Rom. 3: 8.

* The words "through whom we have received grace and apostleship" may be interpreted as "grace *and* apostleship" or "the grace *of* apostleship". Since with Paul conversion is inseparable from vocation we must closely connect the two.

39

goal at which Christian apostleship aims; to bring men back into a state of obedience, since their present state is essentially one of disobedience (5: 19); and the obedience to which they are reclaimed is not the vain effort of the slave who cannot break his chains, but a free participation in the liberating action of God in Christ, communion with Him whose life was the incarnation of obedience. It is the faith which receives the promise of the obedience fully disclosed in Christ. Without having any definite polemical intention, the expression well brings out the contrast between the obedience of faith and the obedience which man would like to acquire by his own effort, even if on the basis of the Mosaic law.

Thus is prepared the allusion to the wide field of missionary endeavour to which Paul as apostle is called to devote himself. His work far exceeds the frontiers marked out by the knowledge of Moses and his law. It includes all peoples (cf. Gal. 1: 16; 2: 7, 9). It extends to all peoples the knowledge of the name of the God of Israel. It in fact accomplishes the mission which was that of Israel itself, i.e. to mediate the revelation of the name of God—which is to say, the person of God—to all the nations.

(6) Those to whom the letter is addressed are themselves the proof of the wide extension and efficacy of the saving grace mediated through the apostolic ministry. The existence of their church confirms the truth that Christ gathers His believers from all the nations. "You too have sprung from those peoples."*

(7) The long salutation thus culminates in its second member, by naming the addressees (v. 7 is linked with v. 1: Paul . . . to all God's beloved . . .). The Christians in Rome† are the object of God's love; they are so in virtue of their being believers, and their own love of God echoes the divine love which has struck them. They are saints, not through a holiness which their irreproachable conduct has earned for

---

* We may also understand: you live in the midst of them, in that Rome which is the meeting point of the peoples.

† The mention of Rome is lacking in some MSS., e.g. G and Orig.; as also in v. 15. Zahn (p. 51) considers it an addition.

them, but because the calling of God (cf. 1 Cor. 1:2) has set them apart so that they may shine as lights in the world (cf. Gal. 1:4; Phil. 2:15; Matt. 5:14–16). Holiness consists in being withdrawn from what is profane, and consecrated to God (Lev. 11:44; 19:2). God chooses for Himself a people which is holy for that reason, and because of that divine destiny. The new Israel is, like the ancient κλητὴ ἁγία, an assembly called to be a "holy people".*

Thus, the vocation springing from the love of God has made of these pagans "saints", incorporating them with a communion to which they were originally foreign. It is surprising not to find in this address the word "church" (ἐκκλησία);† but the expressions used by the apostle are vivid enough to imply it.

The Greeks greeted by saying χαῖρε (joy to you!) the Jews by saying שָׁלוֹם (peace!). Paul seems to make a play on words, joining these two terms in a way which recurs in all his salutations.‡ The goodness of God is the source of peace because through Jesus Christ it restores order and effects a new economy in the relations between man and God.§ The pair "grace and peace" evokes both the source and the reality of this new order which is being realized in the life of the church. For Paul there can be no better greeting than that of the angels: "Peace among men with whom God is well pleased" (Lk. 2:14). All graces are indissolubly connected with God the Father from whom they proceed and with the Lord who is the Dispenser of grace to mankind.

⁸First, I thank my God through Jesus Christ for all of you,

* Ex. 12:16; Lev. 23:2–44 (9 times); Num. 28:25, offer the expression מִקְרָא־קֹדֶשׁ. Paul seems to have used this very characteristic expression of the liturgical language of the Pentateuch, by a literal transcription into Greek. Cf. L. Cerfaux, *La théologie de l'Église suivant saint Paul*, 1948 (2nd ed.), p. 89.

† Cf. 1 Cor. 1:2; 2 Cor. 1:1; Gal. 1:2.

‡ He did not however create this formula (cf. Apoc. Bar. 78:2; Strack-Billerbeck, II, p. 25), and he knows how to vary it (Gal. 6:16: εἰρήνη καὶ ἔλεος).

§ In Hebrew thought, peace (שָׁלוֹם) refers to order rather than tranquillity. There is peace when there is order. שלם expresses the idea of integrity. (W. Foerster, *Th.Wb.NT*, II, 398ff.)

41

because your faith is proclaimed in all the world. ⁹For God is my witness, whom I serve with my spirit in the gospel of his Son, that without ceasing I mention you always in my prayers, ¹⁰asking that somehow by God's will I may now at last succeed in coming to you. ¹¹For I long to see you, that I may impart to you some spiritual gift to strengthen you, ¹² that is, that we may be mutually encouraged by each other's faith, both yours and mine. ¹³I want you to know, brethren, that I have often intended to come to you (but thus far have been prevented), in order that I may reap some harvest among you as well as among the rest of the Gentiles. ¹⁴I am under obligation both to Greeks and to barbarians, both to the wise and to the foolish: ¹⁵so I am eager to preach the gospel to you also who are in Rome.

¹⁶For I am not ashamed of the gospel: it is the power of God for salvation to every one who has faith, to the Jew first and also to the Greek. ¹⁷For in it the righteousness of God is revealed through faith for faith; as it is written, "He who through faith is righteous shall live."

(8) As always (except in Galatians) the apostle begins his letter by giving thanks;* for the point of departure of faith and the church is what God has already done; that is the foundation of all doctrinal or ethical reflection. To give thanks in this connexion is to remind both himself and his readers of the sole foundation which can be laid. The act of thanksgiving ascends to God through Jesus Christ since it is through Him that grace has come to men; He is the mediator, the intercessor, the one who speaks perfectly of God to men and of men to God.

(9f.) It is not the quality of the faith of the Roman Christians which arouses gratitude in the heart of the apostle —he did not perhaps know much about this—but the fact that their faith was known in all the world.† This hyperbole is no mere flattery. It is in part justified by the very situation of Rome; the provinces soon get to know what goes on there.

* To judge by the papyri, ancient forms of civility required that a person should begin a letter by pious formulae, generally a prayer on behalf of the one addressed, and sometimes with an expression of gratitude to the gods. See Dodd, p. 6, several examples and sources.

† Comparable situation with regard to Thessalonica (1 Th. 1: 8).

But the chief reason for this allusion is the apostle's plan of going to Spain.

Other territories are waiting for the faith of which they have heard in connexion with the Romans. In the celebrity attained by the faith of the Romans, Paul discerns a call and a promise for his future action. Spain lies before him like a ploughed field awaiting the seed of the Word (cf. Acts 16: 9). The Romans have shone in the world like a city set on a hill.

Yet Paul does not propose to speak of his project at the very beginning of his letter. He does not wish it to be thought that Rome will be merely a halt, soon forgotten, in his march towards the west. He counts rather on making Rome a base where he may strike roots, he hopes to create with the church of the capital deep spiritual bonds which will bear fruit both for it and his own ministry. Thus he calls God to witness the sentiments which he entertains with regard to the Christians at Rome.* God knows that the whole inner life of Paul is dominated by the gospel,† so that the idea of making the gospel resound wherever it has not yet been proclaimed never leaves him. That is why the idea of going to Rome has not ceased to ferment in his mind and has mastered him in his prayers which are the crucible in which his missionary projects come to birth. At the heart of his plans, as the compulsive form of his apostolic obedience, lies Spain; and in consequence the community at Rome, which he incessantly thinks of in his prayers.‡

He mentions the Romans in his prayers of course; but he prays above all that God will open up to him the path that will take him to Rome.§ The terms used betray a certain

* One invokes God, placing oneself under the divine judgment if one lies. Cf. Josh. 22: 27; 1 Sam. 12: 5; Jer. 42: 9; Ps. 89: 35; 2 Cor. 1: 23; Phil. 1: 8; 1 Th. 2: 5, 10.

† "With my spirit": man has a spirit (see 1 Cor. 2: 11; 1 Th. 5: 23) which is the deepest locus of his inner being, his fundamental function, the core of his personality. It is there that the Spirit of God engraves its new certainties (Rom. 8: 16).

‡ From a grammatical point of view, a comma may be placed after ποιοῦμαι and πάντοτε connected with δεόμενος. The sense suggests rather that we should punctuate after ἐπὶ τῶν προσευχῶν μου.

§ Εὐοδοῦσθαι=to have a happy journey; but also to succeed, to attain, to be able (cf. 1 Cor. 16: 2; 2 Chr. 32: 30; Sir. 41: 1; Tob. 5: 16, 21).

note of impatience and some uncertainty as to the conditions in which his prayer will at last find its answer; the close of the letter will reveal the apostle's poignant anxiety with regard to the near future.

(11f.) Paul is very respectful towards this community which he has not founded. He does not present himself as a prince of the church, he does not invoke an apostolic authority which would give him a juridical right over every church and would authorize him to inspect it. He hopes to strengthen these Christians by imparting to them some spiritual enrichment (cf. 1 Cor. 1: 5). He does not say in what department of their life this may come about; the church does not appear to suffer from any perversion of the faith or any grave weakness of charity. Paul does not write as a censor. He hopes that his visit will be profitable (cf. Rom. 15: 29). To wish less would be to refuse to Rome what he owes to all; to claim more would have been to fail in pastoral tact. But at the heart of the Body of Christ no one gives without receiving in return. Paul is speaking to brothers; to a living and healthy church. He will not only give;* he will initiate an exchange, a dialogue as a result of which the members of the Body will gain mutual enrichment according to the measure of faith accorded to each (cf. 12: 3–6).†

(13) In terms which he generally uses whenever he has something important to say (Rom. 11: 25; 1 Th. 4: 13; 1 Cor. 10: 1; 2 Cor. 1: 8) Paul at last makes a point of his idea of going to Rome. The scheme has hitherto been thwarted. He does not say how and we do not know. The passive turn of phrase may be a reverential way of speaking of God (I have been prevented by God); but Satan too may have opposed the plan which would baffle his own purposes (1 Th. 2: 18), or again tasks yet uncompleted may have re-

* Τοῦτο δέ ἐστιν, which is found only here in the NT, has not the meaning of τοῦτ' ἔστιν (that is to say) (cf. 7: 18). It introduces not an explanation but a complement.

† On "consolation", see on Rom. 12: 8. "Consolation" is not to be understood in the psychological sense of encouragement or comfort. It will be noted that "establishing and consoling" are the tasks of Timothy sent by Paul to Thessalonica (1 Th. 3: 2).

tained the apostle in the east (15: 22, 23). In any event Paul felt that his vocation required him to extend the field of his activity so as to embrace the Gentile world in its totality. Rome, the capital of the pagan world, could not remain outside his scope. The gospel of Christ had already been proclaimed there, and Paul himself will state that he avoids towns where others have worked (15: 20). But this was not a reason for not going there at all; the circumstance only explains the reserved and discreet (τινά) way in which he alludes to the harvest he had hoped to garner from such a visit.

(14f.) Thus the travelling plans of Paul are directly connected with his apostolic responsibility. He was not proposing to go to Rome as a tourist but as an apostle and missionary who owes his services to all, whatever their race and culture, and with the conviction that the treasure of his faith lays on him a debt towards all mankind. The terms in which he speaks of this are very emphatic: the grace of God which has made of him what he is imposes on him as it were an obligation which he must fulfil by working at his apostolic ministry (1 Cor. 15: 10). None should be cheated of a spiritual treasure which is meant for them; Paul owes it to them and it is incumbent on him to deliver it. Greeks and barbarians, wise and foolish—these four words divide men and reflect the superiority which those who use them think they possess. All will soon be submitted to the same judgment. This classification of men corresponds to the point of view of the Greeks; it will be seen later that from the Israelite point of view the Jews are opposed to the Greeks or pagans (2: 16; 3: 9, 29) without discriminating among the latter. Romans might be counted among the Greeks;* but the mention of barbarians is certainly an allusion to Spain and the missionary plans of the apostle.† The gaze of the apostle rests first on the inhabitants of Rome‡ but it also embraces a wider horizon. In going

---

* Cicero (De fin., II, 15) contrasts Graecia and Italia with Barbaria. Cf. Seneca, De Ira, III, 2. Cf. Michel, p. 41, n. 4 for Greek authors. Juvenal (Sat., III, 61) calls Rome graeca urbs.

† Cf. H. Windisch, Th.Wb.NT, I, p. 550.

‡ We may understand: my desire, my eagerness (lit. desire as far as I am concerned). Or else: from my own point of view, my wish was. . .

towards the barbarians, he proposes to preach the gospel in Rome also (καί).*

(16) The field to be sown is that of the world. But the immensity of the task does not exceed the treasure of which the apostle is steward (1 Cor. 4: 1). Paul need not blush in face of the new responsibilities imposed on him by his mission to the Gentiles. We are ashamed when we are not certain of our ground. A solid and sincere faith gives rise to a courageous and clear testimony,† for it expects nothing from the fascinations of style or the resources of human wisdom, but everything from the power of the Spirit of God. The failure at Athens and the success at Corinth are here in the background of his thought (cf. 1 Cor. 2: 1–5). Paul has seen how, by preaching, God gives a demonstration of His power to save (cf. again 1 Cor. 1: 18; 4: 20; 1 Th. 1: 5). Through the gospel God has powerfully disclosed His salvation in the eyes of the nations and all the ends of the earth shall see the victory of which Yahweh once spoke.

These words inspired by Ps. 98 (1–3, 8–9) show the kinship of the apostle's thought with that of the psalmist. We must have in our minds the echoes of this psalm in order to grasp the full dimension in which is contained the short declaration of v. 16. The gospel is the decisive act of God who continues to break forth into the course of human history in order to complete the work begun with Abraham. God comes to pronounce upon the world a word that is decisive for its salvation or destruction. God comes to judge the earth, said the psalmist; which is to say that the sentence of God is the final assessment of the values of world history. According to the judgment of God, events have a meaning or else they are but "sound and fury signifying nothing". The life of man, his individual and collective history, are justified if, at the last, the word which God pronounces upon them is favourable

* The omission of τοῖς ἐν ʿΡώμῃ in G springs perhaps from a wish to give the letter more universal scope. Cf. verse 7.

† "Not to be ashamed" . . . (cf. Mk. 8: 38; 2 Tim. 1: 8) expresses by its negative form the effort entailed for the Christian to overcome his resistance to confessing before men a truth which they are not inclined to receive.

46

when the accounts are made up at the term of the process. Not all the fruits of human activity, nor all the results of human history, are stored by the Divine Reaper into His granaries, for He sifts all things and separates the chaff from the wheat on the day when the world comes under His judgment. But this last day can be anticipated and hailed in advance as a day of blessing by those who know the sovereign Lord, for to know Him is to be the object of His goodness and mercy and truth, it is to know the salvation which He has disclosed. The apostle, on the basis of his own Christian experience, renews the psalmist's theme of joy: God has done great things, He has manifested His power to save. The gospel is a valid and effectual word, a mighty action of God who plants in the midst of the present-day world these fruits which endure as seeds of eternal life.

The prophets of the Old Testament already declared a salvation which was, in some way, dependent on the power of the divine word.* The apostle sees the world taken to its conclusion by the supernatural power of the gospel word which he proclaims. The absolute and decisive event in the history of the world is the preaching of the gospel of Jesus Christ, who, in the midst of the developments of natural history, ushers in a supernatural history and, at the heart of the world of man, establishes the world of God.†

Like the psalmist, Paul celebrates the power of God operating to make available *salvation* ($\sigma\omega\tau\eta\rho\iota\alpha$).‡ This word signifies all the blessings which God alone can give in answer to the need and longing of man, who is oppressed and in anguish in face of a destiny which sharpens his need of supernatural beatitude in proportion as it does nothing to satisfy it. The longing for salvation was not the peculiar

---

* Is. 40: 8; 44: 26–28; 55: 10–11, etc. Similarly in Ps. 147: 15 or in Wisdom 18: 14–16, the Word is the agent by which Yahweh executes His will, perhaps even already hypostasized. Cf. L. Dürr, *Die Wertung des göttlichen Wortes im Alten Testament und im antiken Orient*, 1938; H. Ringgren, *Word and Wisdom*, 1947. On the expectation of Messianic salvation in Judaism, see Ps. Sol., Test. XII Patr., Damascus Document; W. Bousset, *op. cit.*, p. 362, n. 2.

† Cf. A. Feuillet, "Le plan salvifique de Dieu d'après l'Épître aux Romains", *R.B.* 1950, p. 338.

‡ *Eἰs σωτηρίαν* is lacking in G.

characteristic of Israel; we find it also in the world of paganism in very varied forms. State religion proposed to satisfy it by magnifying Augustus as a saviour,* and in a general way the soul of the Hellenistic world sought to satisfy it through the mystery cults. However, in Israel Yahweh's self-disclosure had developed more powerfully than elsewhere the feeling that the harsh and adverse destiny under which man suffers is the result of disobedience to God, and that salvation can be found only by a gracious divine intervention forgiving the sinner and restoring what sin had destroyed.

In the thought of Paul, Greeks and Jews are in the same situation, have the same longings and the same needs. The gospel brings to all, whatever be the form of their expectation or the character of their need, the *efficacious power* of God which alone can satisfy it. Δύναμις is very important in this connexion. It suggests the active presence of God, not only in Jesus Christ but also in the preaching of the gospel, by which God continues to manifest in history the effects of sovereign grace. It is by gospel proclamation in fact that men are brought to the confession of Jesus as Lord, and to the obedience of faith, which are the work of the Holy Spirit. The power of God means then at one and the same time the power which God has shown in Jesus Christ, the efficacity which He grants to the preaching of Jesus Christ, and the spiritual power manifested in whoever believes in the gospel of Jesus Christ.†

For Israel, the power of God had been disclosed and, in a way, exhausted in the action which Yahweh took in favour of His people. Of this action, the deliverance from Egypt and the gift of the law were the essential phases.‡ Henceforth it

* It should be noted that σωτηρία in the Hellenistic period, when Stoic influence was very strong, was understood to imply, not deliverance, but the maintenance of order, the conservation of the universe, and prosperity. Cf. H. Haerens, "Σωτήρ and σωτηρία", Studia hellenistica, 5, 1948.

† Cf. Rom. 15: 13; 1 Cor. 1: 18, 24; 2: 4, 5; 4: 20; 5: 4; 6: 14; 2 Cor. 4: 7; 12: 9; 13: 4; Phil. 3: 10; 1 Th. 1: 5.

‡ On Moses as a saviour, cf. Acts 7: 35. The typology Moses-Messiah stresses this point (cf. Renée Bloch, "Moïse dans la tradition rabbinique", in *Moïse, l'homme de l'alliance* (ouvr, collectif), 1955, pp. 93–167).

was no longer to such interventions that one must look in order to know the saving power of the God of Israel. Now it was not by turning to Moses and clinging to the law that one could gain access to the power which God displayed in endowing the life of men, devalued by sin, with a worth that was real and lasting in His sight.* And in consequence this divine power to save is not accessible to the Israelites alone. It is not necessary to be a Jew nor to become one in order to experience its blessings. Its benefits can accrue to whoever believes, whether he be Jew or Greek. The rest of the letter will explain what is meant by "believe". But here and now we may note that this faith transcends traditionally established frontiers within which men had once had to place themselves in order to benefit from the redemptive power of God. It is the dynamic preaching of the gospel which groups together God's people.†

(17) The term σωτηρία is capable of creating misunderstandings. The salvation of which the apostle speaks is not the same as that of which the Greeks spoke. The gospel is the power of God for salvation because in it the righteousness of God is revealed; salvation is here connected with the fact that the gospel reveals powerfully the righteousness of God.

The present tense (ἀποκαλύπτεται) implies an action that is taking place: the revealing power of the gospel is a present fact. In preaching the gospel the apostle is aware of revealing the righteousness of God with the efficacity inherent in such a revelation. The power of his word as a preacher flows from the fact that God, by His agency, discloses the divine righteousness.‡ But in what precisely does this revelation con-

* Judaism had cultivated the idea that the Torah is "power". In the life of the Jew, the Torah, the revelation of the will of God, became a power of salvation. Grundmann, *Th.Wb.NT*, II, pp. 298–299. Paul overthrows the whole scheme by saying that the gospel is power.

† B G and some other MSS. do not have πρῶτον and read: "for the Jew and Greek". Must we take the omission of πρῶτον as a Marcionite correction (Lietzmann) or has this word been added to achieve harmony with 2: 9, 10 (cf. 1 Cor. 1: 24)? As to its meaning, cf. on 2: 9.

‡ "The present tense of the verb is all-important. . . . The revelation is not yet complete; but it is real and even now in process," Dodd, *op. cit.*, p. 13.

sist? What is the character of the salvation which the gospel mediates? Paul qualifies σωτηρία by the term δικαιοσύνη; salvation has to do with righteousness.

The choice of this latter term, quite appropriate in its own literary context, has brought on the head of the apostle the sharpest reproaches. Let Paul only speak of "righteousness" and we conjure up with horror and indignation the juridical approach of the rabbis and the perversions which this Judaic mentality, persisting in Paul despite his conversion, are supposed to have imposed on the message of Jesus. Alas! the numerous critics of the apostle have unwittingly placed themselves in the wrong. They have been deluded by the mirage of mere words. They have forgotten that before judging an author we should learn to understand his vocabulary. The apostle was not even guilty of the mistake of giving a new meaning to the word δικαιοσύνη. It is we who are foolish enough to translate this word by "righteousness" or at least not to explain in what unaccustomed sense this translation should be understood. Paul spoke Greek very well but he thought in Hebrew. The word δικαιοσύνη had, to his mind, the meaning which it had received in the Greek of the Septuagint where it translated the Hebrew צְדָקָה. It is this latter term therefore which yields us the meaning assumed by δικαιοσύνη under the pen of the apostle. Without entering into too much detail,* let us say first of all that the root *tsdq* suggests something which corresponds to its norm and is in conformity with its true definition. So far it has not necessarily a religious or moral significance:† everything depends on the norm and the object or person in view. Hence for a type of thought which is governed by the fundamental fact of

* The bibliography is immense. An adequate one will be found in A. Descamps, "Justice et Justification dans l' A.T.", *D.B.S.*, IV, 1949; this article may be completed and corrected by H. Cazelles, "Àpropos de quelques textes difficiles relatifs à la justice de Dieu dans l'A.T.", *R.B.*, 1951, pp. 169–188. Cf. also E. Jacob, *Théologie de l'A.T.*, 1955, pp. 75–81. (E.T. *The Theology of the Old Testament*.)

† Like ourselves, the Hebrews speak about just weights and balances. A just sacrifice is a correct one. A right way, one which leads to the goal. In this line of thought, "to justify" means to restore to normal; hence the temple will be justified (Dan. 8: 14) because it will be restored and the right worship re-established there.

the covenant between God and His chosen people the essential norm in very many cases will be the fact of the covenant, the covenant life as theoretically defined for the people and its members as also for the divine partner in so far as his responsibilities are concerned. Man is righteous in so far as he behaves conformably with the pact which binds him to his people and his God. Yahweh is righteous inasmuch as He manifests Himself conformably with the covenant. The "righteous acts" of Yahweh are His acts of power wrought on behalf of His people;* but Yahweh may also manifest His righteousness in intervening against His people, in punishing a people that is faithless to the covenant.

The most significant phase in the history of this idea was determined by the sorrows of the exile. To His people in their distress, Yahweh discloses His righteousness first and foremost by His goodness; He will faithfully fulfil His obligations under the covenant by delivering and saving. Quite often, righteousness is made parallel with salvation. Numerous examples could be given from the Psalms and Second Isaiah, where they abound.†

The most characteristic and (for us) instructive example is certainly Ps. 98. We have emphasized above how its tone and theme recall the words of the apostle Paul.‡ V. 2 reads:

* Such is the meaning of צְדָקוֹת in the oldest text of the Bible, the Song of Deborah: Jdg. 5: 11. Cf. also 1 Sam. 12: 7; Mic. 6: 5; Ps. 103: 6. It is of interest to find this word recurring with the same sense in the rule of the Essene community of Qumran (*Rule*, X, 23).

† After quoting Is. 45: 21; 46: 13 LXX; 51: 5 LXX; Ps. 35 (36): 6, 10; 39 (40): 10; 70 (71): 2, 15; 102 (103): 4; 97 (98): 2; Mic. 7: 9; Ps. 85 (4–6 for the wrath and the rest for the saving righteousness), Fr. Lyonnet writes: "Can we doubt that Paul is indebted for the meaning of this expression to these OT texts, so clear and having similar contexts? We should rather be surprised that so many exegetes have attempted to understand the matter otherwise." The author attributes this persistent error to the fact that critics have started from the idea of vindictive or distributive justice and from dogmatic preoccupations. (S. Lyonnet, "De 'Justitia Dei' in Epistula ad Romanos 1: 17 and 3: 21, 22," in *Verbum Domini* (Pontificium Institutum Biblicum), vol. 25, p. 29.)

‡ The most famous is of course the text which played a central part in the thought of Luther: "in thy righteousness deliver me" (Ps. 31: 1). Cf. in the hymns of the Essene community of the Judean desert: "Thou pardonest iniquity and [purifiest man] from his fault by thy righteous-

"The Lord has made known his victory, he has revealed his righteousness in the sight of the nations." It can be seen that the latter words are closely akin to the Letter to the Romans in spirit: God openly vindicates Himself in the eyes of the nations; similarly the apostle proclaims that the divine righteousness is revealed both to Jew and Greek. The parallel is so much the more interesting in that the psalmist, in the preceding verse, has sung of the power of Yahweh (His miracles, His victories, His holy arm) just as the apostle on his side has affirmed that the gospel is the power of God in action.*

When God manifests His righteousness, it happens too that He justifies the accused. Then He acts as Judge. The process of judgment is akin to the idea of justice since the latter implies a comparison between the object or person in question and the norm or the law. There is here a confrontation in which the judge assesses to what extent things are in conformity with their norm. But the judge is also the one to whom belongs the decision—and indirectly the power—to normalize things if they were not normal. His judgment has practical consequences. By his decision he restores a situation

ness" (*Hymns*, IV, 33). Or in the Rule: "I say to God: 'My righteousness!' to the Most High: 'Author of my good!'" (*Rule*, X, 11). And a little further on, these lines which combine the ideas of wonder, power, grace, justification or righteousness, truth, deliverance (or salvation): "I will bless God, I will thank Him for His wonders and will extol Him for His power. Every day I will rely on His grace and will recognize that in Him lies the justification of all men living and that all His works are truth . . . I will praise Him and will sing of His deliverance" (*Rule*, X, 15–17). Cf. again Damascus Document 20: 20: "Until salvation and righteousness come. . . ."

* In the LXX δικαιοσύνη renders צְדָקָה in many texts where the righteousness of God is shown by saving action. Already in Deut. 32: 4, 35, 36; Hosea 2: 19 (M.T. 2: 21); Mic. 7: 9. "With 2nd Isaiah righteousness becomes synonymous with grace and salvation" (E. Jacob, *op. cit.*, p. 80). The same in the Psalter, to such an extent that δικαιοσύνη is used several times for חֶסֶד *mercy*, generally translated by ἔλεος; cf. Gen. 19: 19; 20: 13; 21: 23; 24: 27; 32: 10; Ex. 15: 13; 34: 7; Prov. 20: 22 (M.T. 20: 28). Again צְדָקָה is translated by ἔλεος in Is. 56: 1, and by εὐφροσύνη in Is. 61: 10. Finally δικαιοσύνη renders אֱמֶת =*truth* in Gen. 24: 49; Is. 38: 19; 39: 8; Dan. 8: 12. Cf. A. Descamps, "La Justice de Dieu dans la Bible grecque", *Studia Hellenistica*, 5, 1948.

that was compromised. When he dispenses justice he re-establishes the injured man in his rights according to the norm; he liberates him from his accusers, from those who willed him or did him harm. Similarly when God justifies, He declares what is good and right and establishes it concretely.

Thus we are led to a final aspect of the notion of justice which happens to be, from certain points of view, the most important. Justice, in fact, finds a field of application in social life, in regard to the relation between persons. Law is the summary of the right and the just in regard to the mutual relations of men; it is the canon of a social life in conformity with what the social group requires. Justice is the concrete application of the law, or, for a reflective type of thought, the soul of law. Thus juridical ideas are pre-eminently ideas describing the right relations between persons. This is indeed the most elementary definition of the law, the dictionary definition, and it would be pedantic to recall it here if theologians had not done their best to persuade the readers of Paul to forget this primary truth. The jurisprudence of the west has often had the effect of depriving juridical notions of their human content. The result has been an often incurable suspicion of the Pauline vocabulary; whereas the copious juridical terms which Paul, the heir of Hebraism, uses, should have been interpreted in his writings, as in their sources, in the light of the personal realities which they connote.

If Paul speaks about righteousness and justification, so far from thereby showing himself insensible to concrete human relations and obsessed by frigid and inhuman abstractions, it is because the whole mystery of his faith arises against the background of that drama in which man meets God in personal encounter. Within the framework of the covenant, terms such as "right", "righteousness" and "justification" become keywords in the life of faith; they denote the man who is in the right relation with God, whom God approves and welcomes, or else the act of sovereign divine grace, by which God restores to man a relation which sin has temporarily suspended, and in consequence of which the sinner once more finds access to God. The thought of the apostle

53

could hardly be more seriously misinterpreted than by an interpretation of his vocabulary in the light of the juridical spirit. If we make that mistake we can hardly avoid posing false problems, the most famous of which (a veritable obsession with the exegetes of Paul) arises from the habit of seeing in the Letter to the Romans the juxtaposition of a juridical vein with a mystical vein, of an argument dominated by the idea of justification (ch. 3: 1—5: 21) with an argument dominated by the thought of life and death in Christ and in the Spirit (ch. 6–8). The problem of reconciling these two themes is insoluble because it should never have been posed; for what is considered the juridical aspect already implies personal relations, and hence mystical ones.

To sum up, δικαιοσύνη and the terms akin to it offer an extreme complexity and richness of meaning, a meaning which is far removed from what notions of justice and so on suggest to our minds. It has been pointed out that it has no less than five meanings, often closely linked and in fact to some extent inseparable: a logical meaning (exactness and conformity); a psychological and moral meaning (judgment, the assessment rendered by the judge); a practical meaning (the emancipating verdict and act); a religious meaning (fidelity to the covenant, salvation); a juridical and social meaning (the right relation between persons).

The preaching of the gospel is the power of God for salvation because it reveals the mercy of God operating to make salvation available to man; in other words, what Paul calls the righteousness of God. When the apostle speaks of the revelation of this saving righteousness, he wishes to stress the fact that it emerges independently of all human causality.* It is an event which is rooted beyond all human possibilities. It reflects the sole power of God active in the service of His love, the sovereign intervention promised for the end of the age.

However, this revelation of the saving righteousness of God does not take place in harmony with the ordinary expectations of Israel. It was thought that God would deliver His people when the latter had completely fulfilled the law, were

* Ps. 98: 1, 2 and Is. 56: 1 (LXX ἔλεος) speak of the revelation (גלה; ἀποκαλύπτειν) of the righteousness of God.

54

it only for one day, and as a reward for such obedience.* Some dazzling manifestation was expected which would drive out the foreigner and restore to the elect people its former glory. But the salvation which the gospel declares has nothing to do either with the works of the law or with political action such as was expected from the Messiah. Hence Paul speaks of the coming of a salvation, a disclosure of divine "righteousness" in very different terms from what current opinion would suggest. Hence he insists that the righteousness so powerfully proclaimed by the gospel is intimately connected with faith.

The formula used has given rise to various interpretations.† It should be associated with what the apostle writes further on in 3: 21, for the rhythm of thought is identical in both passages: revelation of righteousness, the means of benefiting from it, those who are intended to benefit from it.‡ The righteousness revealed in the gospel is thus said to be ἐκ πίστεως because it is obtained by faith; it does not lie within human resources; later Paul will explain what this faith is which excludes human co-operation. The righteousness revealed in the gospel is also said to be ἐκ πίστεως because

* The principle of retribution dominated the thought of Judaism to such an extent that faith itself was considered a meritorious work. "He who believes receives his reward ... you will glorify the faithful according to their faith" (Apoc. Bar. 54: 16, 21). The deliverance from Egypt was considered as a reward for the faith of the Hebrews, on the basis of Ex. 4: 31. Cf. G. F. Moore, *Judaism in the First Centuries*, II, 1927, p. 237.

† 'Εκ πίστεως εἰς πίστιν means, some think, the faith of the preacher and the faith of the hearer, or the faithfulness of God and the faith of the believer. Others consider that the expression suggests the profession of faith (cf. 2 Cor. 3: 18; Ps. 84: 7; Jer. 9: 3); "the continual progress every day in the life of each believer" (Calvin) or the passage from *fides informata* to *fides formata* (Thomas Aquinas, *S.Th.* III, 9. XLIV, 1), or the passage from the old faith to the new (Tertullian). The parallel 2 Cor. 2: 16 has led to the supposition that ἐκ ... εἰς constituted a purely rhetorical formula: the revelation of the righteousness of God was exclusively a matter of faith (cf. A. Fridrichsen, "Aus Glauben zu Glauben, Röm. 1: 17", *Conj. neotestamentica*, XII). G. Kittel, connecting the formula with the paradoxical character of the present possession of glory in 2 Cor. 3: 18, suggests that the meaning is that at the same time one has and has not faith (*Th.Wb.NT*, II, p. 255).

‡ πεφανέρωται corresponds to ἀποκαλύπτεται; διὰ πίστεως to ἐκ πίστεως; εἰς πάντας τοὺς πιστεύοντας to εἰς πίστιν.

it is revealed to all those who believe without any restriction of race or culture.* Faith is the one necessary and sufficient condition; it is by faith and for believers that it is revealed in the gospel. Neither knowledge and practice of the law, nor membership of the race of Abraham, constitute preliminary requirements. The salvation proclaimed in gospel preaching is the work of God alone. That is why such preaching is everywhere effectual in mediating salvation, without any discrimination of merit or ecclesiastical affiliation. The gospel is a power for salvation, and an instrument of the merciful righteousness of God, because it is the power *of God*, to which man has nothing to add, nothing to contribute. It is ἐκ πίστεως . . . εἰς πίστιν.†

* This means connecting, as regards meaning, ἐκ πίστεως to δικαιοσύνη and εἰς πίστιν to ἀποκαλύπτεται (thus Zahn, Kühl, A. Oepke, "Δικαιοσύνη Θεοῦ bei Paulus in neuer Beleuchtung", *Th.L.Z.*, 1953).

† Theologians and exegetes have much discussed the question whether the "righteousness of God" means a divine attribute, i.e. God is righteous, or the gift of righteousness which God grants to the believer and as a result of which God can proclaim the believer righteous. It is difficult to take as much interest in the question as was taken formerly. Debates on the matter have been complicated by confessional differences, and have not ceased to be so in the minds of those who think it useful to perpetuate these discussions. The Roman tradition was inclined to insist on righteousness as an effectual gift which transformed the nature of the believer; the reformed tradition tended to emphasize righteousness as an attribute of God in virtue of which God makes a declaration in favour of the believer, who remains in himself what he was before. There is no hope of solving such a conflict between confessional differences. The basic error here is due to the substantialist and static mode of thought imposed by the Aristotelian philosophic tradition on mediaeval theology, and insufficiently rejected by reformed theology (cf. K. Oltmanns, *Th.Bl.*, 1929, c. 110). As a result, it is the nature of the justified believer that has been discussed; his status has been defined by considering him in himself. To do this was to take an unworkable initial hypothesis for any type of thought informed by Hebrew tradition, where righteousness is essentially a condition of relations, suggesting man's situation in so far as he is related to . . . etc. Now one of the terms of this relationship is God. The ideas of righteousness and justification do not express what man or God are in themselves, but a certain status of their relations, and the situation arising from the latter. The righteous God is He who justifies man; the righteous man is he who is justified by the righteous God. When God proclaims man righteous He creates a new situation; He brings man into a new relation with Himself; He bestows

An affirmation of the prophet Habakkuk completes and concludes this brief yet momentous analysis. As in some other cases Paul doubtless quotes from memory without feeling obliged to give an exact rendering of the text.* He appeals to scripture as much, and perhaps more, to illustrate his own thought as to prove a point.† By the mouth of the prophet, Yahweh declares that life and salvation are assured to the

on man His favour; He gives him access to Himself: He allows man to call Him Father; He owns man as His son. God does not speak in vain, and when He speaks He acts. Justification is an efficacious word of God.

This has not been affirmed with sufficient force in reformed theology, as it was desired not to dissolve the cause of Justification (God and divine grace) in its anthropological effects (a so-called infused grace, becoming a second nature). God acts effectively to establish a new relation between Himself and the believer, whom He draws into a new condition of life by bringing him into the sphere of action of Jesus Christ and endowing him with the free grace communicated by the Holy Spirit. In this sense, the believer *is* a new creature. But he is not so autonomously or intrinsically by a change in his nature; yet he is so in reality so soon as he is placed under the action of divine grace; he is so in virtue of the effectual relation which God has established with him. His new life has all the reality which the sovereign action of God imparts, all the reality conferred by grace; we should add nothing to this by claiming for the believer a quality affecting his nature; that would rather be isolating him from the divine source of his new life, by considering the effect independently of its cause. Some Roman theses have not been able to avoid the danger of thus stabilizing in the nature of man the effect of divine action, of thus naturalizing grace. For Paul, the inheritor of Hebrew thought, justification is an efficacious word of God the sovereign Judge, who thus draws the believer into new conditions of existence and so confers upon him newness of life.

* The Massoretic Text says: "The righteous man shall live by his fidelity (to me, his trust in me)." LXX translates: ὁ δὲ δίκαιος ἐκ πίστεώς μου ζήσεται (BS). Paul does not reproduce exactly either of the two versions. Perhaps he knew yet another form of the text? In C, we find a harmonization with LXX by the addition of μου ("my righteous man").

† The rabbis used scripture very freely and had resort to Biblical expressions in the formulation of their own thoughts without claiming to give by this means any special authority to what they had to say (cf. Fr. Torm, *Hermeneutik des N.T.*, 1930; O. Michel, *Paulus und seine Bibel*, 1929). It will be realized that OT quotations were probably the object of fairly firm tradition in the time of the apostle; collections had been formed with the purpose of facilitating discussions with the Jews. Paul must have used some of these and the fact may explain some of the characteristics of his method of quoting scripture.

57

Israelite if he commits himself to the saving power of God; whoever commits to God the care of his salvation and does not seek from some other source, or in his own strength, the help he needs, acts well, is righteous, is well-pleasing to God and God judges him favourably. The declaration of Habakkuk is enough for the purpose of the apostle. There is no need for us to suppose that Paul wished to wrest the prophetic witness by compelling Habakkuk to speak of "him who is righteous by faith". Such an exegesis is by no means irresistible. Had Paul wished to break with the interpretation of the synagogue, he would have written: ὁ δὲ ἐκ πίστεως δίκαιος ζήσεται; especially as it would surely be repugnant to Paul to say of the believer that he is righteous (he is only justified, which is not the same thing, to his mind). Above all we should note that in these vv. 16, 17 the emphasis is placed on the fact that the "righteousness" of God *is revealed*, on the saving power of God revealed in the gospel. It would not have been appropriate to distract attention by suggesting a new idea of righteousness. On the other hand Habakkuk shows clearly that the power of God is manifested to save the one who commits himself wholly to God.* It was quite enough to let him speak for himself.

[18]For the wrath of God is revealed from heaven against all ungodliness and wickedness of men who by their wickedness suppress the truth. [19]For what can be known about God is plain to them, because God has shown it to them. [20]Ever since the creation of the world his invisible nature, namely, his eternal power and deity, has been clearly perceived in the things that have been made. So they are without excuse; [21]for although they knew God they did not honour him as God or give thanks to him, but they became futile in their thinking and their senseless minds were darkened. [22]Claiming to be wise, they became fools, [23]and exchanged the glory of the immortal

---

* Since Theodore Beza, this exegesis has been very common (Lietzmann, Lagrange, Gaugler). Some think the reasons for it absolutely decisive, and feel it to be the only possible one (A. Nygren, *Der Römerbrief*, 1951, p. 68). The authorities which adopt the contrary opinion show that this is not so: Oltramare, Godet, Sanday and Headlam, A. Schlatter (*Gottesgerechtigkeit*, 1935, p. 43), Dodd, H. Schlier (*Der Brief an die Galater*, 1951, p. 91), S. Lyonnet, *Bible de Jérusalem*, Michel, etc.

God for images resembling mortal man or birds or animals or reptiles.

²⁴Therefore God gave them up in the lusts of their hearts to impurity, to the dishonouring of their bodies among themselves, ²⁵because they exchanged the truth about God for a lie and worshipped and served the creature rather than the Creator, who is blessed forever! Amen.

²⁶For this reason God gave them up to dishonourable passions. Their women exchanged natural relations for unnatural, ²⁷and the men likewise gave up natural relations with women and were consumed with passion for one another, men committing shameless acts with men and receiving in their own persons the due penalty for their error.

²⁸And since they did not see fit to acknowledge God, God gave them up to a base mind and to improper conduct. ²⁹They were filled with all manner of wickedness, evil, covetousness, malice. Full of envy, murder, strife, deceit, malignity, they are gossips, ³⁰slanderers, haters of God, insolent, haughty, boastful, inventors of evil, disobedient to parents, ³¹foolish, faithless, heartless, ruthless. ³²Though they know God's decree that those who do such things deserve to die, they not only do them, but approve those who practise them.

(18) If God disclosed His salvation or His saving righteousness by a transcendent intrusion in Jesus Christ, which is extended by the present efficacious preaching of gospel salvation, the reason is that the human situation could not be remedied except by such an intervention from above. Let us notice straight away that Paul here speaks of men in general (ἄνθρωποι)—he does not say "Gentiles". The Jews are included, for he is thinking of their natural condition apart from election and promise.* Like the righteous man of Habakkuk's oracle whose strength was no match for that of

---

* And in consequence Christians are also included. Paul does not speak of men in the abstract in order to inform the Romans about the condition of some of their contemporaries, as though Christians had nothing in common with such people (see on 1: 32). Christians must recognize themselves ever afresh in what is said of "men"; they too were formerly enslaved to shameful sins (6: 21; 1 Cor. 6: 1off.): they should remember that if they wish to have a true understanding of the grace of Jesus Christ. Cf. G. Schrenk, "Der Römerbrief als Missionsdokument" (*Festgabe E. F. K. Müller*, 1933, resumed in "Studien zu Paulus", *A.Th.A.N.T.*, 1954, pp. 81–106).

his enemies, so that his only hope of survival lay in having recourse to the supreme power of God, humanity, as a result of its disobedience to God, has involved itself in a desperate and mortally sick situation, from which it cannot be extricated by its own resources; that is why (cf. the γάρ of v. 18) it becomes the object of the special loving concern of God who comes to save it from its predicament and to restore it to true life through gospel preaching.

In order to look towards divine help, it is not enough to know that such help objectively exists; man must be mastered by the conviction that he needs it. The existential anguish of man is what incites him to seek God; but his anguish must be so deep and far-reaching that it ceases to be satisfied by fallacious responses. Man in search of God must be enlightened with regard to the true facts of his situation. He must become convinced that his search will not be successful. Only then will he realize that he himself is the object of God's search. Paul will describe in turn the situation of failure of which man is the slave, and the plan by which God comes to his rescue in Jesus Christ. Before being saved man is condemned; but he is condemned *in order to be* saved; his condemnation is the first phase of his salvation, for only he who knows he is lost, has recourse to grace and is able to appreciate its utter gratuity. That is why the "good news" itself implies as a prerequisite the proclamation of the "wrath of God".*

We might go so far as to think that it is the gospel itself which reveals the "wrath of God" (the repetition of ἀποκαλύπτεται in vv. 17, 18 suggests this thought);† for it is the

* This anthropopathism is traditional in Hebrew thought. Wrath is, among the reactions ascribed to God, one of the most frequently mentioned. All religions have given a place to this violent and mysterious reaction of divinity by ascribing to it an arbitrary and irrational character; we see here one of the fundamental characteristics of natural religion, reflecting a certain aspect of that existential anguish which drives man in search of God. Among the Hebrews the wrath of Yahweh was qualified by the fact of the covenant; it is a special manifestation of divine jealousy, of that exclusive love which does not tolerate any infidelity. Cf. E. Jacob, *op. cit.*, p. 91, and the very well-documented article on ὀργή in *Th.Wb.NT*, V, pp. 382–448.

† Paul says that the wrath of God is revealed ἀπ' οὐρανοῦ; this note seems to contrast the way in which wrath is revealed as against the way

gospel which reveals the radical failure of the religion and ethics of man, and brings man to confess with the prodigal son: "I have sinned. . . ." By revealing in Jesus Christ true God and true man, the gospel suggests the judgment of wrath which God makes on the false gods and the aberrations of mankind. With the gospel there begins for every man the great assize of God, the eschatological and ultimate age.*

God reacts against all ungodliness and wickedness; the phrase conjures up all the religious and moral wretchedness of men.† The essence of this misery lies in a sort of absolute falsification, a basic adulteration of the truth.‡ Men, in fact, do know God and His will (Rom. 1: 21 and 2: 15) but they have deliberately effaced this truth,§ distorting and inverting it. ‖ 'Aλήθεια is not to be taken in an abstract sense; truth is what really exists and so what must be if man does not wish to live in vain.

(19f.) We can speak of a truth which is disregarded by men because we can speak of a truth which is known to them. "What can be known of God" was plain to them¶ and fully in which righteousness is revealed (through the gospel: ἐν αὐτῷ). Paul does not explicitly say that wrath is revealed by the gospel. But we should take ἀπ' οὐρανοῦ as a respectful designation of God: wrath is revealed from the sphere in which God dwells so that men should realize what they did not understand, at least they were not aware of the divine wrath as it appears to one who welcomes the gospel. The reaction of God to sin (wrath) is not fully known and lived in all its truth except in the light of the cross of Jesus Christ.

* It should be stressed that the apostle is here moving in eschatological perspectives. The idea of the wrath of God is often related to eschatology (Enoch 91: 7; 99: 16; Jub. 24: 30; Wisdom 5: 20; Matt. 3: 7; Lk. 3: 7; 1 Th. 1: 10; Rev. 6: 17). Cf. Stählin, Th. Wb.NT, V, p. 432; G. Bornkamm, "Die Offenbarung des Zornes Gottes", Z.N.W., 1935, p. 239, and Das Ende des Gesetzes, 1952, p. 9. Schrenk has underlined the solidarity binding wrath and love (righteousness) as the two modes of the action of God (Unser Glaube an den Zorn Gottes nach dem Römerbrief, 1944).

† The two words refer to the two tables of the law (A. Schlatter, Gottesgerechtigkeit, p. 49).

‡ "The devil is the father of lies, and has nothing to do with the truth" (Jn. 8: 44).

§ Κατέχειν ἐν . . . to keep shut up, prisoner: to oppress.

‖ 'Aδικία as antonym of ἀλήθεια; Rom. 2: 8; 1 Cor. 13: 6; 2 Th. 2: 10–12 (=ψεῦδος).

¶ 'Ἐν αὐτοῖς, in them, in their conscience—or, among them, adapted to their level?

accessible.* In fact God was not hidden from them but manifest, if not in Himself, at least in His works by which His invisible being allows itself to be known. Paul is serious in affirming that natural man has a knowledge of God, and he presents this natural human knowledge of God as the effect of the special purpose of God. It is not adequate to say that God is known, as an object is known which remains passive as man examines and comes to know it; God is known because He makes Himself known (καθορᾶται); He is Himself active in initiating the knowledge which man has of Him.†

This knowledge is certainly also ignorance. The paradox suggested by the association of τὰ ἀόρατα and καθορᾶται is deliberately intended by Paul.‡ The invisible God (cf. Ex. 33: 20; Jdg. 13: 22) makes Himself known by visible realities in which His presence is sufficient for the inner vision of man to apprehend it. Since its very existence, creation yields a certain degree of knowledge of its Creator§ to the man who exercises upon it his reflective and contemplative faculties. God cannot be known directly, but neither is He unknowable; man must allow himself to be caught up in the dialogue into which God coaxes him through the work of creation; the knowledge of God is not thrust on a passive

* The expression τὸ γνωστὸν τοῦ Θεοῦ may suggest the partial character of the knowledge (only what is knowable) or, on the other hand, the knowability of God (God as knowable). Cf. Bultmann, *Th.Wb.NT*, I, p. 719. It has been pointed out that if τὸ γνωστόν meant "what is known" it would form a tautology with φανερόν ἐστιν (Lagrange).

† Godet, p. 215, G. Bornkamm, "Die Offenbarung des Zornes Gottes", *Z.N.W.* 1935, and *Das Ende des Gesetzes*, p. 20. In Wisdom 13: 1–9 it is man who tries to know God, who seeks God and goes astray in his effort to find God. If he thus fails, it is because he has been thinking on the wrong lines. The knowledge of God is thus understood as an ascent of man in an effort which if properly directed should succeed. For Paul it is God who makes Himself known and gives Himself as an object of knowledge; man does not discover Him; man receives the knowledge which God imparts. If, in spite of this, man does not know God, it is because man refuses God's gift, and is not simply a failure.

‡ On ἀόρατος and καθορᾶται, discussion in Michaelis, V, p. 370 and 380; καθορᾶν = *take into account, consider*.

§ Ἀπὸ κτίσεως = since the created world has existed (since the act of creation), rather than: on the basis of the fact of creation.

subject; it obliges man to adopt a positive creative inner attitude.

Man's inward contemplation of the world considered as the work of God has two objects: δύναμις and θειότης. *Power* first of all; not so much because man can trace phenomena back to their primal cause; rather because through his life in the world man experiences being and nothingness. He is cast into the world without willing it; he chooses neither the time nor the place of his birth and death; some "power" presides over his existence; through it he comes to be, and in face of it he recognizes his own nothingness. Compared with the flux of historic time, this power shows itself to be eternal; it is both anterior and posterior to the unfolding process of history. Secondly, *deity*; the mystery of being implies that of end; the articulation of my life underlines the mystery of my death; to the "through what" I have come to be is added the "for what". The universe is not moved by blind power. The "human comedy" is after all justified; the adventure of life is not senseless and absurd, for anyone who is willing to assume it in fullest sincerity. If anguish springs from refusal, consent initiates man into the ultimate meaning of things. The power which philosophic contemplation of the world enables us to recognize is of divine character. For it is no blind power; it nourishes thought for the world; it is love; it is God.*

The knowledge of Himself which God willed to give through the works of creation was sufficient to confront men with the basic alternative spelt by their existence and to induce them to make a responsible choice. Paul says that God disclosed Himself to men through His works so that they should be "without excuse". This does not mean that God wished them to make a choice by which they could legiti-

* Cf. the formula of Cicero: *"vis et natura deorum"* (*De nat. deorum*, I, 18: 44). The sources of Paul's thought are chiefly Jewish (for the OT cf. Ps. 33: 6–9; Ps. 8: 3; 19: 1; Job 38 to 42; for Judaism, Wis. 13. 13: 1–9; Apoc. Bar. 54: 17–18; etc.); but Stoicism had influenced Hellenistic Judaism: Ps. Aristotle, *De Mundo*, 6; Cicero, *Tuscul.*, I, 28: 68–70; *De nat. deorum*, II, 6: 16; III, 10, 25, 26. More complete references in Lietzmann. On this point cf. Michel, p. 55, and esp. A. Fridrichsen, *Zur Auslegung von Röm.* I, 19ff., *Z.N.W.*, 1915.

mately be accused as responsible for their guilt, but that God wishes them to choose in conditions which would make quite clear the malice of their choice, and prevent them from being unaware of their malignity; unless their alleged good conscience itself be the climax of their bad faith! It was not in order to be able to accuse them that God enlightened them with true knowledge, but in order to prevent them from seeking vain excuses and to convince them that they are without excuse.*

(21f.) Hence the responsibility of man is securely based, since the revealing action of God culminates in giving man a true knowledge of Himself; men knew God (γνόντες τὸν Θεόν).† This formula cannot be toned down by means of some theological axiom such as "*finitum infiniti non capax*". For the apostle of the Gentiles, man was created capable of knowing God and in fact does know Him; the responsibility which has just been affirmed implies this.‡

It is not a question of denying man's capacity to receive the proffered knowledge, but of knowing to what use man has put this capacity. Man has known God; how has he profited by this knowledge?

To be capable of knowing and effectually to assimilate the knowledge of which one is capable are two entirely different things. One may understand and disobey. One may know a certain truth and refuse to recognize it, that is, refuse to integrate it with one's conscience, and take account of it in regulating one's life. Men who in reality have known God, have not misunderstood; but they have refused the real and

* Cf. A. Schlatter, *Gottesgerechtigkeit*, 1935, p. 51. Besides Wis. 13: 6, cf. Assumption of Moses: "He created the globe of lands for His people. But it pleased Him to manifest the end of creation from the beginning, so that nations should find in it their condemnation, condemning each other" (1: 13).

† On the origin of Paul's argument cf. J. Dupont, *Gnosis*, 1949, p. 21, and the bibliography there.

‡ Not only is there objective responsibility in that God manifested Himself, thus making Himself knowable; but also subjective responsibility because man was capable of receiving this knowledge offered in God's active self-disclosure through His works.

valid knowledge which God offered them.* Men, having known God, should have recognized Him "as God"; they should have made of that knowledge a rule of life, by offering to His "power" and "deity" the sentiments of respect and acknowledgment which are their due. But in fact, men were unwilling to treat God as God; they were unwilling to recognize that the world and their own existence were shaped and governed by God, at once the origin and end of all things. To "honour" is said with regard to a superior power. To "give thanks" is said with regard to a good intention. Men have evaded the homage which they owed to the sovereignty and goodness of the Creator. It is possible to know that there is a God and to tremble (James 2: 19); it is the characteristic of the devil to tremble before God and to arouse in man the fear of God by distorting the kind and fatherly face of God, His "power" and "deity", and by lending to Him the features of a suspicious, jealous and vindictive being (cf. the way in which the serpent distorts the words of God to the first human couple, Gen. 2: 16 and 3: 1). Instead of recognizing God as Creator and Father, men's slavish fear has incited them to invent "religion", "human religion".†

Along this path, they have shown the vanity of their thoughts and the blindness of their hearts. These two consequences of the refusal of God well correspond, it would seem, to the two aspects of God's self-manifestation (power and divinity). The "thought" which is not nourished and focused by faith in God the Creator becomes "futile". Its starting point is sheer nothingness and it can only lead to nothingness; it remains enslaved to the powers which dominate this world, as can be seen in so-called primitive pagan religions; or else it senselessly and recklessly enslaves the world to itself, as can be seen in modern pagan religions;

* Lagrange, after Thomas Aquinas, writes: "Paul does not blame (the pagans) for having refused to worship God as known . . . a worship they knew they owed Him. . . . The first fault of the Gentiles is already a fault of ignorance." But Paul wrote: γνόντες τὸν Θεόν.

† Paul does not wish to deny that men have a natural knowledge of God. They know that God exists. Their error is not an intellectual one. But they do not treat God as God. They do not give Him true worship. Their error is religious, it is sin. Salvation will consist not in better information, but in repentance.

it is a thought which because it has refused to confess the "power" of God has rendered itself powerless. Similarly the "heart" when it is not nourished and focused by thanksgiving for the goodness of God which assigns its end to every creature can no longer know how to guide the steps of created being; it becomes blind, darkened, mad.* Futility of thought and blindness of heart are the two major characteristics of the human condition after its refusal of God.

(22–24) The consequences of this refusal are seen in the tragic disorders in which man makes shipwreck of his life. The apostle classifies them in three groups: perversion of the relation of man with God (idolatry), with his own kind (immorality), with his neighbour (various animosities). Each group will be presented in the same way, the human cause preceding the divine reaction,† and the triple repetition of διό (διὰ τοῦτο) παρέδωκεν αὐτοὺς ὁ Θεός, *for this reason God gave them up*, will sound like so many hammer blows to mark the straits in which man finds himself as a result of refusing to give glory and thanks to God.

Men were free to refuse God, but they were not free to remove the consequences of this refusal. In face of God, so long as man is in communion with Him, man is free; the presence of God is creative of freedom because God is Lord of all. But as soon as man ceases to dwell in the divine presence, he ceases to share in God's sovereignty; he loses freedom; the slavery of man begins. God is not foreign to the necessity which thus weighs upon the sinner, for He has established an order which cannot be broken without causing that order to react against the one who violates it. Order and necessity are implied by disorder and this also is due to the

* Καρδία = *the heart*, the seat of sentiment and volition. It is the sphere of man's deepest life, and of the decisions which commit him in his entire existence.

† E. Klostermann, "Die adäquate Vergeltung in Röm. 1: 22–29", *Z.N.W.*, 1933. The keywords of each paragraph correspond: vv. 22–24: δόξαν = ἀτιμάζεσθαι; vv. 25–27: μετήλλαξαν = μετήλλαξαν; vv. 28–32: οὐκ ἐδοκίμασαν = εἰς ἀδόκιμον νοῦν. Klosterman has also shown that this kind of charge was familiar in Hellenistic Judaism. But he neglected two very interesting parallels noted by J. Jeremias ("Zu Rm. 1: 22–32," *Z.N.W.* 1954), one in Acts 7: 41–42, the other in Test. Napht. 3: 2–4.

creative will. The will of man alone comes into play when he refuses God; but it is God who determines sanctions and He alone can lift them.*

Verses 22, 23, 24 expound the consequences of man's refusal of God in so far as man's relations with God on the cultic level are concerned, and they describe the corresponding sanctions. Men violently assert their wisdom, whereas in truth they have become fools. No doubt they reason correctly from a purely logical point of view. Madness does not here connote mental disorder but that ignorance of God† which leads man to act foolishly in the matter of cultic worship; for, says Paul, it is not reasonable to exchange knowledge of the God of all creation in favour of the making of idols which represent human or animal creatures. Having refused to recognize the true God as God, man will fabricate for himself a god which is not God. In this sense idolatry is indeed madness.

In order to make vivid this degradation into idolatry, the apostle recalls the typical episode of the making of the golden calf (Ex. 32) and he borrows from Ps. 106: 20 the terms in which he refers to it (cf. Jer. 2: 11 and the prohibition of idolatry in Deut. 4).‡ Israel exchanged§ that knowledge of Himself which God had granted to man, the divine radiance (i.e. the invisible presence of God) and the word vouchsafed to Moses (Ex. 24: 17; 25ff.; Deut. 4: 12) for the image of a creature. Thus, in refusing God, men still make for them-

---

* In Gen. 3 the penalty decreed by God has an inevitable character, since the couple are excluded from the garden where they were able to live in the presence of God and receive from Him their liberty.

† Cf. Deut. 32: 6 ($\lambda a \dot{o} s$ $\mu \omega \rho \dot{o} s$ $\kappa a \dot{\iota}$ $o \dot{\upsilon} \chi \dot{\iota}$ $\sigma o \phi \dot{o} s$), Jer. 5: 21 ($\lambda a \dot{o} s$ $\mu \omega \rho \dot{o} s$ $\kappa a \dot{\iota}$ $\dot{a} \kappa \acute{a} \rho \delta \iota o s$), Is. 32: 5, 6; Sir. 4: 27; 21: 22a; 50: 26; Prov. 17: 21 (S). The theme is more broadly treated by Paul in 1 Cor. 1: 18, 21.

‡ Deut. 4: 15–19 forbids the making of any graven image ($\gamma \lambda \upsilon \pi \tau \dot{o} \nu$ $\dot{o} \mu o \acute{\iota} \omega \mu a$) in the likeness of man, woman or any animal for the reason that at Horeb, when Yahweh spoke, Israel saw no image or figure ($\dot{o} \mu o \acute{\iota} \omega \mu a$).

§ '$H \lambda \lambda a \xi a \nu$ $\dot{\epsilon} \nu$ according to Ps. 106: 20 (LXX) is a semitism for הֵמִיר בְּ. W. Bauer (art. $\dot{\epsilon} \nu$, IV. 5) refers however to Soph. Ant. 945. In the background of Paul's text we shall recognize moreover Jer. 2: 11 and Deut. 4: 15–18 (N. Hyldahl, "A reminiscence of the Old Testament at Rom. 1: 23", New Test. Studies, May 1956, p. 285).

selves a god suggested by their darkened minds. And in making their own god, they prove to themselves that they are not his creatures, just as in driving him in front of them, like the golden calf, they convince themselves that they need not obey him.

Thus "religion" is born, springing from a rejected knowledge of the true God and finalizing man's seizure of God, the triumph of gods over God.* Religions would not exist, had not God revealed Himself; revelation explains the existence and the quality of religions;† but the latter are the fruits of the rejection and inversion of revelation; they seek to know God who cannot be known except in the movement by which He makes Himself known; they aim at attaining by means of their technique a God who is pure and gracious self-giving. Here lies the source both of their truth and their error. Paul believes that there is a natural knowledge of God, because God makes Himself known through His works; but this natural revelation has been refused, and the dialogue to which God invited man, suspended. Human religion knows that there is a God but does not know who He is; He alone can name Himself; the religions of mankind are in search of God but the God whom they worship is, at bottom, unknown to them and when they attempt to name Him, they make for themselves idols.‡ "*Quaerite quod quaeritis, sed ibi non est, ubi quaeritis*" (Augustine, *Confessions*, IV, 18; "Seek that which you seek, but it is not there, where you seek it").

As though the law of retaliation were in question, the divine sanction strikes the impious man at the very point where he failed. Man has mocked the honour of God by deifying the bodies of creatures erected into idols; God therefore abandons man to passions which dishonour his own body. The reference here is to sacred prostitution; idolatry and shameful lusts are very closely connected.§ Such prostitution associated with

* On the Jewish idea that the heathen worship animals, cf. Strack-Billerbeck III, p. 60.

† Cf. A. Nygren, *Römerbrief*, p. 83.

‡ One cannot read without emotion Simone Weil, *Intuitions préchrétiennes*, 1953. But for completion and clarification see H. Kraemer, *Religion and the Christian Faith*, 1956.

§ Gal. 5: 20; 2 Cor. 12: 21; Col. 3: 5; Eph. 5: 3. Cf. Strack-Billerbeck,

68

the cults which centre on procreation show that man no longer realizes from whom he derives life and being, and to whom he is responsible for it. The powerlessness of the idols is manifested in these very cults which are intended to sustain and renew the δύναμις, i.e. the power of material vitality, by means of appropriate techniques; thus finally man the sinner imagines that he derives from himself and from the techniques which he controls the power of creative vitality.

(25ff.) Following an identical pattern of thought,* Paul indicates a new consequence of the rejection of God, and the proper sanction which such rejection has entailed. Those who pervert the truth of God deviate at the same time from the right use of nature which is the work of God; they deprive themselves of those natural truths which they might read in the face of nature if they did not regard it in isolation from its author and its goal. Paul assumes that nature gives man indications as to its true and natural use; but the reading has become indecipherable as a result of the rejection of God. The true knowledge of nature once lost, man no longer knows whence it comes or whither it goes, nor, in consequence, its true purpose and use. Unnatural sexual relations offer the most striking example of that corruption of the truth of God which He has imprinted on His creation, what Paul calls the "natural use". When man ceases to worship the Creator, he begins to worship the creature; he becomes the puppet of its manifold possibilities: instead of dealing with things as though one were not dealing with them (1 Cor. 7: 31) he on the contrary abuses them; it is enough for him to be "available" (André Gide) to the forces of his nature. The apostle emphasizes this passive attitude and the violence of the passions which then arise (ἐξεκαύθησαν ἐν τῇ ὀρέξει αὐτῶν). The corruption of the natural order which ensues is the punishment which creation inflicts, as from God, on those who pervert its use. In verse 25 Paul turns aside to insert a formula of benediction, as was the custom with the Jews; disturbed by

III, p. 62. Israel also had known the practice of sacred prostitution: 1 Kgs. 14: 24; 22: 46; 2 Kgs. 23: 7, etc.

* To the perversion of God's truth (v. 25) there corresponds the perversion of sexual life, v. 26; the natural is set in contrast with the unnatural.

69

his reference to the blasphemy of which men have made themselves guilty, he reaffirms his faith in the Creator God.

(28–31) Men have refused to allow the thought of God to shape their own thoughts (i.e. to acknowledge God, to remain in awareness of God) with the result that they have become incapable of considering sanely the question of τὸ κάθηκον.* The word is of Stoic origin; it connotes what it is right to do in view of what one is, or the conduct of man as man, or *duty*. The rejection of God thus deprives man not only of the true knowledge of God and of nature, but also of the true knowledge of himself and of others, so that his mind becomes incapable of discerning what it is right to do: he is ἀδόκιμος, i.e. disordered. The enumeration of the consequences brought about by this condition of the inner life in regard to human relationships is overwhelming in its severity.† The logic which governs it is not altogether clear. Godet thinks that the first four points refer to injustices in respect of the well-being and property of others: the next five, to injustices whereby we harm the person of our neighbour; then comes an allusion to six dispositions of mind centring in pride; finally the last six terms relate to the destruction of all natural human sentiments, such as tenderness and pity.‡ By thus drawing up an inventory of the evil deeds of man, Paul was conforming to a widespread custom among both Jews and pagans, namely that of making lists of virtues and vices for pedagogic purposes.§

* The correspondence of sin and penalty is again expressed by the words οὐκ ἐδοκίμασαν . . . εἰς ἀδόκιμον νοῦν.

† There is some confusion in the order of the first three words. Some eastern MSS. have replaced πονηρία by πορνεία.

‡ Θεοστυγής may be taken actively: those who hate God; this meaning is not appropriate in a list of punishments. The word has also a passive meaning: hated of God. The latter meaning is also out of place in this enumeration of social vices. Lagrange wonders whether this is not a parenthesis.

§ Similar catalogues: Rom. 13: 13; 1 Cor. 5: 10–11; 6: 9–10; 2 Cor. 12: 20; Gal. 5: 19–21; Col. 3: 8; Eph. 4: 31; 1 Tim. 1: 9–10; 2 Tim. 3: 2–5. There is found in Philo (*De Sac.* A and C, ed. Mangey, II, p. 268; cf. Lagrange p. 41) a list with 147 headings! On this subject cf. M.-J. Lagrange, "Le catalogue de vices dans l'Épître aux Romains", *R.B.*, 1911, pp. 534–549, and the literature given by Michel, p. 61, n. 1.

(32) Those who have fallen into the threefold depravity which has just been described cannot claim their ignorance as an excuse. They had some knowledge of God and consequently also of His will and commandment (ἐπιγνόντες recalls γνόντες τὸν Θεόν). Just as they refused to acknowledge God, they also refused to obey a divine will, disobedience to which, they realized, would mean conflict with the very laws of their life, and as such would necessarily incur the Creator's punishment. Paul takes into account the moral teachings of paganism;* but he does not in consequence mitigate the severity of the picture. Men who are capable of entertaining lofty moral convictions are so much the more culpable when they betray them, whether by their own action or by approving the guilty action of others.† If it is true that adultery, for example, was "almost always punished by death" in the ancient East,‡ the ancient world did not wait for the *Corydon* of André Gide in order to justify homosexuality.§

In this passage, Paul was not proposing to furnish a com-

---

* He will recur to it in 2 : 15, and we too.

† "Have not all peoples hated iniquity? (Yet) because of them it continues its progress. Does not the declaration of truth come from the lips of all peoples? (Yet) is there a tongue which cleaves to it?" one reads in a fragment of Qumran (cf. *R.B.*, 1949; Vermès, *Les manuscrits du désert de Juda*, 2nd ed. 1954, p. 199).

‡ Walter Kornfeld, "L'adultère dans l'Orient antique", *R.B.*, 1950, pp. 92–109.

§ Plato (*Banquet*), Plutarch (*Lycurgus*) make homosexual love the highest form of love, the path of virtue, the power capable of overcoming tyrants (A. Gide has added: the source of Greek art . . .). Among many peoples homosexuality, although not specially esteemed, was not punished as illicit. Mazdaism and Hebraism considered it a crime only to be expiated by death (Darmsteter, *Sacred Books of the East*, IV, XXXVI: Lev. 18: 22–24; 20: 13. Cf. Edward Westermarck, *Origin and Development of Moral Ideas*, II, pp. 440–472). There were of course Israelites who shared the manners which Paul condemns in the pagans (Test. Levi 17: 11; Sanh. 7: 4; cf. Strack-Billerbeck, IV, p. 71), but it cannot be said that there were any who justified them. That is a further difficulty about admitting that Paul is speaking of the Jews from 1 : 32, as has been maintained by F. Flückiger, "Zur Unterscheidung von Heiden und Juden in Röm. 1: 18; 2: 3", *Th.Z.*, 1954, pp. 154–158. The expression τὸ δικαίωμα τοῦ Θεοῦ does not necessarily refer to the knowledge of the Jewish law, as is shown by 2: 26.

71

plete and exact account of the state of affairs in regard to paganism and the natural man. He was well aware that pagans too fulfil what the law prescribes (2: 14) as also that the teachings of certain philosophers denounced most of the forms of depravity which he mentioned. We should find the picture drawn by the apostle excessive and unfair if we supposed his intention had been to give a portrait of all men. The aim of Paul is different. He wishes to describe an orientation of the human being, its inner tendencies. Doubtless no one goes as far as he suggests. No one illustrates in his individual life all the depravities which he conjures up. But this is not the point. The apostle's purpose rather is to bring his reader to ask himself whether he recognizes in his own character and inner condition the reflection of any of the features which Paul lends to his portrait of man without God.

Such a self-examination is intended to bring him to the realization that he too is in solidarity with a humanity which is thus ravaged to its depths by its rejection of God. "Let him who is without sin among you be the first to throw a stone at her" (Jn. 8: 7) said Jesus on one occasion in order to bring His interlocutors to the realization of the solidarity of mankind in sin, even though any one of them has not committed such and such a particular sin. Paul writes not as a moralist but as a preacher of the gospel and in order to make us realize that all men whatsoever stand under the "wrath" of God. No one is guilty of so many sins in their totality, but no one is altogether innocent and no one can claim that what is said here does not concern him at all. Each one is involved, although the picture brings together features which are scattered among multitudinous individual lives. This portrait resembles no one man because it resembles all men.‡

‡ See note on v. 18.

CHAPTER

2

¹Therefore you have no excuse, O man, whoever you are, when you judge another; for in passing judgment upon him you condemn yourself, because you, the judge, are doing the very same things. ²We know that the judgment of God rightly falls upon those who do such things. ³Do you suppose, O man, that when you judge those who do such things and yet do them yourself, you will escape the judgment of God? ⁴Or do you presume upon the riches of his kindness and forbearance and patience? Do you not know that God's kindness is meant to lead you to repentance? ⁵But by your hard and impenitent heart you are storing up wrath for yourself on the day of wrath when God's righteous judgment will be revealed. ⁶For he will render to every man according to his works: ⁷to those who by patience in well-doing seek for glory and honour and immortality, he will give eternal life; ⁸but for those who are factious and do not obey the truth, but obey wickedness, there will be wrath and fury. ⁹There will be tribulation and distress for every human being who does evil, the Jew first and also the Greek, ¹⁰but glory and honour and peace for every one who does good, the Jew first and also the Greek. ¹¹For God shows no partiality.

(1f.) It is not easy to decide to whom Paul is addressing himself in the interpellation of the section 2: 1–11. Exegesis in general* has decided that Israel is intended, because of the Israelite tendency to despise the Gentiles† and to abuse

* Except Zahn, who insists on the logical relation which διό establishes between 2: 1 and what precedes; also Kühl, *ad loc.* Cf. E. Weber, *Die Beziehungen von Römer 1–3 zur Missionspraxis des Paulus*, 1905, pp. 6off. G. Schrenk, "Der Römerbrief als Missionsdokument", *Studien zu Paulus*, p. 90.

† "Weigh in the balances our iniquities and those of other nations and it will be seen on which side the scale dips. When have the inhabitants of other lands not sinned against you? And what nation, like ourselves,

its conviction of election. Was it not proper to remind precisely Israel that the principle of retribution which it claimed in favour of its own merits did not allow any leniency towards demerits and showed no respect of persons?

To this it may be objected that a paragraph thus addressed to the Jew would interrupt the flow of a discourse on mankind (including the Jews), for the apostle indisputably returns to the theme of the natural man at v. 12. Moreover in several particulars it would duplicate what is said of the Jews from v. 17 onwards. The vocabulary used here has nothing in common with that which is characteristic of the apostle when he speaks to the Jews or of the Jews (here he apostrophizes "man, whoever you are"* . . . and he makes no mention of the law but speaks of the "truth", etc.).

Hence we would prefer to understand the sequence of ideas as follows.† In reply to the severe evocation of the consequence of the rejection of God one is tempted to say: "Men in general may be capable of all that, but not I; I do not abandon myself to such grave disorders." The Pharisee is always present in each one of us: "God, I thank thee that I am not like other men" (Lk. 18: 11). We have noted that Paul wishes to induce in his readers the realization of their solidarity with a humanity, all of whose members, no doubt, do not surrender themselves to all the vices he depicts, but not one of whom avoids them completely. It is of no use condemning the sins which others commit, urging that one is not guilty of such sins oneself, when at the same time one does commit other sins. That man is without excuse who uses the vices of others, even the worst, as a screen for his own faults, even the slightest. What counts is not the evil that one does not do, but the evil that one does do, and the good which one omits to do.

has kept your commandments?" (4 Ezra 3: 34–35). Not only were all the heathen relegated to Gehenna (Sanh. 13: 2; Sifre Deut. 32: 8; 2 Bar· LXXXV: 9) but they were regarded not as men but as beasts (Yeb· 61b). Cf. Strack-Billerbeck, IV, p. 778, 1180. J. Bonsirven, *Le Judaïsme Palestinien*, 1934, I, p. 101.

* Kühl notes that ὦ ἄνθρωπε resumes the ἄνθρωπος of 1: 18.

† The difficulty offered by 2: 1 has led to the supposition that the text has been tampered with. It has been thought that 2: 1 is a gloss (R. Bultmann, "Glossen im Römerbrief", *Th.L.Z.*, 1947, p. 198) or that it formed the reply to the question of v. 3 (Michel, p. 64).

This is the reason for what is said about retribution in vv. 6–11.

Following the style of the diatribe, Paul addresses himself to a fictitious opponent.* The latter tries to cover himself by denouncing the vices of others. "You don't do that particular thing, but you are just as bad," retorts the apostle. "You judge and condemn? That proves that you know the will of God, and you condemn yourself by that very fact." The judgment which God pronounces on men is in accordance with the truth. In the sight of God, man is not what he knows, nor what he says, but what he does.

(3f.) To be sure, in showing himself capable of discrimination and condemnation, man gives proof of his dignity as man. But by exercising this faculty in regard to others and invoking it to escape the judgment of God in regard to himself, man is forgetting why he has been given this power of moral judgment. God has given it to us in order that we may judge ourselves rather than others and thus be brought to repentance and a turning back to God, our Creator. To know the good does not furnish us with a claim to divine indulgence. The fact that the hour of divine judgment has not yet struck does not by any means show that God judges us favourably. Knowledge of the good is one of the conditions of repentance; the second is the time of respite granted by the patience of God. The whole history of humanity, like the life of each of its members, has taken place under the controlling fact of God's patience ever since sinners have existed.† History is the school of repentance, but we must learn the lesson and not squander our time.

* The apostrophe to a fictitious objector has always supplied orators with a convenient means of amplifying their points in lively fashion. The dialogue, which since Socrates had been well established in philosophy, had become a normal method of persuasion with public exponents of the popular Stoic ethic in the Hellenistic period. The influence of this literary procedure on Paul is obvious. Cf. P. Wendland, "Die philosophische Propaganda und die Diatribe", *Hell. Röm. Kultur*, 1907, pp. 39–53; A. Oltramare, *Les Origines de la Diatribe Romaine*, 1926.

† ". . . For a long time the Most High showed patience towards the inhabitants of the world, and not for their sake, but because of the times which he had foreseen" (4 Ezra 7: 74).

(5f.) He who has not understood that history develops under the governance of the merciful patience of God, misses the ever-present opportunity of repentance and uses his time wrongly. He lives as if the intermissions granted by the patience of God signified divine indifference or weakness. But history marches on to its goal, each day counts, life is not a vain jest, something ultimate takes place in it. The art of living might be compared with the art of guiding a commercial enterprise: on the day of its liquidation it is seen whether wealth has been accumulated or debts. Paul writes ironically: "You are storing something up," and his meaning is that man is storing up the abundance of the wrath of God.* When God makes known His judgment on impenitence, then will be disclosed the justice of His government of the world, which the ambiguous windings of history might have caused us to doubt.† The Greeks could not fail to countenance the idea of a final retribution which was well known to them: "For great crimes, there are great punishments stored up in the hands of the gods," wrote Herodotus (11: 120);‡ as a Jew, Paul expresses himself on this point by a formula which is perhaps borrowed from Ps. 62: 13 (cf. Prov. 24: 12) but without saying that he is quoting scripture, for he has the Gentiles in view as well.

(7) The prospect of strict retribution is by no means a pleasing one for him who has no illusions about the demands of God. Paul reminds us of the character of a good action. In the first place it is marked by perseverance; it is not enough to act well from time to time; a deed is good only if it is persisted in. Further, it is done in view of a transcendent end which excludes all mundane cupidity. 1 Pet. 1: 7 and Rev. 2: 9 express in similar terms the ultimate perspectives of faith.§

* The image of the treasure is sometimes positive, sometimes negative. Cf. Matt. 6: 19; Lk. 12: 21-33; 6: 45; 12: 34; Mk. 10: 21; Matt. 19: 21; Lk. 18: 22; Col. 2: 3. It is often used in an eschatological context.

† $\Delta\iota\kappa\alpha\iota\alpha\kappa\rho\iota\sigma\iota\alpha$, an uncommon term, of recent formation, suggesting the justice of the judge in the exercise of his functions (cf. Test. Lev. 3: 2; 15: 2). In the same sense, $\delta\iota\kappa\alpha\iota\alpha$ $\kappa\rho\iota\sigma\iota\varsigma$ 2 Th. 1: 5; Jn. 5: 30.

‡ Cf. Plato, Laws, 716d.

§ Cf. Matt. 5: 12; Lk. 6: 23; Matt. 6: 1; Mk. 9: 41; Matt. 10: 42; 1 Cor. 3: 8; Col. 3: 24; 2 John 8.

(8) The evil deed is motivated by the spirit of faction which always springs from the chicanery of refusing to God what one owes Him in order to grant it to oneself.* A man thus calls in question what in his inner self he knows he ought to do. It is the way in which the serpent of Gen. 3: 1 proceeds —namely to contest what God has said in order to do as one likes. Truth consists in what God has said. To depart from it is to obey the ἀδικία (cf. 1: 18), i.e. injustice, personified in Gen. 3: 1 by the figure of the serpent. The wrath of God strikes all those who ridicule His will.†

(9–11) In speaking of men in general (cf. 1: 18), Paul was also speaking of the Israelites in so far as they share in the universal human condition. If grace has separated Israel in order to make it the instrument of revelation, the Israelites as men must consider that what is said of mankind as a whole is valid also for them. Their special situation as members of the elect people will be examined later. But they will never be able to understand the truth of this situation until they have consented to be classified among men in general who hold the truth of God captive within their own unrighteousness. The Jew cannot escape from the universal human condition; what is said of the pagan is therefore valid for him in so far as he is a man, for him as he is in himself, aside from the grace of election, and as he knows he must be so soon as he ceases to rely on divine grace.

In order that there may be no misunderstanding, Paul repeats what he has just said concerning the double judgment of God, to remind his readers that this concerns the Jew, who is too much inclined to rest in the divine favours and to forget his weakness as man. God is no respecter of persons so far as concerns the severity of His condemnation or the

* Ἐριθεία probably comes from ἔριθος =reward and not from ἔρις =dispute. This rare word no doubt suggests the vile dispositions oı those who succumb to bribery. However, the meaning of the word according to Phil. 1: 16; 2: 3 (cf. 2 Cor. 12: 20; Gal. 5: 20; Jas. 3: 14–16) seems to be a quarrelsome haggling spirit (thus Lagrange, Lietzmann, after Vulg. Pesh. Chrys.).

† Ὀργή and θυμός together constitute a formula; cf. Rev. 16: 19; 19: 15. There is no real difference between the two terms. Cf. Büchsel, Th.Wb.NT, III, 168.

generosity of His rewards. If He has given to Israel a special knowledge of His "truth", this implies an additional responsibility. The judgment will thus strike in the first place those whom a special revelation was designed to remove from evil (cf. Jer. 25: 29; Ez. 9: 10; I Pet. 4: 17).

Along these lines, the apostle affirms the principle of exact retribution: man will be rewarded or punished by God according to his works. This does not imply any contradiction with the principle of the free justification of the believer independently of his works. The two principles have not the same object. In his present discourse Paul is describing the condition of men before God quite apart from the divine grace of redemption. In His created works God yields a knowledge of Himself which makes men capable of, and responsible for, offering to Him the worship and obedience which are His due; according as to whether they refuse or render Him this offering, God punishes or recompenses. This divine consideration of the right and the good does not however mean that God recognizes the pretensions of man to accumulate merits which are of value in His sight and so to acquire a right over against God. For the right which Paul envisages here is the conduct of a humanity responding to God's general revelation, of a humanity unaware of the drama of the fall, and consequently acting outside the sphere of all juridical questions and all preoccupation with merit. It is fallen man alone who is concerned about his merits. In fact, the state of humanity here envisaged has never been realized in our human history; no man renders to God the worship and obedience which are due to Him; no man lives in His sight without raising pretensions to some righteousness of his own. In the actual situation of men it is only the path of repentance leading man to receive through faith the promise of gratuitous justification which can open up to mankind the hope of a favourable judgment from God. It is by faith that fallen man is restored to that state of life which God's general revelation should have made possible for him; it is by faith that he becomes willing to submit to the condemnation and forgiveness of God all his previous works; it is by faith that it is henceforth possible for him to obey by walking humbly before God. We shall have to consider later the question of the judgment of God on the works which spring from faith.

[12]All who have sinned without the law will also perish without the law, and all who have sinned under the law will be judged by the law. [13]For it is not the hearers of the law who are righteous before God, but the doers of the law who will be justified. [14]When Gentiles who have not the law do by nature what the law requires, they are a law to themselves, even though they do not have the law. [15]They show that what the law requires is written on their hearts, while their conscience also bears witness and their conflicting thoughts accuse or perhaps excuse them [16]on that day when, according to my gospel, God judges the secrets of men by Christ Jesus.

(12f.) All men are placed therefore under the judgment of God. Yet there are distinctions between them which raise many questions. Some are in the situation in which mankind has become involved through its rejection of general revelation; others have been the object of an intervention by which God has made known His will in the law revealed to Moses, so that man might be reinstated in his original destiny. We might ask in what way the judgment of God operates with respect to the two classes.

Paul first recalls the general principle which determines the judgment of God; the determining fact is the measure of concrete obedience, what man does with the knowledge of the divine will which he has. Those who are without the law will be judged without the law. Since the general condition of humanity is under consideration, it is known that they are disobedient to God as the previous sections have affirmed. Paul can therefore say that they will perish without the law. Yet again, those who have special knowledge of the divine will may not presume on their privilege by supposing that for them also the judgment of God will not be in accordance with the obedience which they have shown. They hear the law read in the synagogue, but to be righteous it is not sufficient to know God and His will.*

* "The chief thing is not to discuss but to act" (Pirke Aboth 1:17; cf. 3:18) the rabbis used to say. On the other hand: "Even when we sin, we are still Thine, for we know Thy power; but we would not sin for we know that we are counted among Thine own. To know Thee is perfect righteousness, and to know Thy power the root of immortality" (Wis. 15:2).

79

(14) The application of this principle of divine justice to the Gentiles evidently raises a difficulty: if they are ignorant of the law, how can they be reproached with not accomplishing the divine will? It had been asserted, it is true, that the Gentiles had refused the law, whereas Israel had had the merit of recognizing it (Mekh. 19: 2; S. Deut. 33: 2, etc.). Hence their ignorance of the law would in itself render them guilty. Paul adheres to the principle he has laid down: *nullum crimen sine lege*, which he proposes to apply also to pagans. In point of fact, the latter are not altogether without law as is shown by the fact that they do at times fulfil the will of God (ὅταν, *when*, suggests what is occasional); doubtless, not after formal obedience to its authority but after an inward struggle which shows they realize that they should do certain things and avoid doing others. As Paul asserts twice here, they have not the law, but "they are a law unto themselves" which is to say that spontaneously they have sufficient knowledge of what God wills or forbids, with the consequence that the judgment of God can be exercised without any injustice.

The somewhat enigmatic terms in which the apostle expresses himself do not permit us to decide what concrete content he gave to this inner law of which man disposes, and this point does not concern him; for the extensiveness of the knowledge of what God commands or forbids has no bearing on the argument, which is only concerned to explain how God judges those who stand outside the Mosaic law. There is no reason to take what the apostle says as grounds for affirming—or denying—that he attributed to the Gentiles an extensive knowledge of the will of God in general.* The apostle simply notes the fact—which is indisputable and sufficient for the problem under discussion—that the Gentile is a moral agent, having at his disposal a knowledge and a faculty which justify us in regarding him as such. The word φύσει does not greatly help in the analysis: it serves to indicate that the pagan, in the given case, acts on his own initia-

* Still more must we avoid supposing that the apostle wished to show "how the Gentiles can be saved in spite of their not having received the law" (Lagrange). This remark is against the whole argument which tends to establish the responsibility and culpability of all mankind.

tive, spontaneously, apart from any special revelation such as was granted to the Jew. Φύσει has been understood in various ways, but we should not give it a philosophic meaning; it simply serves to contrast the Gentiles as such with the Jews who have received the law.*

(15) For the Israelite, the law means the text of the law: the knowledge of the law of God which Jeremiah proclaimed as characteristic of the eschatological age springs from a law divinely written in the heart (Jer. 31 : 33).† The Gentile who does the τὰ τοῦ νόμου acts in conditions comparable, though not identical, with those of the Israelite in his confrontation by the law of Moses. In his heart is written the "work of the law", i.e. *what the law prescribes*.‡ By means of this formula Paul suggests that the Gentile has a certain knowledge of the law, not perfect and complete (for this would imply the fulfilment of Jeremiah's prophecy) but none the less real: he knows in truth what the law commands, without knowing that it is God who commands it, and also without knowing the nature of the God who commands it.§

* Bengel has connected it with what precedes: "those who have no law by nature", but this construction is not natural to Paul. Connected with what follows, the word has generally been understood in an emphatic sense, as an allusion to the natural law, which would supply some knowledge of the will of God. But φύσει has not this meaning in Gal. 2 : 15; 4 : 8; Eph. 2 : 3, where it suggests the given nature of some one, his special characteristics, and not nature in general and the universal law. (Cf. F. Flückiger, "Die Werke des Gesetzes bei den Heiden nach Röm. 2: 14ff.", *Th.Z.*, 1952, p. 31, who writes: "What man as such does, he does φύσει, and what he as such is, he is φύσει.")

† Cf. the moving appeal of Antigone to unwritten and immutable laws (Soph. *Ant.*, 454).

‡ Bo Reicke, "Syneidesis in Röm. 2: 15", *Th.Z.*, 1956, p. 160, understands "the work of the law" in the light of 3: 20; 7: 7 to refer to the awakening sense of sin in view of justification by faith (3: 21, 31; 5: 20; 10: 4) which seems forced and incongruous with the description "written on their hearts".

§ Stoicism professed that man has by nature the knowledge of the good: to obey nature is to obey God, for φύσις is God; texts in Lietzmann, p. 40; we will cite only Cicero: "*lex est ratio summa, insita in natura, quae jubet ea quae facienda sunt prohibetque contraria*" (*De leg.* 1 : 6, 18). Paul's use of φύσις should not deceive us; when he speaks of nature Paul still thinks in Hebrew; he does not find in nature the anonymous law and

The work of the law engraved in the heart manifests itself by the inner struggles to which it gives rise. In all ages, humanity has pondered on the worth of its conduct and made a judgment of value on the possibilities open to its choice. This implies the characteristic activity of the moral conscience. It seems that Paul imagines an inner process of debate which proceeds as follows: the "heart" suggests a decision; the conscience supports it by its own testimony (cf. the συν of συνμαρτυρούσης); what was merely a possibility without moral qualification now becomes a matter of obligation; the more one thinks of it, the more one feels that in some particular direction lies the path of duty. Then arises opposition of all kinds springing from false reasoning and false pretexts, etc. Arguments are developed on conflicting lines, contradictory thoughts clash.* When Gentiles, after such inner debates, accomplish the things of the law, their deeds are moral in character. This dialogue which man conducts with himself, this debate in which he is in turn the accuser and the defender of himself, shows that, for the appreciation of his conduct, he has at his disposition some objective term of reference, something in fact which God has ingrained in his heart and to which his conscience brings a subjective confirmation.†

reason (λόγος) underlying all things, but the action of the living God who writes His will in the heart, the central organ of the personality.

* The passage has also been interpreted thus: the existence of the "requirement of the law written in their hearts" is attested on the one hand by the debates of the individual conscience, on the other by the judgments which men make on each other (Sanday and Headlam, p. 61, Kühl, p. 81, Heidland, *Th.Wb.NT*, IV, p. 289). In the *Bible de Jérusalem*: "proved by the witness of their conscience as also by the interior judgments of blame or praise which they make on each other".

† After the belief arose that there was a direct influence of Stoicism on the Pauline notion of conscience, and even that the apostle was indebted to Stoic circles, it then came to be thought that the relation of Paul to contemporary philosophies and religions was more complex than had been imagined. The word συνείδησις bearing a moral significance appears only with Wis. 17: 11, Dionysius of Halicarnassus and Diodorus Siculus. It has been possible to affirm that the NT συνείδησις has no analogy in Stoicism (A. Bonhöffer, *Epictet und das Neue Testament*, 1911, pp. 156–157). If such an assertion goes too far, since the reality of conscience is a universal fact which the Stoics like every one else recognized, it is none the less true that the facts seem to suggest that "the Pauline

Hence the judgment of God on the Gentiles rests on an adequate basis; God cannot be accused of unfairly incriminating beings who were not properly informed.*

(16) Of course the conditions in which these inner debates take place elude the investigation of any other person. We cannot set ourselves up as judges of our neighbour. But this is not so for God. It is impossible to suspect that the judgment of God is distorted by the conditions under which it is made. God knows the secrets of all hearts;† He sees what we do not see; He sees what we hide from others and so often too from ourselves. Thus those who have sinned apart from the law will be judged apart from the law, but nevertheless in com-

---

conscience is a ripe fruit of the Israelite ethic", even if the popular currency of συνείδησις supplied the apostle with a word and an idea ready to be fertilized by revelation. Cf. many texts on the question and a bibliography in C. Spicq, "La Conscience dans le Nouveau Testament", *R.B.*, 1938, pp. 50–80, and his excursus "La bonne conscience et la foi", in *Les Épîtres pastorales*, 1947, pp. 29–38.

* Since Augustine (*Contra Jul.*, IV. III, 25; *De spir. et litt.*, c. 7) it has several times been maintained (Luther, K. Barth) that in these vv. Paul is not speaking of the heathen but of Gentile Christians; it is felt that Paul could not have attributed to the heathen this degree of moral knowledge after he has traced the terrible picture of their immorality which has just been read. This opinion cannot be sustained. First, it seems to spring from a forced interpretation of the text where Paul does not say that the heathen are patterns of moral conduct, but that they sometimes do τὰ τοῦ νόμου. Next, Paul did not deny that the heathen have an at least relative capacity for forming moral judgments, since he alludes to the duplicity of some who, while realizing that certain deeds are wrong, yet approve them; Paul even writes that "they know God's decree" (1: 32). Nothing could be clearer! Let us note again that the evidence of facts should have excluded such an interpretation. Calvin took good care not to follow Augustine on this point; as a jurist he knew very well that the heathen elaborated systems of law which show a secure understanding of morals: "There never was a nation so barbarous or inhuman that it did not regulate its life by some form of law. Since then all nations spontaneously seek to establish laws, we see clearly from that that there are certain original conceptions of right which are imprinted on the hearts of men by nature" (*Commentaries on NT, ad loc.*). Finally if φύσει were intended to refer to τὰ μὴ νόμον ἔχοντα it would be normal for it to precede these words. Exegesis, history, and grammar conspire against this interpretation.

† Cf. 1 Cor. 4: 5; Mk. 4: 22; Matt. 6: 6, etc.

83

plete justice.* And all this reasoning is in harmony with the gospel which the apostle preaches, as is shown by 2 Cor. 5: 10 which confirms Rom. 2: 6. We should see no difficulty in the fact that the gospel which proclaims salvation by faith is evoked in a context affirming that God judges man according to his works. The two doctrines are not mutually exclusive. It is arbitrary to attribute the one to the Jewish background of the apostle who was unable to rid himself of his inheritance, and the other to his Christian inspiration and thus to see in Paul a wretched being tugged this way and that by two contradictory systems. It is the Christ Himself who is to preside at the last judgment (2 Cor. 5: 10). The apostle did not preach that justification by faith freed us from the necessity of performing good deeds, but that we should understand in a new way both the source and the significance of the latter. His present concern is to show that the answer which man makes to God by the way in which he lives is something which cries out in accusation against him. The question of knowing how he who has accepted the condemnation he deserves and the grace offered in Jesus Christ *should* live is quite another matter, which will be discussed further on; it will then be seen that the judgment of God falls upon believers also.

> [17]But if you call yourself a Jew and rely upon the law and boast of your relation to God [18]and know his will and approve what is excellent, because you are instructed in the law, [19]and if you are sure that you are a guide to the blind, a light to those who are in darkness, [20]a corrector of the foolish, a teacher of children, having in the law the embodiment of knowledge and truth—[21]you then who teach others, will you not teach your-

* *Ἐν ᾗ ἡμέρᾳ* has been connected with v. 13: "those who fulfil the law will be justified *on the day when* . . ."; vv. 14 and 15 are a parenthesis (Godet). It is simpler to connect these words with ἐδείκνυνται; the present is durative: "they show (will show) that the work of the law is written in their heart on the day when God judges them (will judge)" (cf. Lietzmann). The text is uncertain. S D etc. gives ἐν ἡμέρᾳ ὅτε. A and some of the versions: ἐν ἡμέρᾳ ᾗ. Only B gives ἐν ᾗ ἡμέρᾳ. In any event, these vv. present great difficulties; J. Weiss has suggested considering vv. 14, 15 as a gloss; Bultmann (*Th.L.Z.*, 1947, p. 200) suggests the same for v. 16. "*The stylistic difficulties in our context are almost insoluble*" (Michel, p. 70).

self? While you preach against stealing, do you steal? [22]You who say that one must not commit adultery, do you commit adultery? You who abhor idols, do you rob temples? [23]You who boast in the law, do you dishonour God by breaking the law? [24]For, as it is written, "The name of God is blasphemed among the Gentiles because of you."

[25]Circumcision indeed is of value if you obey the law; but if you break the law, your circumcision becomes uncircumcision. [26]So, if a man who is uncircumcised keeps the precepts of the law, will not his uncircumcision be regarded as circumcision? [27]Then those who are physically uncircumcised but keep the law will condemn you who have the written code and circumcision but break the law. [28]For he is not a real Jew who is one outwardly, nor is true circumcision something external and physical. [29]He is a Jew who is one inwardly, and real circumcision is a matter of the heart, spiritual and not literal. His praise is not from men but from God.

(17) Since the judgment of God takes place on the basis of the principle already affirmed (vv. 6–11) it is now a question of explaining the condition of the Jew in the sight of God. Now God judges according to the measure of obedience, not according to claims, and the obedience due to God is in proportion to the knowledge of Him that one has been granted. Thus in the last analysis the privileges of Israel are but added responsibilities, and far from ameliorating its situation they do but aggravate it. Paul mentions these privileges: to call oneself a Jew,* to rely upon the law,† and to glory in a special relation to God.‡ Here one feels an undertone of irony, and this enumeration becomes the formulation of a charge.

(18) The practical consequences of these privileges (which are true) are further privileges and hence imply further responsibilities; to know the will (absolute sense: the will of God);§ to be in a position through the study of the law to know the right way of life, or "what is excellent".||

* Cf. Acts 18: 2, 24; 22: 3; Rev. 2: 9; 3: 9.
† Cf. Mic. 3: 11; 2 Kgs. 5: 18; 7: 2, 17; Ez. 29: 7; 1 Mac. 8: 12.
‡ Jer. 9: 24; Ps. Sol. 17: 1.
§ Cf. Schrenk, *Th.Wb.NT*, III, p. 58.
|| "*Non modo prae malis bona sed in bonis optima*" (Bengel on Phil. 1: 10 where we find the same formula).

(19f.) These responsibilities extend to the part which the Jews should play in the world as a guide to the peoples and a light to the nations, for by vocation and in accordance with prophecy* they are those of whom the Book of Wisdom (18: 4) states that the unfading light of the law of God must, through them, irradiate the world. It is their sacred mission to bring to all nations the treasure of the Mosaic revelation, and to apply themselves to the education of the "foolish" and of "children" whose knowledge is still erroneous (perhaps as a result of godlessness or ignorance of God) or incomplete (perhaps through lack of maturity). A difficult task but one which the children of Israel are equipped to fulfil, since they possess in the law both knowledge and truth (both what should be known of truth as well as a true knowledge) explicitly formulated and embodied.†

(21f.) The period begun at v. 17 remains suspended. Each of its members contained an implicit reply; it is readily understandable that Paul was speaking ironically; the Jews are not what they ought to be; they are worthy neither of their name, nor of their law, nor of their faith.‡ Paul takes up the thread again by using οὖν, thus drawing out the consequences. It would be fitting if Israel began by examining itself, by learning the lesson which it is engaged in teaching others, and by abstaining from doing what it condemns.§ The severity of the apostle echoes that of his Master, and the opinion of certain rabbis confirms that he was not exaggerating. ‖ The practice of casuistry facilitated such contradictions.

* Gen. 12: 3; Is. 42: 6, 7; 49: 6; Mic. 4: 1. Cf. Matt. 15: 14; 23: 16, 24; Lk. 11: 39–52; En. 105: 1. Or. Sib. 3: 194; Jos. c. ap. 2: 41.

† Since the various phrases of these vv. are not pejorative in themselves, μόρφωσις will be understood positively as in 2 Tim. 3: 5. Here Paul seems to be quoting expressions familiar to some of his contemporaries; perhaps he is borrowing them from some catechism for proselytes? (cf. Lietzmann; J. Behm, Th.Wb.NT, IV, p. 762.)

‡ It is not necessary to make of vv. 21–23 interrogatives as does Nestle.

§ Διδάσκων concerns instruction; κηρύσσων preaching, λέγων authorized quotation and its explanation (Michel).

‖ Cf. Matt. 23: 15; Ps. Sol. 4, 8: 7–14: "no sin which they have not committed, worse than the Gentiles": Strack-Billerbeck, III, pp. 66–74, 107–115.

The morality of Israel was certainly lofty and Paul does not wish to deny it. What he wished to insist on was the fact that inner contradictions ruined all this positive good, and to show that man is not in a position to raise any serious claim against God. As for the robbing of temples, one would like to believe that the Jews did not do such things themselves, but on the other hand they did not scruple to profit from such misdeeds, which seem to have been fairly frequent (cf. Acts 19: 37); perhaps this kind of sacrilege in respect of pagan temples was justified by the argument that they were thus destroying the object of idolatrous cults.

(23f.) In conclusion, those who should honour God by their knowledge of His will, actually dishonour Him by their faithlessness. And what is worse: they glory in their special knowledge of the divine will, and their disobedience is only rendered worse by this fact. Whereas they think they are accumulating merits, they are in fact only bringing upon themselves a severer condemnation. Because of Israel whose mission it was to bring the nations to the worship of the true God, the name of Yahweh is blasphemed.*

(25) The tone now becomes more didactic; the charge seems to be completed and the argument proceeds on the following lines. In practice, circumcision sums up for the mind of the Jew the privileges of Israel; it is the sign and token of God's covenant with Israel and the perfect commandment. To elude it constituted an almost unforgivable sin; to receive it gave protection against Gehenna.† Hence in the end circumcision became a magical action. Now in fact, circumcision was the sacrament of that election of Israel which God in His grace had determined; it referred to the covenant and was the very sign and symbol of Yahweh's ownership of Israel. By its permanence and visibility it was calculated to

* Allusion to Is. 52: 5, regardless of the sense of these words in the context. Ez. 36: 30 is more appropriate here. Cf. also Lev. 26: 32.
† "The principle is so often repeated that it may be considered traditional" (J. Bonsirven, *Jud. Palest.*, II, p. 70). Texts are too numerous to be cited. Cf. also Strack-Billerbeck, IV, pp. 37–40; 1063–1067. W. Bousset, *Rel. Jud.*, p. 197, denies that circumcision gave a real assurance of salvation.

remind every Israelite that God had made him a member of the holy people. Like every other sacrament, circumcision was the sign of an action of God which believers had to answer by their faith and obedience, so as not to blaspheme and deprive themselves of the proffered grace. Paul does not dispute the usefulness of the sacrament but he refuses to recognize that it has any sort of magical efficacy (v. 25a). Further, circumcision signifies the enduring reality of God's work; the transgressor of the law is not therefore simply breaking divine commandments; he is also denying, repelling, and destroying what God has done for him in the original election of his people; he is ruining God's work both in regard to the Israelites and to mankind in general; he is casting himself outside the sphere of the statute of which circumcision is the seal and sacrament. Thus his circumcision becomes for him uncircumcision (v. 25b).*

(26) Reciprocally, the Gentile† who fulfils the will of God (cf. 2: 14, 15) by obeying it in so far as he is acquainted with it will be judged by God without any unfavourable prejudice. No more than the presence of circumcision is an automatic guarantee of the divine favour, is its absence a sign of divine prejudice. For every one the divine demand is proportionate to grace. The remark of Paul is double-edged.

(27) Such a Gentile will therefore find himself in a better position on the judgment day than the faithless Jew; the former will judge the Jew; not by assuming the role of judge, but by serving as a witness for the prosecution, for his obedience will make plain to the Jew what he ought to have done and could have done.‡

* Other peoples practised circumcision, notably the Egyptians. Gen. 17: 23 mentions the circumcision of Ishmael. Cf. A. Alt, *R.A.C.*, p. 445ff. This rite was thus not at all original; the covenant alone gave it its true theological bearing.

† 'Ακροβυστία: foreskin; by extension, the state of being uncircumcised, or the Gentiles as the uncircumcised.

‡ Cf. Strack-Billerbeck, I, p. 650. The same idea in Matt. 12: 41; Lk. 11: 32 (κατακρινοῦσιν). This is probably also the role of the Twelve in Matt. 19: 28; Lk. 22: 30 (κρίνοντες).

(28f.) Summing up, external things are futile unless inner realities are joined to them. God does in fact act, contingently, by means of external things but His aim is always the heart. Circumcision is indeed of value (v. 25) not because it creates a Jew who is recognizable by this external sign, but because man accepts that his heart should become the object of an operation comparable to circumcision; the ablation of the foreskin is the sacrament of God's will to remove all impurity from the heart.* The Jew who surrenders his body to circumcision without at the same time offering his heart to a process of purification is not truly circumcised, at least in the eyes of God, who looks at the heart and demands an inward and not a superficially literal obedience.†

There may be in v. 29b a play on words: Judah means praise (Gen. 29: 35; 49: 8).‡

---

* Cf. Deut. 10: 16; 30: 6; Jer. 4: 4; 9: 26; Ez. 44: 7, 9; Od. Sol 11: 1, 2; Acts 7: 51. In Col. 2: 11, περιτομῇ is synonymous with ἀπέκδυσις.

† The opposition ἐν πνεύματι οὐ γράμματι is not easy to understand. It generally refers to the contrast between the servile obedience of the Jew to the letter of scripture, and the interior action of the Holy Spirit which frees the believer and leads him into a new understanding of scripture and a new life (7: 6; 2 Cor. 3: 6). In this case, Paul is alluding to the circumcision of the heart which scripture teaches when understood spiritually, but not in its letter. Lietzmann interprets on similar lines: (Circumcision) which takes place at the dictate of the spirit, but not merely because the letter so orders it. Others think that Paul is speaking of the circumcision effected by the spirit and which the letter is incapable of effecting. Finally others tone down the expression: Paul is opposing the deep, soul-searching circumcision of the heart ("spiritual") to that which is only "the fulfilment of the letter of the law"; "thus the apostle simply explains what must be understood by the circumcision of the heart; he is not alluding to the action of the Holy Spirit" (Lagrange). This last exegesis might be the best were it not for the significance which parallel texts give to the opposition Spirit—letter.

‡ Cf. Sanday and Headlam, p. 68.

CHAPTER

3

¹Then what advantage has the Jew? Or what is the value of circumcision? ²Much in every way. To begin with, the Jews are entrusted with the oracles of God. ³What if some were unfaithful? Does their faithlessness nullify the faithfulness of God? ⁴By no means! Let God be true though every man be false, as it is written,

> "That thou mayest be justified in thy words,
> and prevail when thou art judged."

⁵But if our wickedness serves to show the justice of God, what shall we say? That God is unjust to inflict wrath on us? (I speak in a human way.) ⁶By no means! For then how could God judge the world? ⁷But if through my falsehood God's truthfulness abounds to his glory, why am I still being condemned as a sinner? ⁸And why not do evil that good may come?—as some people slanderously charge us with saying. Their condemnation is just.

(1f.) THE APOSTLE WAS too deeply Israelite himself not to raise the burning question: what then is the significance of the function of Israel? If in some cases uncircumcision is the equivalent of circumcision, why was this sacrament instituted at all? The dealings of God with His people thus become enigmatic. Was God mistaken? Has He forsworn Himself?

Paul's reply completely inverts the position of the question. The latter asked what constituted the superiority of the Jew or the usefulness of circumcision:* questions which are addressed to God from man's point of view; they concern what *man* has received. Paul now wishes us to place ourselves at God's angle of vision and to look to God who has given. The acts of God in history must be considered as such in

---

* The two questions are the same since circumcision is characteristic of the Jew.

their origin and intention (i.e. as acts *of God*) but not as *acts* in their earthly manifestations or effects. Judaism had in the end forgotten that the historical, the immanent, the horizontal was suspended to the eternal, the transcendent, the vertical; it had endowed institutions, the law and circumcision, with an absolute value because it had failed to consider them seriously in the light of election grace and of Israel's vocation as the people of God. It had come to believe that these gifts were the intrinsic and inalienable possession of Israel, whereas they were but the means of facilitating its obedience in the accomplishment of its mission.

Thus then Israel is superior to the Gentiles, most certainly; but superior from the point of view of responsibilities: the "oracles" of God have been entrusted to it. By this we must understand the promises rather than the law, as is suggested by what follows where the emphasis is placed on the promises as the vital centre of God's plan.

We should expect that after the promises Paul would quote other manifestations of the grace of God (cf. the list in Rom. 9: 4) especially as he cites the "oracles" as a beginning (πρῶτον μέν). In fact he yields to the attraction of a play on words (ἐπιστεύθησαν-ἠπίστησαν) in order to address himself already at this point to a new aspect of the question which it was indeed necessary to consider. The rest of the enumeration is omitted and πρῶτον μέν, i.e. *first of all*, remains suspended.*

(3f.) Israel, at least as regards the majority of its members, never really answered the trust which God reposed in it (Paul by using τινες is content to suggest a bigger question)†. Its defection, however, must not be taken to imply that of God, for the primary point is not Israel but God.‡ The faithfulness of God is assured, but it concerns His promises, not those to whom He addressed them. God is true when He speaks; His faithfulness is anchored in His veracity. He is

* The textual tradition has been disturbed by the anacolouthon. Origen read πρῶτοι. . . .

† It may also be punctuated: τί γὰρ εἰ ἠπίστησάν τινες, Tischendorf. Cf. however Phil. 1: 18.

‡ 'Απιστία connotes also the idea of incredulity.

91

always the God of the promise, of the covenant. Now the truthfulness of God, which means His fidelity to His promises, must be safeguarded even though it were to the confusion,* at least temporary, of those who have shown themselves to be unworthy of His confidence. Unless God be a liar, the lie of men must turn to their confusion. If they are willing to confront God, instead of sheltering themselves behind His gifts as if they had a right to them, the Jews cannot but confess their own lie and declare that God is just both in His words and actions. This is what the prayer of the psalmist recognizes (Ps. 51: 6, quoted from the LXX). The example of David is particularly significant; by his faults he showed himself unfaithful, but the very solemn promises that were made to him were maintained, and this fact makes clear the faithfulness of God: "I will not lie to David" (Ps. 89: 35).

(5) Thus the fickleness of David served to throw into relief the constancy of God. Did not the psalmist say in fact that the defection of man arose so that (ὅπως) the justice and the power of God might be made manifest? God turns to His own glorification the consequences of man's inconstancy; if we carry this idea to its logical conclusion, we might say that God can profit from the weakness of man. This raises an immense problem. Our "unrighteousness" as men serves to establish the "righteousness" of God,† and evil in the last resort contributes to good. But is not this tantamount to relativizing evil and finding some advantage in it? In that

* Ἀληθής does not denote intellectual abstract veracity; but the quality of what is solid, firm, consistent, reliable and trustworthy. The "lie" contrasts with this consistency as something fickle; it reveals the inconsistency of man. With God on the contrary it is the truth of God which makes His promises solid and unshakeable (Rom. 15: 8). See Bultmann, Th.Wb.NT, I, p. 233.

† Ἀδικία-δικαιοσύνη is the equivalent of ψεύστης-ἀληθής. The righteousness of God is His fidelity to His word of grace embodied in the covenant. Συνιστάναι: 5: 8; Gal. 2: 18; 2 Cor. 6: 4; 7: 11; in Rom. 16: 1, commend. Τί ἐροῦμεν is found only in Rom. (6 times) and shows clearly the influence of the dialogue style of the diatribe. Ἄδικος applied to God connotes His supposed fickleness, inconstancy of purpose, meaning that He would be false to Himself if He broke the covenant and repudiated His promises.

case can it still be termed evil? And can God legitimately react to it by His "wrath", i.e. by condemning man who is the author of it and destroying this evil which He was able to exploit in the interests of the good?

(6) The reply is contained in the concise statement: "By no means, for then how could God judge the world?"* The sufficient answer is to be sought in the ultimate ends pursued by the divine Providence; the judgment of the world is the final summary act of the government of God and by it His ways will be illuminated and receive their justification. This laconic reply is elucidated by the way in which 4 Ezra answers the same problem: "For a long time the Most High showed Himself patient with the inhabitants of the world, and that not for their own sake but because of the times which He had foreseen" (7: 74). The apostle had already told his readers that the patience of God is the key to His guidance of history; He is patient with sinners, not because He need be, not by minimizing their faults, but in view of the repentance which He hopes for. By the very fact of God's patience, evil seems to increase;† but as this divine patience is the condition of repentance, it prepares the way for forgiveness. Thus God will triumph over evil in regard to those who have repented. His severity towards those who have despised His forbearance (2: 4) will show, however, that evil is always abhorrent to Him.

(7) After the problem of the justice of God, comes that concerning the culpability of man. The latter sins against God, but is not the divine patience responsible for this, since it has the effect of multiplying the possibilities of sinning? And is

* Paul did not avoid the problem as Lagrange claims when he says that the apostle "prefers not to involve himself in this difficult question".

† From God's point of view, the evil is not worse *because* sins grow. Evil consists in the fact that there are sinners. Whether the latter show their deeper corruption by a greater number of guilty acts, does not change their fundamental attitude and does not increase the condemnation which God makes. The tree is judged by its fruit, whether the crop be scarce or plentiful; the tree is really cut down because it bears bad fruit; the fact that it bears little does not affect the situation if the fruit is bad. If the fruit is good, on the other hand, it is just as abundant!

not man the sinner to that extent relieved of guilt?* In reality
the problem has already been resolved. The patience of God
is not the cause of sinning and has not an aggravation of sin
in view. Such a contention would be absurd and above all
blasphemous. Paul does not even take time to expose its
absurdity, especially as his thought on this point, which has
been expounded on previous occasions, seems to have
brought upon his head severe criticisms and even calumnies,
from narrow-minded or evilly-disposed persons.

(8) The doctrine of the divine patience was clearly liable to
be misunderstood. Evil looked as if it were becoming a stage
in the achievement of good; God seemed to be making of it a
positive factor in the situation. Hence the mocking slogan
which the enemies of the apostle had devised and imputed to
him as a means of combating him: "Why not do evil that
good may come?" (cf. 6: 1). Paul turns round on them to say
that to invent such opinions and impute them to him, the
apostle, is to call down the righteous judgment of God.†

⁹What then? Are we Jews any better off? No, not at all; for
I have already charged that all men, both Jews and Greeks,
are under the power of sin, ¹⁰as it is written:
"None is righteous, no, not one;
¹¹no one understands, no one seeks for God.
¹²All have turned aside, together they have gone wrong;
no one does good, not even one."
¹³"Their throat is an open grave,
they use their tongues to deceive."
"The venom of asps is under their lips."
¹⁴"Their mouth is full of curses and bitterness."
¹⁵"Their feet are swift to shed blood,
¹⁶in their paths are ruin and misery,
¹⁷and the way of peace they do not know."
¹⁸"There is no fear of God before their eyes."
¹⁹Now we know that whatever the law says it speaks to those
who are under the law, so that every mouth may be stopped,
and the whole world may be held accountable to God. ²⁰For
no human being will be justified in his sight by works of the
law since through the law comes knowledge of sin.

* Ἀλήθεια. Cf. 1st note, p. 92.
† Καὶ μή (ἐστίν) interrogative (cf. 3: 3) with Lietzmann.

(9–18) The argument now proceeds to its conclusion. It has been asked if the Jews have any superiority over against the Gentiles (3: 1). The reply emphasized that such superiority certainly existed, if one considered the matter from the standpoint of the gifts of God which the guilty behaviour of the beneficiaries themselves had not been able to nullify. On the other hand, if one considers it from the standpoint of the beneficiaries, the alleged superiority is debatable; it cannot be affirmed without adding that it is a question exclusively of the divine gifts and, that being so, the excellence of the gifts will make manifest at the last day the unworthiness of their depositaries.*

Thus the apostle ends with this idea and emphasizes further the dominion which sin exercises over all men, a demonstration of which he has previously conducted. Relying now on the authority of scripture, Paul will oblige his reader, whether he be Jew or Greek, to examine himself and to recognize before God that he is "under the power of sin".

From v. 10 to v. 18 we have a long series of quotations very freely given. Paul shortens or modifies his texts without staying to consider whether the text in the original applies to the sins of Gentiles or Jews. Has this mosaic any plan? Some critics have thought that they could trace in it the intention of showing that the entire human personality (throat, tongue, lips, mouth, feet) as well as all men without exception, lie under the dominion of evil.† This would explain the exceptional length of the passage. With less subtlety, one notices the tripartite structure of the period; the first strophe concerns sin as spoiling the relations of man with God (vv. 10–12); the second suggests the corruption of the human personality itself, evinced in the wrong use of speech, through which the heart is expressed (vv. 13–14); the third,

---

* $Προεχόμεθα$ (middle voice) =to put forward as a pretext or excuse. Here in active sense. The text can be variously punctuated, $τί οὖν$ may be attached to $προεχόμεθα$. $Οὐ πάντως$ is in favour of separation from $τι οὖν$. One can also take $οὐ πάντως$ in the sense of "not at all" (*nequaquam*, Vulgate) which would make it out of harmony with v. 2a. The difficulty of the text has caused some alterations: $οὐ πάντως$ is replaced by $πέρισσον$ in some MSS. of which a certain number have $προκατέχομεν$ instead of $προεχόμεθα$.

† A. Feuillet, "Le plan salvifique de Dieu . . .", *R.B.*, 1950, p. 350.

the corruption of human relations (vv. 15–17). It is possible that we have here a sort of psalm, in use already among the Pauline communities.

(19f.) The Jew will be convinced by this massive condemnation both because it is scripture* which pronounces it (ὁ νόμος λέγει) and because all that scripture (ὅσα) says is authoritative. In particular they will have to note what Paul declares to be the general intention of scripture; to render all men silent and inexcusable before the divine judgment which condemns them, both Jew and Gentile (the latter being customarily considered by the Jews as the special object of the divine severity).† Scripture itself is already, *via negationis*, a witness to justification by faith;‡ by the mouth of the psalmist it denies the possibility that any creature (Paul insists by writing πᾶσα σάρξ instead of πᾶς of the LXX) may be justified in the sight of God; and Paul stresses his point again by adding "by the works of the law".§ Finally he points out that through the law we gain the awareness of sin. The law does not enable us to remove the evil of which it makes us aware through its letter; it does not victoriously strive against the forces of evil; it leaves man in servitude to the powers which hold him in bondage; it does not make available any liberating strength or newness of life. The law provides even an occasion for sinning, by the very fact that the man who obeys it at one point thinks that thereby he has gained the favour of God, whereas in reality he needs all the pardoning grace of God to cover the transgressions which he has other-

* *Νόμος* is very rare in the sense of scripture (cf. 1 Cor. 14: 21).

† *Τῷ Θεῷ*: in the presence of God (cf. לִפְנֵי?).

‡ After διότι, γέγραπται is understood.

§ Cf. Strack-Billerbeck, III, pp. 160–162; Bertram, *Th.Wb.NT*, II, p. 642–645. E. Lohmeyer, *Z.N.W.*, 1929, pp. 177–206. The Jews were aware that the law is not sufficient to preserve from sin. "The generally received principle was that no one is sinless. . . . Hence there cannot be complete confidence in the holiness of any man as long as he is alive . . . hence the fear of so many of the righteous. . . ." (J. Bonsirven, *Jud. Palest.* II, pp. 90ff.) "There is no son of woman who has not been guilty of impiety nor any living who has not sinned. This, in fact, is why we shall praise your justice and mercy, O Lord—because you will have pity on those who cannot rely on their good works" (4 Ezra. 8: 34–36).

wise committed; obedience itself brings out the nature of the sinner by nourishing his pride. The principle laid down in 2:13 is not thus contradicted: were there a human being who fulfilled the whole will of God and if in addition he were exempt from all καύχησις (boasting) so that he could render thanks and glory to God alone, God would unreservedly rejoice. But where shall we find such a man who is well-pleasing to God in all that he does and in all his thoughts about what he does?*

We cannot say whether Paul, in quoting Ps. 143, wished to remind the reader of what the psalmist had said immediately before: "Hear my prayer, O Lord; give ear to my supplications! In thy faithfulness answer me, in thy righteousness!" This appeal to the faithfulness and righteousness of God finds its exact response in the subsequent verses of the letter; the prayer of the psalmist is answered and the "righteousness" of God has been disclosed.

[21]But now the righteousness of God has been manifested apart from law, although the law and the prophets bear witness to it, [22]the righteousness of God through faith in Jesus Christ for all who believe. For there is no distinction; [23]since all have sinned and fall short of the glory of God, [24]they are justified by his grace as a gift, through the redemption which is in Christ Jesus, [25]whom God put forward as an expiation by his blood, to be received by faith. This was to show God's righteousness, because in his divine forbearance he had passed over former sins; [26]it was to prove at the present time that he himself is righteous and that he justifies him who has faith in Jesus.

[27]Then what becomes of our boasting? It is excluded. On what principle? On the principle of works? No, but on the principle of faith. [28]For we hold that a man is justified by faith

* Does 'Επίγνωσις (cf. Rom. 1:28; 10:2) reflect Hellenistic influence? Epicurus would have said: ἀρχὴ σωτηρίας γνῶσις ἁμαρτήματος which Seneca comments on thus: "Initium est salutis notitia peccati. Egregie mihi hoc dixisse videtur Epicurus. Nam qui peccare se nescit, corrigi non vult; deprehendas te oportet antequam emendes" (Epist. mor., 28, quoted by Michel, p. 87). Interior experience may explain this agreement of the moralists with the apostle; but the thought of Paul goes further, as will be realized in 4:15; 7:7. He does not merely speak of a psychological experience, he implies the divine intention which the gift of the law has concretely manifested.

apart from works of law. ²⁹Or is God the God of Jews only?
Is he not the God of Gentiles also? Yes, of Gentiles also, ³⁰since
God is one; and he will justify the circumcised on the ground
of their faith and the uncircumcised because of their faith.
³¹Do we then overthrow the law by this faith? By no means!
On the contrary, we uphold the law.

(21) We must emphasize the crucial importance, both
historical and theological, of the νυνὶ δέ, but now.* Paul has
been describing at length the situation of historical, natural
man, both Greek and Jew; over this history there broods the
negative reaction of God, His "wrath": man is on the way
towards death. "But now" things are different because an
event has supervened which objectively modifies the situation
of mankind. There is now set in contrast to the revelation of
the "wrath" of God (1: 17) the revelation of His righteousness: the contrast is significant and well calculated to confirm the interpretation given above of δικαιοσύνη; the
"righteousness" of God saves men from His "wrath"; it consists in God's fidelity to His promises, in His action for man's
salvation.

Formerly God has disclosed His will to save mankind
through the graces granted to Israel (election and law).
These remain because God does not revoke His word; but
the abuse of them of which Israel is guilty has transformed
them into occasions of falling. Furthermore, these graces
were only preparatory; they foreshadowed a perfect and
final form of grace. This final grace has now been disclosed,
and it has been so without the concurrence of the old dispensation;† rather as something new and untainted by the
imperfections of its antitype. The law and the prophets which
attest the self-revelation of God to Israel bear a positive
witness in the latter's favour; there is no rupture of continuity in the works of God, but rather a consummation of

---

* Note the importance of νῦν in the Letter to the Romans alone: 3:
26; 5: 9, 11; 6: 21; 7: 6; 8: 1, 18; 11: 5, 30, 31; 13: 11; 16: 26. Cf.
Stählin, Th.Wb.NT, V, pp. 1092–1117.

† Χωρὶς νόμου may be related to the principal idea expressed by the
verb (a manifestation which owes nothing to the law); or specially to
δικαιοσύνη (righteousness which owes nothing to the law). The construction favours the former. Essentially the idea is the same.

what has gone before. The subsequent chapters will demonstrate this repeatedly.*

(22f.) The saving action which God takes in favour of man is not meant as a reward for his obedience to the law; it has already been seen that man does not obey. God now grants man a favour which he can only receive, for he does not merit it. The attitude of the man who thinks he possesses claims to the favour of God is opposed by that of the man who realizes that he has no such claim and who trusts in the divine pity alone for the graces to which the other thinks he can show some right; in contrast to the Pharisee of the parable is set the publican. This contrast completes and confirms the one which v. 21 had established between "wrath" and "righteousness": the attitude of the Pharisee draws down upon him the divine "anger" while the publican returns to his house justified (Lk. 18: 14). This inner spiritual attitude is faith. Paul will explain at length his understanding of faith in ch. 4. But we may notice straight away in connexion with διὰ πίστεως, *by faith*, that the apostle never says διὰ τὴν πίστιν which would suggest the idea that faith is an instrumental cause.† Faith does nothing except to receive what is the gift of God. The hand of the beggar is empty, and because empty, useful; but to beg does not constitute a work, it is neither a merit nor a claim. What grace uses gains value from the fact that grace uses it, but it has no value in itself.

The object of faith is God active in Jesus Christ, or, in other words, Jesus Christ as the manifestation of the "righteousness" of God. The formula which Paul uses here might lead to misunderstanding. It should not be taken to indicate the faith of which Jesus Christ is the subject,‡ a faith

* The gift of the law characterized the second of the three periods into which the rabbis divided the history of the world; the third was to be that of the Messiah. Paul, in becoming a Christian, thinks that this third period has arrived. Hence the importance of νυνὶ δέ. The Messianic period was to suspend the authority of the law. Cf. L. Baeck, "The Faith of Paul", *Journal of Jewish Studies*, 1952.

† Rom. 4: 11: Δικαιοσύνης τῆς πίστεως. 4: 13: Δ. πίστεως. 9: 30; 10: 6: Δ. ἐκ πίστεως. Phil. 3: 9: τὴν διὰ πίστεως Χριστοῦ, τὴν ἐκ Θεοῦ Δ. ἐπὶ τῇ πίστει.

‡ Also O. Schmitz, *Die Christusgemeinschaft Paulus' im Lichte seines Genitivgebrauchs*, 1924.

99

proposed as a pattern of obedience and trust. The genitive can refer to the object (Phil. 1 : 27). None the less Christ is an object who is known as an object only if He communicates Himself and becomes active in the very faith of which He is the object. Subject and object are not mutually exclusive in this context.*

Since the righteousness of God is disclosed outside the sphere of what man himself can contribute, it overflows the frontiers which up till then had been constituted by integration with the elect people and knowledge of the law. Every man can open his hand to receive. Faith being accessible to all, righteousness is likewise offered to all. It will be recalled that all need it, Israel as much as the Gentiles, since all are equally deprived of the "glory" of God, i.e. deprived of the radiation of Yahweh, of what is visible of the essence of this invisible God, of what is communicable in the being of this transcendent God. The expression means being deprived of the presence of God and communion with Him.† The effect of this disclosure of God's righteousness is thus to restore to men access to God and participation in His glory (5: 2), hence in His essence and very being.‡

(24) Before saying how this disclosure of divine "righteousness" is operative concretely in the life of men by their justification, Paul wishes to lay securely the objective foundations of the redemptive work of God. *Δωρεάν, gratuitously*, first of all emphasizes that the beneficiary has no contribution to make: he receives all and gives nothing. *Τῇ αὐτοῦ χάριτι* explains why this is so; it is the kindness, the lavish grace of

* A. Deissmann, *Paulus*, 1925, p. 53 has spoken of a mystic "genitive".

† Those who approach God are surrounded and clad with His glorious effulgence. In the apocalyptic tradition, glory is the clothing of the righteous (4 Ezra. 7: 122–125; Apoc. Bar. 51: 1, 3; 54: 15). Glorification is the achievement of salvation. (Apoc. Bar. 54: 21.) Cf. later on 8: 17 and 30.

‡ Incidentally it is interesting to note here that rabbinic theology held that the first man shared in the divine כָּבוֹד, a privilege which he lost after the fall, but which was to be restored to men on the achievement of ultimate salvation. The idea that man has lost the image of God is however foreign to Judaism (Moore, *Judaism*, I, p. 479, n. 2; Kittel, *Th.Wb.NT*, II, pp. 249, 391).

God which has arranged the new order of things thus; the two words are again found together in 5: 17. Thus both by its mode of realization and by its deep origination in God, justification is far removed from the principle of retribution which dominated the dispensation of the law (at least this was how the Jews understood the matter): man has not to furnish some work, whose difficulty would in fact compromise the whole plan of salvation. What man cannot do, Jesus Christ has done. The sinner was the slave of a certain situation: Jesus Christ intervenes to liberate him. So far all takes place on his behalf but without his co-operation. 'Απολύτρωσις, i.e. *redemptive action*, suggests this liberating intervention, while ἱλαστήριον, i.e. *expiatory victim*, will explain how it comes about.

The ideas of liberation and redemption* must have suggested both to the mind of Paul and to that of the majority of his readers, two facts, very different in character and equally striking: the deliverance from Egypt† on the one hand, and on the other the emancipation of a slave by the payment of his *peculium* to the liberating gods.‡ In the latter case a vivid contrast was implied: the gods did nothing to effect emanci-

---

* 'Απολύτρωσις refers to eschatological liberation in Rom. 8: 23; Eph. 1: 14; 4: 30, or to present liberation in connexion with the forgiveness of sins, with which idea it almost merges (Col. 1: 14; Eph. 1: 7; 1 Cor. 1: 30). The word is very rare in profane Greek and also in the NT; it is used only in Lk. 21: 28; Hebr. 11: 35, in an eschatological sense, and in Hebr. 9: 15 it denotes forgiveness and "purification" (Héring). It is found in an inscription at Cos, together with ἀπελεύθρωσις, to connote the liberation of the slave in the temple through ransom (cf. A. Deissmann, *Licht vom Osten*, 4th ed. 1923, p. 278; E.T. *Light from the Ancient East*).

† Λυτροῦσθαι in Ex. 6: 6; 15: 13; Deut. 7: 8; 9: 26. In Daniel ἀπολύτρωσις refers to final salvation. We should note that Paul never uses this verb, nor the nouns λύτρον and λύτρωσις.

‡ Deissmann has been severely criticized for interpreting Paul in the light of categories of thought which were foreign to him (e.g. Büchsel, *Th.Wb.NT*, IV, p. 358). Since the word is rarely found in Paul's writings, such strictness is exaggerated, as Médebielle stresses (*D.B.S.*, 1938, *Expiation*, c. 161, 162); this word must have evoked personal memories among those readers of Paul who were freed slaves. The amount of the ransom was τιμή, a word also used by Paul, and connected with ἀγοράζειν as Paul also connects it (1 Cor. 6: 20; 7: 23). Δωρεάν also implies ransom operations.

pation, it was the slave who had slowly amassed the necessary sum of money; God in Christ, however, had done all that was necessary to effect emancipation. "In Christ Jesus" affirms at one and the same time the objective character of the liberating act wrought by God (ἐν being instrumental) and its subjective mystical aspect: liberation is the work of Christ effective through the communion which unites the believer to Him. The two aspects of meaning are equally necessary, as we see in Phil. 2: 5. The grace present in Christ is offered and available to believers through their union with Him and His ecclesial body.

(25a) How does God effect in Jesus Christ the liberation of sinners? In order to clarify this Paul has resort to the traditional vocabulary of sacrifice:* Christ by His death plays the part of an expiatory instrument; His sacrifice takes the place of those sacrifices whose blood was sprinkled on the ark as a plea for pardon and an offering acceptable to Yahweh.†

* One cannot reject the thesis that Paul is using OT notions simply because his readers were chiefly heathen. Otherwise the whole letter would be incomprehensible, both in substance and style. The term ἱλαστήριον shows quite clearly that the background of his thought is the doctrine of Levitical sacrifice. This is what makes it difficult if not impossible to understand our text in the light of passages where Paul recurs to the theme (notably Colossians) and where the presuppositions are very different. On the whole problematics of these vv. cf. W. G. Kümmel, "Πάρεσις und ἔνδειξις. Ein Beitrag zum Verständnis der paulinischen Rechtfertigungslehre", Zeit.f.Th.u.Kirche, 1952.

† On the plaque covering the ark dwelt the majesty of Yahweh, between the four cherubim which veiled this mysterious spot with their wings and hid it from the reckless gaze of men. It is there that Yahweh spoke to Moses, and that the blood of sacrificial victims was shed. This locus was therefore the very centre of religious life, it was the place of encounter with Yahweh in His self-revelation, and where the sinner found it possible to renew with Yahweh relations which had been broken by sin. ἱλαστήριον connotes this plaque (at first as an adjective with ἐπίθεμα, cover (Ex. 25: 29), then alone as an adjective used as a noun); but the function becomes decisive for the meaning of the word; the dominant idea is that of expiation (or propitiation) since the word is found in Ez. 43: 14, 17–20; 45: 19, to denote the framework or plinth of the altar which likewise served for purposes of expiation. In 4 Mac. (17: 22) God saved Israel by the blood of the young martyrs and their expiatory death (τοῦ ἱλαστηρίον θανάτου). Although rare, the word is

Formerly God had instituted sacrificial rites with a gracious intention so as to manifest and effect His purpose of pardoning the guilty. Sacrifice is the means used by the sovereign power of God who approaches thus the sinner with the object of blessing him.* But the efficacity of this gracious approach of God is dependent on man's repentance, a condition *sine qua non* of forgiveness.† For it is not God who needs to be delivered from some kind of anger against the sinner; the fact is rather that sin is abhorrent to Him and He wills man to break with it; man needs to be delivered from his own hostility to God. If there is no repentance on man's part, divine forgiveness does but conceal God's condemnation of sin, it leaves the sinner in ignorance of his true condition and does not avail to deliver him from it. Hence the sinner must associate himself in heart and mind with God's objective condemnation of his sin.

The immolation of the victim does not primarily mean the condemnation of the sinner, nor is it intended to symbolize his death as an ultimate form of punishment. Immolation is rather the prerequisite enabling the blood, which is the vital principle and symbol of life (Lev. 17: 11) to be brought directly into contact with the altar where God mysteriously resides. Thus is symbolized the process by which the sinner, whom the animal victim represents, surrenders his former condition of life, and allows his existence in its most vital aspects to be abandoned to God in self-consecration and self-offering. The sinner associates himself with the victim by placing his hand upon it; such is the sign of a unity which the penitent wishes to affirm and effect. Moreover he recognizes that his sins have made this sacrifice necessary and he recognizes it by making confession of his sins. The communion thus realized by sacrifice gives to the believer access to the renewing and revitalizing forces released by contact with the

found in Greek inscriptions and dedications to denote a monument for expiation. A masculine use of the word is not found. On this subject, cf. Ex. 25: 17–22; 30: 6; Lev. 16: 2–15; Num. 7: 89; 1 Chr. 28: 11. Strack-Billerbeck, III, pp. 165–185; Hermann, *Th.Wb.NT*, III, pp. 319–320, and W. Bauer, where a bibliography will be found.

  * Harold H. Rowley, "The Meaning of Sacrifice in the Old Testament", *Bulletin of the John Rylands Library*, V, 33, Sept. 1950, p. 95.

  † Yoma 8: 8. Cf. G. F. Moore, *Judaism*, I, p. 498.

altar, that is, with God, through this vicarious sacrifice.

There was no difficulty in integrating the death of Jesus Christ with the framework of this sacrificial theology. We ourselves are so accustomed to meditations on the cross that it is hard for us to realize the scandal involved for the zealous pious Jew, such as was Saul of Tarsus, by the idea which the Christian sect maintained that the Messiah had undergone the ignominy of crucifixion. Did not this fact in itself radically disqualify Jesus as Messiah? A Greek was not offended by the death of a god: the tomb of Zeus was shown in Crete. But an absolutely decisive reason was necessary to persuade a disciple of Gamaliel to accept the death of the Messiah. Paul found such a reason when his meditation on the scandal of the cross revealed to his mind the central significance of sacrifice in the old Mosaic law; when he realized that the centre of the law was the grace of the divine will expressed in the institution of sacrifice, and that the law in its concrete prescriptions was intended to prepare the believer to make confession of his sins so that he might receive worthily the grace of pardon through sacrifice, and not to merit the favour of God by his allegedly good works. The death of the Messiah was no longer a theological impossibility; through the rebellion of a generation blinded by the "powers of this world" (1 Cor. 2: 8) the same design was accomplished. God provided the victim in the person of His Son, so that this divine sacrifice should consummate the latent purpose of the ancient sacrifices.

When he writes ὅν προέθετο ὁ Θεός Paul is thinking of this providential will which ordains the cross as the new and supreme sacrifice superseding all others.‡ The formula stresses the fact that the victim in this case was provided by God Himself (cf. Rom. 5: 8; 8: 31, 32, 39; 2 Cor. 5: 14). The generous freeness of forgiveness is rooted in the depths of the love of God who does not spare His own Son.

‡ Προέθετο certainly alludes to a public proposition. The essential point is that the cross is exhibited before the eyes of the public as a spectacle of high significance (cf. Gal. 3: 1; the vb. προτίθεσθαι is used for the public exposition of bodies; cf. Médebielle, *art.* quoted, c. 166). Apostolic preaching less probably alludes to the public proposition of the cross and its theological significance (cf. 2 Cor. 5: 18, 21. Cf. Büchsel, *Th.Wb.NT*, III, p. 322).

The death of the Son is effective as an expiation διὰ πίστεως. Faith is necessary to recognize why God has ordained this sacrifice and why He has openly shown it in the face of the whole world. Faith in fact is that inner submission by which man agrees with the divine intention and trusts the initiative which God has taken in his favour while yet a sinner. By raising the cross on this hill, which becomes as it were the centre and "high place" of the world of the spirit, God offers to the gaze of all mankind His Son surrendered in sacrifice for all. Thus He invites all men to pose the question of their destiny in the light of this offering: He invites them to make of this sacrifice their own sacrifice, one which, symbolizing their own death, will draw them into an inner and spiritual sacrifice, a death to self. Faith is the answer to this divine address which, like every word of God, is both a promise and a question: do you wish to be saved? As the Israelite associated himself with the victim by placing his hand on the victim's head, so the believer associates himself with the sacrifice which God has ordained so as not to remain alien to what God has done for him.

The formula relating to the blood (ἐν τῷ αὐτοῦ αἵματι, in His blood) has been much debated. The position of the words seems to imply that the object of faith is the blood itself; the sense thus obtained is inacceptable if it is a question of believing in the blood of Christ. Paul never spoke of believing in an inanimate object and the idea seems contrary to his thought in general, since he regards faith as presupposing a personal exchange of words, promise and reply, an engagement on either side. This difficulty has led some to think that the mention of the blood in this context merely suggested that the sacrifice was a bloody one (ἐν τῷ αὐτοῦ αἵματι is linked with ἱλαστήριον): the sacrifice of Christ has expiatory efficacy for faith because it involved an effusion of blood. But this exegesis has the defect of attributing to Paul a superfluous formula, almost a pleonasm, since every ἱλαστήριον was a bloody sacrifice. Thus it is better to take ἐν τῷ αὐτοῦ αἵματι as an independently valid phrase, and we are encouraged to do so by the very weighty significance which sacrificial theology gave to the sprinkling of blood on the altar. In fact, after the sacrifice itself and the laying on of the hand, the sprinkling of blood on the altar was the third essential element in all sacrifice. The life of the guilty person, represented by the blood of the victim with which he has closely associated himself, is abandoned to God and thus enabled to receive the new forces of life which restored communion with God will impart. The blood is not primarily a sign of death and still less is it a sign of the satisfaction of divine vengeance.* It is the sign of a life which is at first offered to God and then given back by God, renewed, restored and forgiven. Jesus Christ is thus the means which, in His infinite mercy, God has made available to sinners, so that they might receive new life through their participation in this sacrifice by faith. The blood which has been shed is the sign of this gift of new life.†

Paul the apostle adopts the same interior attitude before the cross as before the altar of the temple. But since God has offered up His Son, all is objectively changed. A new order of grace has succeeded the old.

(25b ff.) Paul had declared that *now* (νῦν) the righteousness of God stands revealed. He has just said in what this open revelation consists; he now wishes to clarify the way in which such a public manifestation promotes the revelation of God's righteousness. The period is a long one, constructed in two parallel parts; it has been much discussed !‡

* Nothing is more contrary to Biblical thought than the popular hymn: "A blood of an immense price appeases His fury". Nowhere in the Bible do ἱλάσκεσθαι or ἐξιλάσκεσθαι have God as object (exceptionally in Zech. 7: 2, but not in connexion with sacrifice and not as a translation of כִּפֶּר): it is never a question of reconciling God, still less of appeasing His anger by an exemplary punishment (cf. Zahn, p. 190).

† Cf. Otto Schmitz, *Die Opferanschauung des späteren Judentums und die Opferaussagen des Neuen Testaments*, 1910, p. 43. The author stresses the idea that the blood is an instrument of communion; for that reason the allusions to blood must not be interpreted in material but in spiritual categories. It is not so much a question of the physical reality of bloodshedding, which is only a sign, but of the divine action thus signified.

‡ Difficulties in construction and special features of vocabulary have led to the suspicion that Paul is using more or less freely a formula already accepted in the tradition (cf. R. Bultmann, *Theologie des N.T.*, 1948, p. 47). E. Käsemann, "Zum Verständnis von Röm. 3: 24–26", *Z.N.W.*, 1950, considers v. 26 as a correction which Paul has made in

Two interpretations are possible. *Πάρεσις* might signify pardon, remission of sins.* By the death of Christ, God would manifest His righteousness in a double way: in regard to sins formerly committed, the cross makes abundantly plain a verdict which has been long deferred by the patience of God; with regard to present sins it makes possible a restoration of life because it furnishes an adequate expiation.† The objection to this interpretation is that Paul was familiar with the word *ἄφεσις* as expressing the idea of pardon; here he uses *πάρεσις* which he uses nowhere else. This choice reveals a special intention. *Πάρεσις* designates therefore *tolerance*, impunity, pretermission of punishment. This meaning agrees well with *ἀνοχῇ* (cf. 2: 4 and Acts 17: 30). It suits equally the allusion to the great day of atonement implied in *ἱλαστήριον*, for this day was regarded as making expiation for the sins which God had endured throughout the whole year (Yoma 8: 8). The divine pity grants men time for amendment of life by repentance; but this long-drawn-out process of the divine pedagogy may mislead the thoughts of sinners; we see a further allusion to this kind of mistake in 2: 4–5 and 3: 6–7. The condemnation of sin which the cross implies and makes plainly manifest dispels all such misunderstanding: the patience of God does not spell a compromise with sin. The sacrifice of the cross discloses the true nature of divine "righteousness": the essence of the latter is pity. In past times it patiently tolerated sin because it was aiming at the inauguration of a day when true repentance would fully seize the grace of forgiveness. God has never willed the death of the sinner, but rather that he might repent and live (Ez. 33: 11; 18: 32; Wis. 1: 12–13).

Thus the cross reveals to the man of today that God is both "righteous" and "justifying": He is righteous through His justifying grace. It was this total disclosure of the saving righteousness of God that the ancient sacrifices foreshadowed order to underline the character of the saving righteousness of God in the present.

* Thus Origen, Luther, Calvin, etc. A. Deissmann, *Paulus*, 2nd ed. 1925, p. 134. W. G. Kümmel, *art.* quoted from *Z. Th. K.*, p. 154. Bultmann, *Th.Wb.NT*, I, p. 306.

† On this hypothesis, *δικαιοσύνη* must be taken in the sense of vindicative righteousness.

—sacrifices which are now consummated and superseded by the sacrifice of the cross (εἰς τὸ εἶναι. ..). The beneficiaries of this new age are believers, and not merely the descendants of Abraham according to the flesh.*

In these few lines Paul has summed up the objective side of justification by faith, what God has done so that His righteousness might be manifested to men and might benefit them apart from the works of the law, in fact by the sole resource of faith. It will no doubt be thought that this concise statement might well have been amplified. Its pregnant terseness leaves open important questions with regard to the thought of the apostle, and dogmatic theologians have sometimes exploited Paul's conciseness to impute to him theories which he did not formulate and some of which are certainly foreign to his mentality.

(27f.) The dispositions which God has made in Jesus Christ inaugurate, in a sense, a new era in the history of the relations of man with God. We have to say "in a sense" only, because the law and the prophets already testified in favour of such a disclosure of the saving righteousness of God (v. 21) and this will be confirmed in ch. 4. Nevertheless, the new way of faith will inevitably appear as an innovation to anyone who understands the law as the masters of legalistic Judaism understood it. It differs on two essential points: in its essential structure it rests on faith, and no longer on works; while in its intention and end it is open to all, Gentiles as well as Jews, and no longer reserved to the elect people only.

In the measure in which the law serves as a support to the pretensions of man over against God, it nourishes his pride and gives birth to καύχησις, that sentiment so characteristic of a piety focused on merit and obedience to the law. This word expresses the inner dispositions of the man who makes calculation of all that gives him the right to claim from the justice of God a recognition and reward of his good works and

* Τὸν ἐκ πίστεως Ἰησοῦ: he for whom his faith in Jesus is the vital principle (cf. 4: 16). For the construction cf. οἱ ἐκ τοῦ νόμου 4: 14, 16; οὐκ ἐκ περιτομῆς 4: 12; τοῖς δὲ ἐξ ἐριθείας 2: 8; οἱ ἐκ πίστεως Gal. 3: 7, 9. In Rom. 4: 16, τῷ ἐκ πίστεως Ἀβραάμ can only mean he who has the same faith as Abraham.

his fidelity to the law. Such a man is a righteous man; he knows of course that he has not observed all the commands of the law but he has two reasons for quietening his conscience, as is shown so interestingly by the Psalms of Solomon:* he will attribute some failures to ignorance and inadvertence and he will rest assured that his good works are, in spite of everything, of such a nature as to justify God.† Thus the righteous man can count on the mercy of God, which is envisaged as a kind of slackness of His vindictive justice in favour of those who are called righteous by reason of their membership of the elect people and their adherence to the law. Καύχησις is not only the pride springing from what one actually accomplishes in the matter of good works; more basically it is the pride of being what one is. It is to this background of thought that we must go in order to understand why it is that Abraham the believer will be presented, not only as he who has performed no work (4: 5), but also as he who could not perform any work (4: 18–19).

When he says that all pride and boasting are excluded, Paul defines in a word the central characteristic of the life of faith, by contrast with life under the law.‡ The believer is then justified by faith without his works being taken into consideration, which means to say that he is *justified by faith alone*. It is well known that Luther translated thus. He has been much criticized on this score, and accused of creating a dichotomy between faith and works which is foreign to the text (Lagrange still echoes this reaction). But in this matter

* Cf. Herbert Braun, "Vom Erbarmen Gottes über den Gerechten. Zur Theologie der Psalmen Salomon", *Z.N.W.*, 1950–1951, pp. 1–54.

† It is characteristic that in the Ps. Sol. δικαιοῦν never has God as subject and man as object. It is man who justifies God. But the righteous can count on the mercy (ἔλεος) of God (in 8: 23 and 9: 2b δικαιοῦσθαι means "to show oneself just").

‡ Νόμος, it seems, is taken here in the general sense of system, rule or principle (cf. also 7: 23; 8: 2); but this sense somewhat conflicts with the context, hence another interpretation has been proposed. Paul envisages the law under two aspects, as a pretext for merits or as a gift of grace, helping to establish the truth of free justification. He is asking here: What excludes boasting? what law? the law which serves to produce meritorious works? No, but the law which bears witness to faith and of which ch. 4 will speak by presenting Abraham as the typical believer (cf. G. Friedrich, "Das Gesetz des Glaubens, Röm. 3: 27", *Th.Z.*, 1954).

the prejudice does not start with Luther; long before him the *Ambrosiaster* and Thomas Aquinas had understood thus the function of the faith of Abraham: *"reputabitur fides eius, scilicet sola sine operibus exterioribus, ad justitiam"*.* To clarify that the faith which is the mark of the new life implies the exclusion of works as a contributory factor in the justification of the sinner, and, to this end, to make the meaning explicit by speaking of faith alone, answers well indeed to the sense of the text.†

Of course we should misunderstand the thought of Paul (as has been done and is still done today in the most cultivated circles in regard to the thought of Luther) if we attributed to him the idea that works are a matter of indifference. In answer to this reproach, which Paul must have refuted even during his lifetime, it may be said that faith would not be what the apostle says it is, if it were sluggish and did not express in action its objective essence. What furthermore must be correctly understood is that Paul radically excludes works in the matter of justification; they do not count either prior to or concurrently with the work of justification, which is really gratuitous because it is χωρὶς ἔργων,‡ without

* "His faith—that is, alone, without external works—will be reckoned as righteousness." Ed. Migne 17, 53c; 79d; 83a; 154c. Th. Aquinas, *Opera Omnia*, Paris, 1876, 473b, 41 (following K. Holl, "Die Rechtfertigungslehre in Luthers Vorlesung über den Römerbrief", *Aufsätze zur Kirchengeschichte*, III, der Westen, 1928, pp. 111–154).

† Proof of this is seen in the fact that the Council of Trent in quoting Paul (Denzinger 801) notes the apostle's mention of faith and free grace, but omits the expression, "without works". This silence is evidently deliberate (cf. J. Rivière, *D.Th.C.*, VIII, col. 2186) since this detail contradicts the conciliar doctrine of "formed faith", i.e. the thesis of a co-operation of the believer in the work of his justification. Roman Catholic theology maintains that works are a collaborative effort furnished by the believer for the increase of righteousness and grace (Denzinger, 799, 803, and c. 834, 842). Fr. Prat thinks he finds these doctrines in the letter to the Romans (*La Théologie de Saint Paul*, II, 1937, p. 300). His explanations are in agreement with the decisions of the Council of Trent but not with the Pauline texts.

‡ In his preface to Romans, Luther wrote, "Faith is the work of God in us. It transforms and regenerates us, gives us new birth from God, kills in us the old Adam, makes us quite other men, changes our heart, mind and thought and gives us the indwelling Holy Spirit. Oh! what a living, active, effectual and powerful thing is faith! It is impossible that

works. Paul's point of view is that the status of man in the eyes of God is totally the work of God and is totally God's gift; to it man can add nothing. Further on he will speak of adoption as sons; now one cannot be more or less a son; one either is a son or one is not. And man is not a son of God because he is worthy to become one or because he deserves to remain one. But once the sinner has been adopted into sonship, either he behaves as a son to his own joy and that of his heavenly Father, or he scoffs at the grace with which he has been endowed and in the latter case will receive the just recompense of his ingratitude. For one does not mock at God and His grace with impunity; the less so, that one has recognized it to be a free gift. Man is not saved by works; but he is not saved either without works, the latter being the fruits of justification and not its cause, nor even precariously co-operative. Justification precedes works as the seed scattered on the ground precedes the harvest, or as the tree (planted by God: Matt. 15: 13) precedes the fruit; but one is not more or less the tree which God has planted.

Χωρὶς ἔργων νόμου, *without the works of the law*, expresses very well the point of v. 28. The idea will be re-examined from a different angle in ch. 7 of the letter in the analysis which man, at last illuminated by faith, will make of his condition under the law. Νόμου clarifies the notion of works and shows well that it is a question of works performed with the intention of accumulating claims to the divine favour. Ἄνθρωπον is equally very expressive;§ any man is called to justification by faith: the gratuity of the justification is the guarantee and condition of its universality; it makes it possible and secures it. If God alone is operative, every man is able to receive His gift, having nothing to bring except his poverty.

(29–31) The second characteristic of this new divine
it does not always do the right. It does not ask if any good works are to be done, but before the question arises, it has done them; it is ceaselessly active. Whoever does not do works of this kind has not faith; he gropes like a blind man to discover faith and good works, and does not know what either faith or good works are, of which he speaks without rhyme or reason."

§ It corresponds to πᾶσα σάρξ of 3: 20 and to ἀνθρώπων of 1: 18.

economy is indeed its accessibility to all men. Thence arises both the possibility and the necessity of preaching to the Gentiles; and likewise the possibility and the necessity of the unity of those who believe. All men have the same God, but not all know Him. The Jews who boast of this knowledge forget that it has been freely given them. Others have just as much right to receive this knowledge, since no class of men has any right to it. The pride of the Jews excludes the Gentiles because the latter are not "righteous"—as though they themselves had not first to be justified, purified, and forgiven. Truly God is the God of all and He wishes to treat all in the same way, now justifying the Gentiles as formerly He had justified Israel.* This logic implies that Israel was justified not by the circumcision which was reserved to it, but by the faith which is open to all. There is no difficulty here, even from the point of view of Israel itself, if only Israel knew how to understand the true significance of the law. It is the law itself which undertakes to testify to the divine intention of justifying both circumcised and uncircumcised on the sole basis of faith. Abraham the father of the circumcised is precisely, by the testimony of the law itself, the champion of justification by faith alone.†

* To vary his style, Paul uses ἐκ πίστεως then διὰ τῆς πίστεως but there is no reason to seek a difference between them (cf. Lietzmann).

† "We uphold the law": νόμος denotes here the Mosaic law as a whole, the old system called to bear witness in favour of the new and not what God commands, His general requirement (Augustine and Gaugler). Especially as the antithesis "annul—uphold" goes back to current rabbinic formulae (A. Schlatter, *Gottesgerechtigkeit*, 1935, p. 156).

CHAPTER

4

¹What then shall we say about Abraham, our forefather according to the flesh? ²For if Abraham was justified by works he has something to boast about, but not before God. ³For what does the scripture say? "Abraham believed God, and it was reckoned to him as righteousness." ⁴Now to one who works, his wages are not reckoned as a gift but as his due. ⁵And to one who does not work but trusts him who justifies the ungodly, his faith is reckoned as righteousness. ⁶So also David pronounces a blessing upon the man to whom God reckons righteousness apart from works:

⁷"Blessed are those whose iniquities are forgiven, and whose sins are covered;

⁸blessed is the man against whom the Lord will not reckon his sin."

PAUL WAS WELL aware of the supreme place of honour that the Israelites reserved for Abraham. The patriarch had acquired incomparable prestige as the ideal believer. But his faith itself was understood as a meritorious work, just like the faith of any other man; for every good deed of man is meritorious, the more so as faith is commanded by the law. "Abraham was given possession of this world and of the world to come, solely from the merit of the faith by which he believed in God" (Gen. 15: 6).* For this purpose great emphasis was placed on that pre-eminent work constituted by the offering of Isaac, with regard to which Paul on the contrary will observe complete silence, a silence that is eloquent. What interests the apostle is not what Abraham did

---

* Mekhilta Ex. 14: 31; 15: 1. Cf. A. Schlatter, *Der Glaube im N.T.*, 1927, pp. 29–32; Strack-Billerbeck, III, pp. 186–201.

nor what Isaac* did in the matter of good works. He is interested in what Yahweh did for Abraham, in the covenant, and the promise which it implied. He is interested in what God gives. In a word, in the grace of God.

(1) Abraham is called as a witness. Is this because of his claim to be the founder of the Jewish race? It depends on the way in which the text is understood.† If εὑρηκέναι is original, it suggests perhaps the formula of Gen. 18: 3 (χάριν εὑρίσκειν, Michel).

(2f.) However this may be, Paul goes straight to his point. If it is claimed that Abraham was justified by works, he is assured of enjoying great renown among men, as can be seen from his reputation among the Jews; for men are flattered to think that in the person of Abraham the merit of their good works is recognized. But this is contrary to scripture (Gen. 15: 6) which proves that, in the sight of God, Abraham does not enjoy the merits which are assigned to him. He has no reason to be proud, no claim to assert.

(4f.) But if it is admitted that Abraham has no claim to assert, that implies that faith is not a work. In order to clarify this point, Paul contrasts the strictly retributory point of view with that of free donation. A contract for work implies a claim for wages; no element of generosity enters into the situation; the wages paid correspond to the work that has been done; we have here a business arrangement between

* It is typical that Judaism not only stressed the sacrifice of Isaac, but even underlined the active share which Isaac had in the operation. In this way his merits were brought out, and added to those of Abraham. Cf. Sifre Deut. 6: 5 (par. 32): G. F. Moore, *Judaism*, I, p. 539.

† We may grant Bultmann (*Th. Wb. NT*, III, p. 649) that the text is irremediably corrupt. Εὑρηκέναι is lacking in B, Or., Chrys.; elsewhere it is sometimes before, sometimes after the mention of Abraham. No decision can be certain. Two possible translations: "What then shall we say about Abraham our forefather according to the flesh?" or, "What then shall we say that Abraham our forefather . . . obtained?" Or the latter text may be interpreted: "What then shall we say that Abraham obtained according to the flesh?" (Godet, J. Bonsirven, *L'Évangile de Paul*, 1948, p. 200; *Bible de Maredsous, Bible Crampon-Bonsirven-Tricot*).

contracting parties who negotiate on equal terms.* In the case of Abraham, is this the valid point of view? Certainly not. When scripture declares that Abraham believed and God reckoned his faith as righteousness, Abraham is not being regarded as having furnished any good work, demanding recognition in the sight of God. How could he have done so, since he did not know the God who was thus revealing Himself? Abraham was still a godless man at that moment.† The words of scripture concerning the faith and the justification of Abraham therefore apply to a man who had no good work to offer. It was this godless unbeliever with his empty hands whom God justified for the sole reason that he believed in the divine promise. Thus faith is not a work and justification is not granted in recognition of man's merits and to crown his good works.

(6ff.) The psalmist is now introduced to bring his confirmation of this thesis by declaring blessed (a word which must be taken in its strongest meaning, for it conveys the idea of access to supreme grace) those whom God has pardoned. Pardon granted not to the man who has good works to offer, but to him whose deeds are wicked. The force of this argument is only fully appreciated if it is remembered that the juridical mentality of the rabbis (and in this they resembled all men of all times) thought of the believer's relations with God as an account showing debit and credit. The important point was that on the credit side should be listed more good works than there were bad works on the debit side.‡ This

* Λογίζεται thus means: to put to an account a sum which in this case is due. In the other case, the sum of money is not due since no work has been done.

† Jewish tradition considered Abraham as a proselyte, since he styled himself גֵר: a stranger, in a religious sense and had been so called (Gen. 23: 4; Ps. 119: 19; 1 Chr. 29: 15; Ps. 39: 12), (Mekhilta Ex. 22: 21). Cf. G. F. Moore, *Judaism*, I, p. 344. The same tradition connects with the fact of his being a proselyte, the circumstance that the patriarch was not circumcised until he was 99 years old. It seems that Paul is arguing from this kind of tradition.

‡ "In any case, merits had to exceed defects by at least a unity: hence the Jews were enjoined to make sure of such a favourable balance always; it is the anxiety to balance every lapse by a *miswa* that earned for the

theory implied both that sins are not so abhorrent to God that a single one is sufficient to bring about a ruinous condemnation; and also that good works, by their number and quality, are so well pleasing to God as to deserve His favourable judgment. The apostle roughly shatters this whole conception. Man is happy because he is forgiven; he has no valid work to show such as to attract the favour of God, and his sins are not balanced by his merits—this would mean that their gravity was being minimized—but purely and simply forgiven. There is neither extenuation of the gravity of sin nor over-appreciation of the merit of good works; but there is grace for the guilty who, as such, is introduced into the sphere of blessedness, i.e. admitted into the presence of God.

By quoting Ps. 32 at this point, Paul makes parallel the justification of the sinner and the forgiveness of sin. Such an association illuminates the previous train of thought. Just as the godless man (in this case Abraham) is justified without having been able to offer any good work, so David declares that he who has brought before God his sins only is nevertheless pardoned and blessed. The justification of the first and the blessedness of the second have demanded no co-operation on their part.

What function then has been theirs? Have they done nothing at all? The former believed in the word of the promise and the latter in the word of absolution. In either case, belief was indeed the part which they played. It was *their faith* which was brought into operation. Is then their faith a good work? In no wise, if we understand this work in the sense which the context gives it, for in this connexion "work" signifies something which is a source of καύχησις, a claim valid in the sight of God, a meritorious deed, the foundation of a right. Faith is indeed a human act and attitude, but not a work in the theological sense. In fact, in both cases, God comes into action freely, without any right on the part of man

Pharisees their nickname of calculators" (J. Bonsirven, *Jud. Palest.*, II, pp. 58–59). It is true that beside this arithmetical preoccupation with merits, some thought that a single sin was enough to overthrow all merit. But the dominant tone of piety was seen in this anxiety to acquire enough merits to outweigh demerits. "Life thus becomes a game of reckoning, a constant inspection of the account which the pious man has in the divine bank" (W. Bousset, *Rel. Jud.*, 3rd ed. 1926, p. 393).

obliging Him to do so in strict justice; godlessness and sin do not make these men creditors of divine grace. In both cases the word of God is addressed to these men to offer them a grace, which *ipso facto* is entirely gratuitous. Both are confronted by an appeal to their faith, by an invitation to receive freely an undeserved benefit. And in both cases, by replying to this invitation, these men will become fully aware of the wretchedness of their situation. The consequence of God's appeal to their faith will be to unveil to their eyes the gravity of a situation which they could not, by their own human insight, appreciate correctly. It is only when they see the light that they are able to measure the depth of the darkness in which they are plunged. If they still nourished any illusion about their lack of merit, they now lose it by opening their hearts and minds to the new grace which is declared to them. They realize henceforth in unmistakable fashion that they are, the one godless, the other a sinner. Justification and pardon preclude from the heart of the believer any trace of καύχησις.

> [9]Is this blessing pronounced only upon the circumcised, or also upon the uncircumcised? We say that faith was reckoned to Abraham as righteousness. [10]How then was it reckoned to him? Was it before or after he had been circumcised? It was not after, but before he was circumcised. [11]He received circumcision as a sign or seal of the righteousness which he had by faith while he was still uncircumcised. The purpose was to make him the father of all who believe without being circumcised and who thus have righteousness reckoned to them, [12]and likewise the father of the circumcised who are not merely circumcised but also follow the example of the faith which our father Abraham had before he was circumcised.
>
> [13]The promise to Abraham and his descendants, that they should inherit the world, did not come through the law but through the righteousness of faith. [14]If it is the adherents of the law who are to be the heirs, faith is null and the promise is void. [15]For the law brings wrath, but where there is no law there is no transgression.

(9f.) Thus Paul has just presented Abraham as a man who "did not work" (ὁ μὴ ἐργαζόμενος), as an "ungodly" man; and the quotation from Ps. 32 associated with this context

117

almost made Abraham look like a forgiven sinner who had nought but his sins to offer God. The problem of justification is thus forcefully suggested: in what sense are we to understand the declaration of Gen. 15: 6 about the imputation of righteousness on the ground of faith? Paul is anxious to examine in all its bearings this decisive point: he is not satisfied to make affirmations, however well supported by quotations from scripture; he wishes to understand and convey understanding.

He approaches his explanation by clarifying, in the light of Abraham's example, the place which it is right to give to works and the part they play in the pattern of God's design. Abraham, in fact, accomplishes at least one work, and that one of outstanding excellence: namely, circumcision. What are we to think of this work? Does it vitiate the previous argument?

(11a) In fact, observes Paul, this work was a consequence of the call of God.* Circumcision was the sign,† but not the cause, of the imputation of righteousness; it was given to Abraham as a seal, confirming a righteousness which had already been granted to him.‡ It is evident that Abraham thus obeyed an order; but this order was a gift more than a command; by obeying it, Abraham was receiving a grace rather than accomplishing a meritorious work. Paul says quite deliberately: Abraham *received* (ἔλαβεν) this sign as a seal of the righteousness which had already been accorded him. In speaking of circumcision as a seal and sign of grace, and of the command as a gift, Paul is laying the foundations of a general doctrine concerning the works of the believer. The latter, no more than the law which is obeyed, are not anterior to the first touch of divine grace and play no part in the coming of justification.

* Between the covenant and circumcision, 29 years are said to have elapsed (Strack-Billerbeck, III, p. 203).
† The word goes back to Gen. 17: 11 (σημεῖον διαθήκης).
‡ By the sign God speaks to the outside world; the sign is the distinctive mark. By the seal, God speaks rather to the believer himself; the seal is the mark which guarantees authenticity.

(11b ff.) The way in which these things took place in that ancient time suggests clearly the nature of the will of God: namely, to establish in history an economy of grace. God aimed at making of Abraham, not the father of an exclusive race, whose characteristic would have been to be the people of the law and circumcision (considered as values in themselves), but the father of a people who trod the same road as himself, the road of faith, a people of believers.* Abraham was instituted as the father of all believers and not merely as the father of those who practise circumcision, because he is the one to whom righteousness was imputed apart from any consideration of his works.†

(13–15) Here is now the positive side of this explanation of the structure of faith. If the place and function of man's works are what we have just outlined, the reason is that God's manner of proceeding does not permit them any other role, and to attribute to them some other role would be to change the character of God's dealings. When God advances to deliver, man must abase himself; when God proposes, man cannot but receive. In the argument of Paul there emerges the notion of the promise, which is of primary importance since it illuminates the fact that God has taken the initiative and that the realization of the ends which He has

---

* The construction of v. 12 is uncertain. Is Paul speaking of two different classes of people? We may understand: ". . . father of the circumcised for those who are not content merely to be circumcised, but who walk in the steps of. . . ." If so, the Jews are referred to in both parts of the clause. Abraham is their father not only because he practised circumcision, but also because he had the faith which justifies. Or else: ". . . father of the circumcised, not only for those of the circumcision, *but also* for those who walk in the steps of. . . ." In the latter case, Jews would be opposed to the heathen. The latter have already been spoken of in v. 11b. Godet (p. 374) suggests that τοῖς of καὶ τοῖς is a pronoun comparable with that of τοῖς πιστεύουσιν in 4: 24.

† It is going too far to say that for Paul Abraham is the father of the uncircumcised much more than of the circumcised (Michel, p. 104). The passage is not so sharply polemical, and Paul always maintained Israel's rights as the first born. Abraham's spiritual fatherhood of all believers is not an invention of the apostle: cf. Matt. 8: 11 and already Ps. 47: 9 (cf. R. Kittel, *Die Psalmen*, 1922, p. 175). Cf. A. Feuillet, *R.B.*, 1950, p. 355, n. 2.

freely purposed will depend on Him. Now the promise is something alien to the law; by which Paul means that it inaugurates a dispensation in which works are no longer fundamental. They take second place as a consequence of the promise (of which they are a sign and seal), and they have not the character of a cause effecting the realization of the promise.

The fact that the initiative of God consists in a promise shows plainly the graciousness of His intention. This emerges equally plainly from the contents of the promise: to give an inheritance.* Paul insists on this idea of the inheritance, which is well calculated to emphasize the boundless generosity of the Giver and the passivity of the beneficiary. In the matter of an inheritance, unless one kills one's father, one can do nothing but receive. And before entering on the possession of the inheritance, there is really nothing to be done except "believe", i.e. wait in the confident hope that what has been declared will eventually be realized.

Anyone proposing to take active measures to secure for himself an inheritance would be justly baffled and disappointed. Similarly, says the apostle, if the inheritance promised to Abraham were to be obtained by the works of the law,† one would wait for it in vain; for this would mean attempting to secure by one's own initiative what was intended to be received as a gift; it would mean that one had ceased to believe in the good intentions of the testator; and it

* In Gen. 12: 3; 18: 18; 22: 17 the scope of the promise is that the posterity of Abraham shall cover the whole earth. The synagogue had already understood this to mean that Abraham's seed would inherit and possess the earth (cf. Strack-Billerbeck, III, p. 209). Whereas originally the promise concerned the land of Canaan, it was later extended in scope to cover the whole earth. Eschatological thought transcended all historical events and referred the promises to ultimate realities (cf. Ps. 37: 9–10). Paul gives to the promise a varying content: life, righteousness (Gal. 3: 21), the Spirit (Gal. 3: 14; Eph. 1: 13), adoption (Gal. 4: 22–23; Rom. 9: 8); in a word, Messianic salvation as Christ fulfils it. This explains why Paul was able to describe Christ as Abraham's posterity to whom the promise was made (Gal. 3: 16, 17), just as here he refers to his posterity after the flesh. In Christ all the promises are fulfilled, and it is from Christ that henceforth the authentic posterity of the patriarch will spring.

† Διὰ νόμου is elliptical.

would mean succumbing to covetousness. In that case, faith would be null and pointless and the promise would end in nothing (v. 14), for God does not keep His promise to those who, withdrawing from Him their confidence, rely instead on their own resources (their merits) as a means of obtaining the promised graces. There is a way of believing in the promise which implies that one attaches more importance to the promise itself than to its giver, and which tends to eliminate the latter in favour of oneself as the chief agent in obtaining it.

Thus two categories of men and two inner attitudes are contrasted in the sight of the God who has made the promise: either they can be ἐκ νόμου, *adherents of the law* (v. 14a), or else ἐκ πίστεως Ἰησοῦ, *having faith in Jesus* (cf. 3: 26; 4: 16). It is only those who maintain the second attitude who will inherit; not the first group who rely on the law in order to make their own works supersede the promise; they place themselves under the government of the law which arouses the negative reaction of God, namely His anger. In speaking of the law, Paul no doubt is thinking of the law of Moses and of particular transgressions; but his thought at the same time ranges further. The *régime* of the law is typical of a certain situation; it brings out that pretension of man, so characteristic of sin, to find out for himself and in himself the justification of his own existence, and to obtain the inheritance by his own resources. The law engenders the divine wrath because, when misunderstood, it gives birth to pride, καύχησις. As we shall see later when the apostle resumes the present theme, the possession of the law is not the cause of transgression but it brings to light the essential character of the latter.*

[16]That is why it depends on faith, in order that the promise may rest on grace and be guaranteed to all his descendants—not only to the adherents of the law but also to those who share the faith of Abraham, for he is the father of us all, [17]as it is written, "I have made you the father of many nations"—in the presence of the God in whom he believed, who gives life to the dead and calls into existence the things that do not exist. [18]In hope he believed against hope, that he should become the father of many nations; as he had been told, "So shall your

* Cf. Michel, p. 106.

descendants be." [19]He did not weaken in faith when he considered his own body, which was as good as dead because he was about a hundred years old, or when he considered the barrenness of Sarah's womb. [20]No distrust made him waver concerning the promise of God, but he grew strong in his faith as he gave glory to God, [21]fully convinced that God was able to do what he had promised. [22]That is why his faith was "reckoned to him as righteousness." [23]But the words, "it was reckoned to him", were written not for his sake alone, [24]but for ours also. It will be reckoned to us who believe in him that raised from the dead Jesus our Lord, [25]who was put to death for our trespasses and raised for our justification.

(16–17a) The promise was of such a nature as to carry, so to speak, its own guarantee of fulfilment. There are two kinds of promise which differ as a result of the person who formulates them; some promises are solid and one can count on their fulfilment because he who has promised is capable of realizing his promise; other promises are made frivolously by unreliable persons who cannot keep what they have promised. The promise of God assuredly enters into the first category. And that is precisely why (διὰ τοῦτο) God has not matched it with a requirement relative to man's co-operation; He asks to be able to act alone, and not to be embarrassed by an untimely attempt at human collaboration; for all such pretensions in the presumptive heir in reality shut the latter off from the beneficent action of God by imprisoning him within himself and riveting him on what he is. The promise of God is thus obtained only through faith. God has so willed it in order that all should depend only on His grace (ἵνα κατὰ χάριν) and that the promise might be as secure in its historical realization as it was in its divine origination (εἰς τὸ εἶναι βεβαίαν).

Furthermore the promise was not made to the posterity of Abraham as the Jews understand this, i.e. a posterity limited by the rite of circumcision to physical heirs exclusively. Since the promise was given to Abraham before the event of circumcision, it concerns all those who can see in him their spiritual father because he has preceded them on the path of faith.‡ This point is supported by Gen. 17: 5, which suggests

‡ Τῷ ἐκ πίστεως 'Αβραάμ should be understood of the faith of Abraham; cf. on 3: 26.

that the posterity of Abraham will consist of "a multitude of nations" and not of a single one.

(17b) Now if the promise offers such a guarantee of solidity, it is because of the character of Him who made it. It is the promise of the all-powerful and sovereignly good God, of the Creator and Redeemer God, the God of heaven *and* of earth. Stress is placed on the person of God by the formula: κατέναντι οὗ . . . and Abraham is brought *into the presence of his God.** In order to define the God of the promise, Paul has recourse to the strongest language and evokes the two supreme manifestations of divine sovereignty: the power of God the Creator, who creates the world out of nothingness; the power of God the Redeemer who gives life to the dead. Both attributes of the deity were familiar to the Jews (cf. Apoc. Baruch 48: 8; Shemone Esre 2).†

In calling Abraham and in opening up to him by the promise the path of faith, God was breaking into the world with the full weight of His sovereign power and glory. He was opening a new page in the history of His creation, and for this purpose He was assembling all His power, with piercing concentration. Paul must have thought thus with regard to the call of Abraham, since this was the view he took of his own conversion;‡ the person of Abraham itself must be the object of this creative and redemptive power of God. The sequel will show that no less was needed to fulfil the promise.

(18f.) Placed in confrontation by such a God, Abraham could hope. His faith was essentially the assurance that God would suspend that deterministic process which always engenders the future from the matrix of the past: the future would be new since God declared that He was about to

---

* The construction is an attraction for: κατέναντι τοῦ θεοῦ ᾧ ἐπίστευσεν.

† Cf. also 2 Mac. 7: 28; Philo, *Creat. princ.* 7; Sanh. 91a.

‡ In order to account for the birth of his faith, his vocation and conversion, Paul invokes the creative activity of God by his allusion to Gen. 1. In this emphatic sense, the believer is a "new creature" (2 Cor. 5: 17); he belongs to the world of new things which God has announced (Is. 43: 19, etc.).

intervene; it was then possible to entertain a hope that would not be illusory, because it now would rest, not on man and his capacities, but on the power of God. The faith of Abraham was radiant with hope, because it was focused on the future and rested in God. As a believer Abraham no longer looked to himself, for like a dead man he was the prisoner of his past; he looked to God as to Him who was able to do what is impossible to man (cf. Mk. 10: 27; Matt. 19: 26; Lk. 18: 27). The unbeliever is without hope because he is without God (ἄθεος) and consequently stands outside the sphere of the promise (Eph. 2: 12).

In order to show clearly the objective basis of this hope, Paul insists on its paradoxical character; it was a hope which was contrary to all human expectation (παρ' ἐλπίδα) which turned therefore on its own axis alone (ἐπ' ἐλπίδι) i.e. on God; it was fed by its own substance, which was the promise of a posterity. Paul cites once more Gen. 17: 5 in order to remind us sharply that it is a question of a promise, and a promise relative to the posterity of Abraham. By implication he was at the same time stressing the fact that nothing justified Abraham's confidence, since neither he nor Sarah were in a position to give birth to descendants. The decay of their bodies is indicated for each by the word *necrosis*. From a practical point of view and in respect of the promise, both of them are as good as dead. The promise will not be realized unless God intervenes with decisive power (cf. v. 17). The faith did not consist in nourishing illusions about his situation, in trying to minimize it, in caressing in spite of everything the hope that he might be able to father a son. Rather he looked at the situation realistically and for that reason his faith rested only in God.* The believer does not blind himself to the facts which contradict his hope; he overcomes the contradiction by seeing it in the light of the promise.†

* Κατενόησεν and not οὐ κατενόησεν, observes Michel, p. 110; without weakening in his faith, Abraham considered the state of his body. Τῇ πίστει is better attested than ἐν τῇ πίστει. Several MSS. have οὐ κατενόησεν (Koiné, DG it.).

† Philo has spoken of Abraham's faith in a remarkable way; whether showing the patriarch torn between consciousness of his frailty and trust in God, between fear and joy (*Quis rer. div. her.*, par. 6); whether extolling the greatness of this faith which renounces reliance on the creature to

The case of Abraham is considered by the apostle from a purely theological angle, not a historical one. Paul uses it as a parable to illustrate the nature of faith; he wishes to show what faith is and not who Abraham was. This is clearly apparent if we note that the incapacity which Paul attributes to Abraham is directly contradicted by his dealings with Hagar. In this context Paul makes no allusion whatever to this attempt, which sprang from incredulity, nor incidentally to the six children which Abraham had by Keturah (Gen. 25)! The idea concerns him more than the historical facts; he makes a selection from the latter in order to illustrate the former.

(20f.) Thus Abraham was not swayed by the consideration that there was some reason to doubt the promise; his mind did not waver through unbelief or lack of trust.* On the contrary, from that consideration so discouraging (humanly speaking) he derived new strength because it compelled him to look to God alone for the realization of the promise. Confronted by the facts of this world, his faith was strengthened† by the thought of the glory of God and the power which God can bring to the service of His promises. Faith is nourished and strengthened in proportion as it recognizes what God is and what He does.

To confess the glory and the power of God is thus already the characteristic of a true piety; the psalmist did not fail in this (Ps. 29: 1; 96: 7). It will be noticed that this pair of words corresponds to what the apostle had said in his des-

trust in God alone (*De migr. Abr.*, par. 9). On faith in general, see *De Abr.*, par. 46. Cf. Strack-Billerbeck, III, p. 193, 197–198.

* Διακρίνειν has a special sense in the NT where it suggests the doubt which agitates the one who prays or him to whom a promise is made (cf. Mk. 11: 23; Matt. 21: 21). The heart is divided, tossing like the waves of the sea (James 1: 6) between various conjectures. Cf. also Rom. 14: 23.

† ᾿Ενεδυναμώθη τῇ πίστει may be understood in two ways: Abraham was strengthened in his faith, the latter becoming stronger (Lietzmann, Lagrange, Gaugler, Michel). Abraham was strengthened by his faith which gave him new power (Euthymius: εἰς παιδογονίαν, in view of the act of procreation, Godet, Zahn, Sanday and Headlam, who refer to Hebr. 11). The parallelism with μὴ ἀσθενήσας τῇ πίστει favours the first interpretation. To break this parallelism it has been suggested to connect τῇ πίστει with δοὺς δόξαν (Godet).

cription of impiety; men refused to give glory and thanks to God (1: 21). The faith of Abraham thus reverses the situation created by unbelief. By faith Abraham gives glory to God, and his act of thanksgiving is inspired by the full conviction (πληροφορηθείς) that the divine power can accomplish its promises. This further clarification shows vividly that Abraham believed *in God* rather than in the promise itself; he clung to the God who had promised rather than to what had been promised; God mattered to him above all, much more than the promise which derived its objective reality and its potentiality of historic realization from God alone. He believed what God had said because God had said it, and not because he might have found in what had been said good reasons for adherence. His faith neither made a calculation of the probabilities of accomplishment nor a quick estimate of the advantages to be gained. Abraham thought only of that Being who had spoken, and, if one may dare to speak thus, he reacted to this Being as divine (ὡς Θεός, 1: 21).

(22) To conclude, Paul quotes Gen. 15: 6 a third time. The reader is now in a position to understand this text in its true scope and significance. As the apostle has just shown, all merit is excluded, since Abraham is pre-eminently a man who "performed no work", even an "ungodly" man* (v. 5). The Jewish interpretation of this word of scripture is thus excluded. The promise depends on God both for its initiation and its accomplishment. In the light of it, Abraham has discovered his true condition of *necrosis*. The faith of the father of believers consists in cleansing himself from all claimfulness in order to commit himself to the God of the living and the dead, the Creator and Redeemer. The *work* of this faith consists in renouncing works. Faith is thus the self-abandonment of the believer to the working of God.

There has been much discussion as to whether God imputed to Abraham a righteousness which was truly his or

---

* It will be noted however that this interpretation is that of the French Rabbinic Bible (pub. under the direction of the Grand Rabbi, M. Zadoc Zahn, 1930) who translates Gen. 15: 6: "And Abraham had faith in the Eternal and the Eternal counted it to him as a merit."

whether, by the effect of a fiction, he considered the patriarch as though he were righteous when in fact he was by no means so. The way in which the problem has been posed makes it insoluble. If we consider righteousness as a quality inherent in man or attributable to him, we are leaving the background of thought proper to the apostle and the Hebraic tradition. We must above all remember that the idea of righteousness qualifies man's situation only in his relation with God; the relationship is here essential, so that nothing can be said of one side of this relationship which does not imply a statement concerning the other. There has been acrimonious debate as to whether man's righteousness was in fact his own or only the righteousness *of God*. It is both, and both at the same time. In the matter of Abraham's relation with God, the former is never a subject without also being an object; and never an object without becoming a subject. It was "before God" that he believed; he cannot be considered as the subject of a righteousness which God approves of, without also being considered as the object of a righteousness which God gives.

These false dilemmas which have blocked the interpretation of the apostle's thought will be overcome if we keep well in mind, as we should, the function of the promise which is characteristic and primary. The righteousness which is in question here must be defined, not from the point of view of the law and its commands, but from the point of view of the word of God and what it promises. The righteousness which is imputed to Abraham is his human condition as affected by the initiative of God, and answering the promise by a surrender to the hands of the God of the promise. Abraham is in truth just; but he is so not by reason of what he is or what he does; rather he is just in virtue of what he is not and does not do, because he recognizes this and confesses it and submits himself to God. The promise has established a new order of affairs; Abraham is truly just because he responds to the initiative of God by resigning the attempt to create a righteousness of his own; he is just in so far as he recollects not his own ability, but the grace of God; in so far as he surrenders the account of what he achieves in order to give himself to what God has promised to achieve.

127

(23–25) It is evident that the long discourse which the apostle devotes to the father of believers concerned believers as a whole. He was not here writing a historical essay nor even an essay in apologetics, either of which would have been a digression.* Abraham in fact is our father, the father of believers in all ages; his faith is our faith; what is said of him is valid for us. Evident as this is, it is not superfluous to point it out. Our vv. 23–25 are intended to say this, at least in brief. In short, the faith of Abraham is essentially the same as our own faith, because its object is the same. Abraham believed in the God who makes the dead to live and who summons into existence from nothingness. Such is also the God of our own faith since God raised Jesus Christ our Lord from the dead. The link between 4: 17 and 4: 24 is very close.†

By emphasizing that the faith of believers in the new covenant is centred in the God who is sovereign over death and nothingness, Paul created a second link with the condition of the patriarch. Abraham had a posterity in fulfilment of the promise, because God gave new life to his withered body. The birth of Isaac took place, so to speak, out of a dead body; it might be compared to a creation or resurrection;‡ it discloses all the sovereign power and grace of the God of Abraham, as defined in v. 17. The believer of today is equally the object of this divine sovereign power at work in the service of divine grace; he is a new creature (2 Cor. 5: 17), he is one endowed with new life whom God has summoned from the dead (Rom. 6: 13). And for that very reason and by the same means he too is of the posterity of Abraham. By the same gracious dealings God continues to give to Abraham children who share in the blessings which were promised to him. Abraham is in truth *our* father.

Much has been written on v. 25, too often by detaching it from its context and treating it as a theological affirmation in

* As several authors have thought; Dodd, p. 71, has even been able to write that the page has little interest for us and no weight.

† The personal character of faith is strongly marked here too. Just as Abraham believed in God and not in a promise, so we believe in the God who raised up Jesus Christ, and not in the resurrection of Jesus Christ. Godet, p. 395, points this out quite rightly.

‡ Hebr. 11, using the word resurrection of Isaac, alludes not to his birth but to the intervention of God which avoided his death.

its own right. Paul may have here been utilizing a traditional formula, an early confession of the first church, as Lietzmann indeed admits. But it is still necessary to understand why Paul has quoted it here, and what relevance it has to the preceding argument.*

The first member of the formula seems to be a reference to Is. 53: 12. The death of Christ is related to the sins of men, which are the cause of it as of all sacrifices.† $Παρεδόθη$ is the Pauline term used to denote the sacrifice of Christ; it is God who has offered it (Rom. 8: 32; cf. 1 Cor. 11: 23; Gal. 2: 20; Eph. 5: 2). It is somewhat difficult to understand the second part of the verse: what is the nature of the link which Paul makes between justification and the resurrection? Is the resurrection the attestation which guarantees to faith the truth that Jesus is indeed the Christ? Such an explanation yields only a very tenuous connexion between the resurrection and justification. Does the liturgical character of the formula justify us in connecting it with baptism, which is "an efficacious symbol of the death of Christ and of His glorious life"?‡ But why introduce baptism at this point where the discussion of Abraham has not prepared us for it?§

If we bear in mind the analysis which the apostle has given of the condition of Abraham the believer, it would appear that his dual formula must correspond with the two phases which have been thrown into relief: man's *necrosis* and the power of God in the fulfilment of His promise. The necrosis of the body of Abraham was a parable of the mortal state of the sinner who is summoned to have faith in Jesus Christ and His death for the sins of all mankind. The intervention of

* We elude the difficulty if we are content to say that this is a more or less rhetorical formula, which it is better not to press too closely (J. Weiss, *Beitr. z. paul. Rhetorik*, 1897, p. 171). Cf. G. Schrenk, *Th.Wb.NT*, II, p. 228. Nor do we explain anything by pointing to Hebraic parallelism (Dodd, p. 70).

† $Διά$ indicates the reason for a thing, the instrumental cause in regard to a past event, the final cause in relation to a future one. Here: *because of* our transgressions . . . and *in view of* our justification.

‡ F. Prat, *La théologie de Saint Paul*, II, 1937, p. 252.

§ The characteristic feature of our text should not be obscured by uncertain associations. Paul does not connect justification with the death of Christ.

I   129

God to vivify the withered body of the patriarch was a symbol
of the power by which God establishes a new life for the
believer through the resurrection of Christ. The resurrection
of Jesus Christ is the basis of the great Christian hope, the
beginning of that new world and new age which God inaugurates through Christ. It both sums up the promise and
already fulfils it. It is in this light that Paul considers it here,
and this explains why the apostle can make such a close link
between the resurrection and justification. Like Abraham we
are justified by faith in the God of the promise; for us the
promise is disclosed and fully present in the resurrection of
Christ. The latter is the promise manifested in a supreme
degree.*

---

* When Paul says: "If Christ has not been raised, your faith is futile"
(1 Cor. 15: 17) he does not only mean: "in that case there is no proof that
Jesus is the Christ". The resurrection is not at all a proof for the apostle.
He wishes to say something else and much more: if Christ has not inaugurated the new age, our faith is futile since it is addressed to the God
who has declared through Christ that now the Kingdom has drawn
near. If Christ is not risen, faith is useless, since the promise implies God's
triumph over death through Christ, and so on behalf of believers.

CHAPTER

5

¹Therefore, since we are justified by faith, we have peace with God through our Lord Jesus Christ. ²Through him we have obtained access to this grace in which we stand, and we rejoice in our hope of sharing the glory of God. ³More than that, we rejoice in our sufferings, knowing that suffering produces endurance, ⁴and endurance produces character, and character produces hope, ⁵and hope does not disappoint us, because God's love has been poured into our hearts through the Holy Spirit which has been given to us.
⁶While we were yet helpless, at the right time Christ died for the ungodly. ⁷Why, one will hardly die for a righteous man— though perhaps for a good man one will dare even to die. ⁸But God shows his love for us in that while we were yet sinners Christ died for us. ⁹Since, therefore, we are now justified by his blood, much more shall we be saved by him from the wrath of God. ¹⁰For if while we were enemies we were reconciled to God by the death of his Son, much more, now that we are reconciled, shall we be saved by his life. ¹¹Not only so, but we also rejoice in God through our Lord Jesus Christ, through whom we have now received our reconciliation.

THE FIRST ELEVEN verses of ch. 5 form the conclusion of the first part of the letter. They are closely connected by vocabulary with what precedes.* But the tone and style is no

---

* The position of these vv. in the scheme of the letter is subject to debate. Following many other commentators, Michel thinks that the second part of the letter begins at 5: 1. The remarks of A. Feuillet, "Le Plan Salvifique . . .", p. 356, n. 1, with regard to vocabulary should convince that the themes of this passage form the conclusion of previous trains of thought: δικαιωθέντες (5: 1, 9): 2: 13; 3: 4, 20, 25, 28, 30; 4: 2–5 (in the rest of the letter only 6: 7; 8: 30, 33)—καυχώμεθα (5:3, 11): 2: 17, 23; 3: 27; 4: 2 (elsewhere only 15: 17)—ὀργή (5: 9): 1: 18; 2: 5, 8; 3: 5; 4: 15 (elsewhere only 9: 22; 12: 19; 13: 4, 5, but in rather a different sense)—τὴν χάριν ταύτην (5: 2) refers to 3: 24—ἐπ᾽ ἐλπίδι

longer that of theological argument: it is now the believer who is speaking—in fact we might almost say, singing, for he is in communion with the fellowship of the church and is extolling the blessing of justification considered as the work of the love of God. There could hardly be a more complete contrast with the situation of the sinner as sketched out in the first chapter.

(1f.) Whilst rebellion against God had subjected all men to the "wrath" of God, faith, which welcomes the activity of God in Christ, enables the sinner to benefit from the divine reversal of the situation. The believer is thus introduced into a new relation with God which is here characterized by two words: peace, and access to grace. The state of hostility is succeeded by one of peace,* a word which conveys above all the formal structure of this relationship. Peace spells good order, a normal state of things, contrasting with the disorder which any rupture with God at once introduces into the life of the world, and into man's relations with God.† Now the peace of God is not the peace of the graveyard; it implies access to a grace which opens up avenues of life that had been blocked by sin.‡ Sin had completed a breakdown of relations, Jesus Christ came to restore that harmonious communion which had been interrupted; by Him and by faith the believer finds once more a way of approach to God, and

τῆς δόξης recalls ὑστεροῦνται τῆς δόξης 3: 23—συνίστησιν δὲ τὴν ἑαυτοῦ ἀγάπην (5: 8) corresponds to δικαιοσύνην συνίστησιν 3: 5—ἐν τῷ αἵματι αὐτοῦ (5:9) to ἐν τῷ αὐτοῦ αἵματι 3: 25 (found nowhere else in the letter).

* The reading (ἔχωμεν, let us have peace) is the best attested (S, A, B, C, etc.). However, it is impossible to adopt it; Paul cannot be exhorting believers to make peace with God; this idea would be in contradiction with the whole tenor of the letter. Lagrange proposes to understand the reading as follows: "let us remain in peace with God" (cf. Acts 9: 31). It will be recalled that Paul was dictating and that the secretary may easily have confused omicron and omega. Further examples of fluctuation between these two vowels are: Rom. 14: 19; 1 Cor. 15: 49.

† For the antithesis of peace—disorder cf. 1 Cor. 14: 33. We should take care not to give to the word peace a commonplace psychological meaning (peace of the soul, inner rest, etc.).

‡ Ἐσχήκαμεν is equivalent to an aorist (Hellenistic peculiarity): τῇ πίστει is lacking in B, D, G, etc.

his supreme hope is now to be able to appear in the divine presence and contemplate the divine glory with its ineffable radiation.*

The implications of this new hope are expressed by a verb which it is important to grasp in all its significance.† The typical attitude of the sinner is to glory in himself, to assert his own honour and credit by relying on his own strength; it is for this reason that sin is, first and foremost, a refusal to give glory and thanks to God as God (1 : 21). This inner attitude is manifested notably in the aspiration to win the favour of God by meritorious works, which Paul describes as "the works of the law". Now God has declared in Jesus Christ His will to deliver man from this seeking of his own glory; that is why, after speaking of the justifying work of Christ, the apostle is eager to emphasize that now all καύχησις is precluded (3 : 27); the man who has seen Christ as the ἱλαστήριον (3 : 25) can no more nourish the desire for self-glory, nor seek in himself the resources to attain it: he has resigned himself into the hands of God in order to open his heart to the promise which has been fulfilled in Christ. That is why "we are gratified by one thing only, the hope of one day contemplating the glory of God, which is the height of His promise". Faith gives rise to such a hope, because it trusts in the God of the promise, who raises the dead and summons life from nothingness. The believer, like Abraham, waits for the full manifestation of the divine power working to accomplish the promise, the manifestation of the sole glory of God.

(3f.) When Abraham, thanks to the promise, was able to glory in the hope of a posterity, he realized his true condition of necrosis; the promise stood in sharp contradiction with the facts of his situation. Similarly the hope of glory which faith engenders exposes the gulf which separates the present con-

* Sin has deprived man of this glory: 3 : 23. There is no stronger expression of the sense of our text than Col. 1 : 27.
† Καυχᾶσθαι is essentially Pauline and is found thirty times in Paul out of thirty-three in the NT. Καύχησις: ten times in Paul (once in James, 4 : 16); καύχημα: ten times in Paul. Useful information in Bultmann, Th.Wb.NT, III, p. 648 and Theologie des N.T., p. 237.

dition of the believer from the promise made to him in Christ. The believer is anchored in a new world, established by Christ but still mysteriously obscure, in a state of travail in the midst of the old world with which it is in conflict. Hope always arouses a state of tension with the actual. The eschatological hope of the Jews had stressed this contrast between the old world and the new by inserting in the rhythm of events which was to lead from the one to the other, a time of great tribulations; this was tantamount to translating into historical terms an ontological—and psychological—truth, integral to every theology of transcendence.* Nevertheless, the contradiction between what one hopes for and what is now, between what one is and what one will be, painful as it is, cannot but have the effect of throwing back the believer on to the sole power which is capable of triumphing over this tension which it has itself brought about. The weakness of man will make the more manifest the power of God; such was the experience of the apostle;† and it is true in an absolute, ontological sense (cf. v. 6; the sinner is by definition a man without strength, which explains why he is one who does not work, in the sense of 4: 5).

Paul uses three words to describe the advantage which faith derives from its clash with those realities which seem to nullify it: endurance, power of resistance,‡ and hope. The contradiction which faith meets in the first place brings into play its very existence, its stability and steadfastness. Then this opposition, if it has not crushed faith at the first shock of encounter, threatens to wear it down; it tries its resistant quality. This double threat, ever renewed, compels faith to concentrate itself more firmly on the One who having made the promise, possesses also the power to bring it to fulfilment. This double contradiction is overcome by progress in the way

* The NT contains several echoes of this thought, in particular the eschatological discourse of Mk. 13 (and parallels). On the whole question, cf. P. Volz, *Die Eschatologie der jüdischen Gemeinde*, 1934, 2nd ed., pp. 127-131 and *passim*; H. H. Rowley, *The Relevance of Apocalyptic*, 1947, 2nd ed., pp. 166-168. Paul will recur to the theme in ch. 8.

† Cf. 2 Cor. 12: 9, 10; Phil. 4: 13.

‡ Δοκιμή =resistance, the quality of being able to resist testing (e.g. of fire). A very rare word but found several times in Paul (2 Cor. 2: 9; 8: 2; 9: 13; 13: 3; Phil. 2: 22). Cf. *Th.Wb.NT*, II, p. 259.

of hope, the full scope of which, for Abraham, was brought out by 4: 20.

(5) Hope thus rooted in God never confounds the believer; it does not make ashamed (cf. Ps. 22: 5; 25: 3, 20; James 1: 12). The reason for this is the presence or activity of the Holy Spirit, which may be understood in two ways. Either, the Holy Spirit reveals to us the love of God* which guarantees His fidelity in the fulfilment of His promise. Or else, we may understand that in giving us the Holy Spirit according to the purposes of His love, God has already begun to fulfil His promise. The cognitive and ontological points of view are not mutually exclusive; it is the presence of the Holy Spirit in us which facilitates the divine action. Faced with the promise which awaits realization, the believer is not reduced to entertaining a hope which lives by its own strength. Even before bringing about the reality of what is promised, this promise —or rather the God who has made it—inspires in the life of the believer good reasons for hope. The word of the promise itself engenders hope through the agency of the Holy Spirit. When God speaks He already acts in the soul of the believer.†

(6) Now, in this connexion, the promise does not consist merely in a word. The love of God has given, in a sense, its pledges; not only has Christ proclaimed the Kingdom and invited men to repent so that they may enter it, but also He has died and risen again to establish that Kingdom. Not only has the word of the promise induced in men the realization of their ontological "weakness", like Abraham (their condition is suggested in vv. 6–8 by the words "ungodly", "sinners", "hostile"); but He who made the promise of the Kingdom has joined action to speech so as to give already to the promise a degree of actuality: He has died for the ungodly. The cross is not an accident of history, an enormous

* We should understand by this God's love for us rather than our love for God. The context speaks of what God accomplishes.

† 'Εκχέω =to pour. Originally it is used of rain, heaven's supreme gift to man in eastern countries. Then, by extension, of the Spirit (Joel 2: 28; Acts 2: 17; 10: 45); of mercy (Sir. 18: 11); of grace (Ps. 45: 2); of anger; Hos. 5: 10; Jer. 10: 25; Ez. 7: 8).

judicial mistake. It fulfils the compassionate will of God with regard to men: it happened at the time appointed by God,* the right time, and in conditions which make clear a particular intention on the part of God. It reveals His will for man's salvation, and His saving righteousness.

(7) In this context of thought Paul stresses what was already clearly affirmed in the statement that Christ died for the ungodly. His death involves a sort of contradiction, for men sacrifice themselves finally on behalf of the right or the good, for a righteous man or a good cause; in short, for what is intrinsically worth the sacrifice to which they agree.†

(8) A sacrifice which involves the death of such a victim to the advantage of such beneficiaries is thus unheard of; it has something self-contradictory and scandalous about it—unless it be that the event is of such a nature as to demand quite different criteria of judgment; and this is indeed the case here! Love does not justify itself by pointing to the value of the beloved object; it does not rest on the basis of an exchange.‡ God loves without rational justification. It is that

* There are three principal readings of the opening of the verse: ἔτι γάρ, S, A, C, etc.; εἰς τί γάρ, G Vulg. (ut quid enim); εἴ γε B sa. Καιρός means the special time, the seasonable moment for doing something, the hour marked by God. Cf. Gal. 4: 4; 2 Cor. 6: 2; Eph. 1: 10; 1 Tim. 2: 6; 6: 15; Tit. 1: 3; Hebr. 11: 15; Lk. 19: 44; Rom. 13: 11, etc. Cf. Delling, Th.Wb.NT, III, p. 462.

† Vv. 6b and 7 have given rise to various interpretations, sometimes very subtle (they will be found in Godet). The first difficulty is to establish the distinction which the author makes between δίκαιος and ἀγαθός; second, we have to appreciate the significance of the absence of the article before the first word and its presence before the second. Two chief trends in the interpretation: (1) we are less willing to make sacrifices for a man whose virtue consists in the strict observance of the law (the righteous) than for a man who does good and thus attracts sympathy, especially by his generosity; (2) we devote ourselves less willingly for a private individual even though he were what is called righteous than for the public good, τὸ ἀγαθόν; we agree to make a sacrifice for our country which we should refuse for individuals, even those we admire or love the most. The second member of the clause appears to be a correction, and it may be that the first was intended to be erased (Lietzmann). On the duty of sacrifice, cf. Michel, p. 117.

‡ Cf. the argument of Jesus: "If you love those who love you . . . if you

very fact which proves that He loves. His love is intended to give to those whom He loves precisely what they have not in themselves, and what they could not in any way acquire, since they have nothing to give in return. By the death of Christ on the cross God has therefore conspicuously manifested His compassionate will towards mankind.*

(9) In such conditions, the hope which we place in the gospel is fully assured. God sent His Son to proclaim the good news and He sealed His message by the death of His Son on the cross. Such a promise, matched by such a confirmation, must convince us by a sort of logical necessity† that the gracious work thus announced and initiated cannot fail to be completed. Already we are justified; the νῦν=now underlines the fact that justification is not an object of hope but a grace already granted to the believer who, by faith, appropriates the benefits of the passion of Christ (for the meaning of ἐν τῷ αἵματι αὐτοῦ see on 3: 25). Thus God has consented to offer, in our favour, the sacrifice which we could not offer, so as to establish new relations with us, by accepting us into His presence and communion. He has wished to undo the work of sin, not only by cancelling the effects which it has already wrought, but also by furnishing the sinner with the potentiality of new life, of which the blood is already the sign and symbol (see 3: 25). Thus as the believer looks forward to the end of the good work which God has in this way begun in him, assured of the faithfulness of God, he can give thanks that he will be delivered from "wrath" on the day of judgment.

(10) But this judgment has yet to come; it must mark the end of a long process, the landmarks of whose course are all the contradictions which faith encounters and must constantly surmount. The life of the believer is a race, or a struggle in which he must emerge as victor day by day.‡ The

do good to those who do good to you . . . or lend to those who lend to you" (Lk. 6: 32).
* Ὁ θεός is lacking in B Ephrem, doubtless under the influence of v. 6.
† Πολλῷ μᾶλλον recalls the rabbinic argument a minori ad maius.
‡ Cf. 1 Cor. 9: 24; 2 Cor. 4: 16; Rom. 13: 12; 1 Tim. 1: 18; 6: 12; 2 Tim. 2: 5; 4: 7.

same assurance should irradiate the daily path of the believer as irradiates its goal. For justification is not simply a verdict decreed by a judge; it is at the same time the forgiveness granted by a father. To the juridical and formal aspect of the relations between God and the sinner is added the moral and ontological aspect. Absolution for the past is linked with the welcome which triumphant love reserves to its prodigal sons. The forgiveness of sins leads to the restoration of the guilty to their place in their father's house and to participation in the affections of the father who rejoices to have found again his son. The believer finds himself to be, not merely the object of a condemnation and absolution decreed by the divine judge, but also the beneficiary of a love desirous of striking at the root of that hostility which roused the son in revolt against his father.

The reconciliation thus effected is not an addition to justification; it is rather the inner living personal aspect of the latter. The sentence which restores to grace and favour is inseparable from the life of love which welcomes the son to share in his father's goods and to enter into the blessedness of the family circle. What justification permits, reconciliation realizes by materializing for the believer that new life which justification foreshadowed. As he participates in the life of the Risen Christ, the believer is assured of attaining the end which the love of God proposes to him, namely salvation. It is the very life of Christ which will animate and inspire him in the struggles of faith. Thus the power of God richly fulfils what He has promised.

(11) And all this is so certain that the Christian can go further* and, already at this stage, rejoice in God through the Lord Jesus Christ; that is, he can experience already the assurance of the man who will confront the judgment of God by relying on divine grace alone, and on the righteousness which has been disclosed in Jesus Christ.

¹²Therefore as sin came into the world through one man and death through sin, and so death spread to all men because all men sinned—¹³sin indeed was in the world before the law was

* Οὐ μόνον δέ may also be completed by καταλλαγέντες.

given, but sin is not counted where there is no law. [14]Yet death reigned from Adam to Moses, even over those whose sins were not like the transgression of Adam, who was a type of the one who was to come.

[15]But the free gift is not like the trespass. For if many died through one man's trespass, much more have the grace of God and the free gift in the grace of that one man Jesus Christ abounded for many. [16]And the free gift is not like the effect of that one man's sin. For the judgment following one trespass brought condemnation, but the free gift following many trespasses brings justification. [17]If, because of one man's trespass, death reigned through that one man, much more will those who receive the abundance of grace and the free gift of righteousness reign in life through the one man Jesus Christ.

[18]Then as one man's trespass led to condemnation for all men, so one man's act of righteousness leads to acquittal and life for all men. [19]For as by one man's disobedience many were made sinners, so by one man's obedience many will be made righteous. [20]Law came in, to increase the trespass; but where sin increased, grace abounded all the more, [21]so that, as sin reigned in death, grace also might reign through righteousness to eternal life through Jesus Christ our Lord.

(12) The verses which have just been read opened up vast and far-reaching vistas of hope: the line of thought envisaged the final accomplishment of the work of salvation in restored communion with God, the ultimate fruits of the justification of the sinner. Essentially all has been said. What has still to be said can only go back to offer further explanations. In fact, the apostle will go back and the exposition which he now unfolds will enable us to understand how sinners are transferred from their actual condition of wretchedness (Jews as well as Greeks) into the glorious state of which a glimpse has just been given. Salvation, justification and its ultimate fruits are exclusively the work of God. Yet this work strikes deeply into the heart of the man whom it proposes to save. The theological aspect is quite primary because God initiates and brings to pass this new destiny for man. Nevertheless one cannot pass over in silence man's concern in the matter, otherwise we might not truly understand God's concern. It is man who is the object of the compassionate activity of God in Jesus Christ. As such an object, he will now engage the

139

attention of the apostle in the second part of our letter. We shall now see how the gospel preached by Paul displays its saving power for the benefit of the believer (cf. 1 : 16); this is the human historic end proposed by the saving righteousness which the gospel reveals (1 : 17).*

The humanity of which the first chapter sketched the picture is indeed, as the apostle has said, under the shadow of God's judgment. But the insight of Paul is too penetrating and his analysis of the human situation too precise for him to overlook the fact that man in history is always dependent on what has gone before him, and on all those who have gone before him. In the Old Testament itself the judgment of God affected not only the guilty but several subsequent generations. Judaism, also, affirmed that the sin of Adam had had the gravest consequences for all his descendants, in particular by introducing death into the world, by distorting life and by depriving his descendants of glory and righteousness.† Nevertheless each man remained guilty of his own faults and died in consequence of his own culpability.‡ Adam himself had been the object of a vast amount of reflection, the effect of which had been to endow his person with the dimensions of a collective and cosmic being, light of the world and the summing up of humanity, in fact a sort of microcosm;§ the whole of humanity was regarded as sharing in his humanity. ‖

* $Δι\grave{α}$ $το\hat{υ}το$ is very difficult to explain. It is not easy to see with what to connect it. We may see in it a general indication that the author is entering on an explanation of what precedes. The objective aspect of the work of salvation has been explained; and in view of such considerations, God sent His Son in conditions which best enabled Him to reach the descendants of Abraham and annul the consequences of sin. $\ddot{ω}σπερ$ points to the opposition Adam—Christ; in fact this conjunction remains suspended; we may find an apodosis in v. 15 or better still in v. 18.

† Cf. J. Bonsirven, *Jud. Palest.*, II, p. 16.

‡ Cf. Strack-Billerbeck, III, p. 222. G. F. Moore, *Judaism*, I, p. 476.

§ P. Volz, *Die Eschatologie*, . . . pp. 189–190. However, rabbinic theology knows nothing of the expressions first and second Adam (cf. 1 Cor. 15: 45).

‖ The notion of the unity of mankind seems to have been based on the theory that the body of Adam was formed of earth coming from the four points of the compass; it was supposed that men belonged to such or such parts of this body according to their various features. (Cf. W. D. Davies, *Paul and Rabbinic Judaism*, pp. 54–57.)

It is against this background of thought that the apostle will place his exposition of the redemptive work of Christ. Just as the condition of man is determined by the solidarity which unites him to all mankind, unfortunately for the worse (since all have sinned), so the new state of life inaugurated by Jesus Christ is shaped by the solidarity which faith establishes between Christ and all believers. Adam is the initiator of a humanity abandoned to sin and death; Jesus Christ is the initiator of a humanity in which abound the graces of "righteousness" and life. Adam and Christ play parallel but antithetic roles.*

Thus Paul first of all proposes to show the actual condition of man linked in solidarity with the sin of all men, who, by their sin, have determined the situation with which he is confronted when he comes into the world. Adam sums up and symbolizes all this humanity both in his person and in his behaviour, and the conditions of life of every individual are moulded by it. Speaking the language of Genesis, Paul refers to the entrance of sin into the world through the fault of one man, and the dire consequences of that catastrophe, namely death. In this matter he is not moved by any speculative interest. He does not attempt to explain the origin of sin or death. We would like to know whether he distinguishes between death, envisaged as the punishment of sin, and death regarded as a natural phenomenon and an integral part of the world as created. We would also like to know exactly how he conceives the existence and influence of this sin, of which he speaks as though it were a real personage. His metaphorical and almost mythical language does not

* Paul calls Adam the antitype of Christ. Since faith recognizes, in the history of the merciful dispensations of God, one unvarying plan which is realized by diverse means according to historical moments, it can establish alignments between facts which are remote in time, when it sees in those facts despite all their external differences the expression of the same divine will. Since faith also sees that the historical process has been directed from afar towards a culminating and crowning point in Jesus Christ, it can establish between the facts a relation of anticipation and realization, of foreshadowing and fulfilment; the most ancient of events in a sense foreshadows, because it in part realizes, what finds its full realization only later. It is in this sense that Adam is the forerunner of Christ. 'Ο μέλλων is an enigmatic designation of the object of the promise like ὁ ἐρχόμενος (Matt. 11: 3; Hebr. 10: 37).

enable us to grasp his thought with any degree of exactitude, and it would be misleading to take him too literally by ignoring the very approximate character of the expressions he uses. The essential point, for the apostle, is neither to describe nor explain what happened in the past. His aim is different and also deeper, for he is concerned to make us understand the redemption wrought by Christ. What matters to him is to show how the condition of man is totally transformed by the work of Christ; hence he speaks of man's condition apart from Christ, i.e. the condition of the sinner, only in so far as that is necessary to bring into relief the redemptive work of Jesus Christ.

Within this framework of thought, Paul notes that man is in solidarity with the sin which weighs on mankind as a whole. He lives in a world where sin is already rooted, and into which it entered long before he existed. The way in which Paul speaks of this, suggesting as he does the invasion of the world by sin and its acolyte, death, expresses the feeling which is characteristic of all human experience; namely, that man does not invent or create sin, and that a power which is in some way external to himself assails and tortures him until it has at last dragged him down and made him consent to its suggestions of evil.

Paul connects this situation with the fall of Adam; but it would seem that this view should not be taken in a strictly historical sense. We have just reminded the reader that the personage of Adam had been the object of reflective thought such as had endowed him with the traits of a collective being. The pages of Genesis which the apostle has here in mind we shall find exploited in ch. 7 with a freedom, and made relevant with a pertinence, which suggest that Paul was accustomed to read in Genesis a theological doctrine of wide import rather than the narration of an event which took place once, at a given spot, and in connexion with a particular person. The mythical approach which he uses here to speak of sin and death answers well to his general interpretation of Genesis in which he divined the declaration of the basic structure of human existence.

Hence for the apostle it is not so much a question of personal as of collective wrongdoing. Adam is man, humanity as a whole considered in its responsibility for the tyranny of sin which lurks in wait for every fresh human existence. Man inherits a situation of bankruptcy, weakness and death. Every act of disobedience to which man agrees contributes to the condition of sinfulness which oppresses other men; because of the solidarity which binds every being and every generation to all other beings and all other generations, each man who is born into the world finds a compromised situation confronting him. Although actual guilt is personal and not transmissible, those deep inner disorders engendered by sin, whether they be physical, moral or spiritual, persist under multiple and manifold forms long after those immediately responsible for them have gone.

In this heritage of the multifarious malversations by which sin has corrupted the world, there is one which is quite specially grave in its consequences, because it assures the perpetuation of the ills by maintaining their cause. By his example and teaching, man multiplies for other men opportunities of repeating on their own account that fundamental rebellion against God, his father and creator, which corrodes his inner life and actuates his social behaviour. Each generation and each individual act in such a way that the inner strength of rising individuals and generations is enfeebled, deflected, and at times destroyed. The result is that man, coming into the world, experiences a congenital powerlessness when faced by the demands of his spiritual vocation. He becomes an easy prey to temptations of every kind; nothing has prepared him for the achievement of victory; he has neither the reasons nor the means of resistance with the object of overcoming evil by good; he becomes the victim of a feeling of fatality* which crushes him. Theoretically, he is free; he has not undergone a corruption of his nature such as would compel him to sin. Practically, however, the moral and spiritual adventure of each man and of humanity as a

* "The real weakness comes before the experience of temptation. It lies in a spiritual enervation which makes the soul vulnerable. In a sense, when we are tempted it is always too late. . . . It is in the prior weakness that the lapse really lies. Evil is only strong because of the moral energies which we have previously lost." René Schaerer, "La représentation mythique de la Chute et du Mal", *Diogène*, no. 11 (1955), p. 77.

whole is liquidated by bankruptcy, whatever be the local or occasional successes that are registered.

The close of v. 12 can be interpreted in two ways. Either it may be referred to Adam; in which case Paul says that all men have sinned in the person of Adam, as is shown by the fact that they all die, even those who stand outside the law and who, for that reason, cannot undergo death as the punishment of sin laid to their account (this will be clarified in v. 13). Such is the traditional exegesis since Augustine* who understood in this way the Latin version *in quo omnes peccaverunt*.† Otherwise we may understand ἐφ᾽ ᾧ in the light of Phil. 3: 12 (*in quo*) where the phrase means *because*:‡ in that case Paul is affirming that all men die because they have personally sinned. This second interpretation clearly has the disadvantage of introducing the idea of personal responsibility in an argument which aims at emphasizing the corporate, social aspect of the human condition. On the other hand the first interpretation links the ἐφ᾽ ᾧ to an antecedent which is remarkably distant! In practice the two interpretations amount to ascribing much the same idea to the text, if we are careful however not to give to the first the scope which the Augustinian tradition has always seen in it; and this implication should be set aside because the whole context precludes it. Paul cannot have meant to affirm that men die because they have sinned in Adam, that is, because they are guilty and punished like Adam, inasmuch as they share in the culpability of Adam;§ for v. 13 excludes this idea by affirming that men, after Adam, have indeed sinned, but in conditions such that their sin is not counted. Thus death strikes all men, but not guilt. If our interpretation is that

* Augustine, *C. Duas Epist. Pelag.*, 4: 4–7.

† "*In quo omnes peccaverunt*" could mean in low Latin "*in eo quod*", which would favour the second interpretation.

‡ Elsewhere ἐφ᾽ ᾧ (2 Cor. 5: 4) is rendered by *eo quod*; and ἐν ᾧ (Rom. 2: 1 and Rom. 8: 3) by *in quo*.

§ The traditional reasoning, which goes back to Augustine, is as follows: death is a punishment: God only punishes the guilty; hence the universality of death since Adam proves that the general culpability of men precedes the particular active culpability of each man; they are guilty because they have sinned in Adam and for that reason they are punished.

men have sinned "in Adam", then it must be in the sense that the sin of Adam has had consequences which extend his punishment to those who have not committed a similar sin and do not therefore share his degree of guilt. This is the situation of collective sin which we have been describing.*

(13f.) Universal extension of sin and death; such an affirmation gives rise to an objection, or at least demands clarification: sin is a personal matter and cannot be interpreted as something which is part of a heritage and integral to a situation of solidarity. Paul would agree; since the fall of Adam, knowledge of the will of God having been suspended, it is no longer admissible that there exists a purely personal sin and a real disobedience. The heirs of Adam are not in the same situation as Adam himself; their fault is not similar to his (v. 14b). In fact, we must distinguish—as we have already done above in an anticipatory fashion—between solidarity in guilt and solidarity in the consequences of the original transgression. After the latter has been committed, its consequences persist: death and the whole compromised situation which this word in itself conveys. But sin itself is not imputed to those who sin for the simple reason that they have been thrown into a situation so imperilled that their fault is, in the last analysis, much more attributable to their parents than to themselves (v. 13a).

Paul clarifies the character of this situation which is thus compromised by sin, in explaining why those who are plunged into it commit what might be called sin for which they are not fully responsible. In such a case, sin is not im-

---

* It is thus on an error in translation that the Western tradition of original sin or the culpability of men in Adam has been built up under the preponderant influence of Augustine. Another problem is posed by the fact that the Council of Trent (Denzinger, 789; already 175) taught the doctrine of original sin and invoked this text in justification. Catholic exegetes do not attempt to hide their embarrassment (Lagrange, p. 106; F. Prat, *op. cit.* I, p. 297). Fr. Benoit returns to the first interpretation without however speaking of culpability in Adam. Does this silence indicate an opinion? (Cf. "La loi et la croix d'après saint Paul", *R.B.*, 1938, p. 487.) A. Feuillet on the contrary is categorical (participation in sin, ontological solidarity) (*art.* quoted, p. 361).

puted because there is no law (μὴ ὄντος νόμου, v. 13b). Adam was able to commit a sin for which he was fully responsible because he knew the will of God. But it is the very characteristic of sin to break down the relation of man with God and to create a situation in which there is no awareness of God, i.e. atheistic.* The inheritance which Adam bequeaths (and this means in a wider sense the inheritance with which every man is loaded when he comes into a world which has been emptied of the sense of God as a consequence of sin) is just this atheism, this unawareness of God and His will. Such is the situation "up to the time of Moses"; in the absence of the knowledge of the will of God, sin has not the full dimensions of the sin of Adam. It is a material but not a formal sin.†

(15–17) The complexity of the problem thus broached has caused the apostle to lose the thread of his sentence; ὥσπερ (v. 12) remains virtually without sequence. But his idea continues to develop. The state of things prevailing as a result of the fall of Adam is now opposed by a new order which the life of obedience to Christ sets up. If the figure of Adam, understood above all in its corporative implications, is fitted to explain the universality of sin, how much more can the

* Cf. Eph. 2: 12.

† The expression "From Adam to Moses" is conceived in a chronological sense. In order to give Paul's thought its full implications, it seems right to qualify the chronological perspective. We are even compelled to do so, when we notice that the period between Adam and Moses, characterized by the absence of the law, presents features which in fact apply to all those who stand outside the influence of the revelation of the law to Moses, i.e. the world of the heathen. In the picture which Paul gives—if we take it literally—the existence of the heathen is completely forgotten. Such a gap cannot be imputed to the apostle to the Gentiles and least of all in the Letter to the Romans. Hence the true perspective should be logical rather than chronological, alluding to categories of men in various situations, rather than to men in historically successive situations. Paul is thinking theologically rather than historically; he is explaining man to himself, he is not describing man's past. The historical form of presentation naturally occurs to the mind because man is a historical being, and his past explains his present. That is why Adam has his place here, as a symbol of that whole historical past which everyone inherits.

figure of Christ explain the universality of grace!* A new humanity is created "in Christ", for a new situation of solidarity now intervenes in the history of humanity, which is destined to play a part more widely beneficent than the solidarity of Adam was maleficent. On the horizons of Paul's thought, revealed in a flash by the parallelism of Adam and Christ, we should discern the glow of that idea of the "new corporative personality created in Christ"† which other texts call the Church or the Body of Christ. The antithesis of the two régimes inaugurated respectively by Adam and Christ is presented in a balanced way in these verses; but one word stands out sharply to convey the common characteristic of the different aspects of the work of redemption, the word "grace".‡

(18f.) How does grace, which is so lavishly affirmed in vv. 15-17, effect in the history of humanity the contrary of what had unfortunately been effected by the transgression of Adam? Precisely through the obedience of Christ. The terms used by Paul are not without a certain ambiguity. In 18b we find the word δικαίωμα, which had assumed in v. 16 the exceptional meaning of justification. Normally this word denotes what is conformed to the right, the *just deed*. Here it is a question of Christ having fully accomplished the will of God.§

* Πολλῷ μᾶλλον: we recognize the argument *a minori ad maius*. The repetition of this formula gives its structure to vv. 15-17. Vv. 18-21 are not determined by this formula.

† Cf. C. H. Dodd, *Romans*, p. 80. Cf. E. Jacob, *Théologie de l'A.T.*, p. 125.

‡ Τὸ χάρισμα recurs in δωρεὰ ἐν χάριτι, an uncommon expression in which ἐν replaces a genitive (cf. W. Bauer, *Wört.* s.v., IV, 4b). In v. 16b, εἰς δικαίωμα is equivalent to εἰς δικαίωσιν, since δικαίωμα is contrasted with κατάκριμα. The accumulation of terms in -μα gives rise to the suspicion that we have here a studied effect of alliteration (cf. 11 : 12). This would explain Paul's use of the term here in this exceptional sense (cf. Schrenk, *Th.Wb.NT*, II, p. 226). Slight uncertainty in the texual tradition: most MSS. give τῷ τοῦ ἑνός; A G read ἐν ἑνί; D ἐν τῷ ἑνί; Orig. ἐν ἑνός. Further on, B omits τῆς δωρεᾶς doubtless to avoid the three successive genitives.

§ δικαίωμα has also been given the meaning of "act or verdict of justification" with the idea that it would be tautological with ὑπακοή (v. 19) if the meaning were "a just action".

147

The formula δι᾽ ἑνὸς δικαιώματος presents another difficulty. It might be understood: *by a single act of righteousness*, but the context makes irresistible another interpretation: *by one man's act of righteousness*.* Finally εἰς δικαίωσιν ζωῆς speaks to us of a justification which introduces us to divine life; but we know how closely connected are the present and the eschatological aspects of life (ζωή) in the theology of the apostle; so that *"acquittal of life"* suggests equally the idea of a justification which is here and now realized in a life which concretely practises righteousness, as will shortly be said (6: 11, 13, 16, 18, 19, 22, 23). It will be noted that Christ's obedience of which our text speaks becomes also the believer's obedience, an obedience which leads to the practice of righteousness (ὑπακοῆς εἰς δικαιοσύνην, 6: 16). Thus it is part of the logic of Paul's thought that his antithetic picture of the two Adams should lead him to stress the factual obedience of Christ as opposed to the factual disobedience of Adam, in order to show that Christ creates a humanity of righteous men, just as Adam had created a humanity of sinners.† The neat parallelism with which the paragraphs are arranged in this part of the letter confirms this point of view.‡

(20) The new humanity which Christ leads in the path of obedience will receive from Christ's obedience the inspiring principle of its own. The Christ discloses a righteousness of a new kind. To affirm this was to raise the problem of the law, the function of which was usually considered to be that of leading the people of God into the path of obedience and thus

* Ἑνός is used six times in the passage, and always with reference to the uniqueness of the person of Adam or Christ.

† Κατασταθήσονται alludes not only to the eschatological judgment but also to the fact that men will be constituted as righteous on the basis of their union with Christ.

‡ This parallelism is rather striking: 5: 12–17 shows that we are in solidarity with Adam and foreshadows the liberating work of Christ: 6: 1–10 expounds this liberating work of Christ. 5: 18–19 affirms that Adam has established us as sinners and points to Christ as the Saviour who establishes us in righteousness: 6: 11–23 expounds this life of righteousness in Christ. 5: 20 raises the problem of the law: ch. 7 deals at length with this problem. 5: 21 suggests to our minds the vision of the reign of grace and ch. 8 explains that this reign is the creative work of the Spirit.

bringing about the life of righteousness. But what the apostle has told us about the solidarity linking mankind to Adam suggests that the law was in actual fact of very little avail for this purpose. To turn them aside from sin, it was not enough to teach them in what righteousness consisted. It was necessary to break the bondage under which they languished, and to renew their being to its depths. The demands of the law could have no other effect than that of exposing the powerlessness of the sons of Adam and multiplying their transgressions. Paul has already said this in 4: 15, but he adds here that the part thus played by the law corresponds well with the plan of God.

In giving the law, God did not propose to make man a sinner since he was one already, nor to aggravate his sinfulness, but rather to reveal it more vividly. From the point of view of God, man is not a greater sinner because he sins more. The essence of sin is not appreciated by considerations of quantity. All such calculations are foreign to God as to the father of the gospel parable; sin is essentially breaking with God; all is contained in this rupture, and sins merely make current coin of this fundamental sin without rendering it worse. From man's point of view things are different, for the sinner has always good reasons for his actions—i.e. good to his blind eyes: the prodigal son after all did but go off with the share which was intended for him; the hard school of trial was necessary to prepare the way for his repentance. Such also is the role of the law;* it exposes the culpability of man, and reduces him to a condition in which he is likely to repent and implore a grace that will deliver him (cf. 7: 24).

Thus, by the will of God, the law supervened,† not to save, but to open blind eyes. The terrible misunderstanding which led Israel to its ruin consists in its having thought of the law

---

* Paul describes the law as a custodian (Gal. 3: 24) whose role is essentially a negative one (cf. ἐφρουρούμεθα, we were under the restraint of the law, v. 23), consisting in the denunciation of faults rather than the guidance into good, in punishment rather than in education.

† Παρεισῆλθεν is somewhat pejorative: the law has supervened as an additional factor; it was not foreseen in the original plan of God; it was the disobedience of Adam which rendered its promulgation necessary. Its function is moreover a temporary one. On these problems the reader will refer to the Letter to the Galatians.

as an instrument of salvation. The consequence of this fundamental mistake was that the law, in fact, aggravated its situation instead of enlightening its mind. Not so much by multiplying particular material sins; Paul does not say that the law multiplies transgressions but *transgression*, and doubtless we are justified in laying stress on the singular here; Paul means formal sin, i.e. what constitutes sin as sin.* The nefarious role of the law lies in the opportunity it gives to the sinner to lay claim to merit in the sight of God. It excites his pride. It is difficult for one who is under the law to do good without boasting of his deed. Christ comes and finds the sinner locked in that kind of fatality which turns to his disadvantage what should have been profitable to him, and He effects in the sinner a transformation which will be so much the more salutary in that it will restore to him the right use of the law and thus prepare him to find the way of grace. When the law strips man of all pride, he is left with the consciousness of his inner nakedness and so turns in humility towards grace.

(21) The system of sin which Adam initiated is thus suspended by the intervention of Christ who inaugurates a new humanity dependent on grace, living in righteousness and progressing towards eternal life. Such is the work of Christ in contrast to that of Adam.

* The use of the singular from v. 12 is significant; it is a question not so much of sins as of sin, sin in its essence. Paul is speaking as a theologian, not as a teacher of ethics.

6

¹What shall we say then? Are we to continue in sin that grace may abound? ²By no means! How can we who died to sin still live in it? ³Do you not know that all of us who have been baptized into Christ Jesus were baptized into his death? ⁴We were buried therefore with him by baptism into death, so that as Christ was raised from the dead by the glory of the Father, we too might walk in newness of life.

HOW DOES JESUS CHRIST bring to birth this new humanity which is freed from sin? How can the solidarity binding men to Adam be broken and replaced by a new solidarity with Christ leading to righteousness and life? If the law was not given to promote righteousness among the sons of Adam, what then is its role? These questions, arising logically from what has just been said about Christ in contrast to Adam, will be treated in chs. 6 and 7.

(1) Paul makes his argument leap forward again by an allusion to the calumny mentioned in 3: 8. Paul was not able to avoid the inevitable. When it is said that what constitutes the value of human behaviour in the sight of God is not material obedience to a law, even though it were the law of God, but the attitude of the heart which is transparent to God, or in other words the faith which inspires conduct, it is certain that the speaker will incur the reproach of encouraging immorality; he will have every appearance of being a master of libertinism, since the moral agent is thus released from the strict obligations which the law implies and the springs of moral conduct are slackened by the discrediting of merit. The contemporaries of the apostle must have felt alarmed by a type of preaching which was so threatening to

the well established structure of a moralism that had been substituted for the obedience of faith.*

(2f.) The reply of Paul is based on the notation of a fact which the subsequent argument will endeavour to explain: "We believers," he says, "who put this question with regard to our conduct, are dominated by one outstanding fact or event: we have been put to death, we have been buried, as far as sin is concerned; the idea of living in sin is for us a contradiction in terms." But who are these believers and how is this reply valid for them? In what way have they died unto sin?

Paul's argument is now based on the fact of baptism. Although the apostle considered that he had been sent to preach the gospel and not to baptize (1 Cor. 1: 17), the communities to which his preaching gave rise were accustomed to practise the rite of baptism. The baptismal doctrine which his letters give some glimpse of is obviously a corner stone in the structure of his theology. This doctrine was familiar to his readers;† but he now proposes to elucidate it in order to bring out its inner logic, and necessary consequences. He first of all reminds us that baptism is εἰς Χριστόν, *into Christ*.

It is not enough to emphasize in this connexion that εἰς expresses the idea of appropriation, a transfer of the ownership of the baptized, who is now placed within the sphere of influence of the Christ and formally accounted as part of the latter's wealth and property; all of which is clearly conveyed by the use of the formula εἰς τὸ ὄνομα (*in the name of* . . .) which is borrowed from accountancy.‡ We must go further,

---

* It is easy to understand that the teaching of Jesus should have met with the same criticism. If the tax collector who is a sinner (in the story of the tax collector and the Pharisee) is justified rather than the Pharisee who is a truly righteous man, then let us sin like the former, so that grace may abound! What becomes of the moral life of the believer, if for justification it is sufficient to lower one's eyes and prostrate oneself in humility in the temple? See also below on 12: 13a.

† Ἡ ἀγνοεῖτε does not mean that the readers were ignorant of it, but that they might have forgotten it; they are being reminded of what they already know, as in 7: 1.

‡ On these points, cf. Oepke, *Th.Wb.NT*, I, p. 537.

for Paul also wrote that the Israelites had been baptized into Moses (εἰς τὸν Μωϋσῆν ἐβαπτίσαντο) in the cloud and in the sea (1 Cor. 10: 2). If the same formula is applicable both to Moses and to Jesus Christ, it is because of what they have in common.

In regard to the fulfilment of God's redemptive plan, they are both in fact the instruments by which God constitutes His people; to be united to Moses was the necessary condition for having part in God's plan. Paul can say that the children of Israel were "baptized into Moses" because he agrees with the sentiment expressed in Acts 7: 35: Moses was ἄρχοντα καὶ λυτρωτήν, a ruler and deliverer; an expression whose large implications will be understood if it is compared with the formula by which Jesus Himself is designated: ἀρχηγὸν καὶ σωτῆρα, a leader and a saviour (Acts 5: 31). The role of Moses appears thus of great importance and it is clear why Paul can speak of the baptism of the Israelites into him, i.e. their union with him. Baptism in an archetypal sense is here present because the natural elements (cloud and sea) have sealed the unity of the people and their leader, enabling the people to appropriate the benefits of that saving work which God had undertaken in calling Moses: the people were virtually saved by Moses alone; Moses in his person summed up and was engaged in fulfilling the plan of God; it was necessary and it was enough for men to be united with him in order to become integrated with the movement of salvation which this prophet thrust into the historical process. In his person alone, a humanity was constructed, at the very heart of the humanity springing from Adam, and such a group was formed in view of the coming revelation of God. Thus it is easy to understand the scope of the declaration: "We have been baptized into Christ Jesus." The person of Christ recapitulates the new people whom God wishes to raise up; in the thought of God He gathers into His own person all those who will be united with Him in order to share in His saving work. His office is indeed to initiate a new humanity; He establishes here below a new solidarity, thus crowning the imperfect work of Moses.

Paul simply recalls the fact that baptism is the rite by which the Christian is united with Christ and integrated

153

with the Church of Christ, or the people of Christ. The accent however is placed on the idea that baptism into Christ is baptism into His death (εἰς τὸν θάνατον αὐτοῦ); the baptized is united to Christ inasmuch as he is dead. It is a union with the death of Christ. The following verses will develop this point but we must at once seize its full import, in order to understand what is thus added to the formal definition of baptism as union with Christ. Why does baptism effect union with the crucified Christ? and with *Christ* crucified? Precisely because God wishes to create a new humanity. Not simply a humanity instructed in the divine law, as was Israel; for instruction is not enough to ensure obedience. It was necessary to handle the matter at a deeper level; it was not enough to instruct the will, it was necessary to change it. God's aim was directed to the inner being, and the focal point of the personality. That is why Christ, at the appointed time, appeared among men, and in the form of man, to fulfil among them the office of a second Adam and inaugurate a new body of humanity. He accomplishes this work by His death and resurrection which are the culmination of His gospel and His example. He opens up to men the avenues of repentance and of death to self, because God has set Him before us as ἱλαστήριον (3: 25). By surrendering His Son in sacrifice for sinners, God offers in the place and in the favour of all men a sacrifice which abases them beneath the judgment of His condemnation and exalts them by the power of His forgiving word.

For the apostle, this sacrifice is in line with the sacrifices instituted by God in ancient Israel to show forth His holiness and to proclaim His grace; in the sacrifice of the Son, these sacrifices find their culmination and their end. Now the one true sacrifice is set before men, as a result of which their repentance will signify their association of themselves with the condemnation of sin which the cross implies, and it will mean a true death to self because it will be a dying with Christ. Just as the Israelite believer associated himself with the sacrificial victim which he offered on the altar in his stead, so the Christian believer now and more than ever becomes associated with the sacrificial victim which God offers in his stead and in his favour on Golgotha. Paul can write: "One has died

for all; therefore all have died" (2 Cor. 5: 14). The full weight
of this *therefore* (ἄρα) must be realized. In the fact that Christ
died because God consented to offer Him up as a sacrifice in
the traditional and authentic sense of this term, the believer
sees the objective foundation of his own death. God willed
that this death should be my own death; when I look at the
cross, I see there the victim who represents me objectively,
His death includes my own, His death is mine, it is my death
which He dies. In the intention of God with regard to myself,
I have died.

It is essential to bear well in mind this theology of sacrifice
in general and the sacrifice of the cross in particular, if we
are to understand the baptismal formulae of this chapter, for
they imply a far greater range of meaning than is actually
stated. When he speaks of baptism, the apostle evokes that
rite of union which brings the people into solidarity with their
leader, and involves the believer in the sacrificial destiny of
the Christ. To ask for baptism is implicitly to recognize that
Christ having died for all, therefore all have died. The believer asks for baptism with the same attitude of mind as had
the Israelite when he used to bring his victim to the altar.
But now the victim is not offered by the believer but by God
"who did not spare his own Son, but gave him up for us all"
(8: 32). No longer is the believer in a situation to associate
himself with the victim by his own initiative, since he does
not offer it. It must now be that God Himself brings the
believer into communion with the sacrificial victim by a
decisive and particular act. In this case the believer is no
longer the subject but the object of the gesture of association.
In fact, one does not baptize oneself; one is baptized.*
Baptism is the act by which God associates the believer with
the victim which He has offered. When the apostle wrote:
"One has died for all; therefore all have died," this death of
all men which he had in mind was as yet only virtual; it
resided only in the compassionate intention of God; it was
the grace which the sacrifice of the cross was to bring into
operation. The rite of baptism makes this grace actual and
efficacious for those who submit themselves to it. Through

* Except in Acts 22: 16. In 1 Cor. 6: 11 (ἀπελούσασθε) the context
suggests the idea of the passive.

baptism God fully actualizes for believers what the death of Christ declared and promised.

Such is the background of the apostolic declaration of v. 3 which is intended to explain the previous affirmation: "We all died to sin." Thus it becomes clear why this exposition of baptism is inserted at this point of the argument. Baptism is in fact the sacrament of the death of the humanity stemming from Adam; it effects a rupture in the malevolent solidarity which makes men enslaved to the inheritance of sin, and through it God associates the believer with the death of Christ.

(4) Death may be considered primarily as a punishment. But it is not this aspect which the apostle wishes to bring into the foreground. The emphasis here is on the suppression and annihilation of the body of sin, as v. 6 will bring out explicitly. By using the image of burial in the tomb, by saying that we have been buried with Christ, Paul is giving a very concrete and striking expression to his idea: we have disappeared with Christ, we have ceased to be counted in the land of the living, our place has become empty. The metaphor of burial seems to have played an important part in the ideas of the apostle concerning baptism, for in Col. 2:12 it is sufficient to sum them up. The general inference is that baptism is, above all, participation in the death of Christ, even to the point of burial as the terminus and end of the process of dying; while, on the other hand, the resurrection remains outside the horizons of this baptismal theology. It may be noted already that in our verse the apostle speaks in very different terms of baptismal burial and the new life in Christ. Baptism does not effect an association with the risen Christ; the new life with the risen Lord begins after baptism, and as a consequence of the latter, just as the resurrection of Christ followed His burial; the new life presupposes a new act of God, a new dispensation. While Paul can say that all have *already* died because Christ died, he cannot say that all have already been resurrected to newness of life because Christ is risen. Naturally the indissoluble link which connects the death with the resurrection of Christ excludes any real dissociation of the negative and positive aspects of baptism; the fact is that the believer

156

is linked with the death of Christ only in order to become linked with His life; the old life is buried only with a view to clearing the ground for the emergence of the new life. In Col. 2: 12 the apostle does associate, in connexion with baptism, the ideas of death and resurrection. Nevertheless his thought does not confuse them logically, and ch. 6 will give ample evidence of this by its use of future tenses in regard to the new life and of aorists in regard to baptismal death.

This contrasting use of tenses gives us occasion to emphasize that Paul closely connects baptism with a precise historical event;* the use of the aorist is to be explained by the reference to a unique event, fixed in the process of the past, namely, the death of Christ on the cross, an event which from God's point of view contained by implication the death of all whom baptism would associate with it. The resurrection of Christ, on the other hand, is not a fact of history in the same rigid and exclusive sense; it opens up within the historical sphere potentialities of new life, it ushers in the "life of the world to come", the new transcendent aeon; it is inscribed as a moment in the past because it marks the initiation of this new age, but it escapes from the past because it does not cease to develop its life-giving powers.

From this point of view we are compelled to refute that interpretation of the Pauline doctrine of baptism which connects it with the contemporary mystery cults. We have just seen that Paul's doctrine of baptism is essentially to be explained in the light of Jewish sacrificial theology, which enabled the apostle to give a new interpretation of the practice of baptism which he found rooted in the Christian communities.† The essential connexion of Pauline baptism with

* It has in fact been possible to speak of a "mystical sense of the historical" in regard to the Pauline doctrine of baptism (E. Sommerlath, *Der Ursprung des neuen Lebens*, 1927, p. 99).

† The history of the rite of baptism is not quite clear in all the phases of its development. Its origin seems to have been the Jewish practice of baptizing proselytes, which John the Baptist transformed into a Messianic baptism. Jesus Himself does not seem to have baptized. The early Christians practised baptism from the start, but the question of the laying on of hands and the gift of the Holy Ghost, both their relations with each other and with the rite of baptism itself, still remains an open

the historic event of the cross conferred upon it a character which was utterly different from that of contemporary rites of initiation which derived their significance from myth. Baptism associates the believer with a person, and with an act of His historical life in which was concentrated and expressed all His will to love, whereas initiation introduces into a mystic communion with cosmic forces. Whereas initiation may be repeated, for example after the lapse of twenty years, baptism is never repeated. The devotee of the mystery cults is penetrated with a power which endows him with the essence of immortal life, but which does not concern him as a moral being (the robber Pataikion is victorious over the virtuous Epaminondas, because he has had himself initiated) whereas baptism implies that the whole human personality is claimed by Christ, its daily life and conduct passing under the authority of the Lord Jesus.* These differences are so radical and far reaching that one cannot admit that contemporary ritual practices had any considerable influence on the thought of Paul.†

Burial with Christ prepares the believer for participation

question. To all this must be added the problem raised by the fate of the disciples of John the Baptist, whose role may have been more important than our sources suggest.

* For texts, see Lietzmann, on 1 Cor. 10: 5–6. The remark about Pataikion comes from Diogenes the Cynic (ibid.).

† Recently R. Bultmann, *Theologie des N.T.*, p. 139, has denied that baptism sprang from a Hebraic origin, because the tradition of Israel is unaware of cultic acts based on such ideas of divinity but is familiar with rites connected with the history of the people. This argument is in conflict with the fact that Paul himself in 1 Cor. 10 interpreted baptism in the light of the history of the people of Israel; furthermore Jesus Christ is not simply to be equated with God, nor are His life and death those of God; it is rather that baptism derives its significance from the role of Jesus Christ as the "eschatological Adam" (1 Cor. 15: 45), the "second man", the head of the people of the new covenant, the One who recapitulates the history of each member of His body, as we have just seen from ch. 5. Finally 3: 25 reminds us that for Paul the death of Jesus Christ is a sacrifice. Thus in 3: 25 and in 5: 12–17 we see the essential basis of thought which enabled Paul to build up his whole theology of primitive Christian baptism. The influence of current ideas was not profound; the environment may have stimulated Paul by compelling him to provide a truly Christian interpretation of a practice which had received other interpretations.

in the potentiality of new life which His resurrection disclosed,* so that, after the act of baptism, a new life opens
before him. But this life is not new in the chronological successive sense; it is new in a metaphysical sense, because it is
the intrusion of something novel, flowing from an act from on
High which interrupts the succession from Adam by an
absolute new beginning. The conjunctions ὥσπερ, οὕτως
which were the landmarks in the passage expounding the
parallelism between Adam and Christ, recall that train of
thought here with the purpose of emphasizing that the new
head of the line is not Adam but Christ.

⁵For if we have been united with him in a death like his, we
shall certainly be united with him in a resurrection like his. ⁶We
know that our old self was crucified with him so that the sinful
body might be destroyed, and we might no longer be enslaved
to sin. ⁷For he who has died is freed from sin. ⁸But if we have
died with Christ, we believe that we shall also live with him.
⁹For we know that Christ being raised from the dead will never
die again; death no longer has dominion over him. ¹⁰The
death he died he died to sin, once for all, but the life he lives he
lives to God. ¹¹So you must also consider yourselves dead to
sin and alive to God in Christ Jesus.
    ¹²Let not sin therefore reign in your mortal bodies, to make
you obey their passions. ¹³Do not yield your members to sin as
instruments of wickedness, but yield yourselves to God as men
who have been brought from death to life, and your members
to God as instruments of righteousness. ¹⁴For sin will have no
dominion over you, since you are not under law but under
grace.

(5) In the following verses the apostle develops his thought
in so characteristic a manner that it is useful to the compre-
hension of the text to note its literary construction. Verses 5,
6, and 7 are symmetrically balanced by 8, 9 and 10, the first
triplet affirming of the baptized believer what the second
affirms of Christ; these last three verses then give the Christological foundation for the anthropological affirmations of the

* Διὰ τῆς δόξης τοῦ Πατρός is lacking in some Latin MSS. The word
"glory" is here used in a broad sense; the effect suggests the cause, for
glory manifests power. In the LXX, δόξα translates words which connote the idea of power (cf. Th.Wb.NT, II, p. 247; cf. Jn. 11: 40).

first three; what is said of the Christian derives its truth from what is true of Christ.*

It is true to say of the baptized Christian that he is as closely associated with the crucified Christ as the young branch is with the trunk to which it is grafted.† The image is a very strong one; it brings out the communication of vitality from the trunk to the new branch, but not the communication of the nature of the first to the second. The image must not be abused in order to speculate on φύσις. The Israelite did not concern himself with questions about nature, in the philosophical sense of the term; but every day he observed that the sap passed from the wild stock to the engrafted branch and vivified the latter. The image of the vine and the branches (John 15) has the same point. Through baptism the believer shares in the new dynamism which has been thrust into human history by the sacrifice of the cross.

It is more difficult to know exactly how the apostle understood the matter. The expression "a death like his" has been referred to baptism itself which is thought of as reproducing the death of Christ and thus associating the believer with it: "We have been assimilated to, brought into conformity with, naturalized into, the image of his death. . . ." But we may also understand it as follows: "We have become one single plant with him" (αὐτῷ is understood after σύμφυτοι as after συνετάφημεν in v. 4) "by means of an imitation of his death, a death like his own." Baptism is presupposed, but the thought centres not on the external fact of baptism but on the inner fact of the sharing of the death of Christ, a death of the believer assimilating him to the death of Christ.

Considered apart from the resurrection, the cross of Christ has no more meaning than would have the immolation of a victim on the altar independently of the forgiveness which it proclaims as from God, and its instrumentality in conveying to the repentant sinner that forgiveness. Sacrifice implies

* Günther Bornkamm, "Taufe und neues Leben bei Paulus" (*Th.Bl.*, 1939) in *"Das Ende des Gesetzes"*, *Paulusstudien*, 1952, pp. 38–39. A. Feuillet, "Le plan salvifique de Dieu", *R.B.*, 1950, p. 364, n. 2.

† Σύμφυτος, i.e. innate, natural; of the same nature or kind; something which grows along with. The word is not used elsewhere in the NT.

death only to liberate the life which is contained in the blood and ensure renewed communion with God; it puts an end to a bad state of things, in order to inaugurate a new one, favourable and beneficent to the sinner.* Sacrifice is in the last resort a joyous feast, since it is ordained for the liquidation of the past and the communication of new life. Similarly the cross is inseparable from the resurrection.

Participation in the resurrection life of Christ is indicated by a verb in the future;† is this future chronological or logical? Is it an allusion to the general resurrection, or to the present participation of the believer in the life of the Risen Lord which should flow logically from his participation in the death of the Crucified? The second meaning is preferable both because of the indissoluble unity constituted by the cross and resurrection as also because of the parallel thought expressed in Col. 2: 12. Further on, Paul will make another allusion to the new life of the believer which cannot be understood except on the basis of his sharing in the life of the Risen Lord (v. 11).

(6f.) We now come to the culminating point of this argument. All that has just been said about baptism was intended to show that the inheritance bequeathed by Adam has been engulfed in the death of the cross, so that a new humanity might begin flowing from the Risen Christ. You should understand, says Paul, that baptism marked the annihilation of the old man that is in us. This old man, this decadent being is ourselves considered in our status as sons of Adam, in our likeness to the aged Abraham, moribund and enfeebled; παλαιός, i.e. *old*, is opposed to καινότης, i.e. *newness* (v. 4); the word qualifies what belongs to the economy of Adam, the old aeon, which the cross brings to an end for the believer, who has undergone baptism.‡ The expression "sinful body"

* Cf. E. Jacob, *Théologie de l'A.T.*, p. 238.

† As regards the construction, σύμφυτοι τῷ ὁμοιώματι should be added.

‡ Paul does not use here—not as yet—the image of the new man who must be put on after the believer has cast off the old man (Col. 3: 9; Eph. 4: 22). The problems raised by these expressions are complex. It will be noted, however, that the idea of the disappearance of the old nature springs up, under the apostle's pen, in connexion with the anti-

clarifies the thought, by pointing to the old man in respect of his external corporal condition.

This does not show any trace of dualism. Paul does not contrast the body with the personality. The body is not only the necessary instrument of personal existence, but the appropriate organ through which the personality expresses and realizes itself. Paul might have said: "My body is myself; I am my body."* Hence when he speaks of the destruction of the sinful body he wishes to stress the end of the inner sinful condition, which in practice is reflected in the deplorable way in which the sinner uses his body.†

The annihilation of the "sinful body" has as its aim the liberation of man who is enslaved by sin. Union with Christ in His death and participation in the power of His resurrection impart to the believer new potentialities of life; the solidarity of men in Adam is thus broken and the solidarity of men in Christ has begun.‡ In order to show plainly that an old status has been cancelled and a new one instituted, Paul borrows from juridical language an expression implying that death annuls all obligations in respect of the law.§ He who

---

thesis Adam and Christ. We should expect the theme of solidarity with Christ to lead to the idea of the creation, or the putting on, of a new humanity, just as the theme of solidarity with Adam had led to the idea of the destruction of the old nature. Perhaps we should not seek the origin of these much discussed images elsewhere but in this deep meditation on the human condition. See again on 13: 13.

* The unity of the human personality and the indivisible responsibility of body and soul are illustrated by the rabbinic parable of the two gardeners of the king, the one blind, the other paralysed, who pillage the garden and then accuse each other of the misdeed; but the king refuses to dissociate them and judges them together (Sanh. 91, a, b; cf. G. F. Moore, *op. cit.* I, p. 487).

† Paul's theology of the "body" is very surprising to our false spirituality. Cf. J. Héring, *Comm. du N.T.*, *Première Épître aux Corinthiens*, p. 47; E. Käsemann, *Leib und Leib Christi*, 1933.

‡ In 1 Cor. 12: 13 baptism is related to the constitution of the Body of Christ (cf. E. Sommerlath, *op. cit.* p. 112).

§ Sab. 30 a, 151 b. Cf. Strack-Billerbeck III, p. 232. It does not seem opportune to introduce here the idea of death as furnishing a sufficient expiation (cf. K. G. Kuhn, *Z.N.W.*, 1931, p. 305; Schrenk, *Th.Wb.NT*, II, p. 222).

dies with Christ is freed from the claims of sin and owes
nothing to it any longer; he is now free.*

(8) Vv. 5, 6 and 7 considered the baptized believer from
the point of view of his participation in the death of Christ;
vv. 8, 9 and 10 will now consider Christ as the bringer of new
life. Πιστεύομεν suggests persuasion (*we know*). This is a confession concerning a fact which faith already grasps; the
resurrection of Christ implies the fullness of true life shed upon
believers, as flame implies heat. God has raised up Jesus
Christ not in order to advertise the gospel, nor to confirm the
Messianic status of the crucified Jesus, but to make possible
for believers the plenitude of new life. It is the divine will that
men should be associated with Christ in His glorious life. The
Risen Christ is the first fruits, the first born of the new
humanity (1 Cor. 15: 20; Col. 1: 18); He has opened up the
avenue to God-centred life and He draws His church into
this new way.

(9f.) It is this supreme function of the Risen Christ which
the apostle suggests and further clarifies by the twofold declaration that it will have no end and that it is wholly
centred in God. Doubtless the way in which Paul expresses
himself here is not too explicit;† but we may recognize in
these two verses his doctrine of the Lordship of the Risen
Christ, called to reign in glory after triumphing over all His
enemies, and finally committing to God the powers which He
has exercised to lead into the way of life those whom sin was
leading into death. The contrast between the death which
sin imposed upon Christ and the life by which He triumphs
over it is well brought out by the word ἐφάπαξ: the death is a

* The use of δεδικαίωται in this sense is not so surprising as appears
at first sight. To be justified is to be the object of a judgment which
exculpates and restores to the accused freedom of person. For a comparable use see Acts 13: 39; Sir. 26: 29; Herm. vis. 3: 9, 1; εὐνὴ
δικαίων ἀφ' ἁμαρτιῶν (funerary inscription in Syria); ἐδικαιώθημεν, ὦ
τέκνον, ἀδικίας ἀπούσης (Poim. 343, 5). Cf. Lietzmann, Michel, p. 132.

† Ὁ ἀπέθανεν: the fact that He died once. ὃ δὲ ζῆ; the fact that He
lives. Death and life are considered in their particular relation to the
unique death and life of Christ: the fact of *His* death, the fact of *His*
eternal life.

unique event. His life, on the contrary, unfolds itself on the plane of eternity, in the filial relation which unites Him to the Father. In speaking of Christ, Paul is thinking also of the believer who is united to Him by faith. For this unique death objectively includes the death of all; the believer too dies but once because his death is gained by the death of Christ. But his life begins anew every day; he too lives to God (Gal. 2: 19; cf. 14: 7; 2 Cor. 5: 15). Hence the need for the exhortation which is to follow.

(11) The unique death of Christ is an objective fact which lends to the history of the world and of every man new possibilities and new obligations. It is important for each man to recognize* that this sacrifice implied his own death, since the plan of God is that each should be involved by faith and baptism in the death of Jesus Christ itself. But beyond this death, the Risen Christ offers to each one the possibility of a new life in communion with His own, a life lived in God like the eternal life of Christ. "Dead to self" and "alive to God" are brief and sufficient formulae which sum up the break with the inheritance of Adam symbolized by baptism, and the installation of a new order of things, the promise of a new heritage (8: 17). This epitomizes the work of Christ both in its unique historical aspect, what it finally accomplished, and also in its more permanent aspect, that is, its present efficacity and future consummation.† The future of the believer is thus closely connected with the death and resurrection of Christ; which explains why Paul, in order to give a secure basis to his ethics and to the conduct of the believer, should make his appeal to the fact of Christian baptism rather than directly to faith.‡ The presence of εἶναι is certainly of use in removing a purely psychological interpretation—in which also a direct appeal to faith would run the risk of getting bogged down, for it would be too easily misunderstood as an

* Λογίζεσθε is an imperative.

† Ἐν Χριστῷ Ἰησοῦ evokes the two aspects: the historical work and the believer's unique participation by baptism in the ἐφάπαξ; the heavenly work which is especially abiding through the agency of the Holy Spirit. Zahn, p. 310 is right to emphasize the second aspect, but the first should not be forgotten.

‡ Cf. A. Juncker, *Die Ethik des Apostels Paulus*, 1904, I, p. 7.

appeal to the pious imagination. It is not a question of imagining that one is dead, or of killing oneself in pious thought. We should consider rather the fact of our "being dead", we should take seriously, as a primary and objective datum implied by baptism, the fact that we have died, since the sacrifice of the cross is the moment of our own death, and was offered as our sacrifice.* On this point see above, from 3: 21.

(12–13a) By a sort of internal necessity, he who has just offered a sacrifice cannot deliberately return to the sins which he has just confessed by the sacrifice of a victim on the altar, since he has expressed in this way his determination to abandon his evil deeds. The οὖν, i.e. consequently, which opens this verse underlines this impossibility; faith and baptism have united the sinner to the sacrifice of Christ; it would be blasphemous mockery to allow things to proceed as before. On the contrary, faith and baptism introduce for the sons of Adam a real possibility of no longer allowing themselves to be subject to the tyranny of sin. The bondage of sin is broken for those who are one with Christ;† in communion with Him they find available for them the powers of the Kingdom; they turn towards God and cease to live for themselves. It is thus that they overcome the passions by which otherwise their servitude to the powers of this world is revealed.‡ It is thus again that they can no longer yield their members to ἁμαρτία which used them as weapons§ for the violation of the will of God. Ἁμαρτία is pictured as a reigning prince, who has subjects and armed troops at his disposal for the accomplishment of his plans and the consolidation of his reign of *iniquity*.

The reader will appreciate the striking nature of the paradox by which Paul concludes his refutation of the objection alluded to in v. 1. Whereas the apostle had been accused of

* Some MSS. (A D G) have omitted εἶναι, doubtless as a result of a psychologizing, subjectivizing interpretation.

† This is perhaps what Paul wishes to suggest by describing the body as "mortal", instead of saying σῶμα τῆς ἁμαρτίας. Θνητός stresses the human character and the weakness of the body, not its degenerate state.

‡ On the idea of ἐπιθυμία cf. 7: 7.

§ Ὅπλα in the sense of arms: 2 Cor. 10: 4; 6: 7; Rom. 13: 12.

encouraging sin by discrediting the law and merit as the principle inspiring right conduct, he boldly states in reply that the very reason for which sin will cease to wield authority is the end of the reign of the law and the extinction of all καύχησις which is the consequence of that reign. We must most firmly hold fast to this paradox if we do not wish to misunderstand the very essence of the apostle's thought. To be sure, the experience of every day shows plainly that sin is not entirely banished from the life of the believer; far from it! The facts of daily life would seem to give a formal contradiction to the thesis of Paul. Are we to suppose that he was unaware of these counter-attacks launched by the power of sin? On the contrary his letters suggest that his readers, particularly the Corinthians, must have reminded him sharply of this cruel contradiction. There is nothing in Paul of the fanatic or the doctrinaire blinded by the obsessive force of his own theories. How then did he interpret the continuing reality of sin in the Church—he who declared roundly that believers are dead to sin and that sin has no more dominion over them?

In order to solve this apparent contradiction we must remember that the apostle, like his Master, situated the essence of sin in the heart, not in particular acts or external matters (cf. Matt. 15: 18, 19). If the law provides the occasion for sinning, it is evidently not because it commands evil deeds; it would be blasphemy to think so; but for the man who concentrates his attention on it in a wrong way it provides the opportunity for nourishing sentiments of pride, for claiming to deserve the divine favour; the law fosters καύχησις which is the very essence of sin. To accomplish the will of God with the pride of the Pharisee, to claim that one's rights, based on merit, should be recognized by God—that, in the eyes of Paul, is the real sin, is sin *par excellence*. Yes, the Pharisee of the parable, a *virtuous* but proud man in the sight of God, went away without having received the divine forgiveness which he did not implore in humility, whilst the publican, a man devoid of virtue but a man who abased himself before God, was forgiven. What makes the believer is not his conduct but his heart; not the excellence of his virtues but the lowliness of his soul before God.

This is the revolutionary affirmation of the gospel, so precisely understood by the apostle Paul, so scandalous for his contemporaries and for moralists of all times, Christians included. It is better to be the publican who was a sinner, than to be the righteous Pharisee! *Pecca fortiter* (sin wholeheartedly), wrote Luther to Melanchthon.* How greatly has this remark been misunderstood by the opponents of the reformer, who were as little perspicacious in their attitude towards him as were the critics of the apostle who reproached him with saying essentially the same thing! He who desires to justify himself in the eyes of God is lost; he spurns the grace that is offered him. One must face one's sin. There is a way of sinning by half measures, of trying to tranquillize one's conscience, either by invoking fallacious arguments in extenuation of the fault, or by not carrying the sin to extremities with the idea of neutralizing the extent to which one has sinned by the extent to which one has abstained from sinning. A candid sinner is nearer to the despair that prepares the way for salvation than a crafty sinner. The pleasures of the world have made saints but not bourgeois morality. The presence of material sin in the life of believers is a sign of their weakness and of their unfaithfulness. But as long as and in so far as he who commits sin abases himself and asks God to forgive him, one may say what Paul will say in 8: 1: there is for such a one no final condemnation.

It is not in fact actual (*material*) sin which excludes us from communion with God, but *formal* sin, which consists in attempting self-justification like the Pharisee. At bottom it is lack of faith, if it is true that real faith consists essentially in committing oneself to the grace of God for the forgiveness of one's sins. When Paul writes: sin will no longer have dominion over you, he is not speaking of material sin, of acts of sin, as is shown by the fact that he amplifies his thought in the statement: "you are not under the law but under grace". He is speaking of that fundamental sin which consists in having recourse to the law in order to claim a righteousness

* Letter to Melanchthon, 1st August, 1521 (*Luthers Briefwechsel*, W. A. II, p. 372). Cf. on this matter F. Kattenbusch, *Stud. z. Syst. Theol.* (*Häring Geburtstag*), 1918, pp. 50–75.

of one's own. For the man who is in Christ there is no *formal* sin.*

(13b–14) The reign of ἁμαρτία has been shattered; the reign of God has drawn near "with power". By the way of repentance and faith, Jesus Christ tears away from ἁμαρτία those whom it holds in bondage. By associating them with His sacrificial death, He frees them from the necessities with

* The persistence of sin in the church and, more concretely, in the life of every Christian is a self-evident fact. No one can deny it, nor does anyone think of doing so. The institution of confession and the sacrament of penance show clearly that this is the point of view of the Roman Church. But in spite of that fact, Roman theologians go on reproaching protestants with the *simul peccator et justus* of Luther. The obstinacy with which they express this criticism is incomprehensible. They claim to be contrasting two ontologies; in their view, protestants do not really believe in baptismal regeneration, with the result that for them the believer, though justified, is still and remains a sinner. It is a most fantastic quarrel, since those who criticize protestantism in this way recognize (and here we cite only one instance among hundreds) that "the greatest saints themselves have admitted themselves to be sinners, and every Christian must be on his guard against the danger of falling into sin to which he is ever exposed" (B. Häring, *La Loi du Christ*, I, 1956, p. 395). Hence Roman theologians do not conceive baptismal grace in such a way as to suggest that it so transforms our nature that the believer, righteous as he is, no longer sins. Hence why such bitter dislike of Luther's dictum? The distinction between formal and material sin, in the sense outlined above, might throw some light on the debate. The Christian is always a sinner, materially, at all events. But as long as he abides "in Christ", as Paul would say, or, in Luther's language, "in faith", or, as the Roman theologian would put it, "in the church", the believer does not give formal consent to sin; he is able to repent of a fall which has revealed his weakness—for he is still "in the flesh"—but not his deep and true intention; he has recourse to the means of grace, to prayer, to the Word of God, to the sacraments. It is in this sense that Paul declares sin no longer to reign over believers. And this is what catholic theology means when it affirms that baptismal grace has effected a unity with the Body of Christ which communicates to the believer the graces necessary for the struggle against sin. This again is what Luther means when he declares that the faith which unites us with Christ suffices to conserve our salvation even if we happen to sin. And when catholicism speaks of the sacramental grace which the church dispenses, it presupposes that the believer has the faith without which sacraments are vain. Likewise when Luther speaks of union with Christ through faith, he presupposes that the believer has recourse to the sacraments of the church, apart from which faith is fluctuating and incomplete; what then is the argument about?

which their former condition of life burdened them; they are thus free to enter the service of God, and to yield their members to His divine control in the struggle for righteousness, i.e. the struggle to attain obedience to His holy will.* They are free, because Christ, who emancipated them by drawing them into His death, now draws them into His eternal life to reanimate them with newness of life.† Henceforth it is He who is their leader, their κύριος; sin is dethroned (οὐ κυριεύσει); it is the authority of the new master which alone counts. They are like soldiers who have deserted the ranks of rebellious troops to rally round the legitimate authority; the orders of their old captain have no further currency for them.‡

The conclusion of the section is somewhat abrupt and summary but Paul has accustomed his readers to this kind of procedure. We have already learnt to consider the law as characteristic of the reign of sin (3: 20; 4: 15; 5: 20). Grace on the other hand is the perfect gift of Christ and the mark of the Kingdom which He inaugurates (5: 2, 15, 21). The opposition between the two authorities of which we have been speaking might be reduced to an opposition between law and grace. Thus the writer leaves aside his metaphors and returns to the field of doctrine; the law, considered as a system of salvation, is abolished; Christ has instituted a new régime. We have, as it were, objectively died with Christ; and the sole necessary and sufficient thing that we have to do, rather than have recourse to the precepts of the law which incite us to aspire to merit the favour of God, is to become aware of

---

* Παριστάνω, παρίστημι are used to suggest the act of cultic offering (cf. Rom. 12: 1). But they are also used in military language (Polybius, 3, 109, 9; cf. Horst, Th.Wb.NT, IV, p. 565, n. 58). The present imperative (μηδὲ παριστάνετε) indicates a break with the past, which must be incessantly renewed, and which, in consequence, assumes the character of a definitive break. The aorist imperative (παραστήσατε) emphasizes on the contrary that the act of obedience is accomplished *hic et nunc* in a decision each time renewed.

† ὡσεί =as . . . not "as if".

‡ This combative condition likewise characterizes the life of the believer who is a member of the Essene sects; Paul's anthropology is probably influenced by these sectarians' modes of thought. Cf. K. G. Kuhn, Th.L.Z., 1950; Z.Th.K., 1950; ibid. 1952.

the significance of that baptism by which God has buried us with His Son so that we may live with Him. It is not for us to deserve this grace of God; but it is our part to live according to the grace which has been freely granted us. Live in conformity with what God has made of you in Jesus Christ and by your own obedience, be what you are through the obedience of Jesus Christ. This is the totally reversed situation which the apostle expresses in v. 14.

> [15]What then? Are we to sin because we are not under law but under grace? By no means! [16]Do you not know that if you yield yourselves to any one as obedient slaves, you are slaves of the one whom you obey, either of sin, which leads to death, or of obedience, which leads to righteousness? [17]But thanks be to God, that you who were once slaves of sin have become obedient from the heart to the standard of teaching to which you were committed, [18]and, having been set free from sin, have become slaves of righteousness. [19]I am speaking in human terms, because of your natural limitations. For just as you once yielded your members to impurity and to greater and greater iniquity, so now yield your members to righteousness for sanctification.
>
> [20]When you were slaves of sin, you were free in regard to righteousness. [21]But then what return did you get from the things of which you are now ashamed? The end of those things is death. [22]But now that you have been set free from sin and have become slaves of God, the return you get is sanctification and its end, eternal life. [23]For the wages of sin is death, but the free gift of God is eternal life in Christ Jesus our Lord.

(15) It is only apparently paradoxical to say that the abolition of the system of the law spells the end of the reign of sin. For the Jews, doubtless, the law symbolizes the whole struggle against evil, and its authority supplies the real reason for doing good. But the new era which Christ has ushered in does not leave empty the place which the law filled; the believer is not deprived of the authority of the law in order to be abandoned to his own desires; he is placed under a new authority. Vv. 11 to 14 had shown the logical consequence of participation in the death of Christ; the believer is now free to surrender himself to the authority of a new master, because he is dead as far as the old authority is concerned. Now

baptism may also be regarded as the act of appropriation by which Christ obtains the ownership of a man and the latter becomes His slave. By giving His life for men, Christ has in a sense gained possession of them; in those texts where this idea emerges it is linked precisely to the statement that believers are free from the mastery of all and everybody because they have become the slaves of Christ. This idea certainly lies behind the use which the apostle makes of the dialectic of the liberty and bondage of the baptized believer.*

(16) Liberation from the power of the law thus by no means gives us the option of sinning because such liberation implies that the believer has passed from one authority, now superseded, to the sphere of a new authority! Two things are equally true: "You cannot serve two masters" as Jesus said; but also: "You will always serve one or the other of these masters," as was clearly implied by the dilemma with which Jesus confronted people. Man is never neutral and purely passive. He is embarked on the adventure of life; he will always have a master in whose service he will gain or lose his soul. In choosing his master he is choosing himself and his ends, because from that master he receives his task and his reward. A man without choice or decision does not exist. The critical decision with which the baptized believer is faced is therefore clear and his choice is already implied in the very act of his baptism.†

(17f.) This is why Paul can give thanks to God for the glad obedience which his readers have shown in receiving the gospel that was preached to them. Since their choice has

---

* Hence it would seem useless to try to discover whether in the ancient world cases might have been known in which men chose for themselves a master and made themselves his slave. It is true that this state of affairs did exist, some wretches becoming slaves in order to be able to live. For Paul the choice consists in making the decision for or against Christ.

† To avoid tautology, δοῦλος will no doubt mean in the first place, servant, then slave. The opposition is that between the one who offers his services freely, and the one who no longer has liberty of action, and so can only obey slavishly. Ὑπακοή means both the obedience of faith and ethical obedience, the latter manifesting the former, as the fruit does the tree.

been made in regard to the master whom they wish to follow, the consequence is expressed directly as liberty in regard to the servitude of sin, and bondage in regard to righteousness.*

(19) Of course this way of expressing the matter does not describe very well the Christian state; it is thus implied to be bondage whereas in truth it is liberty (Rom. 8: 15, 21; Gal. 5: 1–13; 2 Cor. 3: 17). Paul apologizes for the way in which he expresses himself; one cannot compare the Christian's obedience to Christ with the yoke which sin imposes.† Perhaps he also wishes to apologize for having said that liberation (from sin) leads to bondage (to righteousness); for those who had had the painful personal experience of what slavery meant must have found something strange about this way of speaking of a liberation which led to a new form of bondage. With these reservations, Paul does not intend to withdraw anything from his use of the metaphor of the slave: the believer has indeed passed into the ownership of Christ who has acquired His rights through His sacrificial death. Although somewhat awkward, the comparison is vividly expressive.‡

* The expressions of v. 17 are puzzling. The best construction is: ὑπηκούσατε δὲ ἐκ καρδίας τῷ τύπῳ τῆς διδαχῆς εἰς ὃν παρεδόθητε. What is meant by the expression τύπος διδαχῆς? What may be this teaching which has thus been standardized? Paul never speaks of his preaching in this way: does he use this particular phrase because he is alluding to a body of teaching received by the Romans, and does not know what exactly it was? Παραδίδοναι in the sense of this verse is not un-unknown (A. Fridrichsen, Conj. Neot., 7, 1942, pp. 6–8; W. Bauer, Wörterbuch, col. 1120). If we cut out the difficult part of these verses (from ὑπηκούσατε to διδαχῆς) the development of the thought gains in simplicity; we see here perhaps a very old gloss (R. Bultmann, Th.L.Z., 1947, pp. 193–198).

† Cf. Zahn, ad loc.

‡ Ἀνθρώπινος in the sense of: adapted to human weakness, cf. 2 Cor. 10: 3. Ancient exegesis interpreted thus: "I am giving you a precept narrowed down to your feeble resources; I am adapting the requirements of Christian obedience to your infirmities." This is certainly not the meaning, for the expression is the equivalent of κατὰ ἄνθρωπον λέγω (λαλῶ), Rom. 3: 5; Gal. 3: 15; 1 Cor. 9: 8. What is in question is a formal adaptation concerning language, not thought. The "weakness of the flesh" is not necessarily an allusion to concrete defects; it may be an allusion to the difficulties and limitations of human language (so Michel).

The antithesis between the two slaveries is completed. The slavery of sin consists in "impurity" and "unrighteousness"; both terms characterize well the behaviour of the Gentiles (cf. Rom. 1: 18, 24); they suggest the guiltiness of man's conduct both in respect of himself and in respect of God. Such slavery leads to ἀνομία; the repetition of the word is surprising;* to avoid tautology we may see in the first the actual concrete disobedience of man springing from his refusal of the law of God, and in the second the state of disobedience in so far as it is judged and condemned by God. Bondage to righteousness thus opposed to ἀνομία certainly conveys the idea of righteousness as a fulfilling of the will of God, and not the righteousness of the believer who is justified by grace. The unrighteousness in which the slave of sin is entangled is set in contrast to sanctification. The people of Israel is holy because it is the people whom God set apart, the people established by election grace in a close relation with God; the holiness of Israel is therefore the result of an act of God, but Israel must respond to this election by obedience and the practice of righteousness. Thus sanctification will be the attitude and behaviour as a result of which he who is holy because God has called him to belong to the holy people, realizes his vocation in concrete practice by his personal obedience.

Similarly the believer is holy because he belongs to the Body of Christ. As a baptized believer, he has become the exclusive property of Christ; he belongs to Christ as a limb belongs to a body; this objective state of affairs will be reflected in a life of obedience through which the ideal will be concretely realized. The members of the believer's body have become the members of Christ.† The believer must therefore advance in the path of sanctification in order to realize the holiness which has ideally been imparted in Jesus Christ.

Lietzmann thinks it refers to a deeper adaptation both of language and content in the sense of 1 Cor. 3: 1. The expression is found again in Gal. 4: 13 in quite a different meaning.

* Some MSS. (B. Pesh., etc.) have simplified by eliminating εἰς τὴν ἀνομίαν which however should be kept for the sake of the parallelism.

† The image of the body and members will appear again in 12: 4, 5. It is especially amplified in 1 Cor. 6: 15; 12: 12–27. Cf. Eph. 5: 30.

Nῦν, i.e. *now*, stresses the fact that the objective condition of the believer, as determined by the work of Christ, is the basis of the exhortation to progress in the way of sanctification through the practice of righteousness.*

(20–22) The antithesis is continued from the point of view of its results, its "fruits", its ultimate consequences. He who is the slave of a master does the work which has been commanded him; if he has a good master he may hope, by his work, to prepare his liberation; if he has a bad master, all his trouble will only serve to increase his wretchedness and hasten his death. The believer who surveys his past recognizes that he has served a bad master under whose command he has done things of which he is now ashamed; especially as the condemnation of God weighs upon his work, so that he has worked not in order to gain life and blessedness but to prepare his perdition.† Things have now changed; *νυνὶ δέ* insists once more on the reality of this change, which has been objectively effected: "You are the object of a liberation which has given you a new master; hence, from now on, bear fruit conformably to your new status; act in such a way as to show clearly to whom you belong (*εἰς ἁγιασμόν*). Faithfulness to your master will lead you to eternal life."

(23) However, there is an extreme contrast between the way in which the bondage of sin leads to death and the way in which the bondage of righteousness leads to life. The contrast does not lie merely in the result. To the antitheses sin—righteousness, and death—life, is added a third antithesis: wages—free gift. Death is the wage‡ which sin pays to those who live under its commands. For a moment Paul seems to have returned to the image of military life. Hence the slave could serve as a soldier and receive his pay. How ironic to suggest that wages, normally intended to maintain life, are in

* Cf. the formula of Rev. 22: 11: "Let the holy still be holy."
† There are two possible constructions: "What fruit did you then bear? (Fruits) for which you blush now." "What good have you derived from those actions for which you now blush?"
‡ *'Οψώνιον* denotes supplies or military pay; translated into Hebrew or Aramaic, it means wages.

174

fact death! Sin deceives its slaves. At least it keeps to its terms; the wages are due; one is certain not to escape death; this master pays cash down. Life eternal, on the other hand, is not something due; it is a gift, undeserved and freely granted by God, having no other source than the lavish grace of God in Jesus Christ.*

Thus finally the economy founded by Adam becomes bankrupt. It shows how much it is worth by this double fact: that it gives rise to works which make ashamed, and its ultimate term is death.

A word will suffice at this point to suggest the character of the holiness which Paul exhorts Christians to attain; Christians are thus exhorted inasmuch as they are slaves of righteousness (v. 19). What they are objectively because God has restored them to communion with Him by grace, they must become in subjective reality. They have to maintain themselves in this new status, to show themselves worthy, to live as sons, because the forgiveness of God has already fully reintegrated them into the fellowship of the divine home.

* Zahn, p. 326, compares with χάρισμα the *donativum* or bounty which was dispensed by a victorious general or a new emperor. Cf. also Heidland, *Th.Wb.NT*, VI, p. 592.

¹Do you not know, brethren—for I am speaking to those who know the law—that the law is binding on a person only during his life? ²Thus a married woman is bound by law to her husband as long as he lives; but if her husband dies she is discharged from the law concerning the husband. ³Accordingly, she will be called an adulteress if she lives with another man while her husband is alive. But if her husband dies she is free from that law, and if she marries another man she is not an adulteress.

⁴Likewise, my brethren, you have died to the law through the body of Christ, so that you may belong to another, to him who has been raised from the dead in order that we may bear fruit for God. ⁵While we were living in the flesh, our sinful passions, aroused by the law, were at work in our members to bear fruit for death. ⁶But now we are discharged from the law, dead to that which held us captive, so that we serve not under the old written code but in the new life of the Spirit.

(1–3) THE ISRAELITES HAD for long been aware of the requirements of "righteousness"; the centre of the Mosaic legislation was the basic precept, "Be holy for I am holy" (Lev. 11: 44). In explaining that the believer must practise righteousness with a view to attaining sanctification, was not Paul saying the same thing? Was he not referring his readers back to the law? This question is implied not merely by the expressions he uses but by the substance of his thought. The law was God's gift to His people to guide them in the path of holiness. Its very origin would seem to require that it should always play this part in the divine plan of salvation. Hence it was necessary for Paul to show that the authority of the law is now revoked for Christians who by baptism and faith have participated in the death of Christ. This demonstration will be expounded in three sequences of thought, which will in turn show: (a) that the law itself does not claim more than a temporary function; (b) that the law does not pretend to do more than provide knowledge of what sin is; (c) that experience confirms the powerlessness of the law to commit man decisively to the way of holiness and obedience. The first point is discussed in a paragraph whose close literary correspondence with the preceding lines should be noted.*

Paul embarks on his theme abruptly. The reader is at once challenged by the question whether the law has permanent authority. Well, it should be remembered in the first place that the law itself foresees a situation in which its power would be suspended: that is, the case in which a wife loses her husband by death. A woman is bound to her husband as long as he lives; but if he dies, she will not be committing adultery by marrying another (cf. 1 Cor. 7: 39).† What law is Paul discussing here? Since he is addressing himself to Romans who were eminent jurists, is he alluding to some well known and universally recognized juridical principle?‡ It would seem rather that the apostle is thinking of the Mosaic law,§ since v. 4, which draws the consequences from the principles posed at the beginning of the argument, speaks of the Mosaic law. If the argument had been based on a pagan juridical principle its demonstrative value would have

* As regards the structures: 7: 1–4 corresponds to 6: 16–19 (obedience of one submitted to an authority and his liberation for the service of another authority); 7: 5–6 corresponds to 6: 21–23 (antithesis between what previous ways of life have led to (notably death) and what the new way of life will result in. As for the vocabulary; καταργεῖσθαι (6: 6; 7: 6); κυριεύειν (6: 9, 14; 7: 1); καρπός, καρποφορεῖν (6: 21, 22; 7: 4,5); δοῦλος, δουλεύειν (6: 20–22; 7: 6). Cf. Godet, II, p. 70; Michel, p. 141.

† For the formula ἀπὸ τοῦ νόμου τοῦ ἀνδρός: law *concerning* her husband, cf. ὁ νόμος τοῦ πάσχα, Num. 9: 12; ὁ νόμος τῆς ἁμαρτίας, Lev. 6: 25.

‡ Several authors have thought so (B. Weiss, Kühl, Jülicher, etc.). If so, Paul would be addressing his Roman readers by appealing to their juridical competence.

§ The terms used recall the OT: ἡ ὕπανδρος γυνή: Num. 5: 20, 29; Prov. 6: 24, 29, etc. γένεσθαι ἀνδρί: Deut. 24: 2; Hosea 3: 3. It will be noticed that it is likewise from the law of Moses that Paul borrows the terms of argument in vv. 7–12; again it is the law which bears witness to itself. None of this could have been so conceived and expressed had not Paul been thinking of Moses.

been lost. Thus Moses himself foresaw a situation in which the authority of the law would cease to be valid. The law recognizes its own limitations. Its power is suspended by death.

(4) Now, is not the situation thus foreseen by the law the very situation of Christian believers? Paul says of them that they have died to the law by the body of Christ. The formula is strikingly terse. We have learnt from 6: 6 that the death of the believer, buried with Christ by baptism, strikes his "old self" and involves the disappearance of the "body of sin"; this is emphasized by 6: 7 which affirms that death frees a man from obligations towards the law, as the present argument with regard to the decease of a husband reminds us. In such circumstances the death of believers to the law means in reality the death of their old self (or their body of sin); by the fact of this death the believer has in some sense been widowed of his old self (or his body of sin); he is no longer bound to it; he is therefore free to transfer his loyalty to anyone he likes to choose; the law which bound him to his old self (his body of sin) has ceased to exercise any valid authority over him. Thus in bringing him to share in His own death, Christ has caused the believer to die to the authority of the law.*

(5f.) The contrast between the old status and the new is further expressed in a number of memorable formulae. "To live in the flesh"† obviously does not mean to live in our present physiological conditions; no more than in v. 24 does the apostle invoke an intervention which would separate his soul from his body and release it from the dead weight of the latter. Believers are no longer "living in the flesh" simply because Christ has made them to share in His sacrificial death; henceforth their inner life is governed by the promise of God in Jesus Christ; it has ceased to be dominated by

* Another interpretation is that Paul is here alluding to the death of Christ in the flesh; after the death of Christ, Christians are free to give themselves to this new husband, namely, the risen Christ (L. Cerfaux, following A. Feuillet, *art.* quoted, p. 368). However, Paul is surely here speaking of the death of the believer (ἐθανατώθητε).

† On the significance of ἐν in this expression, cf. later on, 8: 9.

178

egoistic and worldly interests, it is now shaped by its answer to the manifestation of the divine love in Jesus Christ; the old self and the old world have passed away. The old status was characterized by the nefarious influence of the law which had the effect of inciting man to sinful deeds, thus leading him in the way of death.* In this way the apostle attributes to the law a function which the rest of the chapter will give him occasion to analyse, v. 5 clearly foreshadowing the trains of thought which are developed in vv. 7 to 25. Once again, *vuví*, *now*, emphasizes the utter newness of the state of the believer—a newness which springs from the fact that the believer's participation in the death of Christ frees him from the burden of the law;† his new way of life is determined by a new loyalty.

The question arises here as to whether the apostle is thinking of a new interpretation of the law or whether he is suggesting, in contrast to the obedience which is based on the law, an obedience which stems only from the agency of the Holy Spirit. In 2 Cor. 3: 4–18 the dialectics of the Spirit and the letter gives rise to an argument in favour of a new reading of the scriptures. But it will be noticed that further on, in ch. 8, Paul speaks very explicitly of the Spirit without at the same time alluding to scripture. We should prefer this near context to that of the Second Letter to the Corinthians. Paul contrasts the old type of obedience, arising from the authority of the letter of the law, with the new type, which is engendered by communion with the resurrected Christ and the power of His Spirit. Thus v. 6 foreshadows ch. 8 as v. 5 has just anticipated the sequel of ch. 7.

⁷What then shall we say? That the law is sin? By no means! Yet, if it had not been for the law, I should not have known

---

* "Sinful passions" may be those which lead to acts of sin, or those which are characteristic of sin.

† $Κατηργήθημεν$ in v. 6 corresponds to $κατήργηται$ of v. 2. $Ἀποθανόντες$ may be completed by $τούτῳ$ $(τῷ νόμῳ)$ in order to make construction easier, in which case $ἐν ᾧ$ will be masculine ("dead to the law which held us enslaved"). $ἐν ᾧ$ may also be taken as a neuter, ("dead to what held us enslaved"). Some MSS. (D G Vulg., etc.), have corrected $ἀποθανόντες$ to $τοῦ θανάτου$ (cf. 8: 2): "freed from the law of death which held us enslaved".

sin. I should not have known what it is to covet if the law had not said, "You shall not covet". [8]But sin, finding opportunity in the commandment, wrought in me all kinds of covetousness. Apart from the law sin lies dead. [9]I was once alive apart from the law, but when the commandment came, sin revived and I died; [10]the very commandment which promised life proved to be death to me. [11]For sin, finding opportunity in the commandment, deceived me and by it killed me. [12]So the law is holy, and the commandment is holy and just and good.

[13]Did that which is good, then, bring death to me? By no means! It was sin, working death in me through what is good, in order that sin might be shown to be sin, and through the commandment might become sinful beyond measure.

(7) The law does not merely indicate the temporary nature of its role; it says precisely what this role is. It is esteemed for what it does not claim to be when the Jews expect it to be a source of righteousness and to enable man to deserve the favour of God. The law makes clear what sin is; Paul has already stated this (3: 20; 4: 15) and now proposes to explain it (vv. 7–12) and to show further, in negative terms, that while it makes aware of sin, the law does not impart the capacity to do the will of God (vv. 13–23).

The difficulties of this section are famous.* There is one which overflows all the others; from v. 7 onwards the writer uses the first person singular—a grammatical point which suggests that he is speaking of himself; the dramatic and apparently intimate character of certain of his declarations strengthens the reader's impression that he is drawing on his own personal experiences and making confidences.

The opinion that the apostle is speaking of himself has been defended under two forms, according as to whether it is believed that the author is referring to his past as an Israelite or to his present Christian experience.

The first thesis involves considerable difficulties. The picture here drawn of the struggle of the man who is subject to the law reflects neither what we know of the experience of

* On this matter, the reader may refer especially to W. G. Kümmel, *Röm. 7 und die Bekehrung des Apostels*, 1939; Stauffer, *art. ἐγώ Th.Wb.NT*, II, pp. 335–360, and R. Bultmann, "Römer 7 und die Anthropologie des Paulus" (*Imago Dei, Festschrift für G. Krüger*), 1932.

the Israelite in general nor the view of Paul in particular concerning his religious life before his conversion. The nature
of Pharisaic piety is expressed more accurately in the parable
which depicts a Pharisee giving thanks because he is not a
sinner, and enumerating to his own satisfaction his various
good works; likewise Paul bears witness to his own experience
as a Pharisee in similar terms when he declares that he was
blameless as regards obedience to the law (Phil. 3: 6). The
drama of inner conflict described in these verses is not in
harmony with this type of consciousness. The conversion of
Paul was not that of a heart devoured by remorse for its acts
of disobedience, but rather that of a proud soul exalting itself
before God because of its obedience to the law.*

Since Augustine the second thesis has often been maintained: it is then supposed that Paul is here speaking of his
Christian experiences.† It is said that only the Christian has
such a dramatic awareness of the nature of sin; only he takes
a true delight in the law of God. All this is true; the man who
is a stranger to the cross of Christ minimizes the gravity of
sin so as to escape the strain and stress of it, at least in his own
eyes. In spite of the undeniable truth of this, which has deep
implications and may not be neglected in any attempt to
solve the problem, it is hardly possible to see in this passage
an echo of Christian experience as the apostle at least knows
and describes it. In the study of ch. 7 people have been too
much influenced by the recollection of the inner drama experienced by the young Luther in his despairing struggles to
attain an unattainable obedience to the divine law.¶ Nothing compels us to believe that Paul was Lutheran on this
point. The text and the whole context of this chapter in fact
preclude the hypothesis. In point of fact, it will be noticed
that Paul speaks in the first and second persons plural both

* "The traumatic condition which it has been desired to see in Rom. 7
and which has been linked with the painful failure of Paul in the observation of the law, is now relegated to the museum of exegetical absurdi-
ties" (P. Demann, "Moïse et la loi dans la pensée de saint Paul", in
Moïse, l'homme de l'alliance, 1953, p. 229).

† It is rare to find exegetes defending this opinion, which is espoused
by a number of varied dogmatists, such as Thomas Aquinas, Luther, K.
Barth, Nygren and many others.

¶ Cf. P. Althaus, Paulus und Luther über den Menschen, 1938.

before and after the passage in question, that is, when he is indisputably declaring what the faith of the Christian is. The change of style may be not unconnected with a change in the point of view. This change of viewpoint becomes quite evident as soon as we compare the essential affirmations of the passages using "we" with those of the fragment which uses "I"; these affirmations are mutually exclusive* and their opposition is further emphasized by the use of past tenses; the old self has been crucified and the body of sin destroyed (6: 6). While we were living in the flesh, the law aroused in us sinful passions (7: 5), but *now* we have been discharged from the law (7: 6); at 8: 1 this "now" is repeated in order to introduce the positive description of the existing condition of the Christian which is marked by the liberating action of the Spirit, and the passage culminates in the affirmation: "but you are not in the flesh, you are in the spirit" (8: 9).

It is not that believers are immune from the necessity of struggling in their endeavours to attain holiness. Paul has exhorted his readers on these lines in ch. 6, and he will take up the theme again at 8: 12. But the tone is totally different, because the very basis of the struggle is quite other. In his efforts towards sanctification, the believer is not alone, abandoned to his incurable weakness, as is the man of ch. 7. It is by the power of the Spirit that he is called to put to death the deeds of the body (8: 13); he has changed his master, and his effort now consists in being faithful to the new master, in surrendering himself in the way of obedience (6: 13, 19; cf. 12: 1). The result is evidently quite different in the eyes of Paul, since he can tell his readers that now they have no need to blush at what used to make them ashamed (6: 21-23).† It is difficult to see how Paul can say about the Christian at the very same time what he writes in 6: 21-23

* The climax of the development lies in the despairing cry: "Who will deliver me?" This declaration evokes God's condemnation, henceforth unavoidable. Nothing underlines the opposition better than the first words of ch. 8: "There is therefore now no condemnation for those who are in Christ Jesus." Despair is possible only if this truth is unknown or unappreciated.

† We find the same points of view in Gal. 5: 13-25; the Christian participates in the life of the Spirit and that fact basically qualifies his whole moral existence.

and what we read in ch. 7: 13–24. So much the less so, moreover, in view of the fact that the position itself of the one who
is speaking in ch. 7 is incompatible with what the apostle
says about the Christian in regard to the law. "You are not
under the law," says Paul to his Christian readers in 6: 14.
Why then in this disputed passage such a persistent and despairing confrontation with the law? Again, why this obsessive self-scrutiny? The Christian may not analyse the state of
his soul with such keen interest. Such a degree of introspection
springs surely from an anxiety to attain an egocentric type of
perfection, it betrays a hypertrophy of the ego which is suspect in the light of what the apostle declares in Gal. 2: 20:
"It is no longer I who live but Christ who lives in me."
Christ delivers the believer from this tragic and useless self-
examination, and the look with which the individual thus
studies his own self is a look which it would have been better
to focus on Christ. Hence we have here a hypertrophy of the
ego and a hypertrophy of the law, both equally contrary to
what we read from the pen of the apostle when he develops
his ideas about the Christian's duty of obedience to the will
of God: in such passages there is no trace of introspective
self-analysis, and in his exhortations Paul never appeals to
the authority of the law nor asks his readers to consider it.*

These two explanations which for a long time have shared
the approval of Paul's interpreters have one defect in common. They presuppose an autobiographical passage, written
in a personal style and referring in content to personal experience, to have been intercalated into an argument wholly
devoted to an exposition of the divine dispensations for the
salvation of mankind.† Of course the expressions used may at
first sight bewilder the modern reader, who is less accustomed
than was the reader in the ancient world to a proceeding
which has become obsolete but which was very familiar to

---

* It will be noted that the vocabulary of these verses offers some very
special features. The following expressions are not found elsewhere in
Paul: ἀφορμὴν λαβεῖν (vv. 8, 11); ἀναζῆν (v. 9); σύνφημι (v. 16);
παράκειται (vv. 18, 21); συνήδεσθαι (v. 22); ἀντιστρατεύεσθαι (v. 23);
ταλαίπωρος (v. 24). This fact may suggest borrowing. It may also imply
that the apostle is adopting a point of view which is not familiar to him.

† Cf. Stauffer, *Th.Wb.NT*, II, p. 355, 39; p. 356, 13.

Paul and his contemporaries.* It is however quite understandable that Paul should have felt warranted in having recourse to it, and that not only for reasons of tradition but by his own spontaneous initiative. Jewish piety was used to hearing the psalmist speak in the first person to express, nevertheless, a state of mind which was common to all believing Israel; the "I" or "me" served to make more concrete and living an experience which was quite general and collective.† One individual spoke out what all thought; in speaking of himself he spoke of man in general; when he said "I" he implied "we".‡

Let us notice further that in the development of Paul's thought it is a question, not of any individual case, but of the case of man in general, of all the heirs of Adam considered in their collective condition. Now, we have seen with what dramatic vigour the apostle depicted sin and death in ch. 5, evoking, as it were, living personages. It was necessary for him to complete the picture in order to show the end of that state of things which the disobedience of Adam introduced. These living personages entitled sin and death aim at the complete subjugation of man and display the full extent of their maleficent activity in the inner life of the human being. To describe this activity it was necessary to speak of man in general; but to do so by referring to ἄνθρωπος would have been very abstract, and the picture would have lost in dramatic force. Paul therefore introduces a new personage, the "I" or *ego* whom he intends to speak in the name of all.§ The procedure was so much the simpler because neither author nor reader have forgotten that it has just been a question of Adam who is not so much a particular man as the

*. W. G. Kümmel, *op. cit.*, pp. 121–132.

† E. Jacob, *Théologie de l'A.T.*, p. 126.

‡ K. G. Kuhn connects with Rom. 7 the "I" of the psalmist and the "I" of the rule of the Judean desert community. However, he stresses that the latter is closer to the Paulinian "I" because connected with the idea of an inner conflict, and because it means "I in so far as I am a sinner" (*Z.Th.K.*, 1952, p. 210). Hans Bardtke thinks that the "I" of the hymns is individual, but that it is applicable to any member of the sect, and has thus a certain universality ("Considérations sur les cantiques de Qumran", *R.B.*, 1956, pp. 220–233).

§ Fr. Benoit, *art.* quoted *R.B.*, 1938, p. 484.

representative of all mankind, the man who I also am, the man by virtue of whom I am what I am, the man who tells me who I am. To enable man to speak with dramatic cogency it was natural to create an imaginary Adam as the speaker. The kinship of vv. 7–12 with Gen. 3 shows that the apostle thought out the scene which he here constructs on the basis of the picture of Adam as at once individual and collective.

If Christ causes us to die to the law, as has been affirmed in vv. 1–16, the reason is that the law is not an instrument of salvation. Is it then an instrument of perdition, a contributory factor in sin? It is not this either; and in fact Paul repudiates vigorously the blasphemous suggestion which reflects on God Himself, who is the Giver of the law. The function of the law has already been outlined in 3: 20; 4: 15; 5: 20; quick indications which it was necessary to resume and amplify. They are now expressed in the form of a personal declaration: "If it had not been for the law, I should not have known sin." Thus the law makes us aware of sin, but does not incite us to commit it. It gives knowledge of sin, but does not bring it into existence. It denounces sin but is not responsible for it. Its true function is to enlighten man as to what he is and the nature of what he does. It is not in question but it does bring man into the question, personally, by obliging him to choose and by revealing to him in his inmost conscience that he chooses for sin.

It plays this part in fact by virtue of its very essence. Paul sums up the law, in characteristic fashion, by referring to the command: "You shall not covet" (Ex. 20: 17; Deut. 5: 21).* He shortens the Mosaic formula in order to give it a more general and fundamental bearing. The prohibition against covetousness is the very essence of the law because covetousness is the impulse which subjugates man to things and leads him to make of things his gods. It deprives God of His rights over man to transfer those rights to things which have become man's idols; and if man surrenders himself to the tyranny of things from motives of covetousness, the fact is that he covets them for himself; he desires to exploit all things for himself

* Philo also singles out this commandment as typical of the law (*De cal.*, 142; 150; 173; *Opif. mund.* 152).

out of egoism and pride. Covetousness includes both idolatry of the world and idolatry of the self. When the law intervenes to forbid covetousness, it faces man with the obligation of choosing to live for God and by the help of God, and, instead of making his own gods and building his own self-security, of submitting himself to God and receiving from God his life. To confront man with this fundamental decision is the business of the law and its impingement on human existence.

(8) The intervention of the law is meant to enlighten man with regard to his general situation. Apart from the law, man cannot know what his position is, since he no longer has adequate knowledge of the will of God; he is in that uncertain situation pictured in ch. 5: 13ff.: his actions are performed without reference to any criterion which would give them the value of an act that is morally and religiously conditioned. Apart from the law, man does not realize in particular that he is in a state of rupture with God. The law restores the original situation of man or a situation similar to it by confronting man once more with the consciousness of the will of God and thus presenting him with the theoretical possibility of obeying it. Moral choice is once again possible. The thought of Paul goes back to the position described in Gen. 3: the man Adam hears the word of God. Thanks to the law, the situation is once more the same, and this is the underlying reason why the apostle describes the function of the law in terms clearly reminiscent of the Genesis story.*

God having spoken, the law having been given, what happens? The reply of Paul is by no means speculative; following the myth of Genesis, he notes that the obligation of choosing sets man on an evil course (v. 8a). This is expressed in vivid terms if it is read in the light of the story of the fall. The suggestion that sin is "dead" apart from the law reminds us of the serpent lying inactive, motionless, hidden, and as it were dead in the garden:† nothing resembles a dead serpent more than a living serpent so long as it does not move!

* Cf. Schrenk, *Th.Wb.NT*, II, p. 547.
† James 2: 17, 26 speaks of a dead faith, giving to the adjective the same meaning, namely, an inactive, inert faith which bears no fruit.

(9) Before the law intervenes, that is, before God has spoken, man lives in ignorance of his true condition. He may put his foot on the serpent but he does not know that a serpent is there. He may do good or evil, but he does not know that he is doing good or evil.* He lives a life that is devoid of quality or authentic value. He is so deeply ignorant of his real situation that he thinks it satisfactory and without danger. He may say that before the law came, he lived. The remark is imbued with irony, for such an existence was indeed rich with all potentiality, yet it realized none.†

The intervention of the law changes the whole situation. God speaks and His word obliges man to choose for or against Him. The life of man will now take on the value of quality; henceforth it will be a life that is qualified. In fact man now becomes aware that his choice brings him into a situation of conflict with God; he yields to covetousness. This choice of his implies the deepest significance. It is not a question of particular actions; it is a question of an attitude which is decisive of personal being in all its interiority and depth, and endows existence either with the character of obedience and dependence, or with that of negation and revolt. It would not be suitable to inquire at this point whether Paul yields to a pessimistic view of man; his conviction is clear; when man enters deeply enough into existence and with sufficient frankness, when he is confronted with the clearly known will of God, he discovers himself as a being who is hostile to God. This discovery is indicated by the image: "sin revived"—an allusion to the serpent springing to life and

* We should think of the situation of the innocent sinner suggested in 5: 13.

† This dictum of the apostle has been connected with the rabbinic opinion which suggested that the young man is not fully responsible for his deeds until after his initiation into the law, i.e. after he had attained the age of thirteen (Strack-Billerbeck, IV, p. 470; Bonsirven, *Jud. Palest.*, II, p. 22). Is Paul alluding to the period of his life prior to his Mosaic initiation? One can hardly think so; the points of view are too diverse; among the rabbis the law is presented as an efficacious help in the struggle against the "tendency to evil" which exists prior to the knowledge of the law and prevails until the law enables one to combat it; for Paul the law multiplies the nefarious effects of sin.

beginning to play its part in the Garden of Eden drama.*

(10) Paul has already said that the wages of sin is death (6: 23). He does not say in detail in what way sin works after its intervention. The contrast between "sin revived" and "I died" is so much the more striking: a contrast which is further emphasized by the observation that the activity of sin perverts the work of God itself. For after all, the commandment had been given by God and had man obeyed it, it would have led him in the way of life. In giving the law, God was acting already for man's salvation: "Do that and you shall live" (cf. Rom. 10: 5; Gal. 3: 12; Lev. 18: 5; Deut. 4: 1, etc.). But man receives the wages of that master in whose service he is engaged!

(11) Faced by the absurdity of the choice, one may wonder how man can have taken such a tragic decision. Is he blind or idiotic? He is neither. He is deceived. Sin has lied. The allusion to the Genesis story is still evident, for the woman complains of the serpent in similar terms (Gen. 3: 13 LXX; ὁ ὄφις ἠπάτησέν με).† The function of sin (i.e. of the serpent) consists in distorting what God has said. If man remained truly in the presence of the authentic word of God, he would not resist that authority, for God has created him with the capacity to feel the compelling power of divine love. But man eludes the presence of God by fallaciously subtle arguments. In the Genesis myth the role of the serpent symbolizes in a very vivid manner this furtive activity which culminates in attributing to God the exact opposite of what He said.‡ In-

* Ἀνέζησεν: waken to life. Here it means, become active once more. The particle ἀνα should retain its value. Ἁμαρτία renews its activity on every fresh opportunity; in the intervals, it is dead, or inactive. Man is essentially a sinner before the intervention of the law brings to light his sin as sin.

† Quoting the text in 2 Cor. 11: 3 Paul uses, as here, ἐξηπάτησέν. Cf. also 1 Tim. 2: 14.

‡ Let us recall that God allowed Adam to eat of all the trees of the garden (an act of divine goodness which placed every good at man's disposal) with the exception of the tree in the centre (a prohibition intended to enable man to develop his freedom within the framework of obedience to God). The serpent completely distorts all this by asserting

188

stead of receiving the law as a sign of the love of God, man stumbles against the word of God as though he were being made to run the gauntlet in humiliating fashion; he persuades himself that he is a victim of the jealousy of God. Hence he comes to think in all sincerity that he must disobey in order to free himself from an irksome tutelage and realize his true destiny. Sin and lying are closely connected (cf. Jn. 8: 44).

(12) The answer is therefore clear: the fault does not lie in the law, in the sense that it is not the law, intrinsically, which leads us into sin, although it is as a result of the law that man, faced with the necessity of choice, discloses that he is a sinner by his own initiative.* The law in itself is holy because it springs from God; it is righteous because it expresses the righteous will of God; good, because it is meant to serve the beneficent will of God.† These three epithets thus characterize the law in respect of its origin, its nature and its effects. If the law in practice seems to provoke man into sinning, he cannot lay the responsibility at its door; let him blame sin.

(13) But what is sin which is thus made responsible? The paraphrase of the Genesis myth might lead us to think that sin is a power external to man on which the responsibility could be loaded so that man would be discharged. This is in fact the natural impulse of the guilty person; he casts the blame on someone else: Adam on Eve, and Eve on the serpent. The guilty tries thus to exculpate himself. He wishes to escape from his true situation by deluding himself about his true responsibility. He cannot do so, however, without deceiving himself. Paul wishes to bring his reader to a degree of lucidity about himself which will exclude every avenue of escape. By putting the question whether it is the law, intrinsically excellent, which brought death to "me", he confronts

that God has reserved for Himself alone the use of this tree; hence the revolt of man seemed to be justified. May we refer to our study: "La situation de l'homme d'après la Genèse" in *Das Menschenbild im Lichte des Evangeliums* (*Festschrift E. Brunner*, 1950, pp. 1–29).

* Νόμος: the law in general. 'Εντολή: the commandment or order—what has imperative character (cf. Schrenk, *Th.Wb.NT*, II, p. 548).

† Cf. Gaugler, I, p. 205.

us with the alternative around which his thought will revolve. Either the law is bad, or else "I" am. The function of the law was to throw into relief the true nature of sin (ἵνα φανῇ ἁμαρτία). This is what it does by exercising the authority with which God has endowed it (διὰ τῆς ἐντολῆς): for it makes the authority of God effectively present and obliges man to make a choice between obedience and revolt, God and self. Thus it makes man nonplussed. Sin might have been present but, as it were, dead, lurking unknown. The law puts an end to this fallacious situation by enlightening man about the nature and reality of sin and thus about his own true condition as a sinner.

[14]We know that the law is spiritual; but I am carnal, sold under sin. [15]I do not understand my own actions. For I do not do what I want, but I do the very thing I hate. [16]Now if I do what I do not want, I agree that the law is good. [17]So then it is no longer I that do it, but sin which dwells within me. [18]For I know that nothing good dwells within me, that is, in my flesh. I can will what is right, but I cannot do it. [19]For I do not do the good I want, but the evil I do not want is what I do. [20]Now if I do what I do not want, it is no longer I that do it, but sin which dwells within me.

[21]So I find it to be a law that when I want to do right, evil lies close at hand. [22]For I delight in the law of God, in my inmost self, [23]but I see in my members another law at war with the law of my mind and making me captive to the law of sin which dwells in my members. [24]Wretched man that I am! Who will deliver me from this body of death? [25]Thanks be to God through Jesus Christ our Lord! So then, I of myself serve the law of God with my mind, but with my flesh I serve the law of sin.

(14) For if the law brings death to me in spite of the fact that it is spiritual*—and it must be spiritual since it is the gift of God—then the reason why my encounter with the law proves mortal to me must lie in myself. It is not what the law is but what I am which explains why the law brings death. The argument is simple. I am then the opposite of what it is:

* Οἴδαμεν. The statement that the law is spiritual is not a personal opinion, but the faith of all. Thus it is a question here of a credal confession with the community. Hence the use of the plural.

it is spiritual but I am carnal; it expresses God's sovereignty over me and is intended to give me the occasion for my obedience; but I have become the slave of sin, I am sold, in fact! The latter expression is very strong; it puts very forcibly the condition of the sinner whom the law enlightens with regard to his wretched servitude; it shows how hopelessly he is subjugated to the implacable authority of an evil master who has every right over him because he is a slave duly purchased.

(15f.) The apostle has now to explain how this slavery imprisons him in the desperate situation which has just been described. If such slavery were external to myself, perhaps I could to some extent remain aloof from it in my inner self? In fact, however, it strikes me at the heart of my being, for it destroys the unity of my inmost self. It is manifested by a division which rends my being to the core. Sin cannot cut me off from among the living; only the power of God can do that; but what it cannot utterly destroy, it can ruin from within. In fact, I approve the law, I recognize its formal authority and the excellence of its precepts; I would like to obey it. But now, when I contemplate what I actually do, I cannot recognize there the man I was when I was reflecting face to face the will of God; I cannot but detest what I do; and in the light of what I actually do, I detest myself as the doer. I justify the law by the direction of my will, and it makes me odious to myself.

(17f.) It is as a result of the painful discovery of this inner schism that I begin to understand the true nature of my condition as a sinner. Sin is not external to myself; it is manifested by this rent in my being which divorces in me the faculties of doing and willing. It is *in me* (ἐν ἐμοί) because it is *in my flesh* (ἐν σαρκί μου).* The linking of these two expressions should prevent the misunderstanding which would see in the "flesh" an external peripheral factor, not altogether

---

* Τοῦτ' ἔστιν is not restrictive but explanatory, simply. Σάρξ is synonymous with σῶμα: cf. v. 24. It is man as he reacts in the world by his concrete decisions, man as he makes or ruins himself by his concrete choices. Cf. on 6: 6.

myself; something in the nature of what moralists have called sensuality. For convenience Paul localizes action in the flesh or the members; but my body is still I myself. The distinction which Paul makes between willing and doing should be understood in the light of what has just been said about an approval given to the law of God which nevertheless is in conflict with actual behaviour and concrete decisions.* On the one hand, when I hear the law, when I hear God speaking to me, I can well recognize in this voice the declaration of God's will; but when I act, I fail to regulate my actions by this assent. So long as only a theoretical kind of will is in question, I assent to the excellence of the law; but when I come to commit myself by actual concrete decisions, my pride and my egoism prevail. And it is then that I realize just how much my mental assent is worth. I approve the law, because I am subdued by it and own its authority; but as soon as it requires me personally to translate it into deeds, then in fact I scoff at it, however much I may extol it in theory. I will . . . but I do not. This antithesis is not concerned with the weakness of a will which is not capable of carrying out pure and lofty intentions. It goes much deeper; it affirms that between my "conscience" which wills the good and my "will" which produces action, a discord has arisen as a consequence of which my action no longer reflects my moral judgments.†

(19f.) Here the thought does not seem to progress. V. 19 resumes what was said in v. 15, and v. 20 what was said in v. 17. These two verses are perhaps glosses.

(21–23) We come here to the conclusion of the analysis. Εὑρίσκω indicates that the author now notes the logical result of what precedes: this then is the summing up. Two essential thoughts. Firstly it is I who will the good, but this same "I"

* Τὸ θέλειν: theoretical will to which the power of judgment belongs. Τὸ κατεργάζεσθαι: practical will to which the power of decision belongs.

† It is this idea of an inner rupture rending man's being at its core which is the new idea introduced by νυνὶ δέ —sometimes conclusive. (e.g. 7: 6) and sometimes introductory (e.g. 3: 21). At the end of v. 18, D G Koiné read οὐχ εὑρίσκω; others οὐ γινώσκω.

discovers that it is reflected both in willing the good and in practising evil. *Secondly, this "I" which is capable of taking a real delight (συνήδομαι) in becoming acquainted with the law of God and which finds in it every reason to obey it, discovers that it is not free; it lives under a law which conflicts with the injunctions stemming from the law of God; it is captive of the law of sin. The word νόμος is here used in a figurative sense—that of authority; it is by the promulgation of the law that an authority exercises its power over its subjects; the subject obeys the law of his sovereign, the slave that of his master. Confronted by the law of God, the "I" discovers that in reality it behaves as the subject of an alien sovereign; like a slave it is submitted to the law of sin. Previously this inner conflict had been illustrated by the antithesis between ἐγώ and σάρξ; but as the "I" includes the flesh in the problem now being discussed Paul clarifies matters by speaking of the "inmost self" and the law of the "mind".†
We should interpret these words in a psychological and secular sense; the inmost self is the natural man considered from the point of view of his faculties of moral judgment, the "invisible personality" (Belser) "the loftiest part of the soul"

* The same word παράκειται is used in v. 18 to suggest that man has the will to do good and in v. 21 to suggest that in fact he accomplishes evil. It is not found elsewhere in the NT.

† Ὁ ἔσω ἄνθρωπος; this expression is certainly of Hellenistic origin, and was current in the religious and philosophical vocabulary of the apostle's contemporaries. The opposition between the inner and the outer man is found already in Plato (Rep. IX, 589 a); it is perpetuated in Philo and the hermetical literature; the outer man is a prison house in which the inner man groans (Corp. Herm. I: 15, 18, 21; XIII, 7). The "inner man" is here placed in parallelism with the νοῦς, a very widespread term which assumes varied meanings: e.g. insight, practical reason, thought (in a subjective or objective sense); Paul uses it twenty-one times in varied senses. The idea expressed by these two words is implied also by others: καρδία (2: 29); συνείδησις (2: 15); πνεῦμα (1: 9). Among the Israelites the opposition between "inner" and "outer" was known (Mk. 7: 21; Lk. 11: 39, or even Matt. 6: 4, 6, 18) (cf. Strack-Billerbeck, I, p. 465), but it was not connected with the expectation of deliverance. The same must be said of the inner conflict implied by the poet's words: "video meliora proboque, deteriora sequor" ("I see and approve the better, I follow the worse"; Ovid, Met. 7: 19). The pessimistic tone of the despairing moralist is emptied of any idea of transcendence. The despair of v. 24, on the contrary, is full of transcendent meaning.

(Allo); it is not yet the "new man", or the "new creature"; the action of the Holy Spirit is absent from the drama of the man who speaks in Rom. 7.*

(24) The verses which follow offer some difficulties for the exegete. Verse 24 is well in line with what has preceded. The believer expresses his despair in face of the hopeless situation which has been described. From the literary point of view, an interjection of this kind is familiar to Jewish piety.† It is based on the recognition that his weakness is such that only a complete inner change can restore to the man enslaved by sin the liberty to act in conformity with what he approves. What the despairing sinner asks for is not deliverance from his body as such; for the power of the Holy Spirit can control the body itself, and the crown of faith is the offering of the body as a living sacrifice (cf. 8: 13; 12: 1, 2). The Old Testament prophet had visualized the resurrection of dry bones into living bodies (Ez. 37); apart from the body, Jewish thought cannot conceive life in any sense. The deliverance asked for is required to bring an end to the domination of sin which enslaves the body to both sin and death. We should understand the sense as: who will deliver me from this body to the extent in which it serves, through sin, as an instrument of my death.‡ This deliverance will have neither the ascetic character of a frantic struggle against the lusts of the flesh, a struggle in which it would still be the "I" which would try, but in vain, to shatter its own bonds, nor the philosophic character of a liberation of the inner being by the destruction of the imprisoning body; for such a liberation, which would come only when the fight had ceased through lack of fighters, would not imply the victory of God over sin. The

* On the other hand, "the inner man" of 2 Cor. 4: 16 is the man renewed by the Holy Spirit; "our personality as it is regenerated and transformed by supernatural communion with God". . . . "The renewed inner man" is fully equivalent to the "new man" (E. B. Allo, *Seconde Épître aux Corinthiens*, 1937, p. 135). Similarly Eph. 3: 16.

† Ps. 14: 7; 53: 6; 4 Ezra. 7: 116–121. For other ref., Michel, p. 155, n. 1.

‡ Τούτου may be connected with σῶμα if we think of Hebrew which puts the suffix after the second noun (ex. Jer. 20: 10; Ps. 41: 9). Cf. Acts 5: 20; 13: 26.

deliverance here awaited required the sovereign manifestation of the power of God, the advent of His Kingdom to restore His authority precisely where sin had shattered it. But the man who expresses himself in these lines cannot do more than call for a saviour. He does not know such a saviour.

(25) The reply to the despairing cry of v. 24 given in v. 25a seems brief and inadequate.* Doubtless ch. 8 will add to this reply all the amplification it needs, but it is difficult to see how this anticipation is justified here, since the second part of the verse, with an olympian and somewhat didactic serenity, brings us back to the problem set by the divorce between the person who reflects and the person who acts. In order to explain this kind of abruptness we might remember the Jewish habit of intercalating doxologies which seem to break up the sequence of ideas.† But it should also be noted that 25b does not give a satisfactory summary of what precedes, for the man who expressed his experience earlier, while approving the law of God, could not have said that he served it—which would presuppose that he obeyed it.‡ Must we then consider that this v. 25b does not belong to the original text?§

At the conclusion of this study of ch. 7 we must reply to the question which we left undecided: what kind of man have we heard speaking in this dramatic page? He recognizes the authority of the law of God under the jurisdiction of which he is placed, and therefore he cannot be a pagan. Such a knowledge of and affection for the law of God must spring from the heart of a Jew; the psalms reflect similar sentiments, though not the despair, which cannot be attributed to

* An attempt has been made to strengthen it by reading: εὐχαριστῶ . . . S A Koiné, etc.

† Gaugler I, p. 232, who recalls 1: 25.

‡ R. Bultmann, "Glossen im Römerbrief", Th.Z., 1947, p. 198. The fact had already been noted by Jülicher, who had concluded there was a gloss.

§ F. Müller, "Zwei Marginalien im Brief des Paulus an die Römer", Z.N.W. 1941, pp. 249–254, has suggested putting some order into the arrangement of these vv. as also in the beginning of ch. 8: 7: 23, 25b, 24, 25a; 8: 2, 1, 3.

a Jew. Only the Christian can denounce the false security of those who trust in the law and are blind to their failings: that is what the apostle did at the beginning of his letter. But the Christian is not confronted by the law, nor by his ego, in the way we find this expressed here. In other words, we have here an account of the situation of man under the law, but from the standpoint of one who is not a victim of the illusory satisfaction which the law gives to the Jew who trusts in it blindly. What the Jew did not understand about his own situation, the Christian has learnt in the light of the gospel. And what is true of the Jew in particular, is true of any man face to face with any law, i.e. any man entangled in the situation of the legalist and claiming to obtain through good works the favour of God. In this sense the situation of the Jew under the law is typical and its bearing goes far beyond the special framework of Judaic legalism.

This explains why the apostle has given to his account of the basic function of the law an implication and a form which make us forget that what is in question is a specially acute problem for the religious conscience of the Jew. Each time that man becomes concerned with his own self or with the law, each time that he fails to concentrate his gaze on Christ and on the manifestation of His will that God has given us in Christ, he becomes the victim of a hopeless situation and eventually of despair and condemnation. Every man, whether he be faced by the law of Moses, or by the "moral law" or by any other law whatever (ecclesiastical, sociological, etc.) finds in the implied idea of obligation the basis of a "right" and the opportunity to attain "merit", i.e. a claim to divine favour. He justifies himself by what he does. His obedience is an entitlement to be shown to God. He cherishes the sentiment which lies at the root of all sin: pride.

The apostle Paul had broken with Judaic legalism because the cross of Christ had given him a just appreciation of the economy of grace which culminated in the Messiah Jesus. Legalistic piety had relegated to the background the piety that was based on the sacrificial cult; sacrifice played only a very secondary part in consequence; the emphasis was placed on what man achieved for God to the detriment of what God was doing for man. The sacrifice of Christ brought to the apostle a revelation of the theology of grace, the capital point in which, together with the doctrines of the promise and the covenant, was the doctrine of sacrifice. The law could not disclose the saving righteousness of God because it had led its champions to a deluded state of mind which was destructive of the idea of God; and if God did not spare His own Son, was it not because this sacrifice, the crown and end of the whole ancient system of the cult, reflected the same will to forgive man which had ordained the ancient sacrifices so as to create the right background for a divine pardon that was always necessary despite the law? The latter, no more now than when it was first given, did not offer the possibility of meriting the grace of God, for such grace is always free and redemptive.

What is more, a misinterpretation and misuse of the law gave birth to the fatal illusion of the meritorious act and encouraged man to foster the sentiment of καύχησις. It was necessary to shatter this false delusion. False, because the pretension to acquire merit always implies a fundamental duplicity. One is proud of what one does and closes one's eyes to what one does not do. Such a man counts on his positive achievements to balance his omissions. Thus it is supposed that God will overlook what He disapproves. From the divine angle this is mocking God, for His will in its totality is equally holy, so that it is utterly despised if it is not obeyed at every point. From the human angle it is compromising with this duplicity and using it as a screen. It is acting as though one were responsible for the works of which God approves and not responsible for those which He reprobates, since one claims the reward due to the former and repudiates the punishment merited by the latter. At the bottom of all the legalism which Paul denounces, there is this eternal rent in man's being which leads him to make others responsible for the evil of which he is the author, because he is ashamed of it and does not wish to bear its responsibility. The scene in the Garden of Eden illustrates this attitude: it is another who did that. . . . Now the apostle wishes to block this fatal attempt of man to escape from himself. The whole development of his ideas is aimed at exposing

197

to man his real situation: he is himself responsible for what he does not care to admit; at the very heart of his being is a deep schism which robs him of the power to accomplish the will of God. The law brings this schism to the light. It reveals the essence of sin. It brings to the light of day not merely sins but sin itself. It imposes on every man the despairing knowledge of his ontological decadence.

Thus the way in which Paul expresses himself in ch. 7 is theological rather than psychological; anthropological, rather than personal. It describes what man is, faced by the law, if only he could realize it, if only sin had not blinded him to his real situation. It is thus that God viewed him when He gave him the law to disclose to him his fundamental state as a sinner. It is thus that he views himself when the cross of Christ has exposed to him what God thinks about his situation. But this means that the Christian who might wish to put himself once again under the law, forgetting that he is under grace, the Judaizing Christian desirous of completing his salvation through grace by means of works, of perfecting the pardon of God by the merits of his human obedience, would in fact be living through the drama described in this page; he would be casting himself into this self-contradictory and hopeless situation of realizing himself to be moribund like Abraham, and yet wishing to secure his future by his own resources.

This relapse into legalism and moralism is a failing characteristic of Christians, and Paul's converts very soon showed signs of it which worried him. It is in struggling against Judaizing temptations of this kind that he wrote a sentence which might be considered a real *résumé* of ch. 7: 13–25; a sentence so much the more interesting because he speaks here too in the first person: "If I reconstruct what I have destroyed, I make myself a transgressor of the law." We have offered here only a hypothesis, but it is verified by the Judaizing adversaries whom Paul struggled against. As soon as the principle of justification by works is re-established, he says, and merit is sought through the law, one finds that one is a guilty transgressor; and since one's hopes have been pitched on one's merits, the only issue is despair. But in the Letter to the Galatians, as in Rom. 7, this is not the doing of

198

the Christian: that is why Paul adds immediately that he is dead to the law. The return to the law was a menace like every form of incredulity. Both a menace and a temptation, ever present moreover.

CHAPTER
8

¹There is therefore now no condemnation for those who are in Christ Jesus. ²For the law of the Spirit of life in Christ Jesus has set me free from the law of sin and death. ³For God has done what the law, weakened by the flesh, could not do: sending his own Son in the likeness of sinful flesh and for sin, he condemned sin in the flesh, ⁴in order that the just requirement of the law might be fulfilled in us, who walk not according to the flesh but according to the Spirit. ⁵For those who live according to the flesh set their minds on the things of the flesh, but those who live according to the Spirit set their minds on the things of the Spirit. ⁶To set the mind on the flesh is death, but to set the mind on the Spirit is life and peace. ⁷For the mind that is set on the flesh is hostile to God; it does not submit to God's law, indeed it cannot; ⁸and those who are in the flesh cannot please God.

⁹But you are not in the flesh, you are in the Spirit, if the Spirit of God really dwells in you. Any one who does not have the Spirit of Christ does not belong to him. ¹⁰But if Christ is in you, although your bodies are dead because of sin, your spirits are alive because of righteousness. ¹¹If the Spirit of him who raised Jesus from the dead dwells in you, he who raised Christ Jesus from the dead will give life to your mortal bodies also through his Spirit which dwells in you.

(1) IN THE PRESENT order of the verses it is clear that 8: 1 comes unexpectedly and presupposes a totally different situation from that which has just been described. We must go back beyond vv. 7–25 to the beginning of ch. 7 in order to find a real point of contact. On the other hand we shall have a normal progression of thought if we connect 8: 2 with the thanksgiving of 7: 25a which is thus explained. Then would come v. 1 to draw the conclusion, namely, emancipation from the law frees from the condemnation which the law implies, and v. 3 following v. 1 would finally explain why

condemnation too is avoided (κατάκριμα of v. 1 connecting with κατέκρινεν of v. 3).

We have seen that the situation described in 7: 7–25 is not that of the believer. In 7: 5 the condition of life implied by such phrases as "under the law" or "in the flesh" was presented as something past, and in v. 6 a νυνὶ δέ emphasized that this past was now opposed by quite a new present: liberated now from the burden of the law, the believer can serve God in the new life of the Spirit. The argument of ch. 8 naturally links up with this conclusion (v. 6) just as the passage 7: 7–25 connected with 7: 5. In this new argument Paul proposes to show the new system of life inaugurated by faith and baptism into the death of Christ, and how the son of Adam now lives after he has been drawn into the humiliation and the triumph of the second Adam. "Those who are in Christ Jesus" are the baptized believers of whom it has been asserted in 7: 1–6 that they are no longer "in the flesh" or "under the law". For them there is no more condemnation: v. 3 will explain why union with Christ in His death removes the condemnation. The theme approached in this way continued consistently the teaching on the law, since the law, by revealing to man his real situation in the sight of God, brought him to despair and the certainty of condemnation.

(2) The expression "law of sin" (already used in 7: 23) denotes the enslaved state of the man who is fettered by sin, and rewarded with the wages of this tyrant, namely, death (6: 23).† The formula cannot be a direct reference to the régime of the law, since the law is holy and spiritual; if the law brings the consciousness of sin and so makes the sinner aware of his state and thus guilty, it simply clarifies a situation that is confused and insoluble; Paul could not possibly describe it as the "law of sin".

The transitory dispensation of the law was intended to

---

* A, Vulg., Pesh., etc., here read: ". . . for those who are in Christ Jesus and who walk not after the flesh but after the Spirit"—text harmonized with v. 4.

† Νόμος in the sense of an order of the day, a statute; or better, in the sense of authority, that which expresses the will of the sovereign. The meanings are interconnected.

open to sinners a new possibility which is finally realized with the coming of Jesus Christ. The dispensation of the law is succeeded by the dispensation of the "Spirit of life in Christ Jesus" which can be understood in two ways: either "the life-giving Spirit in Christ Jesus" or "the living Spirit who is the source of all life". Since there is an implied contrast with the system which leads to death, the first interpretation will be preferable, and it is confirmed by vv. 10 and 11 as also by 1 Cor. 15: 45 ($\pi\nu\epsilon\hat{v}\mu\alpha$ $\zeta\omega\sigma\pi\sigma\iota\sigma\hat{v}\nu$).* The passage from the one dispensation to the other is most certainly a liberation; ch. 7 showed clearly in what state of slavery man found himself as a result of sin; it is not so much a question of liberation from the law as from the slavery which the law brings into light; however, it will be recalled that the death of the "body of sin" in consequence of union with Christ does in fact bring to an end the authority of the law over the believer (7: 4–6); the believer has found in Christ a new authority.

(3) The new régime will effect what the law could not.† The law certainly discloses to man the will of God; but sin makes use of the law as a pretext for the acquiring of merit. In fact, before Jesus Christ, the law did not even reveal to man the full despair of his situation. If he had not been a captive of sin, man would have made a good use of the law; hence God wishes to deliver him. He sends His Son, so that by putting to death the "body of sin" the latter should finally be out of the question. It is the sacrifice of the cross which must accomplish what the law could not. In every sacrifice the death of the victim manifests the verdict of condemnation which God passes against sin; it shows that the condemnation of sin which the law pronounces should be respected, recognized and accepted. Not in order to appease the blind de-

---

* Several of the best MSS. give $\sigma\epsilon$ (S B G pesh., etc.); A C D, etc., give $\mu\epsilon$ and a few rare witnesses $\dot{\eta}\mu\hat{a}s$. These two latter readings appear to be adaptations made in order to harmonize the text, either with the style of ch. 7 or with that of ch. 8.

† The beginning of the phrase remains suspended in the void. $T\grave{o}$ $\dot{a}\delta\acute{v}\nu\alpha\tau\sigma\nu$ $\tau\sigma\hat{v}$ $\nu\acute{o}\mu\sigma\nu$ means: the incapacity of the law (active) or preferably, what is impossible to, inaccessible to . . . (passive). Cf. Rom. 9: 22.

mands of some abstract justice, but because the pardon of God can be granted only to the one who repents and who by repentance cries out for forgiveness and divine grace. Sacrifice substitutes for the guilty sinner a vicarious victim whose death vicariously fulfils the condemnation due to sin; the sinner associates himself with the victim sacrificed for sin by those feelings of repentance and acts of intercession which God in His patience awaits from sinners.*

The sacrifice of Jesus Christ also implies the objective condemnation of sin. By faith and baptism, believers are associated with it in such a manner that their "body of sin" is destroyed (6: 6); the objective condemnation of sin in the body of Christ produces thus a subjective condemnation in the sinner. The baptized believer, converted to God, is no longer "in the flesh" (7: 5). For him the law has ceased to exercise its provisional function which was related to his ambiguous condition as a sinner, for the latter needed to be exposed and clarified. Thus the situation of man the sinner is radically changed by faith in Christ crucified. The end which God had purposed is now attained. He had sent† "his own Son"—the expression is intended to emphasize the unique bond of love uniting the Father to the Son—for this purpose and in conditions calculated to assure the intervention complete efficacy. The phrase "in the likeness of sinful flesh" is designed to suggest that the Son truly became man so that in His person He could offer Himself as a sacrificial victim validly acceptable as a substitute for man; at the same time it is intended to show that the victim was not enslaved to the tyranny of sin but was holy.‡ This makes clear that the Son does not die for His own sin; it is for the sin of others

* Cf. commentary on 3: 25.
† Πέμψας alludes to the mission of the Son as a whole. Gal. 4: 4 with ἐξαπέστειλεν insists also on the human status of the Son.
‡ In the LXX ὁμοίωμα has two meanings: image and form. The second denotes the object according to its appearance (cf. Rev. 9: 7); it does not mean a simple external likeness; it means roughly σῶμα (Lietzmann). The argument about docetic tendencies proposed by J. Weiss, *Urchristentum*, 1917, p. 376 is refuted in *Th.Wb.NT*, V, p. 196. ὁμοίωμα is found again with an identical meaning in Phil. 2: 7, applied also to the human condition of the Son; truly man, but unlike other men, obedient. Hence the word implies both similitude and difference.

that He came and was delivered up.* Thus sin is condemned in the very sphere where it is manifested ("in the flesh" should be connected with "condemned" and not with "sin"). By faith and baptism the sinner is associated with this condemnation, so that with Christ he dies to his sinful state and there is no further condemnation for him (the κατέκρινεν of v. 3 is evidently to be linked with the οὐδὲν ἄρα νῦν κατάκριμα of v. 1 for an explanation).†

(4) The mission of the Son had as its object to provide an ultimate consummation to what had been the basic purpose of the law, namely that reprobation of sin which now at last was clearly exposed, and recognized as sin. The result is that he who accepts this exposure of his sin and submits to the inner spiritual consequences of this acceptance, encounters the essential will of God; he accomplishes the law,‡ not by

* Περὶ ἁμαρτίας indicates the aim of the mission of the Son. The context makes the detail superfluous, which is doubtless the reason why some MSS., followed by certain critics, have removed it. We may see in it a distant allusion to Lev. 5: 6; 7: 37 as in Hebr. 5: 3; 10: 6, 8, 18. It is wrong to say that this passage does not deal with the sacrifice of Christ, because it deals, not with the fault to be expiated, but with the power of sin which is to be broken (cf. Godet II, p. 148). The sacrifice of Christ on the cross, as is shown at great length by the argument in ch. 6, is intended precisely, on the anthropological plane, thus to destroy the power of sin by the destruction of the "body of sin".

† Those commentators who do not wish to admit that Paul is here alluding to the condemnation of sin through the sacrificial death of Christ understand the meaning to be that sin was condemned by the holy life of Christ; for the first time, and that in exemplary fashion, sin is no longer in control of a human life. This exegesis has the grave defect of shattering the unity of the exposition in the course of chapters 6 to 8. It leads thought in a new direction by presenting Jesus Christ as the model of a holy life—a theme, moreover, which will not at all recur in the parenetic passages; on the contrary ch. 12 will recall the theme of sacrifice. Cf. Fr. Benoit, "La loi et la croix d'après saint Paul (Rom. 7: 7—8: 4)", R.B., 1938.

‡ The meaning of δικαίωμα is much debated. The word means: commandments, prescriptions (Lk. 1: 6; Hebr. 9: 1; Rom. 2: 26); in the singular, the essential will of God, even apart from its crystallization by Moses, and as a unity (Rom. 1: 32; 8: 4); action conforming to righteousness (Rom. 5: 18; Rev. 15: 4); as contrasted with κατάκριμα, justification (Rom. 5: 16), (cf. Schrenk, Th.Wb.NT, II, p. 226). Nygren, p. 233, appeals to the fact that κατάκριμα and δικαίωμα are opposed in 5: 16,

particular acts which are in conformity with the law, but above all by the fundamental attitude of his whole being; he shows that he is no longer ἐν σαρκί, *in the flesh*; henceforth he will live a new life, issuing from his burial with Christ in baptism. He can serve in the "new life of the Spirit" (7: 6).

(5f.) Those of whom the apostle had said that they are no longer "in the flesh" (7: 5) cannot evidently live "according to the flesh". In v. 8 we shall meet again the expression "being in the flesh" as opposed to "being in the Spirit". These formulae do not denote, as will be understood, a physiological locus of being, but a certain mode of living according to contrasting realities to which are assigned a determinative function for human acts and thoughts.* Those who are determined by their relation to Adam and the dead weight of the Adamic heritage (which is to say, "setting the mind on the flesh") garner the harvest of their service of the flesh, which is death (6: 23): it may be said of them in elliptical fashion that their thinking is "death". On the other hand those whose lives are shaped by their union with Christ in His death gain access to a new life which is opened up to them, following their baptism, by their communion with the Risen Christ whose ever-living presence is with those whom

18 as here κατέκρινεν and δικαίωμα, and he understands in the light of 5: 16 "the state of righteousness"; Paul is thus supposed to be making an allusion to the righteousness which springs from God, to justification. This meaning hardly fits into the context. And why πληρωθῇ? (cf. Godet, II, p. 152.) With more reason, Fr. Benoit is inclined to understand δικαίωμα in the sense of "verdict of condemnation entailing punishment with the object of death" (*art.* quoted, p. 500); he points out that we should be surprised by the fact that Paul gives, as the goal of the incarnation of the Son, the fulfilment of the commandments of the law, when he has just demonstrated that the Christian is dead to the law. Paul never invokes the theme of obedience to the law in his parenetical passages (Prat, *op. cit.* I, p. 278). The meaning which we give to δικαίωμα includes that given to it by Benoit: the fundamental will of God, expressed by the gift of the law, was the revelation of sin, and the condemnation of it by the sinner's death to sin, which the cross was to make possible (6: 2).

* Φρονεῖν uncommon in the NT (Mk. 8: 33—Matt. 16: 23; Acts 28: 22) frequent with Paul, expresses the totality of inner dispositions determining the behaviour and mode of thought actuating a certain style of life.

He has adopted as His own. Since the essential gifts of Christ are peace with God (5: 1) and, consequently, participation in the divine and eternal life (5: 21) it may be said of them in elliptical fashion that their thinking is peace and life. Death, life and peace, are realities which have a resonance both eschatological and mystical; they are future realities and yet we taste them already in some sense (cf. v. 10).

(7f.) The interpretation of this antithesis which has just been affirmed reminds us that the word "flesh" denotes man's condition in his hostility to God (cf. 5: 10). The man who is "in the flesh" shows the fatal bent of his nature by his persistent refusal to obey the law; if not in some of its precepts, at least in its fundamental intention and especially as an instrument of grace. In fact, it would be untrue to say that Paul considers all men to sin all the time and in all matters; he said with regard to himself that he was blameless touching the law (Phil. 3: 6). But this very obedience—concrete and tangible—however perfect it might be, was only a travesty of the divine intention in the giving of the law; man prides himself on his obedience to the law whereas the law should have brought him to a state of self-abasement.

(9f.) Those who are united to Christ by faith and baptism are thus led into the way of new life.* Paul tries to suggest its character by the use of opposing formulae: living, not "in the flesh", but "in the Spirit". Such phrases are strikingly vivid, but they resist a close analysis. It is evident that we cannot give them a locative meaning as some commentators have done who have attributed to Paul the idea that the Spirit was a quasi-material atmosphere in which the believer had his being.† The antithetic but parallel expression ἐν σαρκί, *in the flesh*, cannot be given a meaning of this type, in spite of the fact that σάρξ (*flesh*) more than πνεῦμα (*Spirit*) denotes a material reality. But it obviously has not this significance in

---

* Εἴπερ has not an adversative sense (if however). Cf. Rom. 3: 30; 2 Th. 1: 6. Paul is recalling a fact and he invites his readers to recognize it too so as to take it into account.

† Summary of the problem in Oepke, *Th.Wb.NT*, III, pp. 534–539. An interesting and more ample survey in F. Büchsel, " 'In Christus' bei Paulus", *Z.N.W.*, 1949, pp. 141–158.

the mind of Paul, since he can write to his readers who were of course still living in their physical bodies: "You are not in the flesh" (cf. 7: 5). To be in the flesh means to live under the domination of what 7: 5 calls the sinful passions. It is clear then that ἐν is instrumental and not locative; it indicates a way of life and not a place. The same applies to ἐν πνεύματι, *in the Spirit.*

Thus it is understandable as it would not be if these phrases had a locative significance, that the apostle can say without difference of meaning: "you are in the Spirit" and "the Spirit is in you". Both expressions have a common meaning, namely, the Spirit governs your existence. The same considerations will apply to the phrase of v. 10: "Christ in you", and the parallelism of the various formulae contained in these two verses will be noted: "you are in the Spirit", "the Spirit of God dwells in you", "you have the Spirit of Christ", "Christ is in you". Not only is the Spirit the Spirit of God and that of Christ, but also Christ is substituted for the Spirit. None of these expressions conveys in itself completely all that has to be suggested concerning the mysterious action and energy of God. Paul uses them to complete each other, since he visualizes in turn the restored communion with God from the point of view of its origin or efficient cause, from the point of view of its realization or instrumental cause, and from the point of view of its completion or final cause. The Spirit is at one and the same time the author of this communion, the essence of this communion, and the consummation of this communion. Similarly with regard to Christ, whose presence is the very foundation of this communion which in turn consists in* and is secured by this presence.

* The use of ἐν in these texts should be compared with its use in regard to possession by evil spirits: it can equally well be said that the unclean spirit dwells in the sufferer and that the sufferer is in an unclean spirit (Mk. 5: 2). In either case the main idea is the possession of the sick man by the spirit in question. In v. 9b Paul says that he who is not "in the Spirit" (since he has not the Spirit in him) does not belong to Christ (οὐκ ἔστιν αὐτοῦ); this shows that ἐν denoted the agency and effective authority of the Spirit. This represents an extension of the instrumental sense of ἐν. Hence, similarly, the parallel expressions οἱ κατὰ σάρκα ὄντες (v. 5) and οἱ ἐν σαρκὶ ὄντες (v. 8): one is "in the flesh" when one is under its sway and behaves according to its dictates, when it possesses one (literally and figuratively).

The indwelling of the Spirit or the presence of Christ are realities which for want of a better term may be called mystical. It is not enough to say that Paul exhorts his readers to remember what Christ has done for them, once for all (Gaugler, I, p. 276). Paul wishes to suggest more because he thinks that the saving work ἐφάπαξ has a continuing reality for believers through its consequences, that is, what Christ means for them and does for them every day at the heart of their lives, having *once* done it for them objectively. The objective work of Christ is inseparable from His subjective work. The former has obtained for Him a right of ownership, which He exercises by dwelling within the believer.* He who indwells and guides is the Master. In saying that the Spirit, or Christ, dwells "in you" Paul is suggesting this act of dominance in virtue of which God exercises His authority, by Christ or the Spirit, at the centre of the personality of the believer. One might say that justification is the objective or juridical side (because it concerns an established relationship) of the change of ownership which the saving work of Christ effects, and that the indwelling presence of the Spirit denotes the entry into possession, the installation of the new owner. The objective work thus acquires interior personal and subjective reality. This was its inner aim; the divorce effected by sin is overcome.†

* Cf. Michel, p. 163, 2 and *Th.Wb.NT*, V, p. 138. In Jn. 14: 17 μένειν has the same meaning as οἰκεῖν; the slave does not continue for ever (Jn. 8: 35).

† We have deliberately used above the term "mystic" in spite of the misunderstandings to which it may give rise. We think it more useful to define it than to avoid it. The ostracism of which this word is the object springs too often from an impoverished interpretation of the apostle's thought, and sometimes from a false interpretation. Mysticism is usually understood to connote the belief that the gulf separating the divine and the human may be overcome and a union established between them. The mysticism disclosed by the letters of Paul will answer this definition but only in harmony with the special requirements of his thought. The idea of the mystical will have to be made more precise in view of Paul's idea of; (1) the distance separating the human from the divine; (2) the means by which it may be overcome; (3) the result obtained, given the character of the distance and of the media used. As to the first point, it should be noted that for the apostle the distance separating man from God is of a moral character and concerns the order of holiness, and not

The expression used by Paul nevertheless presents a certain difficulty. Πνεῦμα denotes the Spirit of God (or Christ); is this also the case in v. 10b? The antithesis with the "body (of man) dead because of sin" might suggest that it is here a question of the spirit of man, quickened by the presence of Christ for the attainment of righteousness or obedience. We must point out however that διὰ δικαιοσύνην, *because of righteousness*, would not suit this meaning; one would expect εἰς δικαιοσύνην, for the *attainment of righteousness* (as Lagrange admits). Hence it is rather a question of the Spirit of God, as in the whole context, mentioned as the reality capable of resuscitating the atrophied being of man on the basis of the righteousness already granted.

(11) The Spirit is life, as the animating spirit in a dead

primarily of a metaphysical character having to do with the order of being; although man is doomed to receive the wages of sin which is death, man lives and his death depends on his sin or his repentance and acceptance of God's forgiveness; the distance which separates the Creator from the creature is an effective separation only because of sin. As to the second point, we must remember that the distance between man and God is overcome by God Himself, by a movement which descends from God to the sinner; there is no ascending movement of man, no (purgative) effort, no ascetic discipline such as would render man worthy of the mystical relationship; there is a descent of God in Christ and that is why Paul's mysticism is Christocentric rather than theocentric: the expressions "Christ in you" and "you in Christ" have no parallels such as "God in you" and "you in God". The result of both factors is that the distance between man and God, overcome by the redemptive initiative of God towards the sinner, strikes the latter in his abasement and unworthiness itself, and that with a view to his healing; the guest within becomes his true "I" (Gal. 2: 20), and exercises His authority at the very centre of the human person through the agency of the Holy Spirit; when the gulf between the divine and human is thus overcome man does not attain a good which he enjoys in a state of passivity, but is rather committed to a new life. Thus Pauline mysticism offers special features because it presupposes the holiness of God, the mediation of Christ, and the agency of the Holy Spirit. Perhaps it would be fitting to replace the term union by that of communion, which is more respectful of that dimension of personal reality in which the relations of the sinner restored to fellowship with God through Jesus Christ are situated. Thus we shall characterize the Pauline mysticism as a relation of communion, moral in character, dynamic and based on divine initiative.

o 209

body, because it is the Spirit of the God who raised Jesus from the dead. God on that occasion manifested His vivifying power which He will once again exert in favour of believers. The latter already feel the power of the God of Abraham (ch. 4: 17, 25) who makes a promise and fulfils it. Most commentators see here an allusion to the eschatological resurrection of believers.* But with Paul eschatological and mystical ideas merge with each other. The apostle believed in a present participation in those revivifying forces which broke into the history of the world with the advent of Jesus Christ; the power of God is now active in the believer who yields himself to that action.† In particular the doctrine of the Spirit included the assurance and the present experience of the power of God; on this point Paul shares a very widespread tradition.‡ Hence the allusion here is to the vivifying energy of the Spirit, who liberates from the tyranny of sin, according to the framework of ideas already sketched out in 6: 12–23.§

> ¹²So then, brethren, we are debtors, not to the flesh, to live according to the flesh—¹³for if you live according to the flesh you will die, but if by the Spirit you put to death the deeds of the body you will live. ¹⁴For all who are led by the Spirit of God are sons of God. ¹⁵For you did not receive the spirit of slavery

* Cf. 1 Cor. 6: 14; 2 Cor. 4: 14; 1 Cor. 15: 20; Phil. 3: 21; 1 Th. 4: 14.

† Cf. 6: 5, 8, 10, 11, 13, 23; 8: 2, 6, 10.

‡ To combat sin, Israel expected an intervention which would transform man to the depths of his being. The Messiah would be the Bearer of the Spirit, which He would bestow upon the elect, changing hearts of stone to hearts of flesh, well disposed and obedient: Is. 32: 15; 44: 3; 63: 10; Ez. 11: 19; 36: 26; 39: 29; Joel 2: 28. Cf. Ps. Sol. 17: 37; 18: 7; 1 En. 49: 3; 62: 2; Test. Levi 18; Test. Judah 24; Sib. III, 582; Jub. I, 23. Cf. Bousset, *Rel. Jud.*, pp. 394–395. It will be noticed that in the NT "Spirit" and "power" are often interchangeable terms: cf. parallelism in Lk. 11: 20; Matt. 12: 28; Acts 1: 8, etc.

§ The MSS. show two readings: διὰ τοῦ ἐνοικοῦντος αὐτοῦ Πνεύματος (S A C, etc.); διὰ τὸ ἐνοικοῦν αὐτοῦ Πνεῦμα (B D G etc.). The former stresses the active function of the Spirit, in virtue of which man will be revivified, while the latter suggests the general state of the believer as the temple of the Spirit, in consideration of which God will revivify mortal bodies. The second reading probably stems from the propensity of the Koiné for the accusative after the preposition (Lietzmann).

to fall back into fear, but you have received the spirit of sonship. When we cry, "Abba! Father!" ¹⁶it is the Spirit himself
bearing witness with our spirit that we are children of God,
¹⁷and if children, then heirs, heirs of God and fellow heirs with
Christ, provided we suffer with him in order that we may also
be glorified with him.

(12–14a) Thus, then, the interior guest indwelling the believer offers the latter by His presence and secret agency a
new possibility of existence. It is for the believer to recognize
this and seize the opportunity, one may say; or rather to
allow himself to be seized by it. New obligations are now
imposed on him, if he knows how to appreciate his true situation. In fact, what God in Christ has done for us puts us in
the position of debtors; we "owe" something to the one who
has liberated us. This duty is not based on ideas of moral
obligation; it is a debt to be paid; what we have to do depends
on what has been done for us; it is something rendered in
return and that is why it can never have the value of merit.
It is a debt to be acquitted towards Him who has freed us
from "the law of sin and death" (v. 2) to enable us to live
according to "the law of the Spirit of life". The alternative
thus presented is already known to the reader: life according
to the flesh or life according to the Spirit. Equally known are
the ends to which each way of life leads: death or life. However, Paul now clarifies the nature of this life according to the
Spirit, by saying that it consists in putting to death the deeds
of the body through the power of the Spirit.* But this kind of
mortification has nothing whatever to do with an impoverish-
ing asceticism. The Spirit is mortifying only with respect to
that which is marked by decay; in compensation its function
is to revivify with new life, with a view to total renovation
(cf. the νεκρώσατε of Col. 3: 5 which leads to the ἐνδύσασθε
of v. 12). The members of the body undergo death as it were
(cf. ὡσεὶ ἐκ νεκρῶν ζῶντας 6: 13) in order to become more
alive than ever through the flowering of their virtualities
which sin had suppressed. They now become instruments
available to the Spirit.

* Σῶμα is here synonymous with σάρξ. G D etc. have even thought it
necessary to replace the one by the other.

Gal. 5: 16–25 shows the concrete manifestation of this contrast between the two ways of life, and what are the "fruits of the Spirit". In reality therefore we have not here a negative enterprise, as the idea of "putting to death the deeds of the body" might lead us to suppose; we have here the energy of the Spirit ($\pi\nu\epsilon\acute{\upsilon}\mu\alpha\tau\iota$) which breathes life into the "members of the body", the concrete personality, in order to orientate it in a new direction, and turn it aside from the old way of life which is governed by the thinking of the flesh (v. 6). The putting to death of the deeds of the body resembles very closely the death of the sacrificial victim, a death which is intended to release life and produce a liberating, revivifying effect. This comparison is so much the more justified because it is in terms of sacrifice that the apostle spoke in ch. 6 and will again speak in ch. 12 of the moral state of the believer. Now sacrifice is something positive: there is death only with a view to an approach to God and a restoration of communion with Him. Here, it is the Spirit who realizes and effects this divine presence and communion. On the body which is sacrificed by the putting to death of its deeds, the Spirit descends to resuscitate it so that it may henceforth act according to the Spirit and bear the "fruits of the Spirit".*

(14b ff.) The real significance of the condition of believers is not to be measured by the results obtained. The "putting to death of the deeds of the body" is an everyday undertaking and is every day renewed. Paul is not suggesting that his readers should begin to watch anxiously to ascertain the degree of mortification which they might have attained, so as to multiply the sacrifices if they happened to be severe with themselves or to relax their vigilance if they are content with little. Such attitudes would spell a relapse into legalism and moralism. This would mean attributing an intrinsic value to what is only the consequence on the human plane of a situation established by God. As Paul will emphasize in ch. 12, the sacrifice of the body only has true justification and significance on account of the "mercies of God". Similarly in

* Note the passive $\check{\alpha}\gamma\omicron\nu\tau\alpha\iota$: believers are "acted on" by the Spirit of God.

ancient Israel the practice of sacrifice had meaning and value only because God had drawn near to this people by His gracious election and had ordained this mode of reconciliation. Prior to man's sacrifice, there is the compassionate initiative of God.

Similarly the presence of Christ in the heart of the believer (or the presence of His Spirit) are the result of a change in man's relations with God, a change which God has taken steps to bring about in Jesus Christ. He gave His Son so that His rebellious children might become sons once more by a procedure of adoption designed to reintegrate them into the Father's home. Mortification is not the basis but the result of this divine initiative. It shows that God has re-established filial relations. It flows from the renewed presence of the Spirit of God. Hence all anxious fear is out of place; for such anxieties characterize him who must try to win the favour of the deity, whether like the Jew who nicely calculates his good works or the pagan who, refusing to give thanks to the living and true God (1: 21) lives in fear and creates for himself tutelary gods (Lucretius, *De rerum natura*, V). The believer is delivered from this fear, essential to the man who claims to make instead of to be made, who wishes to conquer instead of to receive; for the believer has recognized in Christ the witness to the will of God to make of him a son by adoption.

Paul in this connexion uses a juridical term which is pregnant with meaning: *υἱοθεσία*.* Adoption integrates the beneficiary with the family of the adopter whose name he receives and of whose wealth he is made heir. In the thought of Paul adoption introduces the sinner to a quite new relationship with God, who henceforth is the Father of the penitent. This process endows the sinner with the inheritance of the heavenly riches by making him joint heir with the Son. These two effects of adoption are equally well illustrated in the parable of the prodigal son who is restored to the family

* *Υἱοθεσία* (rare in the NT; Rom. 8: 23; 9: 4; Gal. 4: 5; Eph. 1: 5) was a technical term in Hellenistic legal language. Adoption was unknown to the Jews. Paul uses the word with reference to the adoption of Israel (Rom. 9: 4) his thought revolving around the election. The term is unknown to the LXX (even in Ex. 4: 22; Is. 1: 2, etc., texts to which Paul seems to be referring). It seems certain that we have here a borrowing from profane Greek (cf. Deissmann, *Neue Bibelstudien*, 1897, p. 66).

circle, although here it is not properly speaking a question of adoption; we find them again at the end of the passage in Galatians, 3: 23—4: 7, which describes the transition from the almost slavish condition of the child to the enjoyment of the privileges which become his when he has attained his majority; a transition which Paul also calls adoption (Gal. 4: 5).

The first privilege of the adopted is to be able to call God Father. Although he is of course a son, the sinner has lost the dignity and status of sonship. He has to receive it afresh by a deliberate and gratuitous act of God which restores to life the dead son ("this my son was dead"). Adoption and resurrection overlap, for God manifests His pardoning grace by showing His power to call back into life what was dead and to create out of nothing. Thus He shows Himself to be the God of the promise (ch. 4: 17, 25).

Κράζω suggests here not a cry but a solemn declaratory word; the herald who makes a proclamation that is authoritative cries in some way.* The word implies perhaps a liturgical proclamation, that invocation which is the first and characteristic word of Christian prayer whether public or private. Doubtless it was from motives of fidelity to the prayer taught by our Lord Himself that the Aramaic formula ἀββά was kept even in Greek-speaking circles.† Its use must have seemed significant in the highest degree and must have constituted a seal and pledge and a confession with regard to the Lordship of Jesus.

The sinner does not derive this prayer from the resources of his own experience. There are things which are not true unless they are affirmed as an integral part of the communion which unites the believer with Christ; they are said "in the name of Christ", by the Spirit of Christ. The role of the

* The term is used in this sense whether it is a question of a word spoken to man (Rom. 9: 27; Jn. 1: 15, etc.) or to God in prayer (LXX Ex. 22: 23; Jdg. 3: 9, 15; 4: 3; Ps. 3: 4; 17: 6, etc.; Gal. 4: 6; Rom. 8: 15).

† אַבָּא : "my father" or "our father". The expression belongs to familiar speech. As applied to God, it must have been considered lacking in respect (rather like "papa"). But it expressed very well the new relation which the Son opened up to the Father, its familiarity and intimate tenderness. Cf. Kittel, Th.Wb.NT, I, pp. 4–6.

Spirit in Christian prayer, which is here very briefly suggested, will be the object of a more complete explanation further on. Man on his own initiative cannot call God his Father with the accents of intimacy and gratitude which the word evokes on the lips of the believer. It is true that religions have often spoken of the fatherhood of God; but in so doing they were extolling rather the creative power of the source of all life and not His love or compassion. Judaism however realized something of the fatherly love of God; the Old Testament scriptures had taught this doctrine; but its essential core had been weakened and its piety preferred to foster feelings of reverential fear towards a remote and righteous God. From this point of view the gospel inaugurated a veritable revolution with wide theological implications: God has shown His love by approaching sinners with the inexhaustible riches of His divine pity.

(16) The presence of the Spirit indwelling the believer makes real and efficacious for each one this compassionate movement of God coming among sinners to adopt them as His children. If we can validly pronounce the name which Jesus gave to God His Father, and take it on our own lips as applicable to our case, that is because the presence of Christ in us and the working of His Spirit makes this adoptive sonship an objective truth for us. As we look towards Christ and recognize what He has done for us, we can know and confess that we are adopted, that God is truly our Father, that *we are* (ἐσμέν) His children, in deed and in truth (1 Jn. 3: 1). We could not know this by looking towards ourselves, what we are and what we do; but the divine Spirit testifies this for us,* and our spirit, yielding to the authority of that witness, gains a conviction that transcends all reasoning.

* The meaning of συνμαρτυρεῖ is debated. If the word is taken in its original meaning (to join one's witness to that of another), it means here that the Spirit of Christ confirms what our own spirit has spontaneously realized. But Paul certainly does not attribute to the spirit of man the knowledge of our adoption. This difficulty has led to the supposition that "our spirit" denotes the ego as regenerated by Christ (Schlatter, *Gottesgerechtigkeit*, p. 266). In order to avoid this subtlety, which in fact means that the Spirit bears witness to itself, we may understand the word to mean: attest, certify (Lietzmann; Strathmann, *Th.Wb.NT*, V, p. 516).

(17) The second privilege of the adopted son is that the wealth of his adoptive father is made available to him. One may say in fact that the aim of adoption is to make someone a beneficiary of goods which otherwise he would have been deprived of. Right is here placed in the service of the heart's generosity. The metaphor borrowed from the juridical domain suits therefore the dispensation of grace. The idea of inheritance emphasizes the gratuity of the wealth received and its transcendence of ourselves: it comes from a source far beyond us and we count for nothing in attaining it. In the Old Testament this imagery already serves to indicate both aspects even when applied to the realities of this world, such as the promised land; but the link between inheritance and sonship is not so strongly marked as here.* Paul insisted on this link because he saw in the fact of adoption a privilege which was passed on to sinners by the Son, the heir *par excellence*, He in whom the promise of inheritance, made to Abraham (4: 13; cf. Gal. 3: 29) had found its supreme and rich fulfilment.† Paul does not actually describe Christ as the heir; but this idea is implied, since we are made fellow heirs with Christ.

Fellow heirs of what? Of glory: we are made sharers with Christ in the radiance of God's glory of which sin had deprived all men (3: 23) since they had refused to recognize it (1: 23) but the legitimate hope of which has been restored to them by their justification (5: 2; 8: 30). Glory is the effulgence of the Godhead; to share in this radiance is to appear in the presence of God and to be struck by the radiation of His divinity. Vv. 18–30 will renew the theme of glory. Similarly they will take up the theme of suffering, which already at this point is connected with that of glory. "To suffer with Christ" does not seem to be an allusion to the death on the cross, for it is not suffering as such which characterizes the cross in the view of Paul. Suffering is the note of every life which has the tension of contradiction; it is impossible not to know suffering if one conducts one's life in

* Cf. Foerster, *Th.Wb.NT*, III, p. 781.

† It may already be found in Mk. 12: 1–12, at least *via negationis*: those who wish to inherit without recognizing that there is only one heir, the Son, are condemned.

216

this world according to the teaching of the Son, and as a child of one's heavenly Father (Matt. 5: 45). The cross is a special case of the general suffering which the hostility of the world imposes on anyone who witnesses against it to the sovereignty of God; it is this same kind of hostility which makes Jerusalem kill the prophets, crucify the Messiah, and persecute His disciples (Matt. 23: 29, 37; 5: 12); it is the same suffering again which brings on the apostle those tribulations which are the very hallmark of his apostolate (cf. 2 Cor. 1: 5; Col. 1: 24; Gal. 6: 17?). In this way suffering is a condition of glorification; not a meritorious condition, but the necessary pathway, for it is unavoidable in view of what the world is (cf. Matt. 5: 11; Lk. 6: 26).*

[18]I consider that the sufferings of this present time are not worth comparing with the glory that is to be revealed to us. [19]For the creation waits with eager longing for the revealing of the sons of God; [20]for the creation was subjected to futility, not of its own will but by the will of him who subjected it in hope; [21]because the creation itself will be set free from its bondage to decay and obtain the glorious liberty of the children of God. [22]We know that the whole creation has been groaning in travail together until now; [23]and not only the creation, but we ourselves, who have the first fruits of the Spirit, groan inwardly as we wait for adoption as sons, the redemption of our bodies. [24]For in this hope we were saved. Now hope that is seen is not hope. For who hopes for what he sees? [25]But if we hope for what we do not see, we wait for it with patience.

[26]Likewise the Spirit helps us in our weakness; for we do not know how to pray as we ought, but the Spirit himself intercedes for us with sighs too deep for words. [27]And he who searches the hearts of men knows what is the mind of the Spirit, because the Spirit intercedes for the saints according to the will of God.

[28]We know that in everything God works for good with those who love him, who are called according to his purpose. [29]For those whom he foreknew he also predestined to be conformed to the image of his Son, in order that he might be the firstborn

* These remarks confirm Michaelis, *Th. Wb. NT*, V, p. 924. Εἴπερ does not imply a condition, but a fact (cf. v. 9; 3: 20). Ἵνα suggests, not a goal which we might deliberately set out to attain as the prize, but "the tie which God has established between suffering with Christ and glorification. This tie lies in the very nature of things" (Lagrange, p. 203).

among many brethren. [30]And those whom he predestined he also called; and those whom he called he also justified; and those whom he justified he also glorified.

(18) Suffering is more than a mere unavoidable necessity; or rather, what makes it inevitable is so closely bound up with the very essence of the Christian life that the suffering is, as it were, a sign and a proof of the authenticity of our Christian condition. Suffering and future glory are inseparable, because the present is a state of transition leading to the future, the visible an anticipation of the invisible; everything must be referred to another world, that of the Spirit which casts all things into a state of tension and crisis, which induces in the heart of being an essential dissatisfaction since it is itself the ultimate reality and therefore exercises an ontological pressure on this-worldly realities.*

From the very start of this train of thought which explains the connexion between suffering and glory, λογίζομαι suggests the deliberate intention of speaking with some degree of solemnity. Paul is not simply going to give a personal opinion but a body of teaching, the bases of which he has duly weighed. Ἄξια implies too, etymologically, that due weight is being given to the judgments expressed, that the balance inclines in their favour (2 Cor. 4: 17). Suffering in fellowship with Christ is framed in a much wider context. It must be considered in its integral connexion with future glory. The present and the visible can be understood only in the light of the future and invisible, i.e. in the light of that new world and aeon which God has begun to establish with the coming of Christ and whose action, secret but certain, is rendered already effective through communion with Christ in the Holy Spirit.

(19) We still live† ἐν σαρκί, in the flesh, although we might

* It is obvious that in these lines Paul is borrowing from the apocalyptic writers who had already meditated on the encounter and conflict between divine eternity and historical conditions of life. Cf. Bousset, *Rel. Jud.*, pp. 242–254; Bonsirven, *Jud. Palest.*, I, pp. 307–321; P. Volz, *Die Eschatologie . . . passim.*

† On vv. 19–22, cf. A. Viard, "Expectatio creaturae" (Rom. 8: 19–22), *R.B.*, 1952, p. 337. For the whole thing, cf. M. Goguel, "Le caractère et le rôle de l'élément cosmologique dans la sotériologie paulinienne", *R.H.P.R.*, 1935, pp. 335–359.

say that it is Christ who lives in us or again that our life is hidden with Christ in God (cf. Gal. 2: 20; Col. 1: 27; 3: 3). Because we live in the flesh, we share in the general destinies of the world. Our state of suffering has something in common with the suffering of the world; our personal situation compels us to think about that of creation as a whole. Now the whole of creation* aspires towards the fulfilment of the ends which God has assigned to it.† Its situation is a historical one; it is engaged in a process of movement; it waits expectantly. The advent of Christ gives a new justification to its expectancy. For in Him creation can recover the orientation towards its original destiny of which it has been frustrated by the disobedience of man. Christ institutes at the heart of creation the new humanity of the "children of God". Through Him, man, restored to his filial relation with God, will be able to subject creation to that useful work which was its original purpose; and thus he will serve creation by mastering it. In this way he will reveal himself to it as the bearer of the image of God placed at the summit of the creative process to exercise there, according to the will of God, his beneficent authority; he will be disclosed universally as the new man for whom creation is longing that it may attain its goal.‡

* Κτίσις has been understood in different senses: creation (inanimate nature), a part of creation (the "flesh"); the human creation; some segment of humanity (believers, non-believers, Jews or Gentiles); angelic creation, good or evil spirits. The word can just as well denote inanimate or animal creation (nature) as created humanity. Since the general thought of the passage is relative to the realization of the redemptive plan, the word must here denote the world in so far as it is distinct from the church, the world as the sphere in which the saving action embodied in Christ and believers is exercised.

† Ἀποκαραδοκία from καραδοκέω: to hold out the head, to stretch the neck, in order to observe and keep on the watch in anxious expectation of what one may perhaps see or discover.

‡ Man, as the image of God, is the representative of God in the created world, and hence he must accomplish the task which in this capacity devolves on him: namely that of dominating creation, and especially by working at it. This domination by work corresponds on a derivative plane to the divine work of creation itself, and in fact extends it. The still ambivalent powers of creation will thus be controlled, and, when the ultimate Sabbath comes, man like God should be able to say of what he has done that it is good. The fall of man explains the fact that his work

219

(20) Since man has not fulfilled towards creation the ministry with which he was entrusted, creation, for lack of guidance and control, is not evolving towards the end that was assigned to it; it moves purposelessly in the void; life leads nowhere except to corruption and death. Ματαιότης stresses this futility of existence, its essential vacuity or lack of substance and meaning.* It is man who is responsible for the subjection of creation to this condition which is contrary to its destiny, for it is man who has failed to direct it towards ultimate meaning. But it does not seem that Paul at this point affirms that it is man who has subjected creation to futility. Man is responsible for his own fault and its consequences, as the criminal is responsible for the actions which his own misdeeds will compel the course of justice to execute. But it is the judge who executes sentences. It is God who intervenes to punish the disobedience of Adam. Another reason would lead us to think that τὸν ὑποτάξαντα, *him who subjected it*, denotes God: man himself could not connect any kind of hope to the subjection of creation. Hence it is God who subjects creation to the consequences of man's conduct.†
He acts as sovereign of the world, judge and executor of the sentence. The disobedience of man sets in motion the machinery of laws which fulfil the will of God and penalize the fault. The unfolding of the consequences of man's revolt is inexorable. Οὐχ ἑκοῦσα, *not of its own will*, well suggests this ineluctable necessity which causes sin to bear such bitter fruit. Paul was not acquainted with the modern idea of law, but he had observed, like everyone else, that evil engenders catastrophic consequences. From this point of view the scientific concept of law found its religious equivalent in the unwavering constancy with which God executes His judgments on those who scorn Him (cf. Ex. 20: 5ff.). By the operation of the order which God has established and which

does not culminate in this happy end. Cf. E. Jacob, *Théologie de l'A.T.*, p. 138.

* Gaugler understands ματαιότης as the deprivation of the "glory" which creation should fully receive. Other commentators regard the word as synonymous with φθορά; however, corruption appears to be the consequence of vanity rather than vanity itself.

† Cf. 1 Cor. 15: 28.

He maintains, the fault of some becomes the inevitable misfortune of others.* This penalizing of sin remains however in line with the axis of divine love. God does not subject creation to a *fatum*: the very sanctions He awards are pedagogic, are aimed at an ultimate good and are the basis of hope.†

(21) In fact, God's sanctions last only for a time (cf. the contrast between the four generations involved in punishment and the thousand which enjoy the blessing, in Ex. 20: 5). God does not keep His anger for ever (Ps. 103: 9). If He maintained its intensity for ever, He would destroy His own work. On the contrary, He punishes in order to save. He wishes to lead His creation to the goal which He has purposed, even though, to attain that goal, He would have to employ other resources such as His pity suggests. His patience is inventive. He has given to the world a final and decisive chance by the mission of His Son, the first born of a new creation, and through whom the believer becomes a new creature (καινὴ κτίσις, 2 Cor. 5: 17). He is the head of the community of those who have become His brothers by adoption and constitute His church, which is His body. They are His members, the bearers of His spirit, the instruments of His action, the weapons (6: 13, 19) in the warfare which He wages against the powers enslaving the world, especially sin and its satellite, death. Through them the tragic consequences of sin will be striven against and overcome.

That liberty over against the "powers", which Christ has secured for them, they will pass on to creation which man was destined to control. What is more, this liberty will find its crown and completion in the final liberation when the last enemy will be conquered (1 Cor. 15: 26). Then will be fulfilled the prophecy of a new creation in which God will be

---

* Διὰ τὸν ὑποτάξαντα has been taken as referring to Satan (Godet, P. Dubarle, "La théologie du cosmos", in *Initiation théologique*, 1952, II, p. 322) and to Adam (cf. Gen. 3: 17; also Zahn, Jülicher). However, Satan is no more than an instrument, and Adam has delivered the world over to futility, but was not able to subject it (Bengel, Gaugler, Michel). The object of the participial form is to avoid a personal mention of God; it evokes the indirect action of God rather than God as agent.

† For the meaning, ἐφ᾽ ἐλπίδι must be connected with ὑπετάγη.

all in all and there will be no more corruption or decay.* This liberty will not be merely a liberation from the tyranny of sin but also a participation in the divine glory; more than a "glorious liberty" in the banal sense but rather a liberty wherein the glory of the Creator is fully manifested, for then the new creature will have fulfilled its destiny within the framework of the new creation. The fundamental renewal of the being of man will be matched by a renewal of the life of the world: the ultimate hope of faith must be extended to the creative process as a whole, for he who participates in the glory of God could not live in the conditions provided by the old and decadent world (Gaugler).†

(22) It is then that the history of creation will reach the goal which God had assigned to it from the beginning. But before this comes about, it waits longingly and suffers like the woman who bears a child. This comparison was usual in speculations on the advent of the Messianic Kingdom.‡ The image suggests well the preparation for a great joy, for the emergence of something altogether new through the crisis of acute and liberating sufferings.§ Affirmations such as these have nothing at all to do with experimental observations. Paul stresses the esoteric character of such ideas by his phrase: οἴδαμεν . . . . Faith alone can discern in phenomena the secret movement which is directing things towards a transcendent goal. It is "we" who know this, and apart from faith it is absurd to affirm it. But *we* who have faith know. It is thus that we are able to divine, about the significance of history, what the groaning creation is itself unaware of.

* Cf. this theme in ancient prophecy (Is. 65: 17; 66: 22) renewed by Jewish apocalyptic (Bousset, *op. cit.* p. 280; Strack-Billerbeck, III, p. 840).

† It will be recalled how the word of Jesus about the conditions of life under which the "sons of the resurrection" will live (Lk. 20: 34–36; Mk. 12: 24–25; Matt. 22: 29–30) puts a stop to disordered imaginings about the future life.

‡ It originated in prophecy: Is. 26: 17; 66: 8; Jer. 22: 23; Hos. 13: 13; Mic. 4: 9. Cf. Strack-Billerbeck, I, p. 950.

§ Σὺν . . . in the two verbs συστενάζει and συνωδίνει indicates, not that creation sighs and suffers with man, but that all its elements sigh and suffer together (as in "symphony"; Lietzmann).

The few lines which we have just read from the apostle's pen raise vast problems. The knowledge available to us today about the origin of the earth and the human species, however incomplete it may be, does not allow us to establish a simple causal relation between man's revolt against God and the existence of the various ills which afflict nature. These ills existed, at least in certain forms, before the appearance of man; they are still observable today in spheres where it is impossible to connect them with human sin. What is more, they are in many cases the necessary condition and hence, as it would appear, the natural basis, for the very life of the creative process. Did Paul plainly attribute these ills in their totality to the fall of man, as has been generally supposed? This question must be asked, because the exegesis of the text does not necessarily require that this was his thought.

We should distinguish two kinds of evil and suffering, for in several passages Paul speaks about tribulations and trials which are the special mark of the Christian state of life, or especially of the apostle, in a world which is hostile to the revelation of God in Christ (1 Th. 1: 6; 3: 3, 7; Rom. 5: 3; 2 Cor. 6: 4; 7: 4; 8: 2; Phil. 3: 10; Col. 1: 24). To describe this, he uses a quite striking expression in writing to the Corinthians: "always carrying in the body the death of Jesus, so that the life of Jesus may also be manifested in our bodies" (2 Cor. 4: 10; in the same sense 4: 17; Gal. 6: 17 is no less striking). We found this idea again right at the start of our section (Rom. 8: 17b; 2 Cor. 1: 5, 7). Paul can write to the Thessalonians with regard to these trials and tribulations: "This is to be our lot" (1 Th. 3: 3). We find ourselves in quite a different context of thought when we read Rom. 8: 18–23. Here creation is envisaged as being "in travail". We may indeed suppose that this painful condition is the consequence of the fall of man; but this is not clearly contained in the texts themselves. For what creation longs to be delivered from is *corruption* (φθορά). Now Paul considered that the plan of God for the world ordained that the physical should be first and the spiritual second (1 Cor. 15: 45); which is tantamount to saying, as the apostle adds, that the perishable comes first and the imperishable later. These notes, unfortunately very brief, are in harmony with the

223

texts of Genesis. Creation was intended to be mastered by man who is the image of God so that it might pass from the physical and perishable stage to the spiritual and imperishable one. Man himself, created mortal, was destined to share in divine life.* His disobedience deprived him of that supreme good and at the same time it thwarted creation of the good which it would have received from a humanity responsive to its divine vocation.

This dynamic interpretation of history may give a less purely negative significance to the evils of creation than does the doctrine that claims to see in them a result of the fall. It is already interesting that Paul was able to write: "Is it for oxen that God is concerned?" (1 Cor. 9: 9) with regard to a Mosaic law which seemed inspired by the very concern to relieve the suffering of an innocent victim of man's sin. The use to which Paul puts this precept seems to prove very clearly that he is not at all concerned about animal suffering. He thinks that God gave this command to teach men to be kind and to relieve human suffering;† it is not animal suffering which worries him. Why not? It is simply because this suffering is natural and is part of the normal travail of a creation which is not yet completed. Suffering becomes intolerable when it can serve no useful purpose; but we know well that suffering with pedagogic aims does not shock us, and the Jews realized this too.‡ In such a case the end justifies the means. But in the hands of men this doctrine is more often than not abused, because their ends are not pure and their means are ill adapted. Nevertheless the Old Testament in its teaching about suffering as punishment attributed the idea to God.

It might be pertinent to add that we are fond of displaying a very anthropomorphic hypersensitivity in discussing these questions, forgetting that every day we derive our life from

* Cf. Paul Humbert, *Études sur le récit du paradis et de la chute dans la Genèse*, 1940, p. 151.

† This was already the interpretation of Thomas Aquinas, *Summa theologica* I a, II a, q. 102, a 6, on 8 (cf. a 6, on 1, and a 3, on 8). Quoted by A. M. Dubarle, "Le gémissement des créatures dans l'ordre divin du cosmos", *Revue des sciences philosophiques et théologiques*, 1954, p. 459. In this article there will also be found a study on recent aspects of the discussion.

‡ Cf. W. Bousset, *Rel. Jud.*, p. 385.

multiple forms of suffering and death in animal and plant life. We are not wrong to do so, but this contradiction should help to dispel certain confusions of thought which are sentimental in origin. There is surely no need to point out that these remarks have nothing to do with the question of cruelty!*

The intervention of sin into the world may nevertheless have had disastrous effects. Unfortunately it is impossible for us to assess these exactly, since we can have no idea of what humanity might have become if its development had taken place in accordance with the plan of God. It is equally impossible to know what would be our relations with nature and our "lesser brethren" on the same hypothesis. In any event, it is clear that, in the line of development from the physical to the spiritual which creation was intended to traverse (1 Cor. 15: 45-46) man has not progressed as he should have done, that on the contrary he has, throughout his history, experienced the detrimental effects of the law of solidarity—a situation arising from his sin.

In consequence, when he meditates on his position in the world, how can man escape the painful consciousness of his responsibility in the sight of God for the control of the creative process that was entrusted to him, beginning with the control of his own body? And in view of the new vistas which are opened up to the eye of faith by the insertion into the world of creation of those potentialities of new life disclosed in Jesus Christ, how should he resist Paul's conclusion that the creation is awaiting from the new man in Christ the means of at last realizing its own original vocation?

* "The mutual destruction of animate beings is, in the framework of a vaster whole, a function necessary to the maintenance of life. The war of animals among themselves is a vital process which is situated beyond the categories of culpability and responsibility. For man in his responsibility towards God, to kill uselessly or to ill-treat or to cause to suffer is something which violates the respect and love which he owes to his Creator. But even when it is legitimate to slay animals one cannot be insensitive to the process. The contradiction into which this throws us can only be overcome if the sacrifice of the creature is not an act to which we are indifferent; we have to consider it in the light of the gratitude we owe to God; instead of seeing in it the exercise of our rights as lords of creation, we should realize that we are creatures to whom the Creator has given, for their good, other creatures like ourselves" (Max Huber, *Mensch und Tier*, 1951, p. 84).

Whatever may have been the real opinions of Paul* on the questions which we have just been discussing, it is evident that his Letter to the Romans did not claim to advance any new teaching with regard to facts. If our modern knowledge yields a very different framework of thought it matters little, provided that the essential arguments of our author are discerned and assimilated. Now the purpose of Paul was to remind his readers, in connexion with the Christian's status in his environment, of the solidarity binding together the creature and creation which Genesis in its own way had already affirmed. We may differ widely from the apostle in our mode of grasping and assessing this solidarity. The fact itself cannot be denied, and faith recognizes in this the Creator's will and thus a responsibility for man. Such solidarity will not be, in his view, either a misfortune or an accident as the various forms of gnosticism and dualism have affirmed. On this absolutely basic point, the anthropological realism of Hebrew theology expresses itself with the widest implications. If then faith affirms the ideas of sin and the fall, it cannot hesitate to think that the fall of man must have had far-reaching consequences for creation as a whole. Similarly if faith believes in the redemption of sinful man, it cannot resist the inference that this redemption will have equal repercussions on creation. Here is the essential point. The guise in which these doctrines are presented to make them more vivid may be a useful support, but may become dangerous if it is confused with the substance of the truth which it covers. And do not let us forget that, in all these matters, the strictest sobriety of opinion is indispensable.†

---

* A. Viard, *art. cit.* p. 343, brings together ch. 7 and ch. 8; Paul interprets a situation (that of man before the law, that of creation) in the light of his faith; he sees it such as it really is in God's eyes; he lends it his voice and renders it articulate even though no man has spoken as in Rom. 7 and no creature as in Rom. 8.

† "We must be on our guard against all concordism and allow the grandiose ideas of the apostle and of scripture in general to retain their exclusively religious meaning. This does not mean, far from it, that such data, which have perhaps been too much neglected, should not be taken into account; but it remains the fact that their true bearing is difficult to make exact and clear" (A. Feuillet, *art. cit.* p. 382).

(23) Inasmuch as man the creature shares the life of creation as a whole, he too must sigh and groan with the latter;
and the believer who still lives "in the flesh" (Gal. 2:20) can
share in the same way the characteristic longing of creation.
But the apostle was not thinking merely of this aspect of the
believer's condition;* he has in mind also the spiritual destiny of the believer as such; no longer his external being, but
the inner man, for the latter too and above all is proceeding
towards transcendent ends, namely that glorification which
v. 30 confirming v. 17 will show to be the goal of his trajectory in history (cf. 2 Cor. 4: 16–17).

What is brute suffering for the creation—and for us considered as an integral part of it—assumes the character of a
real contradiction if we remember that we have received the
Spirit. But this contradiction itself is of the highest significance. The suffering by which it is manifested throws light
on the new reality which travails in secret; it foreshadows the
glory to come. We are indeed sons because God has adopted
us; we rejoice in this blessing by praise and thanksgiving; and
yet we are far from enjoying the liberty of the children of
God. The Spirit within us is the anticipation of the new age,
the reality of what is to come;† and yet our bodies in which
it dwells are mortal (cf. 1 Cor. 6: 19; 3: 16). The natural
creaturely conditions of our existence present an obstacle to
our "Christian" condition, to what we are, from the point of
view of our union with Christ by faith and baptism. We see
only in an incomplete and distorted way the realities which
we greet from afar by faith (cf. 2 Cor. 5: 6–7; 1 Cor. 13: 12;
Phil. 1: 23–24). Hence we would like our external condition

* The beginning of the verse is uncertain: D G etc. add ἡμεῖς after
ἀλλὰ καί, S A C etc. insert ἡμεῖς after ἔχοντες, beside καὶ αὐτοί. All
do not give to the three words ἡμεῖς καὶ αὐτοί the same order. B has
even omitted ἡμεῖς and D G retain only αὐτοί. These variants are not
significant for meaning.

† In ἀπαρχή there are three ideas: (1) a part of the sum total is already
present; (2) there is anticipation; (3) this first instalment is the pledge
and guarantee of the reward to come. Paul does not seem to hold fast as
important the idea that the gift of the Spirit is only partial; God has not
given partial payment. Paul insists rather on the chronological and
logical aspects of the notion: anticipation and pledge: ἀπαρχή =ἀρραβών,
2 Cor. 1: 22; 5: 5.

227

of life to be brought into harmony with our Christian confession about our internal condition; we would like our spiritual status as sons to be embodied in an objective status of adoption,* whereas in fact we as yet apprehend the latter only through the inner witness of the Spirit (v. 16); in this sense then we still wait for adoption. Paul describes the embodiment of our adoption on the plane of our historical existence as the "redemption of our body". The thought of the apostle here may not go beyond the train of ideas in 2 Cor. 5 where is expressed the hope of removing from our "earthly tent" in order to dwell with the Lord. But the eschatological tone of our section would incline us rather to connect this redemption of the body with the vistas of thought in 1 Cor. 15: 45–49 with its theme of the transformation of the physical and terrestrial body into the spiritual and heavenly one. It is not merely a question of the liberating power of death; it is a question rather of the redeeming action of God aimed at endowing humanity with a new status of existence, by bringing the believer to share in the power of Christ's resurrection (Phil. 3: 10).

(24f.) A state of expectancy is therefore the present condition of the believer who lives in the midst of a world in travail, where God pursues His work with patience. What has already been done *for* us permits us to say: "we are saved". What remains still to be done *within* us obliges us to say that this salvation is still an object of hope.† The short argument which Paul develops turns on the idea of hope. "Hope that

* "Witnesses of considerable authority", representing the so-called Western text (e.g. P 46 D G Ephr.), do not have υἱοθεσίαν. Fr. Benoit thinks they are right, because adoption is something definitive, already granted and incapable of augmentation, hence as far as it is concerned there is nothing to wait for (Benoit, "Nous gémissons, attendant la délivrance de notre corps" (Rom. 8: 23), *Mélanges Lebreton. Rev. Sc. Rel.*, 1951–1952). Similarly S. Lyonnet in the so-called *Bible de Jérusalem.* May we point out however that it is not a question of augmentation of the adoption, which is inconceivable, but of a development of its consequences; just as in v. 19 creation awaits, not the presence of the sons of God, which is already a fact, but their manifestation; what they are has not yet disclosed its full effects—the manifestation of the glory which is in them.

† *Τῇ ἐλπίδι* is equivalent to *ἐφ' ἐλπίδι*, v. 20. *Dativus modi* (Bengel).

228

is seen" means: "if you see what you hope for". In such a case hope no longer exists, the end has been attained and there is nothing more to wait for. We possess. Does Paul mean by this: in view of the fact that salvation is eschatological, and thus future, it is only to be expected that we should have to wait and to suffer while waiting (chronological interpretation)? Or does he mean: if the object of hope is visible, as we are tempted to desire for our own inner comfort, then it would belong to the perishable sphere of the visible (cf. 2 Cor. 4: 18) and we could no longer count on it as abiding; in spite of the fulfilment of our hope we should finally be baffled (ontological interpretation)?*

A more strictly theological interpretation might be suggested which would include the two others and would be in better harmony with the structure of Paul's ideas about hope. This interpretation centres in the promise of God; Abraham was the type of him who hopes against hope (4: 18) because his condition was in contradiction with God's declaration. In view of this, the point of the present passage lies in v. 25 in the idea that what one does not yet see one awaits patiently, i.e. with the faith which trusts in God both for the choice of the moment and the means by which He will realize what He has promised. And if we insist on seeing what we hope for, then by an untimely initiative, which is the fruit of our lack of faith, we undertake anticipatory action and seek from the use of our own resources what God had declared that He would accomplish by the exercise of His sovereign power. In that case we do as Abraham did when he went to Hagar. He sought in haste to see the object of his hope; it is true that he gained time, but this gain was a dead loss from the ontological point of view; the son that was born to him did not inherit the promise.†

(26f.) The tension of contradiction from which we suffer as a result of our continuing integrality with the present order of things, is shown further by the obstacles which clash with our inner life, and especially with prayer which is the

* In this sense, Bultmann, *Th.Wb.NT*, II, p. 528; Gaugler, Michel.
† The end of v. 24 is uncertain. C K L P : τί καὶ ἐλπίζει, D G latt syr: τί ἐλπίζει, Pap. 46 B: ἐλπίζει, S A bo: τί καὶ ὑπομένει.

culminating point of our inner life. The feebleness and wretchedness of our prayer should not discourage the believer or cause him to doubt his status of adoption. If the "necrosis" of man is thus evinced, then let him look to God instead of regretting that he is not a virtuoso of prayer like the Pharisee of Lk. 18: 10, or those pious people from whose lips flow an abundance of religious formulae (Matt. 6: 7). The Spirit comes to our assistance and that is enough. But we should understand that the weakness of our prayer does not lie in its scarcity; it lies rather in the poverty of its substance. If it was enough to speak in order to pray, it would be enough to find subjects of prayer, of which there is no dearth. The essential point lies elsewhere. While warning His disciples against pious chatter, Jesus taught them in a short prayer what they ought to ask for. It is not enough to pray: we must pray "as we ought to pray". There is a prayer which God does not listen to, namely the prayer of the Pharisee; but He does hear the very short prayer of the publican, who could say only one thing definitely, namely that he did not know how to pray, so that a single and quite simple phrase, uttered with lowered eyes, expressed his petition for pardon. Prayer is essentially an expression of our ignorance as to what our prayer should be (Gaugler, pp. 315–316). To pray as we ought, we must pray according to the will of God;* but the inspiration for this can only flow from God, who alone knows His mind. The rest is a sterile performance.

If true prayer exceeds what we are able to think or say, our poverty will leave no other course open to us but to express ourselves by "sighs too deep for words". In that case we, like the publican, will have given up the idea of cutting a good figure in the presence of God; for when we pray it is indeed a question of coming into the presence of God.† Now the believer never realizes better his weakness and unworthiness than when he appears before God; then he feels the anguish and shame of an Isaiah or a Peter (Is. 6; Lk. 5: 8–9) or of the publican. Neither the content nor the form of human speech is then

* Michel rightly connects καθὸ δεῖ with κατὰ θεόν.
† . . . and not before men . . . go into your room where no one sees you but God (Matt. 6: 5–8).

suitable. The believer can express only his deep dissatisfaction, his self-abandonment and his expectancy. Paradoxically the very weakness of his prayer is a sign of its authenticity. God who "sees in secret" knows what this poverty of expression means. These words which have no expressive power,* God understands. They have a meaning which does not flow from the one who utters them but from the action of God Himself within us at work in the Holy Spirit. The Holy Spirit plays as it were the part of an intermediary, an intercessor.† He takes up our defence in the presence of God as though He were explaining that our weakness and distress are the very sign of His living presence within us; and He turns our poverty of utterance into wealth.

(28) The condition of the Christian is now envisaged from a final point of view. The movement which draws all creation —and man in particular who is the crown of creation— towards its intrinsic ends, is realizing the thought of God. This was already implied but must now be stated more clearly, so that it becomes more vividly apparent that no obstacle offered by history will be able to check the work of redemptive recreation undertaken by Christ. Neither the corruptibility of the world and of the "outward man" nor the

---

* Στεναγμοί should be connected with συστενάζει and στενάζομεν (v. 22, 23). These "sighs" are a form of the "sigh" of creation. Hence they cannot be assimilated to glossolaly. Moreover Paul is speaking here of the prayer of every Christian, whereas glossolaly is a special charismatic gift. Furthermore, glossolaly is above all an act of thanksgiving, and not intercession (cf. Gaugler, p. 323).

† There are here two ideas difficult to co-ordinate: the Spirit appears to play the role of an Intercessor, as does a third party intervening between two others. On the other hand, God discerns the mind of the Spirit as He sees it in the "heart" of believers, and thus it is there, at the most secret core of the personality, that these sighs are heard; in this case, the Spirit does not act as a *tertia persona* but by uniting with the mind and heart of man (in this sense Delling, *Th.Wb.NT*, I, p. 376). This difficulty should not be stressed too much at the risk of hardening the meaning of words so that reality escapes. When it is a question of the functions of the Spirit, vocabulary and thought must remain very flexible. The Spirit of God is never merely within man, nor is it ever solely exterior to man. We cannot distinguish between the Spirit and its action within man, and still less contrast them.

231

weakness of the "inward man" will prevent God from fulfilling His plan (Michel, p. 180).

For God has a plan. "We know" that such a plan exists,
declares Paul, expressing the faith of the church, as in v. 22.
And we know too that this plan will be realized for the good
of those who love God. The phrase recalls Jewish tradition;
"to love God" is an expression inherited from the Old Testament but remarkably rare with Paul (1 Cor. 2: 9; 8: 3) who
stresses always the love of which God is the subject, rather
than that of which He is the object.* It is God who is in
active control of things and not that things eventually
straighten themselves out.† He guides them, not with the
object of assuring the petty happiness of the bourgeoisie but
with the object of attaining that salvation and glorification
which will be the crown of His work. The phrases used by the
apostle do not suggest the idea of a restricted choice, nor that
of rejection, as Augustine insisted. The point emphasized is
the certainty of ultimate salvation based on God's faithfulness
to His plan (Gaugler, p. 331).

(29) Those who love God are those whom He has known
(οὕς recalls τοῖς ἀγαπῶσιν), for if anyone loves God, it is that
he is known of God (1 Cor. 8: 3): ἔγνωσται ὑπ' αὐτοῦ). V. 29
is intended to explain why God brings to those who love
Him an assistance which is aimed at their supreme good and
salvation. The reason is (ὅτι has a causal sense) that He
destines them to become conformed to Jesus Christ. Such is

* The rabbi Aqiba was accustomed to say: "Let man always say:
whatever the compassionate man does, he does it for the good" (Ber.
60b). In the hermetical writings (9: 4b): πάντα γὰρ τῷ τοιούτῳ
(θεοσεβεῖ), κἂν τοῖς ἄλλοις κακά, ἀγαθά ἐστι. Plotinus 4: 3, 16, 21; cf.
W. Bauer, Wörterbuch, s.v. συνεργέω.

† Pap. 46, B A Orig. have ὁ Θεός which must have been added for the
sake of clearness. In the absence of ὁ Θεός, πάντα might be taken as the
grammatical subject. However, if we replace the phrase within the peri-
cope as a whole, God may be implied as subject ad sensum. If we make ὁ
Θεός the subject of συνεργεῖ, the latter assumes the meaning of "come
to the help of", and πάντα will be taken as an adverb (God collaborates
in all things with those who love Him and thus works for their good: S.
Lyonnet) or again; in all things God collaborates for the good of those
who love Him ... (Bible du Centenaire).

His purpose, and the following phrase will say how this purpose is realized.

Those who love God are then those whom God has "known". This knowledge is not objective intellectual knowledge; it is the kind of knowledge implied by the Hebrew idea of ידע: in this kind of knowledge the subject is inclined towards the object, encounters it and there are no longer an object and subject face to face with each other; there is set up a relationship, a communion. This knowledge is experiential and, as it presupposes an initiative taken by the subject, it often carries with it an elective judgment; to know is to choose, to commit oneself, it is already to love, and to choose from motives of love.* The "knowledge" which God has of man is prior to the love of man for God and is the foundation of the latter (hence προ-έγνω: the προ marks this priority; cf. 1 Cor. 8: 3).

The movement of God's "knowledge" pursues an end. Like the father in the parable who reintegrates his son into the bond of a filial relation, God pursues the reintegration of sinners into His communion through the process of adoption, by which He makes believers fellow heirs who are glorified together with Christ. Paul expresses this with the ideas of μορφή, *form*, and εἰκών, *image*.

The purpose of God is to make us conformed to His Son (the συν recalls those of v. 17) i.e. to enable us to share the form of His Son. In this type of thought the form does not correspond to the external (as opposed to the internal) nor to the peripheral (as opposed to the essential). The "form" is that which permits us to know the reality; it is the content emerging and becoming communicable.† The considerable

* Thus, in the OT, ידע will signify to know by experience, because one has met or experienced (e.g. Ex. 1: 8; Is. 42: 25); in the hiphil: to cause to know in concrete experience (e.g. Jer. 16: 21), to be concerned with (e.g. Gen. 39: 6, 8). To know a man or a woman is to have the most intimate sexual relations with (e.g. Gen. 4: 1; Num. 31: 18). To know God is to be intimately in fellowship with Him, to serve Him, to recognize Him concretely in acts of obedience (e.g. Jer. 22: 16). When God knows someone, He enters specially into relations with him, He is concerned with him, He chooses him and loves him (Gen. 18: 19; Ex. 33: 12; Amos 3: 2; Hos. 13: 5; Jer. 1: 5).

† The sense of μορφή is thus very close to that of δόξα. These two

233

closeness of meaning between "glory" and "form" facilitates the transition from the idea of "conform" to that of "glorify together with" (v. 17). To make conformed is to give participation in the glory of the Son by bringing believers to share the image of the Son—which is what 2 Cor. 3: 18 and Phil. 3: 21 say precisely, where also we find in close connexion μορφή and δόξα.* This conformity to the Son is what preeminently gives the status of sons to those who benefit from it. Fellow heirs, said v. 17; brethren, says v. 29. These things go together; the sons are at one and the same time the former and the latter. Naturally the Son of God has preceded the others. It is through Him that these have received filial adoption; He is their elder brother.†

Hence the predestination of which Paul speaks is concerned with the content of the divine plan of love realized in the person of the Son, and with the means of its realization; it is not concerned with the inclusion or the exclusion of whomsoever.

(30) The prefix προ which we have just met three times in v. 29 implied the priority of the purpose of God to historical

words translate תְּמוּנָה; Job 4: 16 and Num. 12: 8; Ps. 17: 15. Cf. Is. 52: 14 which is translated τὸ εἰδός σου καὶ ἡ δόξα σου (LXX), ὄρασις αὐτοῦ καὶ μορφή (Aq). Cf. Th.Wb.NT, I, p. 759, n. 53. On εἰκών cf. Kittel, Th.Wb.NT, II, p. 395.

* Participation in the image of the Son is central to the plan of God, because the Son Himself is εἰκὼν Θεοῦ (2 Cor. 4: 4; Col. 1: 15). He who is conformed to Christ is in fact conformed to Christ as the image of God. The effulgence of the glory of God in the face of Christ, the image of God (2 Cor. 4: 4, 6) effects the glorious metamorphosis into His image (2 Cor. 3: 18). We must not forget to note that this is the work of the Spirit (2 Cor. 3: 18), and this remark further emphasizes the unity of the ideas developed in that Letter to the Corinthians with those of Rom. 8.

† In πρωτότοκος the idea of generation is vague and secondary. The word expresses primarily the idea of priority. Here it is a question of priority in the order of sonship; elsewhere of priority in the order of creation (Col. 1: 15) or in the order of resurrection (Col. 1: 18; Rev. 1: 5). In all things Christ is the first (πρωτεύων, Col. 1: 18). Priority also suggests excellence; the first-born is the favourite child, the privileged one; the Jews were accustomed to bring out the qualitative importance of something by stressing its age (cf. the Torah, the temple), (cf. Strack-Billerbeck, II, p. 258.) These ideas, without being excluded, play here only a secondary part.

manifestations. Paul now wishes to show what this purpose becomes in its historical embodiment, the historical trajectory which the eternal design of God will trace in time. Vocation, justification, glorification are its three essential phases; God calls, God justifies, God glorifies. The call resounds today through the preaching of the gospel, which conveys to mankind the promise of God in Jesus Christ and arouses the response of faith. Justification is the new status of the believer who accepts the promise; it is a word which implies all the good, all the gifts and all the requirements of the Christian condition here below, as has just been shown in the whole argument of this letter to the Romans. Glorification is the final status which those whom Christ calls to partake of His own glory will receive. Here Paul speaks in the past tense of this phase, but its realization will come only later (cf. v. 17). We may see in his choice of tense at this juncture the assurance of faith; the divine will is already shaped in the eternity of God, and the accidents of history can avail nothing against it. Similarly the believer can say with Paul: "we have been saved", when he considers the objective work of Christ; and he can also say: "we shall be saved", when he takes a historical point of view. In a sense glorification is already included in vocation and justification.*

[31]What then shall we say to this? If God is for us, who is against us? [32]He who did not spare his own Son but gave him up for us all, will he not also give us all things with him? [33]Who shall bring any charge against God's elect? It is God who justifies; [34]who is to condemn? Is it Christ Jesus, who died, yes, who was raised from the dead, who is at the right hand of God, who indeed intercedes for us? [35]Who shall separate us from the love of Christ? Shall tribulation, or distress, or persecution, or famine, or nakedness, or peril, or sword? [36]As it is written,

"For thy sake we are being killed all the day long;
we are regarded as sheep to be slaughtered."

* It might also be thought that glorification, although in its full reality future, has already begun for those who have the Spirit, the first-fruits of that glorious world (Zahn); 2 Cor. 3: 18; Col. 1: 27 seem to support this point of view. It has also been said that Christ is glorified, and that believers are glorified also in the person of their Head (Godet).

[37]No, in all these things we are more than conquerors through him who loved us. [38]For I am sure that neither death, nor life, nor angels, nor principalities, nor things present, nor things to come, nor powers, [39]nor height, nor depth, nor anything else in all creation, will be able to separate us from the love of God in Christ Jesus our Lord.

(31) The scope of God's plan which His faithfulness will accomplish justifies complete assurance; there is nothing more to be said after what has just been said. Yet the peace of God does not exclude the struggles of faith. The world is not yet transformed. If God makes all things concur to the good of those who love Him, it is by leading them to the victory of faith, not in sparing them trials (1 Jn. 5: 4). To the sufferings which he knows, because the Spirit is in travail within him, there are added for the believer threats from without; a new experience of his own weakness, and a new experience of the power of God (2 Cor. 12: 9).

In introducing this final phase of his thought, is Paul putting a question or imagining an objection?* In any event, the question cannot fail to suggest itself to the heart of the believer: God is for us; but are there not against us powers which could tear us away from God by seducing us afresh? Doubt is never excluded from the life of faith in any definitive way (cf. Mk. 9: 24); the last times are, by definition, times of tribulation.

"For us" and "against us" imply the circumstances of a legal process. The text here presupposes a situation like those symbolically described in the Book of Job and Zechariah 3. The evocation of such a scene reflects very vividly the tension of conflict in which the Christian always finds himself.†

* Here we recognize in general the style of the diatribe. The paragraph as a whole may be divided into strophes: 31b–32; 33–34; 35–37; 38–39. The first two speak of God and His love; the last two of the possible enemies of the love of God.

† The introduction of the accuser is mythical in character. It is intended to express the ambiguity of God's judgment, which is sometimes accusing, sometimes favourable. R. Meier interpreted Hosea 14: 2 by saying that Israel must return to God before her advocate becomes her accuser. God is both, according as He exercises His mercy or His justice (cf. G. F. Moore, *Judaism*, I, p. 387).

(32) The decision is in the hands of the supreme Judge and we already know how He judges. He has pronounced Himself in our favour in one decisive circumstance. He then gave us everything. He will not allow the adversary, by his cunning, to destroy the work of His love. The gift which He made of His Son was on our behalf; hence He cannot but be a Saviour for us. The objective accomplishment of our redemption assures us that it will also find its fulfilment on the plane of our everyday life.

(33) The image is further amplified. Satan enters on the scene. He is the professional accuser* (Job 1: 6; Rev. 12: 10); he disputes the fidelity of God's elect: he tries to turn them away from Him or to set Him against them. But what can he do against God's elect?† He accuses them in vain, as was seen in the case of Job and that of the high priest Joshua in the vision of Zechariah. God declares righteous and acquits those who love Him.

The construction of vv. 33 and 34 is much debated. Some consider all the parts of the sentences to be questions. Others adopt the grouping 33b and 34a: 34b and 35, after the pattern of Isaiah 50: 8–9 which the apostle has certainly in mind. Others again make v. 34 a question. In the absence of any criterion it is very difficult to decide. The punctuation adopted by Nestle and lately by Michel well secures the logic and movement of the passage.

(34) In conformity with the text of Isaiah 50 Paul asks: "who is to condemn?" Condemnation involves death. Who would condemn to death those for whom Christ has already died?‡ If any accuser or tyrannical power like those

* Enoch 40: 7; Test. Levi 5: 6; T. Dan 6: 2; cf. Strack-Billerbeck, I, p. 141.

† Ἐκλεκτός: rare with Paul (Rom. 8: 33; 16: 13; Col. 3: 12) although it was current in apocalyptic writings. The term articulated the sentiments of pride fostered by religious nationalism. Perhaps the apostle tended to avoid it for this reason. Col. 3: 12 shows that the elect are above all they who are the object of God's love which they must manifest in their turn. There is no restrictive implication (elect by opposition to reprobate; cf. v. 29). In 16: 13 the word is applied to an individual (Rufus, elect in the Lord).

‡ Ἰησοῦς is wanting in B D E K.

237

of which v. 35 will speak should demand a victim, the victim has already been handed over and has undergone the punishment. And not only has Christ undergone the condemnation and the penalty, but He afterwards displayed His innocence to His accusers by triumphing over death, rather like an accused person who had emerged victor from a trial which was designed to evince his culpability by bringing about his death. Christ the conqueror of death has returned to the tribunal and has sat down at the right hand of the Supreme Judge. Now He has become the advocate of those whom the same accusers would like to overwhelm too. There He intercedes for the victims of Satan, as did the angel whose role was to maintain the cause of the high priest Joshua.

(35) If v. 34 reminds us of the scene from the vision of Zechariah, v. 35 recalls rather the sequence of incidents in the drama of the Book of Job. After Satan has made his accusations against Job, the latter's trial begins. The believer too accused by Satan undergoes trials which risk separating him from God by causing his faith to waver. Such trials are, in a way, personified (τίς, *who*, is masculine; it may be compared with τις κτίσις, *any creature*, of v. 39). In this enumeration of the trials which threaten the believer, we see, with the exception of the sword, the various trials which Paul himself had had occasion to suffer.* The apostle is here conjuring up the whole of his dangerous life as an apostle and his difficulties and sufferings for Christ. It is no rhetorical phrasing that we have here.

(36) This psalm (44: 22) which had already been applied to the martyrdom of the seven brothers narrated in 2 Mac. 7, confirms that the life of faith is lived on the very confines of death.†

(37) Nor is there any rhetoric in what the apostle writes here. While, to be sure, he has triumphed over his various

* Cf. 1 Cor. 4: 9; 15: 30–32; 2 Cor. 4: 8–11; 6: 4–5; 11: 22–28; 12: 10; Col. 1: 24.
† Cf. Strack-Billerbeck, IV, p. 259.

sufferings, they showed him the weakness of his natural resistance. It was by faith that he overcame, by the power of the Master who strengthened him (Phil. 4: 13; 2 Cor. 12: 10). It is more than a victory; for if need be one could meet these difficulties by stiffening oneself, clenching one's teeth and by passive resistance. But this sort of thing is not in question here! What we have here is a participation in the power of the love of God, so that God carries off a super-triumph, as it were, a victory in the deepest sense,* and associates us with it.

(38f.) This evocation of the tribulations of the apostle lends to the πέπεισμαι, *I am sure,* the force of a personal witness even though the vision of the writer here embraces horizons which far surpass the bounds of personal experience. Even if the mysterious powers now to be suggested enter the field, the assurance of the help of God is the same.

The picture of the hostile forces makes use of ideas, some of which are difficult for us to grasp. It is easy to see that death may constitute a threat to faith, for the fear of suffering the supreme punishment that men can devise may in the critical hour tempt one to renounce one's faith and deny the Lord. Similarly but inversely, life itself may turn us aside from the faith by reason of the lusts which it excites. "Angels and principalities" are already more mysterious powers. Behind the great events of history and expressing the metaphysical background of these events, personal energies were detected at work. Paul mentions quite a number of such, but we get the impression that there is nothing systematic about these enumerations.† Angels and principalities suggest then perhaps the secret forces which direct and unleash events and mark with their seal the life and death of men.

"Things present and things to come", by introducing the category of time, powerfully evokes the chronological framework of the history of mankind. We are surprised to find next

* ῾Υπερνικάω =hapax NT.
† Δύναμις goes with ἀρχή and ἐξουσία in 1 Cor. 15: 24. Cf. Col. 1: 16; 2: 10–15; Eph. 1: 21; 3: 10; 6: 12. In 1 Cor. 2: 8 the ἄρχοντες are the invisible authors of the crucifixion of the Lord of Glory. Christ manifests His sovereignty by disarming ἀρχαί and ἐξουσίαι (Col. 2: 15).

the mention of "powers", for the letters of the apostle usually range the "powers" along with angels and principalities. Must we see in this allusion simply a complement to what has just been said, or must we see here a new notion? Perhaps the forces of nature which form the physical framework of the Christian life? "Υψωμα and βάθος are still more obscure. Such terms belong properly to the language of astrology; they denote the proximity or distance of a star in relation to the zenith. Must we suppose that the apostle is borrowing from this specialized vocabulary? In that case, "*height* and *depth*" would be astral powers (Lietzmann). Otherwise we might think of heavenly powers for haight, or subterranean powers (hell) for depth (Origen and Michel); or, more generally again, we might see here an allusion to space as a geographical framework (Lagrange). The list seems exhaustive; but as these beneficent or maleficent forces reigning over the destinies of mankind had not been systematized by any rigid doctrine, the apostle leaves the door open to speculation; there may be some other mysterious adversary rising up to thwart the Christian's hope.

Whatever be the detail, the intention is clear and the three series of possible trials are firmly delineated. The first series suggests the inner struggles of faith against the assaults of doubt. The second (v. 35) brings into view the threats springing from the instrumentality of men. The third (vv. 38–39) conjures up the mysterious forces of the universe which escape from all human control. Three concentric circles, which are not without interconnexion and even mutual connivance, the enumeration of which gives the reader a vivid picture of the dramatic character which marks the Christian life. But the more gloomy the reality, and the more threatening the situation, so much the more clearly emerges in all its luminous assurance the peace instilled into the hearts of believers by the witness which Jesus Christ bears to the love of God. The plan which God has formed for those who love Him will not suffer failure; such is the confirmation and conclusion which these somewhat enigmatic sentences give to the systematic exposition of God's merciful purpose summed up in vv. 28–30.

CHAPTER

9

¹I am speaking the truth in Christ, I am not lying; my conscience bears me witness in the Holy Spirit, ²that I have great sorrow and unceasing anguish in my heart. ³For I could wish that I myself were accursed and cut off from Christ for the sake of my brethren, my kinsmen by race. ⁴They are Israelites, and to them belong the sonship, the glory, the covenants, the giving of the law, the worship, and the promises; ⁵to them belong the patriarchs, and of their race, according to the flesh, is the Christ. God who is over all be blessed for ever. Amen.

⁶But it is not as though the word of God had failed. For not all who are descended from Israel belong to Israel, ⁷and not all are children of Abraham because they are his descendants; but "Through Isaac shall your descendants be named." ⁸This means that it is not the children of the flesh who are the children of God, but the children of the promise are reckoned as descendants. ⁹For this is what the promise said, "About this time I will return and Sarah shall have a son." ¹⁰And not only so, but also when Rebecca had conceived children by one man, our forefather Isaac, ¹¹though they were not yet born and had done nothing either good or bad, in order that God's purpose of election might continue, not because of works but because of his call, ¹²she was told, "The elder will serve the younger." ¹³As it is written, "Jacob I loved, but Esau I hated."

WITH CHAPTERS 9 to 11 the landscape of thought abruptly changes. The question which is now going to be discussed seems to have no connexion with the preceding themes (cf. Introduction). In fact, there is a very close connexion; furthermore a real logical necessity compels the apostle to deal with the subject which he now broaches, and had he not discussed it we should feel obliged to deplore a serious omission.

The whole structure of argument which has been built up

so far rests on the assumption of the primary initiative of divine grace in the promise made to Abraham, of which Christ is the realization. Now the attitude of the descendants of Abraham towards the One in whom the promise is realized, and the present eviction of Israel on account of its incredulity, compel us to ask whether the promises are still valid since they were made to a people now repudiated. The security of the promise is thus challenged, and thus the whole doctrine of justification by faith. At the same time the continuity and unity of the people of God, of which the apostle wishes to convince his readers, becomes insecure. How could the young church feel conscious of belonging to the old trunk of which Abraham is the stem, if the new dispensation develops outside the framework of the elect people of God? After twenty centuries of severance from Israel the question has lost for us the acuteness which Paul felt it to have: the Christian church believes—somewhat too facilely moreover —that the plan of God for man's salvation is fulfilled in the new Israel. Matters wore quite a different aspect for Paul. For him the bonds of blood gave to the theological problem of the unity of the church in time and space an emotional intensity which chs. 9–11 discover to the attentive reader.

To put it in other words, it was a question of knowing what exactly was the scope and bearing of the incredulity of Israel from the point of view of God's intentions towards it both in the past and the future. Events appeared to ruin the past and compromise the future. It was necessary to reinterpret them in order to show how, in spite of appearances, believers of today are the heirs of a valid promise, and remain in ecclesiastical unity and continuity with the elect people of God.

(1) In his approach to this subject,* Paul wishes to assure himself and his readers that he is going to speak solely from the point of view of the faith, as a man in Christ (ἐν Χριστῷ: cf. 2 Cor. 2: 17; 12: 19) without allowing himself to be influenced by any impulse of resentment towards those Israelites who have made him suffer so much. It has often been thought that the apostle was trying here to refute the

* Cf. E. Weber, *Das Problem der Heilsgeschichte nach Röm.* 9–11, 1911.

accusation of being a renegade, so that in the first place he would be endeavouring to make clear the sincerity of his declarations on behalf of Israel: "Believe me, I am not lying when I declare today as yesterday that Israel has been granted the greatest of privileges, and that I am truly sorry for what is happening to it." In reality this is not the point. Paul is not undertaking an apology *pro vita sua*. It is not a question of his own personal life, any more than it was in ch. 7; but, here again, he is concerned about the eternal plan of God and the successive stages of its historical realization. What Paul wishes to affirm is his sincere desire to treat the question with heartfelt truth. His conscience brings to his deepest being, where the Holy Spirit is at work, the testimony that he is speaking without pretence. Questioning himself in the sight of God he can affirm that he is speaking the truth.

(2f.) In the first place, it is his sadness which Paul wishes to express. His grief is evoked by two complementary terms and underlined by two adjectives.* It is such that it drives the apostle to extremes; if only he could be useful to Israel, he would be prepared to accept the worst punishment that a Jew can imagine, namely that of the curse, of banishment, the effect of which was to deprive the unfortunate person of all participation in the material and spiritual wealth of his people and to devote him to physical and moral death.† Judaism was familiar with the idea that a man might take upon himself the suffering due to another so as to spare the latter punishment.‡ Paul would go so far as to accept what, in his particular circumstances, would make his sacrifice the most cruel conceivable: separation from Christ.§ He would

---

* Λύπη suggests rather a suffering of the soul, a sadness; ὀδύνη a suffering in which the body is somewhat more concerned, which does harm and oppresses the heart.

† Ἀνάθεμα: a hellenistic form of ἀνάθημα. In the LXX ἀνάθημα translates ḥērem. Cf. Behm, *Th.Wb.NT*, I, p. 356. In Michel will be found a long discussion on this v. 3.

‡ Phrases such as the following are cited: "Might I become an expiation for such and such." Cf. Strack-Billerbeck, III, p. 260. But the idea goes back further; e.g. Moses had asked Yahweh if he might be blotted out of His book to do expiation for the sin of the people (Ex. 32: 32).

§ Ἀπὸ τοῦ Χριστοῦ includes doubtless separation from the community.

243

take matters thus far and would really make such a prayer if he felt it at all possible to formulate it.*

(4–5a) It is not the bonds of the flesh which constitute the decisive reason for such sentiments, although those bonds are so real that the apostle does not for one moment think of underrating their solidity and permanence. But there is a further consideration, for these bonds derive their value from a higher reality: that of the divine election which made Israel the people of the promise. For the attentive reader, it is enough to say "Israelites" to sum the matter up in one word. This was the supreme title of honour to be recalled at the very start of the argument. Politically speaking there existed at this time only Jews, but the promises were made to Israel—a name which denoted the people of God as such.† The apostle proceeds to explain the scope of this title.

Firstly it implies adoption (Ex. 4: 22; Deut. 14: 1; Hos. 11: 1), for it conferred on the people a special status which was to permit them to enjoy the presence of the God of glory (in the tabernacle, the temple, and special manifestations; Ex. 40: 34; 1 Kgs. 8: 10–11; Ex. 33: 22). This status proper to the people of God is rooted in the successive dispensations or the general dispensation which God ordained for it, i.e. the covenant or covenants.‡ The law applies the covenant concretely to the daily life of the elect people, and provides both an opportunity and a rule for its obedience. Standing at the centre of the law as its culminating point are the ordinances relative to the cult, which reminds Israel that the law draws all its significance from the grace which God incessantly renews for His people. Finally the whole of this economy was and remains placed under the sign of the promises which, from the call of Abraham, constituted the final end towards

However, the apostle is speaking of Christ, not of the church; a fact which is not without importance; one is separated from the church because one is separated from Christ, not the reverse.

* Paul knows very well that the hypothesis is not serious (Lagrange). The imperfect (ηὐχόμην) in the Koiné may express the optative. Cf. Gal. 4: 20.

† Cf. Gen. 32: 29; Rom. 11: 1. Cf. in *Th.Wb.NT*, III, pp. 357–394, the big art. on Ἰσραήλ.

‡ Pap. 46 B D G Cyp. it. have διαθήκη.

which all the ways of God's self-revelation tended; for the God of Israel was the God of the fathers* and of the promise which had been made to them—the God whose fidelity to these promises assured the very continuity of the life of His people. There is no doubt that Paul has here built up a systematic enumeration, the careful structure of which is reflected in the literary arrangement and style.†

(5bc) The strictness with which this enumeration is constructed throws into relief its final term where Christ is named; the Christ thus appears as the essential culmination of this long process of preparation of which Israel had been the privileged instrument. Ἐξ ὧν, *of their race*, clearly marks the bond of origin which connects the Christ to Israel; but Paul seems to have wished to stamp with a special note the link which connects Christ with the enumeration of the privileges of Israel, for he does not simply continue the enumeration. Ἐξ ὧν has something enigmatic about it: yes, Christ has sprung from the fathers, but only "according to the flesh" (cf. 1: 3; Gal. 4: 4).

The restrictive detail "according to the flesh" seems to demand a complement, saying what Christ is "according to the Spirit"; in 1: 4 the two sides are considered in turn. Must we find this complement in 5c (ὁ ὢν, etc.)? It is possible to read the present text in three different ways according to the punctuation,‡ but the chief issue does not lie here. The essential point of the age-long debate which has been carried on around this text§ concerns the question whether we should see here an affirmation referring to Christ who is thus

---

* Cf. Schrenk, *Th.Wb.NT*, V, p. 376.

† There are two groups each containing three members:

| υἱοθεσία | δόξα | διαθῆκαι |
| νομοθεσία | λατρεία | ἐπαγγελίαι |

It is possible that the words correspond, the first to the fourth, the second to the fifth, the third to the sixth (cf. Michel, p. 196, 3).

‡ According to punctuation we shall read: (1) ... Christ according to the flesh who is God over all blessed for ever; (2) ... Christ according to the flesh. He who is over all, God: may He be blessed for ever! (3) ... Christ according to the flesh who is over all. May God be blessed for ever!

§ "Interpretation more discussed than that of any other NT verse," say Sanday and Headlam who devote to it a long excursus (pp. 233–238).

245

described as God or whether we should read this last part of the verse as a doxology. The following are the reasons which would lead one to understand v. 5c as a dogmatic explanation concerning Christ: it is the normal reading of the text; doxologies are usually closely connected with what precedes: the predicate is placed before the noun in doxologies; "according to the flesh" demands a complement: in a passage which is marked by a note of deep sadness a doxology is quite out of place (cf. Lagrange, p. 227). On the other hand, since the fourth century authors have pointed out that the Christology of Paul was not compatible with an affirmation predicating of Christ that He is "God over all"; the Son is always "subordinated" to the Father;* εὐλογητός is typical of the style of doxologies, and Paul never wrote a doxology on Christ;† a doxology would be normal as the conclusion of such a solemn passage and would accord with the Jewish habit of interrupting the flow of thought by such formulae.

One may well hesitate between these two arguments! Hence some commentators have regarded the whole business as a false problem, due simply to an unfortunate inversion. To clear things up it would suffice to read ὧν ὁ (instead of ὁ ὤν). In that case ὧν is ranked parallel to the two other ὧν of v. 5,‡ and like the others it then introduces the mention of a privilege, and of course the last and greatest; namely, the knowledge of the sovereign God, which it would be surprising not to find mentioned here.§

If we wish to adhere to the traditional text, grammar would favour the first exegesis: 5c refers to Christ. However, the objection based on considerations of Pauline Christology which the supporters of the second exegesis emphasize, has in

---

* Cf. 1 Cor. 11: 3; 15: 25, 28; 2 Cor. 11: 31; Phil. 2: 6. Paul does not think out the question of the relations of the Son to the Father on the ontological plane but on the functional plane (*heilsgeschichtlich*). He does not fathom the mystery of what God or Christ is "in Himself"; He declares what He is "for us".

† Cf. Rom. 1: 25; 11: 36; 2 Cor. 11: 31; Gal. 1: 5; Phil. 4: 20.

‡ ". . . to whom belong the patriarchs, and of their race according to the flesh is Christ; it is their God who is the supreme God, blessed for ever."

§ This conjecture goes back to J. Schlichting, quoted by Wettstein (*ad loc.*). It is adopted by the *Bible du Centenaire*, K. Barth.

fact been given much weight. We may take it into account to some extent by connecting ἐπὶ πάντων to ὁ ὢν and not to Θεός: "(Christ) who is over all, God blessed for ever, Amen" (e.g. Lagrange). This construction, while maintaining the affirmation of the divinity of Christ, avoids all confusion between Christ and God, especially as the absence of an article before Θεός allows us to take this word as indicating an attribute of Christ (He is "of divine nature") and not as implying an identification with God (Michel, p. 198).

By taking these precautions the chief difficulty of the first interpretation is much diminished. We should add that those who defended it in the past intended to make, with regard to the essential divinity of Christ, more categorical affirmations than modern exegesis would care to sustain.

(6–8) When we realize how deeply God committed Himself to Israel, we may well wonder whether His initiatives are not nullified by the present attitude of the elect people. Has His foundation declaration become obsolete?* To answer this question it is enough to come to a clear understanding of what Israel is; the promises were made to Israel, but what constitutes Israel? Is the Israel of the promise constituted by those whom carnal generation has made members of a particular race? That would be making the promise of God dependent on human resources. Now it is the will of God alone which made Israel the heir of the promises; the will and initiatives of man had nothing to do with it. Is proof required? Ishmael, born of the works of Abraham, would be heir of the promise if its beneficiaries sprang from human initiatives. But according to the plan of God, Isaac alone (cf. ἀλλά) is to furnish a posterity to Abraham proper to inherit the promise.†

(9) Thus we see that physical generation which is at man's

* Οὐχ οἷον δὲ =οὐχ ὅτι (λέγω): I am not saying, I do not mean that. . . .

† Κληθήσεται constitutes a play on words; on the one hand it has the Hebrew meaning which it derives from the text of Gen. (21:12) quoted here: to receive a name means to come to exist; on the other hand, it implies the special vocation which makes of a son according to the flesh an heir of the promise.

disposal is not the determining factor; one can be a descendant of Abraham and yet not a "child of God". The opposing formulae "children of the flesh" and "children of the promise" are certainly intended to suggest, in the mind of Paul, the contrasting conditions in which Ishmael and Isaac were conceived. The former owed his birth to the fact that Abraham, by going to Hagar, thought that he might be able to provide for himself, out of his human resources, the son whom God had promised; but when man attempts to handle the promise on his own initiative he substitutes his own works for those of God, he acts as though he were master of the situation, as though it were a question of his own resources in the realization of God's promise. The failure of this attitude shows clearly that God is free and sovereign in face of human behaviour and that He intends to pursue His plan by His own mysterious ways. We have only to think of the essential character of the promise to understand that it must be so. It is in the very nature of a promise that he who makes it should undertake to fulfil it himself: if its realization depended on the beneficiary, there would be no promise at all. In the case under consideration, God said indeed that He Himself would *come*, in order that the promise might be realized (ἐλεύσομαι). Hence the initiatives of man are not decisive, neither originally nor finally. God promises, God fulfils: it is impossible that human behaviour should annul a purpose of which God is the author and the fulfiller.

(10–13) The freedom which characterizes God's pursuit of His purpose, and which man's actions can do nothing to restrict, becomes still more manifest in the case of the children of Isaac. One might in fact counter what the apostle has said about the children of Abraham by the consideration that the preference for Isaac was justified by the fact that his mother was the wife of Abraham and moreover a free woman (cf. Gal. 4: 22); hence historical contingencies and the conduct of the man Abraham did have some influence on the realization of God's plan. But Jacob and Esau have done nothing; they are twins;* from before their birth Jacob is

* Κοίτη: the bed, then the sexual act, the male semen (LXX: Num. 5: 20; Lev. 15: 16, 17, 32; 18: 20; 22: 4: κοίτη σπέρματος). This is the meaning here because of ἐξ ἑνός. 248

chosen as the heir of the promises; he belongs to "the fathers" in virtue of a decision anterior to any action whatsoever on his part, whether good or bad.

Thus the place occupied by any man in the unfolding of those events by which God pursues the revelation of His name and the salvation of mankind, depends on the sole choice of God. If Paul is anxious to show by these examples that God is utterly free in the choice of means, it is certainly not for the purpose of exalting liberty as desirable in itself. God is not arbitrary in His decisions and His liberty of choice is not the same thing as caprice. But God is sovereignly free in face of human circumstances, free because His grace owes nothing to anyone, free to choose as He wills the instruments of His redemptive action. Far from being arbitrary, this divine liberty ensures on the contrary the continuity and permanence of God's plan, the realization of which is thus protected from the caprice of man and his conduct whether good or bad. It will be recalled that the intention of the apostle is to show that no obstacle can thwart the work of compassion which God has begun with Abraham, the theological structure of which has been explained in 8: 28–30.

If we bear well in mind the real theme and purpose of the apostle, we shall understand that these sentences are not at all concerned with the so-called doctrine of predestination. For what is in question here is not the personal salvation of those who are called but their utilization as instruments in a saving process. The choice does not depend on man, because the work which is to be accomplished does not originate with him: the choice depends on the One who calls (ἐκ τοῦ καλοῦντος) because only He who has conceived the design may invite collaboration in its execution. If God did not control the undertaking by choosing freely His collaborators, all would go awry and the divine purpose would not continue (μένῃ). This then is the reason why the plan is realized by free choice of means (ἡ κατ' ἐκλογὴν πρόθεσις). There is no question of the salvation of individuals.* This again is

* Bengel already noted that it is here a question of the *status externus* and not of *statu spirituali*. Similarly many other commentators, e.g. "it is not here a question of their becoming saved, but of their historical position and task in life . . ." Schrenk, *Th.Wb.NT*, IV, p. 184.

249

emphasized incidentally by the phrase borrowed from Genesis 25: 23 indicating that Esau will serve as a slave;* the choice of God destines him in this way, but not for perdition. We should cease to exploit these texts to maintain a doctrine of which Gaugler says that it is not only of frightful cruelty but also exegetically untenable.†

In support of these remarks we should stress the fact that the names mentioned certainly do not connote individuals so much as peoples who are thus named after their eponymous ancestors, according to Old Testament practice. It is best to understand the names in this way, since the argument which they are quoted to support concerns the destiny of Israel as a whole, and not the destiny of the individuals who compose Israel. Paul thinks in terms of collectives.

V. 13 (a quotation from the LXX of Malachi 1: 2) has greatly contributed to the misunderstanding which the official doctrine of predestination has crystallized: it is supposed that because God hated, He spurned and condemned Esau. The text of Malachi shows plainly that it is the descendants of Jacob and Esau who are in question.‡ Again, the contrast of "love: hate" has not in the mind of the Biblical authors the emotional character which we lend to it: love and hate suggest less a contrast between affection and hostility than the concrete attitudes of one who turns to and concerns himself with some particular person, or pays no attention to him. In fact, in the thought of Paul, "love, hate" are virtually synonymous with choosing or leaving aside.§

---

* Oltramare, II, p. 272. Gaugler, II, p. 37.

† Cf. Gaugler, II, p. 36; cf. his even more severe comment, p. 40.

‡ And Bengel adds: "*non omnes Israelitae salvati, nec omnes Edomitae damnati*".

§ In spite of the discredit into which this exegesis has now generally fallen, we think it valid. Μισεῖν (שׂנא) is certainly much more subtle and flexible than the ordinary word "hate". שׂנא means also: to disdain, despise, to abandon (Gen. 29: 31, 33; Deut. 21: 15-17; texts in which French rabbis translate as "délaissé", abandoned; Is. 60: 15, where שׂנא means abandoned and solitary). In the NT μισεῖν implies the same idea: to hate one's life (Lk. 14: 26) means to be detached from it, to turn away from it, to surrender it (cf. Lk. 9: 23: ἀρνεῖσθαι). The opposite, ἀγαπᾶν, offers the same concrete character; often it denotes the fact of doing good to someone rather than any feelings of the heart. To love is to do good, and not to foster fine sentiments. Lk. 6: 27 contrasts

Moreover this sense is the only one that is compatible with the argument of the section as a whole; for if the meaning here were a rejection based on real hatred and a judgment of divine condemnation, the rest of the argument would conflict with such a conception of divine decisions and human destinies. In fact Paul wishes to explain in the first place that God is free to choose for Himself some other people than Israel, whom He at the present time rejects; but he will subsequently show that this liberty is further manifested by the reintegration of Israel in the channels of salvation. Thus the casting out of Israel is not permanent. It serves indirectly but definitely the sole purpose of God, which is the redemption of mankind. Israel will be temporarily rejected as an instrument of salvation, but it will not become the object of a reprobation which would completely exclude it from the sphere of salvation itself.*

"hate" with "doing good". To love justice and hate iniquity (Ps. 45: 7; Hebr. 1: 9) means to practise the one and turn away from the other. In Eph. 5: 29 the opposite of hating one's flesh is caring for it. In Rom. 7: 15 it is characteristic that μισεῖν is opposed to θελεῖν: to will, i.e. willing as relative to action. In Lk. 14: 26 the translator of the word of Jesus has mechanically used μισεῖν; but the translator of Palestinian origin in Matt. 10: 37 has more correctly rendered the exact shade of meaning in the original word by expressing the idea of preference (cf. G. Kittel, *Die Probleme des palästinensischen Judentums*, 1926, p. 54). In his article in *Th.Wb.NT*, Michel discusses at length the meaning which we adopt, but rejects it for Rom. 9: 13 without giving a reason.

* The problems raised by the conciliation of divine sovereignty with human liberty are not broached *ex professo* by the apostle. It is not our business to treat the theme here. However, it is evident that, for the apostle, the defection of Israel was not foreseen, still less willed, by God, since it obliges Him to set aside (momentarily at least) the people of the promise, in spite of all His initiatives towards them, which were, as far as the divine intention was concerned, sufficient to enable Israel to fulfil its vocation as the Messianic people. As far as the future is concerned, it will be noted on the other hand that Paul counts on the jealousy of Israel concerning the Gentiles as the motives which will excite its zeal and bring it to Christ; this consideration presupposes a divine pedagogy which takes fully into account man's liberty and indeed human psychology. The existence of more or less clearly formulated predestinarian doctrines in apocalyptic circles or Jewish sects does not oblige us, as far as our letter is concerned, to attribute similar ideas to Paul. On this subject, see the big art. by Quell and Schrenk on ἐκλέγομαι, ἐκλογή in *Th.Wb.NT*, IV, pp. 147–197, and also the rest of our commentary.

[14]What shall we say then? Is there injustice on God's part? By no means! [15]For he says to Moses, "I will have mercy on whom I have mercy, and I will have compassion on whom I have compassion." [16]So it depends not upon man's will or exertion, but upon God's mercy. [17]For the scripture says to Pharaoh, "I have raised you up for the very purpose of showing my power in you, so that my name may be proclaimed in all the earth." [18]So then he has mercy upon whomever he wills, and he hardens the heart of whomever he wills.

[19]You will say to me then, "Why does he still find fault? For who can resist his will?" [20]But, who are you, a man, to answer back to God? Will what is moulded say to its moulder, "Why have you made me thus?" [21]Has the potter no right over the clay, to make out of the same lump one vessel for beauty and another for menial use? [22]What if God, desiring to show his wrath and to make known his power, has endured with much patience the vessels of wrath made for destruction, [23]in order to make known the riches of his glory for the vessels of mercy, which he has prepared beforehand for glory, [24]even us whom he has called, not from the Jews only but also from the Gentiles? [25]As indeed he says in Hosea,

"Those who were not my people
I will call 'my people,'
and her who was not beloved
I will call 'my beloved.' "
[26]"And in the very place where it was
said to them, 'You are not my
people,'
they will be called 'sons of the living
God.' "
[27]And Isaiah cries out concerning Israel: "Though the number of the sons of Israel be as the sand of the sea, only a remnant of them will be saved, [28]for the Lord will execute his sentence upon the earth with rigor and dispatch." [29]And as Isaiah predicted,
"If the Lord of hosts had not left us children,
we would have fared like Sodom and been made like Gomorrah."

(14–16) This unrestricted liberty of choice recognized to be God's right nevertheless sets a problem from the point of view of men. Why this one and not that one? The impartiality of God appears to be compromised. The implied objection is

252

repudiated and a quotation from Exodus confirms that there is no injustice in God. The quotation is a declaration of Yahweh to Moses after the sad episode of the golden calf. It is clear that the mind of Paul is passing under review the chief phases in the life of Israel: after the patriarchs, Moses. Hence the quotation Ex. 33: 19 must be placed in its historical context. Then the divine word to Moses is seen in its full and true significance. It is true that Yahweh has acted freely, but how did He act after the deplorable infidelity which led to the fabrication of the idol? If His reaction had depended on "man's will or exertion", i.e. on what the Israelites decided and fulfilled in this situation, then Yahweh could only have punished with the greatest severity. Instead of that He gave to this rebellious people a new revelation of His grace and at the same time displayed its basic principle: my mercy is utterly free. It is fortunate indeed that God is entirely free in regard to what men do! Seen in the light of its historical context the quotation well answers the question asked (contrary to Michel).

(17f. Thus the rebellion of Israel did not have the effect of revoking the election. Neither did the refusal of Pharaoh frustrate the purpose of God to form for Himself a people under the leadership of Moses. God made use of Pharaoh's refusal in order to continue His work of mercy. And this shows, once again, that these saving events depend neither on man's will nor on his exertion (cf. the γάρ).*

Moses and Pharaoh are individuals but their entry on the scene does not change the point of view. They are both considered in the light of their function, not as individual personalities; they are treated as leaders of peoples, not as believers or unbelievers.

Here it is the word σκληρύνει which has caused misunderstanding. The word has been taken to convey the idea that God rejects whom He wills and so hardens the heart of the rejected that the divine word can find no welcome or re-

* In order to emphasize the action of God, Paul writes twice ὅπως (LXX ἵνα . . . ὅπως). Instead of: "You have been preserved . . ." he writes: "I have raised you up."

253

sponse in it. Things are not quite so simple.* In reality, in the thought of the prophets, hardening appears as the reaction of God to an already existing hardness of heart in the people of Israel; God confirms and seals a situation which He has not created; hardening is a judgment of God on sin. In regard to Pharaoh, the situation is only apparently different;† the Egyptian did not know the God of Israel; it was not the knowledge of God that was proposed to him and it is not that which he refuses. Nevertheless the circumstances created by the redemptive action of God bring into light the inner situation of this man; in hardening his heart God punishes his sinful state which is already presupposed. The hardening of heart is not therefore the effect of an arbitrary decision which God takes to exclude any man from the possibility of salvation. It is a way of suggesting the indisputable fact that God plunges the sinner deeper into his sin when He offers His grace and it is refused.‡ The same is true of the word addressed by Moses to Pharaoh as of the word which he addresses to the people, in both cases a word declaratory of the will of God; by reporting to Israel the words of Yahweh, Moses obliges the people to choose and thus the secret thought of the heart of the people is revealed. The apostle assigns to the law the same function. As the word of God it is given that sin may abound; not that it instigates to evil, but because it makes evil clearly apparent (cf. 2 Cor. 2: 16).§

* They are not so simple even in the texts themselves, taking the latter as they stand, since the hardening of Pharaoh is attributed sometimes to Yahweh (Ex. 4: 21; 7: 3; 9: 12; 10: 1, 20, 27; 11: 10) sometimes to Pharaoh himself (Ex. 7: 14, 22; 8: 15, 19, 32; 9: 7). On the critical problems involved, see Franz Hesse, "Das Verstockungsproblem im A.T.", *B.Z.A.W.*, 1955, p. 74.

† *Antwort, Reaktion Gottes auf menschliche Schuld . . . Gerichtswalten Gottes*, F. Hesse, *op. cit.* p. 55. See also on 11: 7–9.

‡ See also 11: 7.

§ In face of man's rejection of His word, God could react by putting into operation the supreme sanction, namely the death of the guilty. Genesis says, in metaphorical and mythical language, that God chose a different solution: He punishes man's hardness of heart by imprisoning him within his refusal. This does not mean that the imprisonment lasts for ever! On the contrary, it is a reprieve intended to afford the pedagogic action of God as Saviour all necessary scope. Henceforth God patiently endures man as sinner, but solely in order to lead man to

(19f.) After the question of justice comes that of coercion and the attendant problem of responsibility. Can God fulfil His purposes without imposing on His human instruments roles which they did not freely choose? If this be so, can we still speak of responsibility? In that case, what becomes of the judgment of God? The apostle's reply does not consist in imposing silence on the objector by saying to him: "Who are you? You are meddling in matters beyond your understanding!" Instead he wishes to bring his reader to frame the question in its true context. If man presumes to dispute with God, he must at least try to share God's angle of vision, if he can, which is another matter. God's providential government must not be judged by the limited views of man. To help his readers to adjust their field of vision, Paul proposes that they should consider the parable of the potter.

At first sight the comparison hardly seems just and adequate, for the clay is inert and unconscious in the hands of the moulder. How can it illustrate the situation of man? Hence it is important to note that the comparison is not concerned with the nature of the terms compared, but with the functions to which the material is destined. "Why have you made me thus?" does not mean: "Why am I clay?", but, "Why am I such and such a particular vase?" The potter does not create the clay, he moulds it and adapts it to the various uses he has in view (Godet, p. 284). The thought of Paul is certainly influenced by his memory of the prophet's use of the theme (Is. 29: 16; 45: 9).* It has also been thought that the apostle was alluding to the creation of man from the

---

repentance. Hardening constitutes a blocking of the situation as a result of which the final sanction is not applied, so that the sinner may have opportunities of repentance during the season in which God exercises forbearance towards him (cf. 2: 4; 9: 22). This is a very important truth for the consideration of God's government of history; Paul has applied it to the Gentiles in 2: 4; he insinuates it with regard to the Jews in 9: 22. He will express it again in 11: 7, which should be understood in the light of what follows: the Jews are hardened with a view to their ultimate salvation, so that the conditions for their "jealousy" may be prepared (11: 25).

* Cf. Is. 64: 8; Job 10: 9; 33: 6; Sir. 33: 13; Wis. 15: 7. Strack-Billerbeck, III, p. 271. The Wisdom text speaks of man's making of idols, not of God's liberty in the choice of His instruments.

loam of the earth, Gen. 2: 7 (Michel): but it is not here a question of God the Creator but of God as Providence. The image of the potter illustrates the freedom with which God exploits the material given, such as it is: God has conceived a plan and proceeds to execute it. If we wish to understand what He is doing, we must know what He is aiming at.

(21) Thus of the same lump from which we see him make little balls thrown forcefully on to the turning plate, he makes sometimes vessels intended for noble uses, sometimes vessels which will serve menial uses. A very old type of exegesis considers that what is here illustrated is the fact that God destines certain men to places of honour in His Kingdom, and others to perdition; from the same human clay He makes the elect and the damned (Augustine; Calvin). The defect of this interpretation is that it applies the doctrine of the transcendent freedom of God to a point which is not being discussed in this chapter, namely, election to personal salvation.* The prophet himself did not use the comparison for this purpose. The work of the potter furnishes a good illustration of the liberty which a man uses in adapting his methods and processes to the ends he is pursuing. The potter has to satisfy the varying needs of his customers; he does not act arbitrarily in making vessels adapted to different uses. What may appear to be caprice springs on the contrary from a guiding thought and purpose, which fully justifies what he does. We must rise to the height of such a new point of view in order to discover the coherence of actions which are apparently contradictory. The reference to the text Is. 45: 9–13 was well apposite here. The Lord chose Cyrus for the

* It has also the defect of allegorizing too much. It wrongly interprets the expressions εἰς τιμήν and εἰς ἀτιμίαν; these formulae apply solely to the use of the vessels, without implying any judgment of value; those vessels intended for menial purposes are often more useful than the others; there is nothing in common between the idea of a vessel intended for a menial purpose and one intended to be destroyed. The ideas expressed in vv. 21 and 22 are wrongly repudiated because of this confusion between the menial use of the vessel and the idea of reprobation. The potter does not make ordinary vessels only to destroy them! He makes them in order that they may be used. In this sense, A. Feuillet, *art. cit.* p. 496, or Stählin, *Th.Wb.NT*, V, p. 426.

fulfilment of His purposes; the means chosen may have been surprising but must be interpreted in the light of the whole scope of God's work of mercy; this ignoble vessel proved in fact to be very useful.*

(22) The potter's work had supplied the prophet Jeremiah with a different illustration (Jer. 18: 1–10). It here happens that the mould of the clay disappoints the expectations of the potter. Instead of our seeing instantly emerge from the hands of the skilful workman vessels of many forms intended for various purposes, the half-moulded material begins to spoil and the form collapses. Then the potter throws away the abortive sketch and carries on with his work using a different material. Israel, said Jeremiah, was like this refractory material in the hands of the workman; Yahweh repents of the good which He had proposed to do for it.

Paul now thinks of this aspect of the work of the potter which illustrates so well one of the points of his thought. Israel has disappointed God's hopes. Is Israel like the clay snatched away from the plate and cast aside? Oh no, it is not thus that God acts in regard to Israel. The comparison with the potter now shows itself to be no longer adequate: God exercises a patience which has no parallel in the potter's craft.† The introduction of the theme of God's patience, the importance of which we have seen from 2: 4, bursts the framework of the comparison. God shows a patience the aim of which Paul has already suggested: instead of destroying

* The case of Cyrus is of particular interest in connexion with the problem raised by the text. Opposing the exegesis which we here adopt, Michel, p. 209, says that it is impossible to distinguish between the historical part which God allots to a man and the eternal plan concerning him. Yet Cyrus is God's instrument, without there being any question of reckoning him among the elect. His case shows that the advocates of a predestinarian interpretation entertain too human an idea of the resources at God's disposal; they confine God to a dilemma which is valid for us, but not for Him.

† It is the consideration of the facts which leads Paul to introduce the theme of patience; for the history of Israel is to be explained only by the patience of God. The thought of Paul has now freed itself from the image of the potter; it has returned to the facts; hence the use of the historic tenses which resume the thread of v. 17, beyond those verses cast in the present tense (Zahn).

R   257

the guilty,* God wishes to bring him to repentance and salvation; such is the guiding plan of His providential action. God does not cast away as rubbish the refractory clay; His patience tolerates "vessels of wrath" which however are ripe for destruction.† For human clay is after all not quite the same as the material moulded by the potter. Man is capable of repentance. The "vessels of wrath" may become "vessels of mercy", just as the "sons of the kingdom" (Matt. 8: 12) may become "children of hell" (Matt. 23: 15). If Paul himself wrote Ephesians 2: 3 he declared that the believers of today were yesterday "by nature children of wrath".‡ Hence there is no rigid predestination to perdition for the "vessels of wrath". Their call remains, and the patience of God tolerates them in the hope that they will some time commit themselves to the way of repentance. It is clear that the apostle is alluding to the destiny of Israel as in 2: 4.

* Θέλων may be regarded as implying a concession: "although God wished . . ." or a cause: "because God wished. . . ." If we desire to stress the introduction of the new theme of patience it is the former interpretation which is preferable.

† The verb καταρτίζω means: to put an object in order, in such a condition that it may be used for its intrinsic end; to give it a certain perfection: cf. 1 Th. 3: 10; 2 Cor. 13: 11; Hebr. 13: 21; 1 Cor. 1: 10; 1 Pet. 5: 10; Lk. 6: 40; Hebr. 10: 5; 11: 3. It will be noted that the word is in the perfect (κατηρτισμένα). If it is translated "prepared for perdition" the suggestion is that someone has prepared them; and as this agent can be none other than God, the translation implies that God destines these vessels to wrath and has prepared them for this end. The perfect suggests rather that a certain state has been reached—not that an action has been accomplished. The vessels are in a certain condition which makes them ripe for destruction. Paul was familiar with προκαταρτίζω (2 Cor. 9: 5); but he does not use it here in order to avoid the suggestion of a previous divine causality. It is not God who has in advance disposed the vessels for the end of destruction (Gaugler); but the vessels are there and their condition is such that they are fit for destruction. Moreover we should note the subtle complexities of thought which Paul has introduced into his text. Of some, Paul says that they are "quite ready" for destruction, but he does not say that they perish; the patience of God will in fact prevent their destruction. Of others (v. 23) he says that "God has prepared them beforehand for glory", which discloses a divine causality (Lyonnet, p. 104). When creatures attain glory, that is the work of God; but when they move towards destruction, it is their own doing.

‡ Cf. Stählin, Th.Wb.NT, V, p. 436.

Finally we may understand how the patience of God in bearing with the rebellious does at the same time manifest His wrath and power if we think of the case of "hardening of heart" and in a more general way of the consequences brought about by the sinner's refusal of God. The "wrath" of God suggests His reaction of condemnation with regard to sin, and His "power" executes this judgment. Pharaoh is hardened as, in the myth of Genesis, man is subjected to divine sanctions. The patience of God is shown through this process of redemptive chastisement, for thus God does not destroy the guilty in one overwhelming punishment, but sustains his existence in the prospect of his one day repenting. Divine wrath, sanction, and patience are fully compatible in the thought of the apostle and constitute the structure of God's providence.

(23f.) In almost all the manuscripts the sequence is now broken; v. 23 does not follow on from v. 22.* We may understand the argument thus: if God has used patience, it was not only because He wished to allow Israel time for repentance, but also in order to show His mercy towards us. Patience, as we have seen, includes also a note of judgment; it is exercised with a view to ultimate grace, but the restoration is distant. Now God would not tolerate the excessive delay which the disobedience of Israel imposed on the fulfilment of His design. Hence He called men, who, according to His first plan, should have been called only at a much later date. The call of the Gentiles shows the richness of God's glory, that is, the wealth of His purposes. The "vessels of mercy" are its objects; they are "vessels of mercy" because God intends them to share the glory which He bestows upon His elect people: προητοίμασεν, *He has prepared*, refers to the plan of God and not to its execution (cf. 8: 30). The declaration that God calls not only Jews but Gentiles implies at once that the traditional distinctions are now obsolete. There no longer confront each other on the one hand the elect people and on the other hand the Gentiles. But we have on one side those whom the patience of God tolerates and on the

* *Kaí* has been omitted at the beginning of v. 23 in P 46 B 69 vg. Or. This reading has been adopted by S. Lyonnet.

other those of whom His call has made "vessels of mercy". Ἐκάλεσεν, *He has called*, should be connected with τοῖς κλητοῖς, *the elect*, and with ἐκάλεσεν of ch. 8: 28, and 30. God realizes His purpose of mercy by His call, of which preaching is the primary instrument (ch. 10: 14–18).

(25f.) In fact this means that the "vessels of mercy" have become "vessels of wrath"; they are placed under the dispensation of the divine patience (cf. 4th note, p. 254). Anyone who knows the Old Testament prophecies will not be shocked at this: in Hosea God declared that He was not bound to one people and that He was free to choose whom He would. In the first quotation Paul substitutes καλέσω for ἐρῶ (LXX) because he divests the personal names of their symbolic significance.* The second quotation (2: 1) should not be too closely pressed. Paul is not concerned to know the exact spot in which the Gentile world will receive its call; it is the fact which matters to him; God calls the Gentiles where they are to be found.†

(27–29) The rejection of Israel is no less attested by scripture than the call of the Gentiles. The first oracle of Isaiah quoted emphasizes the contrast between the multitude of the people called by God and the quite small number of those who will effectually share in salvation.‡ Now we are here

---

* Paul makes a very free use of the text of Hosea. It is right to note that the prophet was speaking, not of the heathen, but of the ten tribes which most certainly belonged to Israel (cf. 1 Pet. 2: 10)! Paul must have thought that, the inhabitants of the north having fallen into real paganism, a promise valid for them was clearly valid for the Gentiles also. Given similar situations, God may be expected to act in a similar way.

† Exegetes have experienced an almost insurmountable difficulty with regard to this localization. J. Munck, *op. cit.* p. 301, thinks that Paul's move in bringing the collection to Jerusalem will permit him to proclaim, in the holy city of an apostate people, the accession of the Gentiles to the status of a people who are sons of God.

‡ The text (Is. 10: 22) has been slightly modified. Moreover, while the prophet was thinking of those who would escape the disaster brought about by Sennacherib, Paul is thinking of those who will escape perdition. Is this type of transference to be condemned? The acts of God in history realize, in varied conditions, one and the same will to salvation or condemnation; it may be said that what is true of one situation will

faced by a sentence of God (cf. v. 28). God can call or reject whomsoever He wishes; neither the unworthiness of the former nor the grace already granted to the latter prevent Him from doing so.* It is the consequence of His mercy if a remnant, a shoot, a posterity (σπέρμα) subsists (v. 29); God might indeed have struck down and destroyed as He did in the case of Sodom and Gomorrah, of which nothing remained. All this goes to show that in using His freedom, God at the same time manifests His grace; He sets aside the rebellious, but not to reduce them to nothing. His grace is the ultimate foundation and justification of His judgments.

³⁰What shall we say, then? That Gentiles who did not pursue righteousness have attained it, that is, righteousness through faith; ³¹but that Israel who pursued the righteousness which is based on law did not succeed in fulfilling that law. ³²Why? Because they did not pursue it through faith, but as if it were based on works. They have stumbled over the stumbling stone, ³³as it is written,

"Behold I am laying in Zion a stone that will make men stumble,
a rock that will make them fall; and he who believes in him will not be put to shame."

(30–33) Paul's reflections so far have remained on the plane of abstract doctrine; no allusion has been made to the responsibilities which the apostle's contemporaries might have had in the concrete decisions of divine providence in regard to the Gentiles and Israel. But the question inevitably arises whether the rejection of Israel was the chastisement for some grave disloyalty to Moses. Similarly one might ask whether the call of the Gentiles was the result of a more consistent obedience to the law.†

be true of another, which is yet different owing to historical contingencies. Already the LXX had interpreted by writing "will be saved" instead of "will return to the land".

* V. 28: literally "for, by way of completing and cutting short, the Lord will execute His word on earth" (LXX abbreviated); i.e. fulfilling and accomplishing His word, and without wasting time in vain words or vacillation. Or else: He accomplishes His word (relatively to the faithful remnant) and He shortens it in its execution, by cutting out something (relatively to the rejected mass).

† V. 31 may be understood in two ways: (1) Israel tried to obey the

Paul returns at once to the paradox of the righteousness which is attained through faith. The pagan world did not seek righteousness, for they were ignorant of the law, and this ignorance protected them from the difficulty to which Israel succumbed: that is, the bad use of the law, which degenerated into a mere pretext to establish merit and to win righteousness, i.e. a favourable judgment from God by means of works. The words describing the condition of the Gentiles evoke the image of a race (διώκοντα); of course quite intentionally, for the central idea is thus well thrown into relief: it is not the effort of the Gentiles which has gained for them their present favourable position, whilst it is the presumption of Israel to obtain security through its meritorious effort which has deposed it from its original vocation. Those who have taken much trouble have failed. Paul will soon speak of an unintelligent zeal. Abraham inactive (cf. 4: 5) was in a better position to succeed than Abraham "pursuing" Hagar!

Extending the metaphor of the race, Paul now suggests the image of the stone against which the athlete stumbles and which overthrows him, thus snatching the victory from his hands. Israel thus stumbled when Christ, "the end of the law" (10: 4), came: Israel neither understood nor believed that the promise was being fulfilled thus, to the confusion of those who trusted in their virtues.* Once again it was proved that the ways of divine grace produced a catalytic effect. The people of Israel were living in a state of obedience which they thought to be in conformity to the will of God. But when God made an unambiguous declaration of His will, the compromises which satisfied Israel were necessarily dispelled. In fact, however, the people of Israel preferred to repudiate the true and vital obedience of faith, for which God offered them

law which led to righteousness, but did not attain her goal which was the law. (2) Israel regulated her conduct according to the principle (νόμον, cf. 3: 27; 7: 21; 8: 2) of the pursuit of righteousness, but did not attain her goal which was righteousness (in this case εἰς νόμον would be incorrect; εἰς δικαιοσύνην would have been better: Paul may have written εἰς νόμον in order to balance his sentence). Some MSS. have completed in this way: εἰς νόμον δικαιοσύνης.

* Ὡς ἐξ ἔργων: "as though it were possible to attain righteousness by means of works"; ὡς stresses the contrast between the true way, viz. faith, and the false way, viz. works.

the opportunity in Jesus Christ. Thus was fulfilled God's intention to extricate the plan of His self-revelation from the impasse where Israel had blocked it through its vain pursuit of legalistic righteousness. Certainly some stumbled. But however numerous they were, that was better than the frustration of all. The path of true righteousness was now accessible.* Thus, without naming Him, Paul here implies the advent of the Messiah Jesus. His readers must have recognized the echo of the thoughts expressed in Mk. 12: 10; Matt. 21: 42; Lk. 20: 17 (cf. 1 Pet. 2: 7; Acts. 4: 11). Perhaps we should see, in the positive emphasis of v. 33b, the foreshadowing of ch. 11: the same stone which overthrew Israel will become the foundation stone of its rebuilding.†

* Paul combines Is. 28: 16 and 8: 14 which he cited according to the LXX. In Hebrew Is. 28: 16 is very obscure. Judaism already was interpreting this passage in a Messianic sense.

† Cf. W. Vischer, "Étude biblique sur Rom. 9–11", in *Deuxième Cahier d'études juives, Foi et Vie*, 1948, p. 118.

¹Brethren, my heart's desire and prayer to God for them is that they may be saved. ²I bear them witness that they have a zeal for God, but it is not enlightened. ³For, being ignorant of the righteousness that comes from God, and seeking to establish their own, they did not submit to God's righteousness. ⁴For Christ is the end of the law, that every one who has faith may be justified.

(1) No JEW COULD write what Paul has just written without his heart bleeding. The thought of this shattered destiny—and who knows for how long!—inclined the soul to prayer. No one could be resigned to the exclusion of Israel from the salvation of which it had been the first herald. Hence Paul nourishes the hope that Israel will be guided to recover its position. The prayer which rises from his heart to God commits this hope to divine grace. It will be recognized that this inner attitude of soul is not compatible with a predestinarian interpretation of ch. 9. Determinism would automatically exclude such a prayer (Vischer).* Paul would willingly have sacrificed himself for his brethren (cf. 9: 3). Prayer does not take the place of sacrifice, but its necessity is so much the more urgent when nothing else can be done.

(2–4) The severity with which Paul denounces the theological errors of his people neither weakens his profound attachment to them nor does it cloud his judgment. No one knows better than the apostle himself how passionate and sincere can be the zeal of the Jew, but also how blind to the revealed truth of God.† Zeal implies a certain psychological

* Εὐδοκία: will, desire, disposition of the heart. Cf. Phil. 1: 15.
† Cf. Gal. 1: 14; Phil. 3: 6; Acts 21: 20; 22: 3.

state, but it is not valuable in itself; sincerity is not enough, and does not of itself establish the truth. Israel is full of religious zeal, but alas! it is unenlightened; it uses the law in a misguided way, imagining that God has given the law to enable sinful man in some way to deserve grace. This is tantamount to seeking to establish one's own righteousness.

Now the law should be understood in the light of the promise. Paul has already shown what this means: the law is an instrument of the promise, for it should convince man that God alone can give what He has declared it His intention to give. It was necessary to "submit" rather than strain one's energies; there is a complete contrast between those who use every effort (ζητοῦντες, seeking) in their aspiration to secure a righteousness of their own, and the submission (ὑπετάγησαν, they submit) of those who wait trustfully to receive the gratuitous gift of God.* Only an attitude of submission to the word of the divine promise—an attitude of which Abraham had furnished the pattern—could lead to righteousness, that is, to grace. In saying that his Israelite brethren did not submit to righteousness because they were ignorant of the righteousness of God, Paul is certainly not committing a tautology, and this explains why v. 4 begins with a γάρ, for, which makes the mention of Christ, the end of the law, the beginning of this v. 3c. "They did not submit to God's righteousness" is in fact a clarifying addition to v. 3a and 3b; for it shows that the consequence of the Israelites' ignorance of God's righteousness, and of their search for their own, is that they did not recognize (when He came) Him who is the embodiment of God's righteousness, and that therefore they did not submit to Him.

If the second mention of God's righteousness here denotes Jesus Christ, whom Israel failed to recognize in submission as its Saviour, then the verb ὑπετάγησαν is more understandable and the explanation given in v. 4 becomes clear. Since they did not understand the nature of the divine righteousness to which the Old Testament bore witness, they

* Ἡ δικαιοσύνη τοῦ Θεοῦ denotes here again the saving initiatives of God, among which the law was to be counted (. . . *de salvifica Dei activitate*, S. Lyonnet, "De Justitia Dei in Epistula ad Romanos 1 : 17 et 3 : 21–22", *Verbum Domini*, vol. 25, p. 118). See commentary on 1 : 17.

were not able to understand either how that righteousness was a preparation for the gospel of Jesus Christ, nor how Jesus Christ brought the law to its culminating point and at the same time suspended it. Christ is the end of the law because the law attests faith as the way to true righteousness; this has been clearly seen in the case of Abraham. Thus Christ fulfils the underlying intention of the law and supersedes it.*

⁵Moses writes that the man who practises the righteousness which is based on the law shall live by it. ⁶But the righteousness based on faith says, Do not say in your heart, "Who will ascend into heaven?" (that is, to bring Christ down) ⁷or "Who will descend into the abyss?" (that is, to bring Christ up from the dead). ⁸But what does it say? The word is near you, on your lips and in your heart (that is, the word of faith which we preach); ⁹because, if you confess with your lips that Jesus is Lord and believe in your heart that God raised him from the dead, you will be saved. ¹⁰For man believes with his heart and so is justified, and he confesses with his lips and so is saved. ¹¹The scripture says, "No one who believes in him will be put to shame." ¹²For there is no distinction between Jew and Greek; the same Lord is Lord of all and bestows his riches upon all who call upon him. ¹³For, "every one who calls upon the name of the Lord will be saved."

¹⁴But how are men to call upon him in whom they have not believed? And how are they to believe in him of whom they have never heard? And how are they to hear without a preacher? ¹⁵And how can men preach unless they are sent? As it is written, "How beautiful are the feet of those who preach good news!"

* "Christ is the end of the law" may be understood; He is the end, the culmination of the law, revealing its true purpose—or else: He is the term of the process of the law, and abolishes it. These two interpretations are not mutually exclusive: Christ puts an end to the law because the law finds in Him its goal and crown. We may point out that K. Barth, *Kirchl. Dogmatik*, II, 2, p. 269, interprets τέλος νόμου in the light of כְּלָל =ἀνακεφαλαίωσις: sum, total, recapitulation. Judaism does not appear to have officially believed that the Messiah would put an end to the law; however, it was thought that circumstances might lead Israel to declare certain parts of the law inapplicable (cf. Strack-Billerbeck, I, p. 247; III, p. 277). Gaugler, 11, p. 100–118 devotes a long passage to a discussion of the general problems arising from the use of the law in a Christian dispensation.

(5) The law itself confirms what has just been stated, for Moses certainly considered that a complete accomplishment of the law would lead to righteousness.* The law is holy; and it could not be claimed without blasphemy that total obedience to it would have no relevance. Otherwise it would have to be assumed that God—or Moses—deceived Israel.

We should not try to diminish the force of the statement that righteousness can be obtained by the law, according to the text of Leviticus (18: 5) which Paul quotes. The apostle's argument requires that the possibility of the achievement of righteousness through the law should be maintained as an open possibility. Nor does this affirmation contradict the other theses of the apostle. If the law is to play the part which Paul has already assigned to it (the awareness of and multiplication of sin) that is precisely because the law by its nature demands obedience. For it is in endeavouring to practise such obedience that the sinner will discover his powerlessness. This discovery shows the sinner that, through his own fault, he cannot use the law as a means to the attainment of righteousness; it does not prove that it is contrary to the nature of the law to be used for this purpose. The real mistake of the Jews was that they did not take the law sufficiently seriously, rather than that they took it seriously; they drew up a balance sheet showing their failings and their merits, and recording their credit. They counted on the positive achievements partially to compensate their failures, and trusted in the indulgence of God, at times, to overlook any debit balance. Thus in a twofold way they failed to take the law, i.e. the will of God, with sufficient seriousness. They behaved as though acts of positive obedience could by a law of compensation neutralize the evil of acts of positive disobedience, and again as though to trust in the grace of God meant to hope for divine indifference with regard to sin. Had the Jews taken quite seriously the word of Deuteronomy which Paul quotes, they would have reasoned differently, for this word means that he who does not fulfil the law will be condemned in the name of the law (Deut. 27: 26; quoted Gal. 3: 10). The Jews were unwilling to reckon with the

* Paul further cites with the same intention Deut. 27: 26 in Gal. 3: 10 —P 46 B G K C P give a harmonizing reading which is to be rejected.

possibility that their obedience to the law might terminate in bankruptcy and condemnation.*

(6f.) The exegetical argument which Paul uses here has often caused surprise. Bengel calls it *suavissima parodia*. The fact is indeed that at first sight it may well surprise us. Paul quotes texts of Deuteronomy (9: 4; 30: 12–13) the second of which at least was meant to convince the Israelites of their duty to obey the law, by basing this obligation on the fact that the publication of the law made it known to all. Paul appears to wrest this text from its true significance, since he uses it as a testimony to the righteousness obtainable by faith, independently of the works of the law which the text had properly in view. On close examination the matter seems still more complex. Firstly the quotation from Deut. 9: 4 or 8: 17 introduces in that book a declaration which the apostle must have remembered when he cited its beginning: "Do not say in your heart, 'it is because of my righteousness† that the Lord has brought me in to possess this land'," or in 8: 17: "My power and the might of my hand have gotten me this wealth." In writing the words which he here borrows from Deuteronomy Paul knows that they revolve around a thought which is completely in conformity with the doctrine of "justification by faith", which consists essentially in not claiming

* F. Godet (II, p. 328), embarrassed by the affirmation that the law can lead to righteousness, dilutes the meaning of this declaration. Lev. 18: 5, speaking of the fulfilment of the law, would include in that the whole system of ritual practices the purpose of which was to secure forgiveness (with or without sacrifice); to fulfil the law meant not simply to obey by actions more or less meritorious, but also to confess one's sin and to ask God's forgiveness for it according to His prescriptions. Hence, on this view, law included grace and in itself implied grace. Thus Paul did not recognize the principle of a legalistic righteousness. This interpretation seems to blunt the point of the Pauline argument. However true Godet's observation may be—and its truth is confirmed by the use which Paul makes of doctrines of sacrifice in his attempt to grasp the meaning of the death of Jesus—it does not fit in with our passage. As the succeeding verses will show, Paul wished to suggest in the first place the impossibility of satisfying the requirements of the law, in order to oppose to it the new possibilities which God has opened up in Jesus Christ.

† The presence of this word must be emphasized. The rabbis and Dhorme translate by: my merit.

before God a "righteousness of one's own" (v. 3); in other words, in not trusting to the power and might of one's hand.

The second quotation is borrowed from Deut. 30: 12–13, where we must understand the true implications of the text if we are not to feel surprise at the use which Paul makes of it. Moses says to Israel: "You know the commandment; God has revealed it to you; God has drawn near to you to point out to you the way of obedience; consider what He has done and listen to Him when He speaks. His revealing grace has forestalled you in all your ways and doings, and underlies all your efforts; you are not expected to be a race of supermen, to scale the heavens or to descend into the deeps; but you are called to receive, in humble and well disposed hearts, the word of His grace which has come to you in the shape of the law which I have made known to you." This is the meaning which Paul finds in the words of Moses to the people, not by distorting their true meaning but by interpreting them in the light of the idea that the gift of the law is in itself a manifestation of the grace of God.

There was thus no further difficulty in relating all this to the new situation created by the coming of Christ. Let us not forget that Paul has just called Christ τέλος νόμου, *the end of the law.* God reveals His will to Israel by the ministry of Moses who begins the work which Christ completes, fulfilling it and superseding it at the same time. If that be so, the same exhortation can today be addressed to those who see in Christ the revelation of the will of God and the supreme manifestation of divine grace. Just as Moses had disclosed the will of God, so that it was not necessary to scale the heavens, so Christ has come down from heaven to bring to men a fully accessible revelation. The same applies to the second image borrowed from Deuteronomy: as it was not necessary for the Israelite to descend into the abyss to know the will of God, neither was it for the believer, for Christ rose again from the abode of the dead in order to give a striking manifestation of that holy will. We may not even say that Paul has used improperly these Deuteronomic images, although he has endowed them with new meaning: "to climb the heavens" and to "descend into the deep" were used in current speech in order to suggest something impossible.* The Moses of Deuteronomy obviously did not think literally of an ascent into the heavens or a descent into Hades. But in the thought of the Deuteronomic writer these images were intended to illustrate the idea that the exertions and the searches of man had been rendered useless by the initiative of God. Was it not legitimate for Paul to connect them with events which constitute the two essential ways of man's search for God?

The fact that in both cases it is a question of descent and ascent is of no significance compared with the deep meaning which Paul has brought out in his use of Moses' words. The force of the argument does not lie in these two plays on words, which because of their artificial character strike us on a first reading, and so much the more so because we do not normally use such images. But this is not what constitutes the true axis of the argument. Paul has recognized the real bearing of the Deuteronomic text, whereas his modern detractors have failed to see it. This then is the message of righteousness based on faith, that is, this is how the believer speaks who does not try to trust in his own strength and who does not imagine that he is saved because of his own righteousness. In theory the law is indeed a way of righteousness; if anyone fulfilled it he would live thereby; but is it within the reach of our human strength and resources? To believe that would mean being mistaken, not about the law, but about ourselves. We are mistaken about the law if it arouses in us a feeling of pride in our own righteousness. It represents an initiative of divine grace which thus enlightens us with regard to our own weakness, and is intended to help us by inclining us to humility. It is the effect of the love of God of which the coming of Christ and the resurrection of Christ give us the full measure and reality.

(8f.) The revelation of the will of God to Moses has made known the divine commandment: the law could then play its part. It is the same and in a supreme degree with the coming of Christ. The rest of the text of Deuteronomy thus found

* Cf. Lietzmann, p. 96, Strack-Billerbeck, III, p. 281. One might compare the expression used by Jesus, "move mountains", to indicate the strength of one who does the seemingly impossible. Cf. *ibid.*, I, p. 759.

its full and true scope in Paul's line of argument. For Christ came to earth so that man in his lostness and distance from God might be reached; so that the word of the gospel, "the word of Christ" (v. 17) should strike him and penetrate his very being. It is not now the word of Moses, revealing the law. It is "the word of faith which we preach".* This word is both a word which communicates the object of faith and invites the hearer to have faith; the word which Christ charged His disciples to proclaim in His name and which at the same time communicates His presence: it is the word which constitutes the preaching of the Word.

Reading in the Book of Deuteronomy the distinction between the heart and the mouth, Paul sees here an implication which he retains and makes use of. While it is the lips which utter the word, it is the heart which gives it meaning and weight. There can be no question of detaching the one from the other; the mouth speaks out of the abundance of the heart (Matt. 12: 34; Lk. 6: 45); it expresses the heart's obedience. It should however be noted that Paul mentions the "Lord Jesus" as being the contents of oral confession. Now it seems quite clear that for first-century Christianity the confession of the faith consisted essentially in this very declaration: "Jesus is Lord" (1 Cor. 12: 3).† Since confession of faith is essentially a matter of speaking words in the presence of others, it is natural that Paul should connect it with the lips. The word which distinguished the Christian from the Jew or the Greek was: "Jesus is Lord". If Jesus is Lord it is that God has exalted Him to His own right hand by the resurrection (cf. Phil. 2: 11). Lordship and resurrection are inseparable. It is the resurrection faith which provides the basis for the confession of Christ's Lordship.‡

* Τὸ ῥῆμα τῆς πίστεως is a phrase formed on the model of Deut. 30: 14.

† Acts 2: 36 reports a confession of this type. 1 Cor. 16: 22 suggests the liturgical usage of the word κύριος. On this term cf. Lietzmann, pp. 97–101; Foerster, *Th.Wb.NT*, III, pp. 1081–1098. Cf. O. Cullmann, *Les premières confessions de foi chrétiennes*, 1948. (E.T. *The Earliest Christian Confessions of Faith.*)

‡ In speaking of the confession of the Lord, Paul is perhaps thinking of the confession made by the baptized; the connexion with salvation (σωθήσῃ) recalls the baptismal promise of Mk. 16: 16. Several exegetes establish a relation between the two indications about Christ in vv. 6b

271

(10f.) Handling independently his Deuteronomic quotation, Paul in summing the matter up returns to the normal order according to which faith precedes oral confession. He had said (v. 3) that Israel did not submit to the righteousness of God which God had already revealed by Moses. Now it has been brought within the reach of all, for the preaching of Jesus as Lord has gone forth: it is sufficient to believe and confess.

Belief and confession are here clarified. Faith is bound up with "righteousness". From the analysis of the position of Abraham, the reader of Paul knows that faith is the avenue to "righteousness", because faith is the attitude of a person who opens himself to the power of the God who raises the dead (cf. 4: 17, 25b). The confession of the faith is the path to salvation, which must be understood here as final eschatological salvation; credal confession implies the fidelity of the believer in face of the hostile world in which he lives; since he is not ashamed of his Lord in the face of men, he will be acknowledged by his Lord in the face of God.* Scripture attests that the believer is not confounded when he trusts in the Lord (Is. 28: 16, already quoted in 9: 33). Paul adds to the text of the prophet an affirmation of universality ($\pi\hat{a}\varsigma$) which introduces his last remark.

(12f.) In fact all, whoever they may be, must renounce all claim to their own righteousness, for God has established the Christ as Lord of all equally and as the Giver of all good. All must call upon Him as their Saviour and their Lord. The oracle of the prophet Joel referred to the great Day of the Lord when the ultimate purposes of God will be realized (Joel 2: 32). By quoting him Paul seems to suggest that the eschatological design of God is fulfilled in Christ who is Israel's last chance. This application to Christ of what had been said of Yahweh shows that in the economy of salvation Paul does not distinguish between the work of Christ and that of God. The title $\kappa\acute{\upsilon}\rho\iota\sigma\varsigma$, Lord, which the Greek Old Testa-

and 7 (incarnation and resurrection) and the two affirmations of v. 9 (Lordship and resurrection), (Sanday and Headlam, Lagrange.)

* Mk. 8: 38; Lk. 9: 26; Matt. 10: 32; Lk. 12: 8. Cf. Michel, *Th.Wb.NT*, V, p. 209.

ment applied to Yahweh was for this reason appropriate to Christ, and this continuity of vocabulary clearly affirmed the continuity of the covenants.*

(14f.) The revelation of God's will in Jesus Christ has effectively touched all to whom it is addressed; their refusal to submit to it is without excuse. They cannot allege that Christ, who came down from heaven and rose again from the dead, is nevertheless an absent one since He has returned to glory. (His Lordship has just been emphasized!) Moses bequeathed the law and the rite of circumcision, whereas Christ left behind Him no institution, no book, no vicar. Is there not here an excuse for Israel?

The apostle refutes this suggestion. If Israel has remained in unbelief it is not because the conditions for faith have not been fulfilled on its behalf. Israel has known its Messiah by the preaching which He Himself instituted as the primary sacrament of His presence. In a series of questions, Paul goes back over these conditions. To "call upon" the Lord is just what the believer does, it is the very manifestation of a living faith; in reference to Christians, 1 Cor. 1:2 uses the phrase "those who call on the name of our Lord Jesus Christ".† But how does one become a believer? It is necessary that the divine testimony should be proclaimed by duly authorized witnesses; faith comes from hearing (cf. v. 17; Gal. 3:2–5); it is impossible to believe unless one hears the object of faith proclaimed. And who proclaims it? He who has been authorized and commissioned to do so by Christ‡ whom he represents, namely the apostle (1:1). Paul does not feel it necessary to say explicitly that there are apostles; the fact is evident enough; but the quotation from Is. 52:7 implies that this institution is the fulfilment of prophecy.§

* Cf. Gaugler, II, p. 138.
† Cf. Acts 9:14; 22:16; 2 Tim. 2:22.
‡ The κῆρυξ does but convey the message; he is a medium (the mouthpiece of his Lord; cf. Plat. *Pol.* 250d), Friedrich, *Th.Wb.NT*, III, p. 686. Κηρύσσειν relates to the exercise of the mission; ἀποστέλλειν is its basis. If not sent by anyone, the κῆρυξ speaks on his own authority; but this is not the case with the preacher of the gospel, who is commissioned by Christ.

‡ Judaism already interpreted this prophecy in a Messianic sense

¹⁶But they have not all heeded the gospel; for Isaiah says, "Lord, who has believed what he has heard from us?" ¹⁷So faith comes from what is heard, and what is heard comes by the preaching of Christ.

¹⁸But I ask, have they not heard? Indeed they have; for
"Their voice has gone out to all the earth,
and their word to the ends of the world."
¹⁹Again I ask, did Israel not understand? First Moses says,
"I will make you jealous of those who are not a nation;
with a foolish nation I will make you angry."
²⁰Then Isaiah is so bold as to say,
"I have been found by those who did not seek me;
I have shown myself to those who did not ask for me."
²¹But of Israel he says, "All day long I have held out my hands to a disobedient and contrary people."

(16) Thus Christ has been presented to Israel by the authorized preaching of the apostles who form a conspicuously venerable institution. But the preaching of the gospel has failed,* at least as far as Israel as a whole is concerned. The words of Is. 53: 1 have once again been verified: like the suffering servant to whom these words referred, Christ has been an object of scandal.

(17) In short, faith comes from what is heard, on which point no special problem arises. But the important fact is that what is heard is not any sort of word. The apostolic word springs from "the preaching of Christ". This may mean two things: what is heard originates in what Christ has said—the latter is the formal and material source of the preaching; or else that what is heard is proclaimed by the command of Christ (cf. Lk. 3: 2; 5: 5). In both cases the authority of the word is emphasized. It is the very word of Christ.†

(18–21) Might Israel claim that the apostles have not ful-

(Strack-Billerbeck, III, p. 282). Paul uses the Hebrew text but modifies it.

* Munck, *op. cit.* p. 269, p. 272, etc., insists many times on the importance of this mission of the apostles among the Jews.

† Instead of $Χριστοῦ$, A K L P etc. read $Θεοῦ$ and G gives nothing.

filled their mission as heralds of the Word? But the scope and extensiveness of Christian preaching was a well-known fact, and the Romans themselves are the proof that the gospel has been preached throughout the civilized world.* A text from the psalms is cited in support of this affirmation, not without some artifice.†

Again, could Israel assert that the heralds of the gospel have spoken unintelligibly? But in that case, how is it that the Gentiles have understood? The fact is that those who were not prepared by the divine pedagogy have received the Messianic message, whereas Israel, whose education in the ways of God dates from far back, has rejected it. Today is happening the very thing with which God had threatened Israel (Deut. 32: 21).‡

Furthermore, not only has Israel been well prepared but its preparation has had the fortunate consequence that it is full of zeal; alas, it is a blind zeal (cf. v. 2). The more they try to please God, the more they become hardened in their blindness. The Gentiles were more open-minded, more rough-hewn (cf. the ἀσύνετος, *foolish*, of v. 19) but more docile, in fact the poor in spirit. From this point of view the word of Isaiah§ is audacious but the prophet *dared* (ἀποτολμᾷ) to

* Munck, *op. cit.* p. 272, wishes to take εἰς πᾶσαν τὴν γῆν in a literal sense. The apostles have now finished with Israel as a whole. Those to whom the gospel has been preached represent Israel in its totality. Hence Israel as a whole has now rejected the Messiah.

† Ps. 19: 1 says that nature declares the glory of God. This has nothing to do with the preaching of the gospel. Paul is using this text from memory, and has been reminded of it by the idea of a universal extension of the words of Christian preachers.

‡ At the moment when he introduces for the first time the idea that the Gentiles now take the place of the elect people, Paul wishes to adduce a double testimony, that of the law, voiced by Moses, and that of the prophets, speaking through Isaiah. He quotes Moses in the first place, the first (πρῶτος "firstly" says Lietzmann; "as the first witness", says Michel). But one may also understand the text as follows: "Moses said that already before I myself" (Lagrange, who however prints "d'abord" in italics). πρῶτος has also been connected with 'Ισραήλ: "Was not Israel the first to know the gospel?" (Bentley, Zahn): grammar supports this, but the meaning loses.

§ The word of Isaiah is applied by the prophet himself to Samaria. For Paul's readers, the prophecy was even more severe than for Isaiah himself, for the Jews abhorred the Samaritans to such an extent that R.

say that it is better not to seek than to seek perversely. Israel's zeal to create its own righteousness prevented it from receiving righteousness as the free gift of God. God held out helping hands to His people, hands full of His gifts; but the hands of the people were full of their own works. They disregarded the gift and turned away.*

The words quoted from Moses and Isaiah suggested too the ideas of substitution and jealousy; thus was introduced the theme which finds its full development in ch. 11.

Eliezer considered them to be unacceptable even as proselytes (Strack-Billerbeck, I, p. 538; IV, p. 333).

* Verses 14–16 have presented in sequence: invocation, faith, preaching, apostolate, Christ. Verses 17–21 present the same sequence, in reverse: v. 17: Christ, the word of Christ; v. 18: proclamation and hearing; v. 19: faith; v. 20: the encounter of the believer with God.

CHAPTER

I I

¹I ask, then, has God rejected his people? By no means! I myself am an Israelite, a descendant of Abraham, a member of the tribe of Benjamin. ²God has not rejected his people whom he foreknew. Do you not know what the scripture says of Elijah, how he pleads with God against Israel? ³"Lord, they have killed thy prophets, they have demolished thy altars, and I alone am left, and they seek my life." ⁴But what is God's reply to him? "I have kept for myself seven thousand men who have not bowed the knee to Baal." ⁵So too at the present time there is a remnant, chosen by grace. ⁶But if it is by grace, it is no longer on the basis of works; otherwise grace would no longer be grace.

⁷What then? Israel failed to obtain what it sought. The elect obtained it, but the rest were hardened, ⁸as it is written,

"God gave them a spirit of stupor,
eyes that should not see and ears that should not hear,
down to this very day."
⁹And David says,
"Let their feast become a snare and a trap,
a pitfall and a retribution for them;
¹⁰let their eyes be darkened so that they cannot see,
and bend their backs for ever."

(1) PAUL HAS AFFIRMED that the plan of God does not suffer permanent frustration from the contingencies of history (ch. 9). However, we have just seen that God's purpose failed with regard to Israel. How shall we explain this contradition?

However severe, the page which Paul has just written is not a formal charge, and does not call down condemnation on the people which resisted God's purposes with regard to it. In fact it is not Israel in itself which is Paul's concern. No man has the right to institute proceedings between a man and God. Doubtless Israel failed in its vocation. But it is this

vocation which matters to the apostle, not the fact of disobedience. The question is to know how the plan of God,
which was disclosed in the call addressed to Israel, will now
find an instrument suitable for its realization. Paul is in
effect writing a chapter in theodicy in order to elucidate the
problem of the historic initiatives of God in the present.

The guilt of Israel had been so strongly established that
one might have read in the citations from Deuteronomy and
Isaiah a prophecy of the rejection of this people. This is not
so, declares Paul, with the support of Ps. 94: 14* and the
proof of this lies in the personal situation of the apostle himself. Is not Paul an authentic Israelite? A son of Abraham
according to the flesh and a member of the tribe which was
most essentially Israelite?† If God had rejected His people,
He would not have chosen as the principal agent in the
mission to the Gentiles an Israelite of so indubitable a kind
(Gaugler). This very choice is an indication of God's fidelity
to His word.

(2–4) Hence God has not rejected His people. His faithfulness to Israel is that of love.‡ Will it be said that a single
person is hardly a valid and adequate testimony to God's
loyalty towards a whole people? Numbers have nothing to
do with it. Elijah remained indeed alone (μόνος) in his
struggle against a whole people; he was the living symbol of
the fidelity of God struggling with the infidelity of men. The
solitude of Elijah is vividly evoked by the prayer reported in
1 Kgs. 19: 10–14 (freely quoted by Paul, no doubt from

* P 46 G have τὴν κληρονομίαν (cf. Ps. 94: 14) instead of τὸν λαόν.
P 46 A D L add ὅν προέγνω, according to v. 2.

† W. Vischer, *op. cit.* pp. 105 and 125, emphasizes the importance of
these indications by recalling that (1) the basis of Jewish religion and life
is the doctrine of the physical and biological quality of the elect people
(cf. M. Kosmala, *Judaica*, 1947). (2) Benjamin is the only autochthonous
tribe in the holy land (Gen. 35: 16–20), the only one which remained
faithful to David, the one which justified the claim of the kingdom of
Judah to represent Israel as a whole, the one on whose territory was
situated the city of all the promises. Did not the first king of Israel belong
to this tribe and was he not called Saul? (Michel.)

‡ *Προέγνω* is to be taken in the same sense as in 8: 29.

memory).* It would seem that Paul, in calling to mind the sorrows of Elijah, is thinking also of his own; 2 Cor. 11: 22–24 is not without some analogy to this text. God replies to the prophet by showing him that the divine intention is not to leave him in solitude; He has chosen seven thousand men by means of whom He will pursue the fulfilment of His plans. Hence God can maintain His loyalty to His people even when the latter is reduced to a single unit.†

(5f.) This might be so with regard to a faithless people. But Israel has not simply disobeyed; it has crucified the Messiah and Son of God. Paul foresees this objection, but it would be reasoning on Judaic lines to take it seriously. God has always acted by grace; the works of Israel are of no avail either to establish the covenant, or to maintain it, or to annul it. Grace is grace at the present time more than ever. A "remnant" has been chosen to maintain the link of continuity and God by its means will pursue the original plan of His grace.‡

(7–10) In these circumstances the problem is, however, to know what is to become of the greater number. A section only attains the end which all were intended to reach. Are the others henceforth excluded from the race? This inevitable question introduces us to the painful aspect of the subject. Paul replies yes and no. They are not finally rejected, they are "hardened"; they are out of the race, but not for ever.§

"Hardened" is the first reply. When man refuses the call

* Ἐν Ἡλείᾳ: as though Elijah had written the narratives concerning him. It was the custom to name the portions of scripture read in the synagogue after the principal personage concerned in them. Cf. Strack-Billerbeck, III, p. 288. ἐντυγχάνω κατά, intervene against . . . (cf. W. Bauer, s.v.).

† Here no more than elsewhere does Paul pay much attention to the precise historical circumstances relative to the texts he quotes.

‡ B and many MSS. of less value add to v. 6: εἰ δὲ ἐξ ἔργων, οὐκέτι ἐστὶ χάρις, ἐπεὶ τὸ ἔργον οὐκέτι ἐστὶν ἔργον (B; χάρις instead of ἔργον). In the opinion of most critics this phrase is a gloss.

§ Ἡ ἐκλογή: the election. Paul describes the object of the term expressing the action of which it is the object. The "remnant" manifests in history the divine election at this critical moment.

279

which God addresses to him, when he opposes the divine will, he entangles himself in a situation which cannot but get worse, and in living through which he finds that God is not mocked. If the creature refuses to be carried along by the current of divine grace, his very refusal drives him towards nothingness, for one cannot refuse the call of God except by positively opposing Him. God penalizes this opposition; that is, in His turn He refuses His mercy to the man who resists His will (cf. also 9: 17–18). It is in this way that the judgment of God is exercised;* God is active in judging thus, as is suggested by the first word of the quotation from Isaiah: ἔδωκεν ὁ Θεός, *God gave them,*† which may be compared with the threefold παρέδωκεν of the first chapter.

The quotation from Psalm 69 is difficult to explain in detail. We must not try to press the text too closely. The apostle quotes the passage primarily for its allusions to blindness considered as punishment and servitude (συγκάμπτειν τὸν νῶτον is an image of servitude).‡ The infidelity of one section of Israel has brought it into a position which God has "sealed" by the process of hardening. When people have mocked God, they are confined in their attitude by the action of God Himself and only the divine grace enables them to escape. This is how God acts towards man, as scripture says in Deuteronomy (quoted v. 8) and as David asked Him to act towards the enemies of the suffering righteous.§

¹¹So I ask, have they stumbled so as to fall? By no means! But through their trespass salvation has come to the Gentiles, so as to make Israel jealous. ¹²Now if their trespass means riches

* Πωροῦν: to make callous, to harden (medical term). By extension, to render insensitive.

† Paul is certainly quoting from memory. He mingles Deut. 29: 3 (or 4) and Is. 29: 10.

‡ Is the table furnished with delights which are snares? Have we here a symbol of the pleasures which blind the eyes of the soul? If a low table is meant, does the image allude to someone bumping against it and becoming trapped in the decorative cloths? The latter interpretation would explain v. 11a. (See Zahn and Gaugler.)

§ Gaugler points out that Paul is not concerned with the detail of the quotation, otherwise he would not include διὰ παντός, which implies a lasting punishment, when the rest of his argument shows that the punishment of Israel is temporary only.

for the world, and if their failure means riches for the Gentiles, how much more will their full inclusion mean! [13]Now I am speaking to you Gentiles. Inasmuch then as I am an apostle to the Gentiles, I magnify my ministry [14]in order to make my fellow Jews jealous, and thus save some of them. [15]For if their rejection means the reconciliation of the world, what will their acceptance mean but life from the dead? [16]If the dough offered as first fruits is holy, so is the whole lump; and if the root is holy, so are the branches.

[17]But if some of the branches were broken off, and you, a wild olive shoot, were grafted in their place to share the richness of the olive tree, [18]do not boast over the branches. If you do boast, remember it is not you that support the root, but the root that supports you. [19]You will say, "Branches were broken off so that I might be grafted in." [20]That is true. They were broken off because of their unbelief, but you stand fast only through faith. So do not become proud, but stand in awe. [21]For if God did not spare the natural branches, neither will he spare you. [22]Note then the kindness and severity of God: severity toward those who have fallen, but God's kindness to you, provided you continue in his kindness; otherwise you too will be cut off. [23]And even the others, if they do not persist in their unbelief, will be grafted in, for God has the power to graft them in again. [24]For if you have been cut off from what is by nature a wild olive tree, and grafted, contrary to nature, into a cultivated olive tree, how much more will these natural branches be grafted back into their own olive tree.

(11) Grace is never changed into malediction, although sometimes it takes the form of punishment. Israel has stumbled, but it is not God's intention to overthrow it.* In other circumstances it is true that God behaved towards Israel differently and with less severity. How many times has He pardoned her sins! Why then this time did He harden the elect people instead of patiently offering them a further chance of repentance? The reason is that this time there was something quite different at stake. God wills to remain faithful to the primary intention of the election, which was to make known His name to all nations through the instrumentality

* *"Iva* is a final conjunction: "was the purpose of God to make them stumble *so that* they could not rise again?" It is true that the subject of the sentence is not God but the Israelites (cf. Michel, who quotes K. H. Schelkle).

of the people of His choice. It is to this purpose of His love that He must in the first place remain faithful, not to the fact of Israel's election, which is only secondary. God could not give up the idea of realizing His plan of mercy, on the grounds that He had called Israel to be the primary instrument in its realization.

Paul does not claim that Israel's rebellion was necessary in order that salvation might be brought to all the nations. The historical fact is that Israel has fallen. Paul has experienced this himself (Acts 13: 46; 18: 6). Things might have taken place otherwise, but the fact is that they have taken place thus. The hardening of Israel consequent upon its rebellion has produced results for which Israel alone is responsible, although the hardening process was willed by God Himself. Since Israel repudiated the gospel it became necessary for God to remove it as an obstacle. This dramatic consequence of Israel's refusal is rooted in the love of God, who does not wish to limit His revelation to Israel nor to accept the exclusion of the Gentiles as the effect of Israel's own insolvency. But this divine love will likewise make Israel feel again the effects of that grace which does not wish to exclude anyone, although for the moment it sets aside this people which is paralysing the divine intentions. Ei_{ς} $\tau\grave{o}$ . . . suggests this ultimate intention of God, which will find its realization on the historical plane by the fact of Israel's jealousy (cf. 10: 19 and Deut. 32: 21). How could Israel fail to be stirred on seeing itself cast out from the blessing promised and already granted to pagans, when in fact it was Israel itself which had been the primary recipient and depositary of these promises? In these circumstances the pagans will become the true Israelites, in whom Israel, which has been excluded from the race, will be bound to recognize the instruments by means of which its own vocation has been finally realized. This situation will naturally arouse it to desire salvation.

(12) It can now be foreseen what the final result of this holy emulation will be. When Israel becomes converted to Jesus the Messiah it will recover once more the place which God had assigned to it, it will again be the instrument by which God will shed upon mankind His benediction. It will

bring to the world the supreme riches of God's grace. Israel is essential to the fulfilment of the divine plan. Then it will be seen how utterly true it is that God did not will to remove Israel for ever, for it will rise again to a position of pre-eminence and will be wholly saved (v. 26; πᾶς Ἰσραήλ).*

(13f.) Vv. 13 and 14 are not simply a parenthesis, as those authors think who connect v. 15 with v. 12 (Vischer and Barth). It should be noticed that the tone becomes personal and that exhortation now takes the place of theological and scriptural argument (there is no further Biblical quotation from v. 13 to v. 24). This is not because Paul is now addressing himself to a part of the community which is not concerned in the same way with the previous line of thought. But now that the principles have been laid down, Paul proposes to eluci-date the further implications of the matter. If the conversion of all Israel which Paul visualizes as taking place later is to benefit the Gentiles themselves, by the same token the ministry of Paul gains a far richer significance. The full riches of divine grace which Paul has proclaimed to the pagan world will be imparted only after the conversion of Israel. Thus it may be said paradoxically that the final aim of Paul's ministry to the Gentiles is the conversion of Israel it-self, which will be facilitated by the jealousy which the conversion of the Gentiles will provoke in Israel.†

* Parallelism would require παράπτωμα, πλήρωμα, and ἥττημα to be similar in implication. But the only known meaning of ἥττημα is relative to quality (inferiority, degeneration; Is. 31: 8; 1 Cor. 6: 7), whilst πλήρωμα has certainly here a quantitative sense as in v. 25 (cf. ad loc.). We may understand thus: "The failure of Israel and the inferiority which has resulted from it (by contrast with the Gentiles who now pre-cede the Jews in the Kingdom of God). . . ." Or again: "The failure of Israel and its consequent reduced state which makes it inferior (because only a fragment has been converted). . . ." If we give to ἥττημα a quantitative sense = "If their failure and their numerical reduction . . ." (Godet). Apart from the philological objection, the numerical meaning of ἥττημα is contrary to the intention which caused Paul to write, first πλοῦτος κόσμου and then πλοῦτος ἐθνῶν: the inferiority of Israel is contrasted with the advantage which the Gentiles enjoy, not with their greater numbers. For a discussion of this text see Munck, pp. 40–41.

† Δοξάζω τὴν διακονίαν μου: I magnify my ministry, the best title to glory in this ministry is. . . .

Pagans might have a tendency to believe that they have become the chief pawn on the chessboard and have taken Israel's place in the heart of God. This is not so. God loved the pagans already when He chose Israel. Nor does He cease to love Israel in calling the Gentiles to salvation. The love of God will flow back upon and embrace Israel, for it is not partial or exclusive but on the contrary generous, wide-embracing, inclusive. This is attested by the ministry of Paul which, even as far as Israel is concerned, has indirectly the significance of an appeal to embrace the Messianic faith.

The very fact that it is Paul himself, the authentic and true Israelite (v. 1), who has been chosen to open up to the pagan world the salvation primarily promised to Israel, is a fact full of significance. It is designed to show that Israel does not lose its privileges; in the person of him who is the chief apostle to the Gentiles, Israel itself is opening the door of salvation to the latter. It can thus be clearly seen that it is with Israel that the Gentiles are incorporated by this ministry. The goal and the way to it are both marked with the seal of Israel; salvation truly is of the Jews (Jn. 4: 22).

(15) If the true glory of the apostolic ministry is then to witness the conversion of a few Israelites at least, what a marvellous thing it is for Paul to see one of his brethren after the flesh converted to Christ. This gives a veritable crown to his apostolate for here the power of the gospel (1: 16) is manifested in a conversion which is nothing other than that work of God which gives life to the dead (4: 17). After all, Israel is symbolically a people of the dead; it is the most dead of all because of its attitude to the law; its unenlightened zeal has killed it. Its conversion would furnish the most impressive triumph of life over death, the typical resurrection from the dead. And as for the apostle, to welcome an Israelite, a brother after the flesh into the Body of Christ, a member of a people which is at present rebellious and spiritually dead, must have had for him a prophetic significance which we have difficulty in realizing; such a happening foreshadowed the reawakening of the people of the promise,

and its spiritual resurrection by the inspiration of the Holy Spirit.*

(16a) The apostle sees, in the few Israelites whom the preaching of the gospel has converted, the signs which herald the conversion of the whole, the first fruits of the harvest.† He reasons by the principle that the part is a valid expression of the whole, or, expressed more theologically, that the sanctity of the part accrues to the credit of the whole. No doubt he has in mind the texts of Lev. 19: 23–25 and Num. 15: 17–21;‡ the uncleanness of the fruits of the earth is effaced by

* This verse is very much discussed. Since Origen, the great majority of commentators find here an allusion to the final resurrection, and the entry of the church into eschatological glory (Lagrange: the resurrection of the body: Lietzmann: life in Christ for those who are resurrected: Sanday and Headlam: the ultimate consummation which would come *when the Kingdom was completed*. Similarly Schrenk, Vischer, Michel, etc.). The weight of this exegetical tradition is considerable. But one cannot overcome the astonishment aroused by the terms in which Paul would thus have spoken of the final resurrection: his formula is vague and without article (ζωὴ ἐκ νεκρῶν). Hence some exegetes (Calvin, Godet, Gaugler, etc.) take the expression figuratively, rightly pointing to Lk. 19: 24–32 and Ez. 37: 3–14, which apply the idea of resurrection to the people of Israel. Apart from this objection based on the terms used by the apostle, there is a further objection springing from the context. The apostle has just been speaking of his ministry; from v. 13 the perspective is still more restricted and concrete; it is a question of the real conversion of a few Israelites thanks to the ministry of the apostle (τινὰς ἐξ αὐτῶν). Later on, it will again be a question of these converted Israelites, and of the sentiments of Gentile converts with regard to them. All this has nothing to do with the end of the age, but with concrete and present circumstances: Paul will even speak in the second person (v. 17). Πρόσλημψις does not mean "reintegration" (thus Godet whose explanation is more correct: "the welcome which God will give to the Jews when they are converted"), but: welcome, good reception (acceptance; cf. W. Bauer, s.v.). It will be noted that Paul does not put αὐτῶν after πρόσλημψις; this may be deliberate, for this pronoun was used to denote the Israelites collectively in vv. 12 and 15a; this would explain that he reserves πρόσλημψις for the welcome given to individual converts. But the debate goes on; cf. for example G. Fessard, "Théologie et histoire. Apropos du temps de la conversion d'Israel", *Dieu vivant*, 8 (1947), pp. 37–65.

† In Rom. 16: 5; 1 Cor. 16: 15 Paul uses ἀπαρχή in the same sense, to denote the first converts.

‡ The expression ἀπαρχὴ φυράματος from Num. 15: 20 (LXX) shows that Paul is thinking of this text.

285

the hallowing of a crop; the first fruits are offered to Yahweh to permit a free use of the rest of the harvest. Similarly in 1 Cor. 7: 14 with regard to a married couple of which only one member is a Christian, Paul declares that the other is thereby consecrated, a principle which makes possible conjugal life. ¶ Thus the first members of the Jewish people to be converted fulfil, as regards the incredulous remainder, the function of the first fruits in relation to the whole crop, or of the one Christian partner in marriage.

(16b–18) 'Ρίζα, parallel to ἀπαρχή, should have the same meaning and so denote that part of the whole formed by the first converts, who are thus considered as the root which will bear the tree of the future. Unfortunately a certain difficulty lies in the way of this interpretation, since a few lines further down ῥίζα is used to denote the root of the olive tree which bears the newly engrafted branches, i.e. the ancient Israel and especially the patriarchs (Abraham above all) with whom have been incorporated the Gentiles. If this meaning must be given to ῥίζα in v. 17, should it not have the same meaning in v. 16? If so, it is difficult to see why Paul thus returns to the question of the origins of Israel when he has been concentrating his attention on its future.

Thus the vocabulary seems to oblige us to connect v. 16a with what precedes, and 16b with what follows. Just as ἀπαρχή appropriately denotes the newly converted, the first fruits of the whole people, so ῥίζα is suitable to denote the root from which the tree springs. Two images are thus juxtaposed in the mind of the author, and we should not interpret the one in the light of the other. From 16b Paul is thinking already of what he proposes to say to the Gentiles to forestall in them the possibility of a misplaced pride. These Jews, some of whom have been already converted, are part and parcel of the trunk; they are nourished from the root; they too, and they above all, are children of Abraham; if the root which bears them is holy they share this holiness like natural branches springing from this venerable trunk.

Doubtless the faithlessness of the greater number has obliged God to remove many branches which have grown

¶ Cf. Dodd, p. 179.

from the patriarchal root. The Jews as a whole are like withered branches which the gardener has cut away. The true living branches which are now growing on the chosen trunk, the true posterity of Abraham, are not the Jews who have refused the promise but the Christians. True, says Paul (v. 17a). But it must not be forgotten that the divine gardener has not torn away the trunk; far from it, the promise subsists for all Israel. Further, the Gentiles who have been called to share in the benefits of this promise are nothing other than wild shoots grafted on the trunk which remains God's planting;* and it is the sap of this old trunk which now feeds the newly grafted branches. The Christians have been made sons of Abraham, i.e. have been allowed to participate in the promises made to Israel.†

The image is a very striking one and well suited to make the Gentile Christians understand why Paul stressed the importance which the conversion of the Jews had for him, and about which he spoke paradoxically as the very crown of his apostolic ministry.

The end of v. 17 and v. 18 show however that the intention of Paul goes beyond this theological point and that he has in view a practical application. The fact that they are shoots grafted on to the trunk should awaken in the Gentile Christians feelings of respect for any Jew who became converted. It is possible that some Gentile Christians, who formed at least an important section of the church in Rome, did not entertain such sentiments.‡

* The allegory of the olive tree is supplied to Paul by Jer. 11: 16; Hos. 14: 6; cf. 4 Ezra 5: 23; En. 93: 2–10. Cf. Strack-Billerbeck, II, p. 563; III, p. 290.

† The asyndeton συνκοινωνὸς τῆς ῥίζης τῆς πιότητος τῆς ἐλαίας is somewhat strained. An attempt has been made to correct it either by adding καὶ after ῥίζης (S A Vulg.) or by omitting τῆς ῥίζης P 46 D G it, etc. The short reading is generally rejected (though Lyonnet adopts it, saying, "it might be the best"). Lagrange explains that "the very wood of the olive is as though impregnated with oil and burns very easily". The idea is that by the effect of the grafting the shoot benefits from the juicy sap of the olive which is nourished from the root.

‡ Various reasons have been given to explain the existence of a sort of masked anti-semitism among the Gentile Christians of Rome. The latter gladly took advantage of the privileges accorded by the Empire to the Jews, but also kept aloof from them so as not to be obliged to be attached

A horticulturalist usually grafts a fertile branch on to a wild trunk. Paul is here building his argument on the inverse process. Is this because Paul as a townsman was completely ignorant of country life or did he in fact know of a practice of this kind? The latter is indeed possible, for several ancient authors say that agriculturalists sometimes revivified old olive trees by the grafting of wild shoots.* It would also be legitimate to offer a psychological explanation of the passage. Paul's imagery may have been moulded by the idea rather than any care for scientific accuracy; the Gentile world, in relation to Israel, plays the part of a wild shoot; the pagans enter the church as wild shoots are grafted on a noble trunk. Paul may even have realized that he was suggesting a not quite natural process (cf. παρὰ φύσιν, v. 24). The surprising procedure well expressed the fact that the bringing in of the Gentiles was something quite out of the ordinary; nothing less than the grace of God was required to attempt and succeed in so unnatural an operation. This circumstance again should have deflated any possible pride on the part of the Gentiles.

(19) Nevertheless Gentile Christianity might well have wished to support the idea that it had been definitely called by God to take the place of Israel, by pointing out that if the branches were cut off it was not merely by accident or only because they were barren. This means that Israel was set aside not simply because of its attitude with regard to the Messiah. The divine gardener had a further positive intention; He was not content to punish Israel; He willed that it should be replaced by the Gentile world. God declared His will plainly enough in events; the promises have not fallen into escheat merely; Israel has been disinherited to the advantage of the pagans. We should notice the ἵνα, so that.

(20f.) Paul admits that there is some truth in this point of view; the facts in part confirm it. But these facts must be

to the ghetto (Dodd). On this subject, cf. W. Lutgert, *Der Römerbrief als historisches Problem*, 1913.

* Cf. Columella, *De re rust.*, V, 9, 16. Palladius, *De insitione*, 14, 53. A bibliography will be found in W. Bauer, s.v. ἀγριέλαιος. Cf. W. Straub, *Die Bildersprache des Apostels Paulus*, 1937, p. 74.

properly understood. The rejection of Israel is the result of its lack of faith just as the admission of the Gentiles is due to their gift of faith. Now this faith, as formerly the election of Israel, is a gift which God has given and which He ultimately controls. The present advantage of the Gentiles does not therefore flow from any superiority which it is in their power to exploit; they enjoy a grace from which they can profit only if they remain in a state of humility so that they may continue to receive it as the free gift of God. Pride is the ruin of faith and disqualifies one from receiving the fruits of the promise.* The fear of God dispels all conceit.† The horizons oft his train of thought are overshadowed by the idea of God's judgment; God did not spare the original trunk: hence He will be so much the more likely to remove the grafted shoots if need be. He is not any the more tied to the Gentiles by what He has done for them than He was to Israel through His election grace. He is tied only to His love. If the pride of good works caused the downfall of Israel, let the newcomers beware lest the pride of faith cause them to stumble. The faith of which a man boasts is, by that very fact, faith no longer. The branches which the gardener cuts off are the natural branches, not the engrafted ones which are expected to yield their flower or fruit after such an operation. By threatening the Gentiles that they might share the fate of the branches already cut off, Paul is imagining an unreal situation. But he does not worry about these improbabilities; the comparison is most expressive for his purpose. It would be pedantic to take it too literally.‡

(22–24) Since the comparison can only be worth what any comparison is worth, the essential point lies of course elsewhere; what must be understood is the situation in which those whom grace has now called find themselves. The case

* Instead of ὑψηλὰ φρόνει (S A B) some MSS. read ὑψηλοφρόνει (C D G).

† It may be a question of the fear of God (Michel) or the apprehension of some evil (Bengel, Godet).

‡ What Paul calls the "natural" branches are the branches which have naturally grown on the parent tree. He does not mean to say that Israel is "by nature" a people suited to what the divine election has called it to become.

of Israel shows that God is resolute in acting with severity in order to remain faithful to His love. His freedom is the condition of His fidelity. Hence the Gentiles who are called to benefit from the promises must be faithful in response to the faithfulness of God. It is enough for them to "continue in the kindness" of which they have been the object. Otherwise* . . . and there follows the threat of being in their turn cut off as useless branches.

God's liberty with regard to the instruments He has chosen for Himself would thus be manifested again. But there is a further point. Even with regard to those whom He has cast aside, God is still unfettered in His action and His fidelity is unchanged. If they abandoned their unbelief, God would be the first to rejoice to see His people return to Him and He would accept them with the warmest welcome. It will be noticed that Paul again speaks of grafting in connexion with the restoration of Israel to the channels of salvation. The conversion of the elect people to their Messiah will not be a simple renewal of the *status quo ante*. We know that God is not mocked; sin creates a situation which God alone can change: conversion needs God's forgiveness, the conversion of Israel no less than that of anyone else. But Paul can assure the Israelites that this forgiveness will not fail and that God will do all that is necessary to restore Israel to its position. The use in this connexion of the image of grafting emphasizes the point that the intervention of God is necessary and that it will effect the restoration of the chosen people to their former position. Once again, the comparison seems not too well adapted to the demands of the argument. In practice no one grafts the natural branches of the tree back on to the tree. This matters little to the apostle, who is concerned with the idea to be illustrated rather than with the suitability of the illustration. He who can do the greater can also do the less. If the Gentiles have been called to inherit the promises, how much more normally will the Jews be reintegrated in a heritage which has not ceased to be theirs.†

* 'Eπεί: otherwise (Rom. 11: 6; 1 Cor. 5: 10; 15: 29; Hebr. 9: 17, 26).
† Paul is right in opposing a shoot κατὰ φύσιν to a shoot παρὰ φύσιν because it is true that a shoot succeeds the more easily if the original tree and the engrafted shoot are closely related in species.

All these thoughts of Paul about the destiny of the Jews and Gentiles show that history is not a process which consists in the mechanical unfolding of external and immutable divine decrees. The faith or the unbelief of the former or the latter provokes in God the one reaction or the other, and causes Him to punish or forgive. God directs history towards the ends which He has chosen but He takes into account the obstacles which the freedom of man opposes to His will. The liberty of God in face of men is the counterpart of their liberty over against Him. It does not flow from an arbitrary or capricious will. It is the expression of His fidelity to His plan of mercy, the realization of which must not be thwarted even if the chosen instrument of its realization at some time fails.

[25]Lest you be wise in your own conceits, I want you to understand this mystery, brethren: a hardening has come upon part of Israel, until the full number of the Gentiles come in, [26]and so all Israel will be saved; as it is written,
"The Deliverer will come from Zion,
he will banish ungodliness from Jacob";
[27]"and this will be my covenant with them
when I take away their sins."
[28]As regards the gospel they are enemies of God, for your sake; but as regards election they are beloved for the sake of their forefathers. [29]For the gifts and the call of God are irrevocable. [30]Just as you were once disobedient to God but now have received mercy because of their disobedience, [31]so they have now been disobedient in order that by the mercy shown to you they also may receive mercy. [32]For God has consigned all men to disobedience, that he may have mercy upon all.
[33]O the depth of the riches and wisdom and knowledge of God! How unsearchable are his judgments and how inscrutable his ways!
[34]"For who has known the mind of the Lord,
or who has been his counsellor?"
[35]"Or who has given a gift to him
that he might be repaid?"
[36]For from him and through him and to him are all things. To him be glory forever. Amen.

(25–27) The apostle has just visualized the possibility of the final conversion of Israel. Will this possibility become a reality? The question is both irresistible and distressing.

How should one reply to it? Who can say? It is not a question of making calculations, of investigating reasons for hope or doubt. The answer to this kind of question is not a matter for conjecture at all. Only faith can propound it, and it can be propounded to faith alone. Paul declares that it is a mystery because it contradicts all that the reason of man might infer from a study of the facts, and has no other foundation but the will of God.* The apostle does not appeal to any special revelation. It is enough for him to believe in the election of Israel for him to believe also in the final conversion of Israel.

The tone here becomes somewhat solemn because such an assertion of faith reminds the Gentiles more directly of all that their faith requires of them. It is essential that the Gentile Christians should take quite seriously the election of Israel; then they will not wish to press forward to take the place of this rejected people and to imagine that they are sufficient unto themselves. It would be madly conceited for them to aspire to replace Israel, for that would be tantamount to despising God's election of Israel at the very moment when, in the name of the same election grace, they were presuming to claim the position which that grace had assigned to Israel. Cannot the grace which has saved the Gentiles save Israel also? To be sceptical about the salvation of Israel by desiring to take its place would in fact be doubting the efficacy of the grace which saved the Gentiles themselves: it would be sawing off the branch on which they had been grafted. From yet another point of view, they would thus be showing that they have understood nothing about the mystery of the divine dispensations. The shoot cannot be sufficient unto itself. Israel remains the root. The young church is the true church only if it is grafted on the patriarchal stem; the revelation in Jesus Christ fulfils the promise made to Abraham and is unintelligible apart from the latter.

Here is a doubly fatal presumption threatening the Gentiles, against which they have now been duly warned. If they take seriously the election of Israel they will understand this

* Μυστήριον implies the secret thought of God with regard to saving events, a thought which the preaching and teaching of the apostle make known.

mysterious declaration which is true if the fundamental fact of election is true: namely, the hardening of Israel is only temporary.*

For how long will it last? For as long as is necessary to complete what had made it necessary, the conversion of the Gentiles. God will not prolong the abnormal situation as though He had some indignation to satisfy or an expiation to impose on His elect people. When the "full number of the Gentiles" has come in,† His end will have been reached. The words "the full number of the Gentiles" are parallel to πᾶς Ἰσραήλ, *all Israel,* and are intended to denote the Gentile world as a whole, only in a more expressive fashion.‡ Both formulae are to be understood as suggesting collectives or groups without prejudging the condition of any particular individual.§ Paul does not say that all the heathen will be converted just as he does not say that all the Israelites will be saved. He speaks of "all Israel". The exact meaning of this expression is seen if it is contrasted with the idea of the "remnant".

The relation between the salvation of Israel and the entrance into the Kingdom of the totality (the "pleroma") of the Gentiles is not formulated in such a way as to indicate a strict chronological dependence. Paul did not write: καὶ τότε

* A B ἐν ἑαυτοῖς; S C D παρ' ἑαυτοῖς; G vulg. ἑαυτοῖς. Lietzmann and Michel adopt the first reading; Zahn, Lagrange the third: to be wise "in so far as oneself is concerned". "It seems that the Gentiles were tempted to understand the designs of Providence only in regard to themselves, finding it quite natural that His mercy should not extend to the Jews." Lagrange adds: "It cannot be said that this piece of advice was superfluous for Christians!"

† Paul says simply: has entered. . . . Ought we to supplement: "has entered the Kingdom", which would have a synoptic ring (Michel)? It might also be thought that this metaphor refers back to that of grafting shoots (Lagrange).

‡ Delling, *Th.Wb.NT*, VI, p. 300. Apocalyptic thought fixed the stages of future history in terms of years. When the preordained figures were reached the situations would be ripe for the final events. (Cf. P. Volz, *Die Esch. d. jüd. Gem.*, pp. 138–145.) But we should not attribute as much importance to chronological evaluations as to the idea that history ripens and evolves towards the term which God has appointed.

§ The affirmation that "the whole of Israel would share in the world to come" (Sanh. 10: 1) did not prevent the Jews from thinking that certain categories of sinners, of which a list was drawn up, would be excluded (Strack–Billerbeck, IV, pp. 1052–1056).

and then but καὶ οὕτως *and so*. This is to say that the two events are logically related but the relation should not be understood in a rigid arithmetical fashion. It is rather a question of situations which will have matured and will thus permit the fulfilment of the divine plan.* Thus the prophecy of Isaiah will be accomplished which foretells the coming of the Deliverer and the establishment of a new covenant.†

(28f.) All is now said; but it seems as if the apostle's thought, which has now reached its climax, needs to return upon itself in order to feel secure. It is more than a conclusion which will form the end of the chapter. Paul himself still seems to hesitate in contemplation of the mystery. Israel is loved by God because of the election; for the gifts of God are irrevocable, and hence Israel is still the depositary of the promises. God has not withdrawn from her any of the gifts enumerated in 9: 4–5. But the proclamation of the gospel has brought Israel into conflict with its vocation; the people of God has become the "enemy of God". As always in the New Testament, the expression may be understood to convey the hostility of men against God; this is not perhaps the meaning here, at least not the sole meaning, for the hostility of Israel is brought into relation with the call of the Gentiles ("enemies of God for your sake": δι' ὑμᾶς); this hostility is therefore to some extent the present situation of Israel, which God "treats as an enemy" in order that the gospel may be preached to the Gentiles.‡ As far as the gospel is concerned

* Πᾶς Ἰσραήλ has been understood in various senses: the numerical totality of individuals: the people as a whole collectively; or the Israel of God only (Gal. 6: 16), or the "Election" (Rom. 9: 6) as distinct from Israel after the flesh; or again the election as composed of both Jews and Gentiles. The text should be understood, without subtlety, as referring to the whole of Israel, as the elect people, in a view of history which is concerned with collectives rather than individuals.

† Paul, quoting from memory, juxtaposes Is. 59: 20–21 and 27: 9 "without being aware of it himself" (Gaugler). Ἐκ Σιών may be inspired by Ps. 14: 7; 110: 2. Critics have seen in it an evocation of the historic advent of Christ to Zion.

‡ Cf. Foerster, *Th.Wb.NT*, II, p. 814. We may add that ἐχθρός is active in the NT (he who fosters sentiments of hostility); ἀγαπητός is passive (the object of love). Parallelism would require ἐχθρός to be passive likewise.

294

Israel has assumed an attitude of hostility to God and in consequence God has treated it as an enemy by hardening it. Ἐχθροί, enemies, will connote therefore the condition of Israel before God rather than sentiments of animosity in God Himself.*

(30–32) Vocation and the gifts to which it gives rise being irrevocable, God will pursue by new means the accomplishment of His plan, without resigning the purpose of bringing back to Himself His disobedient people. Thus there arises in the history of the divine dispensations a kind of jigsaw puzzle, the complexity of which is reflected in the tangled skein of the apostle's sentence; he who formerly obeyed has now disobeyed; the disobedient have become obedient; those who now disobey after having obeyed will be restored to obedience.† And all is overshadowed from above by the divine mercy which is the ultimate source and motivation of this drama in all its rich complexity. It is likewise the divine mercy which has "consigned all men to disobedience". This does not mean that God has provoked disobedience; otherwise what the apostle has written so far would be incomprehensible, especially what he wrote in v. 14 about the jealousy which the conversion of the Gentiles must arouse in the Jews. Men have disobeyed by their own free will; but their disobedience has been penalized because God is not mocked and it is not a matter of indifference in His sight whether men obey Him or not; He has locked (συνέκλεισεν) the situation and barred and bolted it, waiting for the sinner to realize that he has involved himself in a desperate position, where his only hope lies in repentance and the forgiveness of God.

The gospel message declares this pardon to be possible and indicates the means of access to it: Jesus Christ. God's sealing of Israel's situation is not intended to imprison it permanently any more than the heathen were permanently locked in the situation of rebellion, God's chastisement of

* The apostle never pictures God as the enemy of anyone. Michel cites 1 Th. 2: 15, but the text has not this meaning.

† Notice that in vv. 30, 31 the two datives ἀπειθείᾳ and ἐλέει, although complementary, have not perhaps the same meaning.

which was described in ch. 1.* On the contrary, the sanctions decreed by God are also salutary. Israel is already the object of the divine pity (notice the present tense: $\nu\hat{v}\nu$ $\grave{\epsilon}\lambda\epsilon\eta\theta\hat{\omega}\sigma\iota\nu$) which is urging it to repent. "Thus the liberty of God is triumphant. If He wills, He can save all men. The gospel is the good news that He does so will" (Vischer).

(33–36) The extent to which the purposes of God are seen to be realized in human history from day to day throws the human mind out of focus; but these enigmas of history are puzzling because the understanding of man is so limited and short-sighted. Faith is able to appreciate the narrow boundaries which confine man. It suspends the judgment of the believer by inclining it towards the silence of adoration. It confesses the "depth", that is, the mysterious unfathomable immensity of the resources by which God exploits His treasures of "wisdom" and "knowledge". Wisdom displayed in the execution of His compassionate purposes. Knowledge which characterizes the initiatives of His love electing in order to save.† "It would be tactless", says Lagrange, "to attempt to define too strictly what Paul declares to be unfathomable; however, he spoke in order to be understood...." The four terms which he uses are of special significance in this respect, namely, that Paul is here borrowing from circles whose boast it was to fathom the mysteries of God;‡ a vocabulary which he uses for a confession of ignorance. Paul breaks with a curiosity and speculativeness of which the apocalyptic writers had made a speciality. He returns to the humility of those Israelites who confessed with the prophet that the ways of God are not the ways of man.§ In fact he

* Cf. the triple $\pi\alpha\rho\acute{\epsilon}\delta\omega\kappa\epsilon\nu$ of ch. 1. It is by the term $\pi\alpha\rho\alpha\delta\acute{\iota}\delta\omega\mu\iota$ that the LXX renders סגר (lock) in the hiphil in Deut. 23: 16; 32: 30; Ps. 31: 8; 78: 48, 50, 62; Job 16: 11.

† The word is to be understood in the sense of $\pi\rho o\acute{\epsilon}\gamma\nu\omega$ Rom. 8: 29. Cf. Bultmann, Th.Wb.NT, I, p. 706.

‡ These words belong to the terminology of the "spiritual". $\beta\acute{\alpha}\theta o\varsigma$: 1 Cor. 2: 10; Rev. 2: 24; $\pi\lambda o\hat{v}\tau o\varsigma$: Col. 1: 27; 2: 2; $\sigma o\phi\acute{\iota}\alpha$: 1 Cor. 1: 30; 2: 6, 7; 12: 8; Col. 1: 9, 28; 2: 3; $\gamma\nu\hat{\omega}\sigma\iota\varsigma$: 1 Cor. 1: 5; 12: 8; 2 Cor. 8: 7; Col. 2: 3; Eph. 3: 19.

§ Is. 55: 8; 40: 13; Jer. 29: 11; Prov. 30: 2; Job 9: 2; 28: 23. In Judaism: Bar. 3: 29; Sir. 42: 18; 43: 30; Wis. 13. Cf. Strack-Billerbeck, III, p. 294.

allows the Old Testament to speak for itself on the point by his quotations from Is. 40: 13 and Job 41: 11 (LXX) which emphasize the distance between God and man, who can never be in regard to God either a counsellor or a creditor.*

The last part of this hymn in which Paul dissolves intellectual problems in the adoration of faith borrows from Hellenistic Judaism a formula which philosophy had brought into currency, under many varied forms. The whole springs from the one and returns to the one: God is the principle underlying all things.† Judaism had already made use of formulae of this kind in its prayers and liturgies.

This concluding hymn is of considerable interest as showing us the scope of the literary background of the apostle. It will be observed that Paul has in turn laid under contribution three literary sources (the language of the "mystics", the Old Testament, and Hellenistic Judaism).

To understand the full implications of the apostle's thought and to place in its true perspective this passage on the destiny of Israel, it would be well, before abandoning the subject, to recall what was the basic question which suggested itself to his mind. It may be formulated thus: what bearing has the unbelief of Israel on the actualization of God's plan? Does this unbelief put Israel out of the question? Affirmatively answered, it may be thought that everything crumbles with the exclusion of this people to whom were made promises which in this case turn out to be false. Answered negatively, how are we to understand the present situation of Israel? What can be the basis of the hope that one day its unbelief will cease?

* This humility however is not altogether foreign to the apocalyptic writers: Apoc. Bar. 14: 8, 9; 75: 1-4. Cf. J. Dupont, *Gnosis*, p. 325.

† Cf. Marcus Aurelius, IV, 23 (ὦ φύσις, ἐκ σοῦ πάντα, ἐν σοὶ πάντα, εἰς σὲ πάντα). Paul avoids saying ἐν αὐτῷ (similarly 1 Cor. 8: 6) so as not to give a pantheistic character to his formula. On the contrary he wishes to emphasize the transcendence of God and the dependence of history, directed by a sovereign will which remains distinct from the events in which it is mysteriously manifested. On this subject, cf. the texts quoted by Lietzmann and E. Norden, *Agnostos Theos*, 1913, p. 240. G. Harder, *Paulus und das Gebet*, 1935, p. 51; J. Dupont, *Gnosis*, p. 344.

This question brings us to the essence of the apostle's argument, for he does not seek reasons for hope that are inherent in the character of this faithless people. If we were reduced to thinking that Israel's unbelief will be overcome because one fine day it will decide to believe, we should be flattering ourselves with a delusive hope. There is no reason to suppose that Israel will modify its attitude towards its Messiah, whom it has rejected in categorical fashion and for reasons which from its own point of view were excellent (understanding of the nature of faith and righteousness). Doubtless Paul might have been satisfied to say that God remains faithful to His covenant; but such fidelity would be without real efficacity if it consisted merely in the permanence of His plan which has already been mocked by the chosen people. In reality, Paul explores a difficult avenue of thought but one which has wide-reaching theological implications.

With regard to Israel's situation and prospects he proposes an interpretation which harmonizes with his doctrine concerning the situation of guilty humanity. Since God did not react to sin by putting in operation the supreme sanction, the guilty were placed under the government of the divine patience by which God wills to induce them to repent. Similarly the unbelief of Israel did not provoke God to make a final break with His people; Israel was subjected to the process of hardening which, for it, is the equivalent of the dispensation of divine patience, and thus God wills to bring the Israelites to repentance. God has not exposed Israel to malediction nor abandoned it to the sole consequences of its unbelief. It is not alone in its estrangement: in some sense God has accompanied it in the desert. Here lies the reason for hope, as solid and unshakeable as the love which inspired this attitude in God. Israel will turn away from its unbelief, not because, contradicting itself, it will arbitrarily decide to do so, but because its heavenly bridegroom will have followed it in the barrenness of its exile in order to urge it, in spite of its present remoteness, to return to the paths of obedience, and faithfulness. God secretly prepares the nets of His love. He wills to overcome Israel's repudiation of Him, as He overcomes every form of human sin, by working in the heart of man, by that kind of constraint of which love alone possesses the key and the mastery—the constraint which compels while exalting liberty.

Paul implies this kind of inner travail which God foresees as the means of restoring the faithless one, when he speaks of the jealousy which will be excited in the breast of the unfaithful wife on seeing the benefits loaded on the second wife, if one may dare to speak thus of the Gentiles. That break with its unbelief which Israel could not accomplish on its own initiative, and which there is no reason whatever to expect of it, is being secretly but sovereignly prepared by God. God never abandons the sinner.* The doctrine of hardening—paradoxically to our modern way of thinking—is precisely intended to safeguard this truth. Hence we must conclude that the position adopted by the apostle in these three chapters is as badly interpreted by the exponents of a predestinarian doctrine, as by their opponents, if the latter understand the people of Israel to be abandoned to its solitary decisions and free with an abstract freedom, devoid of any reason to decide because shrunk into utter isolation. Paul considered that man, even in his sin, was always confronted by God; but he did not consider that man, in this confrontation by God, was ever completely determined or completely undetermined. The relations set up by love elude such rigid alternatives.

---

* Although the comparison is not put forward here as an argument, it is interesting to note that a similar idea is found in the parable of the prodigal son, naturally in metaphorical terms. The prodigal does not return home as a result of a decision which he has taken himself arbitrarily, resting on any chance motives. In reality, he remains in his inner life under the secret influence of divine grace. His decision does not spring from himself alone. Even in the far country, he has held a colloquy with his father through intermediate persons ("my father's hired servants . . .", Lk. 15: 17). He too is stirred with jealousy when he thinks that the wealth of his father is going to others; jealousy has converted him and brought him to himself and to home!

¹I appeal to you therefore, brethren, by the mercies of God, to present your bodies as a living sacrifice, holy and acceptable to God, which is your spiritual worship. ²Do not be conformed to this world but be transformed by the renewal of your mind, that you may prove what is the will of God, what is good and acceptable and perfect.

ONCE MORE, THE subject matter and the style of the letter change. Moreover, there is no further systematic and extended exposition, but a succession of varied themes whose unity it is not easy to grasp. Exhortation now takes the place of dogmatic teaching. Nevertheless these chapters are closely connected with the preceding ones. The question arose as to how, in the new conditions of life which the apostle explained to his readers, the ethical function which the law fulfilled in Israel was now to be understood. If the young church is to remain grafted on the old trunk, was it once again to be preoccupied with the law, if not as an occasion for merit, then at least in its practical requirements? What is the exact nature of the righteousness of which believers are now the instruments? (6: 11–23; 7: 4; 8: 13.) How does the church in practice embody the righteousness which is by faith?

The unsystematic character of these last few pages is instructive. Paul was not writing here a short treatise on ethics. Did he consider this impossible or simply inappropriate? In any case he thought it adequate not to go so far. The ethic which flows from his theology of grace thus retains a spontaneity which preserves it from any hint of legalism. It will be realized that this pedagogic advantage is justified by the very way in which he understands the meaning of Christian obedience. Three themes will be touched upon; the relations of Christians among themselves; their relations with those outside the sphere of Christianity; finally a special aspect of the mutual relations of Christians, namely, the problem arising from their different backgrounds.

(1) First of all, Paul lays the foundations. He explains what the Christian should be in his practical conduct by reminding him of what he essentially is in his faith. One word stands out from the start; of itself it forms a bridge with what precedes, it recalls all that has been said and lays a basis for all that is about to be said: οἱ οἰκτιρμοὶ τοῦ Θεοῦ. The divine mercy was at work in Israel's election; it gave meaning to the history of Israel; it brought this history to its culmination in Jesus Christ; it enables believers to share in His sacrifice and His victory. It is the mercy of God which has made of every reader of Paul's letter what he is. Paul bases himself on this primary and decisive fact of the divine mercy, in order to exhort his readers to consider all that it implies for them.*

Now the divine mercy is fully manifested in the sacrifice of the cross to which every believer is linked by faith and baptism. In 6: 11 Paul had already laid a stepping-stone; he now returns to the same thought. Christ is the sacrificial victim offered in favour of and in the place of the sinner, so that he may share in his death and thus no longer live for himself (2 Cor. 5: 15). The verb παριστάναι likewise recalls to us the ideas which have been expounded in ch. 6; Paul had used it to suggest how the believer puts his body and his members at the disposition of righteousness (6: 12–23). The word which means to *offer*, to present, to place at the disposition of, is here related to the idea of sacrifice and thus implies the consecration of the offering on the altar; the consecrated gift belongs no more to the one who has offered it, he has no

* The plural οἰκτιρμοί comes from the Hebrew רַחֲמִים. The fundamental importance of compassion in the new economy of life has led to doubts that Judaism was anything other than a religion of strict retribution. W. Bousset, *Rel. Jud.*, p. 382, protests against the wrong that is done to Judaism when it is thus judged in the light of Pauline or evangelical polemic ardour. It remains true, however, that mercy, to which the Jews often referred, consisted chiefly in tempering justice rather than in triumphing over it. Bousset, *ibid.* p. 386, recognizes that mercy never constituted the basis of Jewish faith.

further control of it.* Hence the apostle is here bringing forward a very bold and vivid image; the believer sacrifices on the altar his own body, and this altar is the cross. The body (σῶμα) signifies the reality of existence, the human person in the concrete manifestation of his life. There is no offering of the heart which is not outwardly embodied; pure interiority would be for the apostle a defect and would spell contradiction.

Why does Paul say that the offering in question is living, holy, and acceptable to God? It is almost inconceivable that these expressions are entirely unconnected with the law prescribing that the animal offered to Yahweh should be, in order to be acceptable to Him, both living and free from contamination by unclean objects. However, it is difficult to see how these requirements would be valid for the "body" which must be put to death because it is contaminated by fleshly thoughts and because death is the punishment of sin. Hence Paul must rather be applying these ancient qualifications to the offering which is already sacrificed and surrendered to the sphere of the divine. What is in question here is not the condition but the effects of sacrifice. Participation in the death of Christ gives access to new life (8: 13); the Spirit of God touches the offering as formerly the fire consumed it on the altar; the Spirit imparts to it new life and sanctifies it. As the odour of the holocaust was agreeable to God (Ex. 29: 18; Lev. 1: 9, 13, etc.), so was the offering of the body when revivified and sanctified by the Holy Spirit. Chs. 6 to 8 are the source of what Paul says here in terms of the sacrificial image.

It is to the same line of thought that the concluding phrase of the sentence should be referred. Sacrifice is an element in the cult (λατρεία) or the service which God expects from the faithful.† The offering of the "body" or the personality

* Παριστάναι θυσίαν is a technical expression for sacrifice (cf. references in Lietzmann and Michel).

† It is useful to recall the fact that the cultus, in the liturgical sense, is only a special aspect of the "service" which God has a right to expect of His servants; doubtless its culminating point, but nevertheless inseparable from all the other forms of service which as it were constitute the base of this apex, which has no foundation apart from them. In the LXX, λατρεύω generally translates the Hebrew עָבַד: (to work, to

302

gathers up all the essential elements in the cult-worship required by the merciful God disclosed in Jesus Christ.

This conformity of the offering of the body with the fundamental requirement of the divine mercy makes very plausible the explanation which many commentators have given of λογικός; what is in conformity with the nature of God and of man (Lagrange).* But we can hardly avoid giving special attention to the use of λογικός in several texts of Hellenistic Judaism and hermetic literature; there it denotes what is interior, what concerns the deepest being of man, in contrast to what is formal, external or theatrical.† In that case the use of the phrase would emphasize the fact that the sacrifice of the body or personality is indeed that of the whole being of man, perhaps by contrast with the ancient sacrificial system where the bodies of animals were merely placed on the altar. The philosophic sense of λογικός (in close and harmonious connexion with the *logos*) was here much weakened;‡ perhaps however it was not foreign to Paul's mind, for the words λογικὴ λατρεία, as he uses them, connote by a characteristic reversal the cult inspired by the Holy Spirit, which for the believer is the ultimate reality, and takes the place of the *logos* of which the Stoics spoke as being the ultimate rationality of things. Thus the rich complexity of the adjective becomes apparent. This reference to the Spirit as the ultimate reality for the believer brings us again into line with the meaning originally proposed: this service is inward and true because it is in conformity with the Spirit; in other words because it is spiritual, because it flows from the action of the

serve), when the word is used in a religious sense. Elsewhere עבד is rendered by δουλεύειν. The predominant idea in λατρεία is service, work which is done for God because He is the Master who commands. Every act of obedience is a form of cultic service and ministry.

* Without using the word "logical", it is this idea which Michel singles out when he speaks of a sacrifice or a cult which conforms to divine revelation or the Word (*Offenbarungsgemässes Opfer*, p. 260; *dem Wort gemässer Gottesdienst*, p. 258).

† Cf. Const. Apost. VII, 34, 6 etc.; Test. Levi 3: 6; Philo, *Spec. leg.* I, 277; *Herm.* I, 31; XIII, 18, 21 (δέξαι λογικὰς θυσίας . . . λογικὴν θυσίαν). Judaism considered prayer as an inner cult, as distinct from the cult in which sacrifice predominated (cf. Sifre Deut. 11 : 13; par. 41. Cf. Strack-Billerbeck, III, p. 26).

‡ Cf. Seneca, *Ep.*, 95, 50; *De benef.*, 1, 6, 3.

Spirit itself.* The inclusiveness of λογικός overflows all the terms by which we attempt to translate it.

(2) Sacrifice is a grace, it introduces us into a renewed and restored existence, because it abolishes all the old debts. After the death of the "sinful body" and the silence imposed on the "mind of the flesh" (6: 6; 8: 6), after the "condemnation of sinful flesh" (8: 3), the mind of the Spirit presides over the inner life. The Spirit gives to the believer quite a new vision of the world and of himself. The present ceases to be governed by the determining effects of the past, by the dead weight of sin, for a double crucifixion has broken the spell which held man enslaved to the law of the world (Gal. 6: 14). A future is now made accessible which God has created through the Risen Christ, the Conqueror of the powers which fetter the human spirit; the Christian is, in Christ, a new creature (2 Cor. 5: 17). Hence he must now behave, not in view of what he once was, but of what he is called to be; not as an heir of Adam, but as a joint heir with Christ. For him, life and the world take on a different meaning, and his reactions to them are different, for he does not regard reality as consisting in the world as it now lies under the control of the various powers which have several times been indicated (sin, death, the flesh, covetousness, etc.). That world passes away (1 Cor. 7: 31); it has no solidity; it plays a part and it holds the stage but it is without ontological reality. Once a man realizes that, what madness it is to join in this puppet show which is displayed on a tottering stage: "Do not be conformed to this world."† In compensa-

* In 1 Pet. 2: 2, the milk on which the Christian feeds is likewise called "logical". The context shows that this milk is so qualified because of its connexion with the "spiritual house" which offers "spiritual sacrifices" (v. 5). On the whole question, cf. Kittel, *Th.Wb.NT*, IV, pp. 145–147. It seems rather arbitrary to wish to save the "rationalist" meaning of λογικός by supposing that the word means spiritual since the reason (νοῦς v. 2) has been redeemed (cf. L. Cerfaux, *La Théologie de l'Église suivant saint Paul*, 1948, p. 114, n. 2); this is playing on words.

† In 1 Cor. 7: 31 Paul concludes an argument about the moral status of the Christian by saying that we should deal with this world as though we had no dealings with it, because the world is like an actor whose form passes away on the stage of life and vanishes; σχῆμα there indicates the

tion, a new world has emerged with the coming of Christ, and it is with this world that we must now reckon.

All this implies a reversal of values (cf. Phil. 3: 8) which is strikingly expressed by that contrast between an earthly and a heavenly treasure which we find on the lips of Jesus (Matt. 6: 19-21; Lk. 12: 33-44) or again by the antithesis between things above and things below (Col. 3: 2). Paul suggests it in a more theoretical manner here by speaking of the "transformation" of the "mind" as the result of a "renewing". The mind here implies much more than the intellectual faculty of apprehension; νοῦς includes the personality viewed in its deepest aspects and suggests, as it were, man's awareness of his total situation in the universe.* Metaphysical and moral self-consciousness will be renewed because a new reality will now confront it.† This transcendent reality is Jesus Christ. In Him is realized God's purpose of making the creature conformed (σύμμόρφους) to the image of His Son (8: 29). As they contemplate the glory of God which radiates from the face of Christ, believers are transformed into His image (μεταμορφούμεθα), that is, inwardly moulded by the operation of the Spirit of the Lord (2 Cor. 3: 18).‡

Since his inner life is thus transformed, the believer is free in his judgments, he is no longer enslaved to the "law of sin" (8: 2), he can decide on his actions with a spirit of understanding and commit himself as a moral personality. Δοκιμάζειν, to discern, excludes all automatism, including that of the law and casuistry. Phil. 1: 10 shows that discernment has its source and criterion in the love of God manifested in Christ. The believer discovers a mode of conduct which reflects his answer to the divine *agape* in the given situation. In such conditions he can accomplish the will of God.

part played by the actor; the word suggests the external appearance (cf. Héring ad loc.). The word recurs in our text: συσχηματίζεσθε.

* "A word expressing the inner bent of a human personality, or its basic moral disposition . . . the inner orientation of thought and will . . . the cast of the moral consciousness." Behm, *Th.Wb.NT*, IV, p. 956.

† In ἀνακαίνωσις, the idea of newness is above all qualitative and metaphysical (καινός), only subordinately chronological and physical (νέος was preferred for the meaning: young, fresh).

‡ A D G read συσχηματίζεσθαι and μεταμορφοῦσθαι; these infinitives are connected with παρακαλῶ; but the imperatives are preferable.

Are the three adjectives direct qualifications of the will of God or criteria of that will such as enable us to discern it? Both interpretations are grammatically possible, but the second suits better the character of the exhortation. Thus in order to discern the will of God we must seek "what is good". For rabbinical theology the good was such both in the sight of man and the sight of God; good works are also works useful to mankind—works which contribute to man's good and are the means of helping, serving and loving him; 1 Th. 5: 15 shows this clearly.* "What is acceptable" is what is acceptable to God (12: 1; Eph. 5: 10).† "What is perfect" suggests an action which does not fail to attain its objective; this formal sense is found too in the gospels.‡ These three adjectives thus qualify in three ways an action in which the believer feels compelled to recognize the will of God; such an action is controlled and inspired by the love of God and one's neighbour; it is good—it is acceptable to God and consequently is performed with a view to pleasing Him; it is perfect, flowing from single-minded frankness; it is not limited to ineffectual gestures and still less to empty intentions. Thus are expressed the concrete implications of the will of God as regards content, purpose and form.

It is surprising to find the apostle using such general terms as criteria for the discernment of the will of God. He is probably taking up an already traditional formula which both Judaism and Hellenism had contributed to mould.§ But if it is not of his own invention, at least he has adopted it, and has been content to do so. Doubtless he saw here an echo of his Master's teaching: Jesus had confronted man with the

* "Only he who is loving towards God and towards the creatures is both righteous and good; he who is loving towards God but wicked towards the creatures is a righteous man but not a good man . . ." Qid. 40a. Cf. Strack-Billerbeck, IV, pp. 536, 559. Grundmann, *Th.Wb.NT*, I, p. 14. Cf. Lk. 23: 50: ἀνὴρ ἀγαθός καὶ δίκαιος.

† In this sense Rom. 14: 18; 2 Cor. 5: 9; Phil. 4: 18; Col. 3: 20; Hebr. 13: 21.

‡ God is "perfect" because His love is not checked by the wickedness of man; He loves all men with a total love (Matt. 5: 48). In order to be perfect, the young man is exhorted to carry his intention to extremities and without reserve (Matt. 19: 21).

§ Cf. Michel, p. 262, n. 6 and 7.

dilemma of doing good or doing harm, "saving life or killing" (Mk. 3: 4). Further, the refusal of men to do the merciful deed, their refusal to do good, had aroused the sorrow and anger of Jesus who thus reflected the reactions of God to the hard heart, as He also rejoiced over the heart that repents (Lk. 15: 7, 9; Matt. 18: 13). Finally, perfection is the hallmark of the acts of the disciple who does nothing in a bargaining spirit (Matt. 5: 48; 19: 21; Lk. 9: 57-62).

At the close of our commentary on these two verses we must once more emphasize the character of the exhortation which they introduce. Exhortation rests on evangelical preaching, ethics on faith. The Christian vigilance is aroused as to what he ought to do, in view of what he already is as a believer. Gospel preaching teaches him what God has done for him in Jesus Christ, what he is, objectively, through grace, what he is inasmuch as God has entered into new relations with him by adopting him as a son in Jesus Christ, by forgiving him and welcoming him into the divine presence. The exhortation is based on this redemptive work, and appeals to it in urging the adopted son to behave henceforth as a son, so that he may be worthy of the grace which has been conferred on him and a good steward of the gifts which he has received. Such exhortation is not made in order to please: ethics are not the same thing as luxury; the obedience of the Christian is as necessary to his faith, as his faith is necessary to his obedience. The imperatives which Paul uses here are real categorical imperatives, and from this point of view the term exhortation might be misunderstood. If no one is saved by his works, yet the works of him who is saved will be judged; and although one cannot achieve salvation by meritorious good works, the believer can lose his salvation by bad works.

[3]For by the grace given to me I bid every one among you not to think of himself more highly than he ought to think, but to think with sober judgment, each according to the measure of faith which God has assigned him. [4]For as in one body we have many members, and all the members do not have the same function, [5]so we, though many, are one body in Christ, and individually members one of another. [6]Having gifts that differ according to the grace given to us, let us use them: if prophecy, in proportion to our faith: [7]if service, in our serving; he who

teaches, in his teaching: [8]he who exhorts, in his exhortation; he who contributes, in liberality; he who gives aid, with zeal; he who does acts of mercy, with cheerfulness.

(3) After laying down this theological principle, the apostle comes down to concrete details in order to illustrate it. The style assumes a somewhat solemn tone and becomes rhythmical even; there is a liturgical note about it which is appropriate to the subject. But it would be going too far to suggest that Paul here invokes his apostolic authority to give more weight to what he is about to say, for the expression: "the grace given to me" is applicable to any Christian, as is shown by v. 6 (cf. Eph. 4: 7 or 1 Cor. 1: 4 in connexion with faith). Paul is concerned to point out that in the Christian community members should seize the first opportunity to perform a spiritual cult in honour of God by making the "sacrifice" of which we have been speaking.

Did local circumstances provide the occasion for the particular theme of this first illustration of the Christian attitude? But everywhere there is urgent need for lessons in humility, an essential form of the sacrifice to which Christ invites and disposes us. Spiritual gifts flatter our pride, they are regarded as individual achievements and become an occasion for vanity. What is more, those thus gifted humiliate others who have been less generously endowed; the mediocre are despised. Nothing of all this is in place among brethren. We should not exalt ourselves, but retain a certain sobriety of judgment. The word $\sigma\omega\phi\rho\sigma\sigma\acute{\nu}\eta$ is borrowed from secular language. Difficult to translate, it conveys the idea of a harmony and balance which assure peace* to the individual or group. This wisdom which secures the right proportion in all things, the Christian will seek from his faith, for the latter assigns to each one his position and function in the group, in view of the harmony of the whole. It cannot be a question here of the faith which justifies, in regard to which it is inconceivable that God bestows different measures. Perhaps we have here a metonymy, a faith being named instead of the fruits of faith, that is charismatic powers. Or rather the

* Cf. Festugière, *L'idéal religieux des Grecs et l'Évangile*, 1932, p. 18, 2; 19, 1.

308

apostle is alluding to faith as an order of life, πίστις hence denoting the fact of walking in faith.* Wisdom will consist in being governed by the varied conditions which God has assigned to each one, without any suggestion of superiority or inferiority, since all is of grace. But the measure of faith thus understood can vary, for the same development has not taken place in each individual; there are in the church children and grown men (1 Cor. 13: 11) spiritual men and men of the flesh (1 Cor. 3: 1) mature men (1 Cor. 2: 6; Phil. 3: 15) and brethren who behave unworthily. We should recognize that such inequalities exist; faith is a living reality which can grow or become weak.† At Rome itself there are the "strong" and the "weak", as we shall see.

(4f.) The basic reason for this wisdom is not that the anxieties of the jealous soul might be avoided, but rather that since diversity exists for the enrichment of all, he who exceeds his appointed part impoverishes all; this wisdom alone can allocate to each one his place and special function for the common good. The "allegorizing parable" of the body illustrates this truth. (Cf. Michel.) Paul makes much use of it in the Letter to the Corinthians.‡ Believers in their inter-relations and their relation to Christ are not only like a body. They *are* a body, the Body of Christ. The emphasis is here on the first idea which is fully sound only in so far as it is inte-grated with the second. It is a question of the unity achieved by the members through the exercise of their manifold functions.§

(6) Grammatically this sentence is badly connected with the preceding one. We might take it as being simply descrip-tive, e.g. "the fact is that we have different gifts. . . ." It is better to take it in an imperative sense: "This is what should

* Cf. Bultmann, *Th.Wb.NT*, VI, pp. 213, 220.

† Cf. 1 Th. 3: 10; 2 Cor. 10: 15; Rom. 4: 21; 14: 5.

‡ This comparison was widespread in Hellenistic circles. Its use by Paul raises special problems. The literature on the subject is immense. Cf. Fr. Benoit, "Corps, Tête, et Plérôme dans les épîtres de la captivité", *R.B.*, 1936.

§ Οἱ πολλοί: a semitism for *all* (as in 5: 15, 19). τὸ καθ᾽ εἷς: εἷς indeclinable as in Mk. 14: 19; Jn. 8: 9; Rev. 21: 21.

be if gifts are to be exercised in due measure." The "charis-matic powers" constitute such gifts, special aptitudes granted to the members of the church for the good of the latter.*

Paul's enumeration of such gifts here does not coincide with that in 1 Cor. 12: 8–11. No exhaustive catalogue could limit the liberty of the Spirit which animates the Body of the Church according to its needs. No ecstatic charisma are mentioned here. Is it that the Roman character was not favourable to that type of gift? The first gift mentioned is that of prophecy. If we refer to 1 Cor. 14 the prophet, it is said, speaks to men for their upbuilding, encouragement and consolation (v. 3) and also instruction (v. 31); he convicts the sinner and abases him in repentance (v. 24).† The prophet is not the author of predictions, but the preacher who declares the word of God so that it makes a vital impact on the community, the man who gives concrete and exact commands. We know from 1 Cor. 14 that the exercise of prophecy gave rise to certain disorders and that it was neces-sary to restrain and control the prophets.‡ With this experi-ence in mind, the apostle here exhorts the prophets to prophesy only "in proportion to their faith". 'Αναλογία connotes a correspondence or proportion. In practice the idea expressed merges with that of μέτρον πίστεως, *measure of faith*, in v. 3; the Syriac version, the Peshitta, renders both μέτρον and ἀναλογία by the same word. This connexion readily suggests itself. The apostle wishes that the exercise of charismatic gifts should take place conformably with the graces which underlie them (v. 6). The expression should neither fall short of nor exceed the controlling inspiration; it should be neither negligent nor pretentious.

In regard to prophecy the risk which is particularly threatening is that it may be practised with the addition of what is superfluous and without authority, or that the pro-

* "Sometimes, it is a question of charismatic gifts in such a broad sense that every Christian, even the most modest, is considered to possess one which will be useful to the community" (Héring, *Comm.* 1 *Cor.*, p. 109).

† This picture of the activity of the prophet corresponds to what we see of the activity of that prophet who wrote the letters to the churches (Rev. 2 and 3).

‡ In Paul's view this was not a reason for silencing them and eli-minating them, as has been done since!

phet continues to speak when he has nothing further to say that is inspired by the Spirit. A practical test enables the authenticity of the exercise of other gifts to be verified, whereas prophecy eludes direct control.* Hence the prophets are exhorted to be vigilant, not to force their gifts but to remain within due limits according to the measure of their faith. Thus this faith is not the *regula fidei*, the apostolic creed, the doctrine taught by the church, and it is not a question of prophecy being subjected to this.†

(7–8a) Then comes brotherly helpfulness‡ and service which demands, if we are to escape from formalism, a special grace. It should be practised as a ministry by which the church is edified. The "teacher" must have had an important part to play and the function was regularly exercised (Acts 13: 1; 15: 35). It continued in fact the task which the rabbis had undertaken but with a liberty in the interpretation of scripture which flowed from the ever living Spirit (2 Cor. 3: 17; Matt. 13: 52). As for "exhortation" or "consolation" (cf. 15: 4) it is addressed more to the heart than to the mind; this is what should distinguish prophecy from exhortation; for the prophet both exhorts and instructs (1 Cor. 14: 3, 31).

---

* Cf. Zahn, pp. 544–545, who insists again on the fact that the faith in proportion to which the charismatic gift should be exercised is not the faith which saves, but, as in v. 3, "the faith as charisma, i.e. a confidence variously based according to the variety of the individual charismata, and relating to different objects, an instrument of the Spirit of God, which engenders and allocates the charismata". Same interpretation of ἀναλογία in Kittel, *Th.Wb.NT*, I, p. 350. Already A. H. Meyer, *Handbuch* . . . 1872, p. 542.

† In this regard, Augustine appeals to the *regula fidei* (*Doct*. IV, 20, 40) and dogmatists have followed him, even when they thought that the rule of faith was scripture and not tradition (*conformitas doctrinae in scripturis*, Calov). There is a painful irony in the fact that, in order to eliminate prophecy to the advantage of a conformist and dogmatizing sclerosis, appeal was made to a text which concerned the exercise of this charismatic gift, and regulated it according to the measure of personal faith. An unjust triumph of the *fides quae creditur* over the *fides qua creditur*.

‡ Διακονία may designate the apostolic ministry in general, (11: 13; 2 Cor. 4: 1; 6: 3, etc.) or a charismatic gift, since all charisma forms a ministry (16: 1; 1 Cor. 12: 5; 16: 15), or again the help rendered to members of the community (15: 25, 31; 2 Cor. 8: 4; Acts 6: 1).

While exhortation rouses the spirit, instruction enlightens the judgment (cf. 1 Tim. 6: 3; Tit. 1: 9).

(8b) The construction changes. Now the exercise of spiritual gifts is seen to call for personal feelings such as simplicity and zeal. "He who contributes" must do so with simplicity of heart; the "leader" must be zealous: church leader (1 Th. 5: 12, 13) or head of the family (1 Tim. 3: 4, 5, 12)—to which does he allude? He who does acts of mercy must do so "radiant with joy" (Lyonnet).* Are these three spiritual gifts exercised within the community life of the church, officially and in the name of the church, or have we here a reference to private life? The context favours the former interpretation. We see here manifestations of Christian ἀγάπη. The personal feelings of those concerned are mentioned by reason of the very nature of the functions specified. "He who contributes" provides the church with wealth which someone ("the leader") organizes and administers† and others distribute by concrete acts of charity.‡ The givers must act without pride or ulterior motive; the administrators must be zealous in the administration of wealth which does not belong to them and from which they will not profit (a hit at the red tape involved in all administration); those who dispense the wealth must not be mere functionaries, so as to spare as much as possible the feeling of humiliation inseparable from dependence on others; they must know how to behave with tact so as to be readily forgiven for offering money to the needy. If you will, such observations are not specifically Christian. But we should not for this reason be surprised, with Michel, to find them connected with the Christian charisma. Firstly, because Christian conduct moves within certain external conditions which are imposed on it as on every man; to be Christian, conduct is not obliged to be practised in a rarefied atmosphere which is inhuman; that would be an absurd aping of the angels. Secondly, because the Christian must consider always to be obligatory, since it is rooted in *agape*, a mode of conduct which the world can

---

* Cf. Prov. 22: 9 (LXX), quoted in 2 Cor. 9: 7.
† In the same role, ἡ προστάτις of 16: 2.
‡ Ἐλεεῖν = ποιεῖν ἐλεημοσύνην. Strack-Billerbeck, III, p. 296.

always criticize, which it has in fact often devalued in view of certain specific interests, and discredited by perverse propaganda.

⁹Let love be genuine; hate what is evil, hold fast to what is good; ¹⁰love one another with brotherly affection; outdo one another in showing honour. ¹¹Never flag in zeal, be aglow with the Spirit, serve the Lord. ¹²Rejoice in your hope, be patient in tribulation, be constant in prayer. ¹³Contribute to the needs of the saints, practise hospitality.

¹⁴Bless those who persecute you; bless and do not curse them. ¹⁵Rejoice with those who rejoice, weep with those who weep. ¹⁶Live in harmony with one another; do not be haughty, but associate with the lowly; never be conceited. ¹⁷Repay no one evil for evil, but take thought for what is noble in the sight of all. ¹⁸If possible, so far as it depends upon you, live peaceably with all. ¹⁹Beloved, never avenge yourselves, but leave it to the wrath of God; for it is written, "Vengeance is mine. I will repay, says the Lord." ²⁰No, "if your enemy is hungry, feed him; if he is thirsty, give him drink; for by so doing you will heap burning coals upon his head." ²¹Do not be overcome by evil, but overcome evil with good.

(9) The thought here takes a new turn. It is not now a question of various functions devolving on various members of the church, but of attitudes and dispositions common to all. Firstly ἀγάπη, *love*, by which the believer responds to the love of God. How can one live by the strength of God's love without exercising love oneself? (Gaugler.) Love is the primary fruit of the Spirit (Gal. 5: 22); it is pre-eminently the mind of the Spirit which was the theme of ch. 8. The Spirit and love are the inseparable characteristics of the age which Christ has ushered in, and of the mode of life conformed to it (cf. vv. 1, 2). Love is hypocritical when we pretend to love our neighbour while secretly thinking only of ourselves; that is giving to receive in return (Matt. 5: 46; Lk. 6: 32-36). True love is a matter of being intensely concerned about the good of one's neighbour, to which one must give single-minded attention* (we have already found this definition of the good, τὸ ἀγαθόν, v. 2) by the removal of all impure motives (cf. the dilemma of Mk. 3: 4).

* Κολλάω; to stick together, to weld, unite closely.

313

(10) The exhortations which follow seem to be grouped in pairs. Φιλαδελφία suggests the ties of affection which tenderly unite the members of the same family; it is manifested in tenderness which according to Lagrange is the very mark of the Christian disposition. With such dispositions there can be no question of one brother becoming impelled to assert his superiority over the others; on the contrary each one will esteem others better than himself.*

(11–12a) Paul now considers deeper zones of the inner life. Because of the eschatological situation (cf. 13: 11, 12) we should not put off what can be done at once. Each set of circumstances confronts us with special tasks; each opportunity has a specific time limit, as fixed by the will of God. Idleness is therefore disobedience. "Let your inner being be ever vigilant, ready for action, mobile as water which boils over the fire." The image is at once intelligible; we say of someone who gets angry quickly, that he boils over like milk. There is no need for allegorization, no need to insist that the Spirit which is fire is the source of this keenness (Is. 4: 4; Acts 2: 3). Τῷ πνεύματι is the spirit of man, of course, when filled and aglow with the Spirit of God. The believer is in an inner state which in its zeal and eagerness reminds us of boiling water. Both exhortations are doubtless a reference to the need for prompt fulfilment of the tasks of love and brotherly affection.

* V. 10b has not yet received a satisfactory interpretation. Προηγοῦμαι means: precede, go in front of, or prefer, esteem more highly (2 Mac. 10: 12). Hence two different ideas: "forestall each other"; or again: "try to outdo each other"; or else: "esteem others more highly than yourselves". Τῇ τιμῇ is equally difficult; it may be understood to mean marks of honour, which would be more appropriate to the first meaning of προηγοῦμαι, or feelings of consideration, which is suitable to the second. It would seem that Phil. 2: 3 favours the second meaning. What is in question is that humility inspired in the believer by the realization that he benefits from divine grace, like an insolvent debtor, and the fact obliges him to offer himself to the service of his brethren. Only humility before God can give rise to humility before men, and that is why Graeco-Roman antiquity did not know the virtue of humility (A. Dihle, art. "Humility", R.A.C., III, p. 737); it understood the necessity for restraint, and condemned "hubris", but it did not consider that man might renounce his rights. The principles of the μηδὲν ἄγαν and γνῶθι σεαυτόν spring from a nobleman's ethic! (p. 738.)

The end of v. 11 is a problem. The majority of manuscripts read: "serving the Lord" (τῷ Κυρίῳ δουλεύοντες);* but an ancient version reads τῷ καιρῷ δουλεύοντες, which is a more difficult formula though one which is in better harmony with the context, for the mention of the Lord is somewhat surprising here. If we read κυρίῳ we shall point out that Paul wishes to bring out the real nature of services rendered to the brethren; in the last analysis they are a service rendered to the Lord, and he who fulfils them is behaving as a faithful servant of the Lord. If we read καιρῷ we shall not merely see here a counsel of opportunism: "adapt yourselves to the given situation, be resigned" (*tempori servientes*), as some critics have suggested. Καιρός has a much more emphatic meaning: *the present age* (ὁ νῦν καιρός, cf. 3: 26; 8: 18; 11: 5) is marked by the Lordship of the Risen Christ; that is why the καιρός has such an important bearing on practical decisions (13: 11; Gal. 6: 10; Col. 4: 5; Eph. 5: 16). Paul wishes us to take into consideration the character of the age in which we live, and to remember that it is dominated by the fact of Christ's resurrection and by the hope of His return. It will be seen that this interpretation naturally links the ending with the initial phrase of v. 12: "rejoice in your hope", which evidently is an allusion to the eschatological hope awakened by the Spirit in the heart of the believer.

(12b) As in 8: 18–27 (cf. 5: 4) prayer, tribulation, patience, and hope are organically connected. His religious hope involves the believer in a conflict with this present world, of which that hope constitutes a radical criticism; hence the reaction of the world and the distressed condition of the Christian of which Paul has already spoken in chs. 8 and 5. Perseverance in prayer both expresses and nourishes faith; God strengthens the one who in his weakness trusts in Him (2 Cor. 12: 9, 10).

(13) In the difficult times in which hope involves believers by bringing them into conflict with the world, there arise special needs among them with which each Christian must feel in full solidarity and sympathy. We must be ready to

* Κυρίῳ : S A B E L P ; καιρῷ: D F G it Ambr.

turn to those in need and share their affliction.* If on the
other hand they come to us, we shall receive them with
brotherly hospitality, for in Christ there are no longer
strangers, only brothers (cf. 1 Pet. 4: 9; Hebr. 13: 2; 1 Tim.
3: 2; Tit. 1: 8). Christian hospitality must inconvenience us
more than that of the world; we do not choose our time or
our guests; it demands a special effort emphasized by διώκω,
to pursue.

(14) By association of ideas, the verb διώκω leads the apostle
to describe the appropriate Christian attitude towards adversaries. Thus we are introduced to a series of exhortations
concerning the Christian's relations with those outside the
church.† Paul is perhaps thinking of Matt. 5: 44 and Lk. 6:
28, under the influence of which some copyists have applied
to the Romans what in the apostle's mind was of more
general purport: those who *persecute you.*‡ To bless and to
curse do not consist simply in speaking a pacifying word or in
hurling sharp invective: it is from the depth of the heart to
invoke on someone the blessing (or the curse) of God, it implies desiring for someone the supreme and ultimate good,
and, when opportunity arises, doing to him the good that is
in one's power.

(15) Our relationship with others should be§ so close
as to enable us to share their deepest feelings, to draw
near to them in the secret recesses of their inner life, to be
present with them at the point where they are most deeply
themselves, in their joys or their sorrows (Gaugler).‖ In
the first instance it is on this secular and psychological

* D G it Vulg. speak of remembering (ταῖς μνείαις) the saints; this
would be an allusion to the contribution to the brethren at Jerusalem
(Rom. 15: 25), (Zahn). The second member of the phrase suggests
rather immediate needs.

† Many commentators think the new section does not begin until v. 17.
In that case v. 14 seems out of place. But it must be recognized that vv.
15 and 16 can very naturally refer to the life of the community itself. The
problem remains open.

‡ S A D etc. add ὑμᾶς.

§ The infinitive has the value of an imperative. Cf. Phil. 3: 16.

‖ Judaism and Hellenism already advocated this kind of sympathy
(Strack-Billerbeck, III, p. 298; Epict. II, 5, 23: τὸ συγχαίρειν).

plane that the believer's encounter with man is situated.

(16) It is certainly very easy to apply this exhortation to the relation of believers with each other, since Paul has used the expression several times in this sense.* However, there is no reason to suppose that it is not a question of the good understanding which the Christian should take care to foster towards people who are outside the church. The sympathy which is the subject of v. 15 concerns of course the plane of feeling; Paul is here enjoining the attainment of mutual understanding on the plane of ideas. We must be able to sacrifice our own special opinions and not desire to assert ourselves at any and every cost. Do not be ambitious in your thoughts nor claim to be constantly scoring points against your opponent; be content with a more modest role. A man who insists on being right every time is by that very fact putting himself in the wrong; he is making his own ideas of truth the standard of truth itself, and is intruding himself between the truth and the person he is addressing. There is a way of clinging to the truth which is no more than a way of clinging to oneself.†

(17) After considering relations with men from the point of view of the difficulties they create for the church, Paul now considers in the same perspective of vision the concrete aspect of things; actions will be added to feelings. The Christian will not return blow for blow;‡ he will be concerned§ on the

* Rom. 15: 5; 2 Cor. 13: 11; Phil. 2: 2; 4: 2; cf. Phil. 3: 16.
† This verse may be understood otherwise: "Be equally complaisant to all: do not make distinctions among men; do not be misled by your own preferences, which always incline towards what flatters your pride, what is distinguished and brilliant; be drawn towards what is humble, in persons or things." Michel applies all these exhortations to the "spiritual" who appeal to their more or less ecstatic revelations and despise the ordinary run of normal piety with its lowly tasks. We do not think that the spiritual are specially alluded to in these passages, from which of course they could profit, as could all other Christians. Paul may have been thinking of them, but he does not refer to them exclusively.
‡ Not only the gospel (Matt. 7: 1), but several Greek authors (Soph., Phil., 679; Plato, Crito, 48) condemned the law of retaliation, which answers injustice or evil by injustice or evil.
§ Προνοέω suggests foresight, providential careful thought; thought which precedes and controls action. Cf. 1 Tim. 5: 8.

317

contrary to perform good deeds, which will be recognized as such by those who are the object of them* (1 Th. 5: 15). The desire to earn the approbation of non-Christians is inspired by the thought of furnishing a testimony to the glory of God (1 Cor. 10: 31–32) which reflects the mind of Jesus (Matt. 5: 16).†

(18) By behaving thus, we create the best conditions for fostering peaceful relationships. Unfortunately we do not always attain the desired objective. We cannot live in peace at any price, nor with anyone whomsoever, if only because truth has rights which charity cannot disregard, or again because some people refuse to co-operate. We can at least endeavour to promote such peace, and the believer must realize that in this regard he has a greater responsibility than anyone, since he is aware of the work of reconciliation effected by Christ (5: 1; 8: 6; 14: 17; 15: 19).‡

(19) It will be said that an exaggerated concern for peace is playing into the hands of the wicked, favouring his schemes, leaving his wickedness unpunished and plunging him further into it; whereas a decisive reaction would dispel such mis-understanding. As far as the sphere of personal relations is concerned the apostle repudiates these considerations.§ In 1 Cor. 6: 1–5, in regard to quarrels arising between Christians,

* Paul quotes freely Prov. 3: 4 (cf. 2 Cor. 8: 21). Under the influence of the original text, corrections have been made: P 46 D G: "in the face of men"; G lat. add: "not only in the sight of God but also . . ."; A: "in the sight of God and. . . ."

† Cf. J. Jeremias, *Jésus et les païens*, 1956, p. 60, n. 1 (E.T. *Jesus' Promise to the Nations*). It will be noted that in Phil. 4: 5, 8 Paul describes the Christian attitude in terms borrowed from Stoic moral philosophy; this fact shows that the Christian ought not to despise what is recognized by non-Christians as worthy of approval; such pride would indicate a lack of charity.

‡ Cf. Matt. 5: 9; Mk. 9: 50; 1 Th. 5: 13; 2 Cor. 13: 11. Epict. IV, 5, 24; εἰρήνην ἄγεις πάντας ἀνθρώπους.

§ It may be said that he who parries the blow, even in defence of a good cause, is in fact defending his personal rights, and this creates a still worse misunderstanding; for on the pretext of defending justice he is giving the latter an appearance of self-interest. Thus a more profound division between men is set up.

Paul advised the arbitration of a brother; he was vexed that people should have resort to pagan judges; it would be better to suffer an injustice or be defrauded (v. 7). As regards quarrels arising with non-Christians the attitude enjoined in our text is not perhaps quite the same. Paul does not tell his readers to suffer injustice; is it because he reckons with the intervention of a court which would forestall it? It may be thought so indeed, for he says: "Leave it to the wrath of God"—that the wrath of God is really in question is clear from the allusion to Deut. 32: 35,* and later (13: 4) wrath is used to denote the activity of civil powers as the vindicators of justice against those who do evil. Hence it would seem that in this text already Paul envisages the wrath of God being exercised through the medium of the civil power. Hence the believer will not need to have positive and direct recourse to civil justice; but he will approve its intervention in his favour and recognize in it an instrument of God's providential government of things, in the sense in which ch. 13 will handle this theme.

(20) The believer will not be satisfied with allowing the justice of men to take its course; he will adopt a positive attitude and will try to show, in regard to someone who is imbued with animosity towards him, that he does not entertain any hostility in return. Quoting Prov. 25: 21–22 (LXX) Paul suggests the simplest and most direct means of doing good. In its sober terseness, this expression implies everything else. In the context it is out of the question to interpret the image of heaping burning coals on the head as an aggravation of divine chastisement, or as a measure intended to attract a further misfortune to the guilty person, which is certainly the sense which the expression has in Ps. 140: 10. The practice, which was probably magical in origin, implied either the execution of a punitive measure or the repentance of one who under-

---

* Διδόναι τόπον: give scope for an action by leaving the field free. The citation from Deuteronomy follows a text which is neither Massoretic nor LXX: perhaps Targum Onk., cf. Strack-Billerbeck, III, p. 300. Cf. Prov. 20: 22; Sir. 28: 1; Test. Gad 6 (ἄφες αὐτοῦ καὶ δὸς τῷ Θεῷ τὴν ἐκδίκησιν).

took voluntarily to expiate his fault in this way. We may see here then, either the idea already expressed by the suggestion of the "wrath" which executed punishment; or else the idea that the guilty man will repent at the sight of the kindness shown to him by his victim. It has often been suggested that the pain of burning coals was the pain of repentance acting like an inner fire burning the conscience.*

(21) Thus the first victory which we must win over evil is to prevent it from triumphing by filling with vengeful feelings the heart of the victim. The essential victory over evil is the work of love. If evil is not securely conquered in the heart of the enemy, it will at least be so in the heart of the believer. This is enough, the rest is the work of God, but this is also the essential matter. The philosophic character of the expressions used did not prevent the apostle from understanding this victory of good over evil as the victory of God and obedience to His will. "The good" is the love of one's neighbour (cf. 12: 2) and generally the will of God (2: 10; 7: 13; 8: 28).†

---

* The Targum of Prov. 25: 21 understands the image in the sense of a repentance which leads to reconciliation (Strack-Billerbeck, III, p. 302). Michel, p. 279, devotes a long note to the question; *ibid.*, bibliography.

† Cf. Test. Benj. 4: 2: "The good man does not scowl, he has pity on all, even if they are sinners and work evil towards him"; 4: 3: "He overcomes evil by doing good, protected as he is by the good."

CHAPTER

13

¹Let every person be subject to the governing authorities. For there is no authority except from God, and those that exist have been instituted by God. ²Therefore he who resists the authorities resists what God has appointed, and those who resist will incur judgment. ³For rulers are not a terror to good conduct, but to bad. Would you have no fear of him who is in authority? Then do what is good, and you will receive his approval, ⁴for he is God's servant for your good. But if you do wrong, be afraid, for he does not bear the sword in vain; he is the servant of God to execute his wrath on the wrongdoer. ⁵Therefore one must be subject, not only to avoid God's wrath but also for the sake of conscience. ⁶For the same reason you also pay taxes, for the authorities are ministers of God, attending to this very thing. ⁷Pay all of them their dues, taxes to whom taxes are due, revenue to whom revenue is due, respect to whom respect is due, honour to whom honour is due.

WE KNOW FROM the Letter to the Corinthians (I, ch. 6) that the relations of early Christianity with public authorities created a serious problem for the Christian conscience; if the Christian was not to be conformed to the present world, should he adopt an aggressive attitude towards all its institutions? The problem was not merely one of practical importance. It was essentially a theological problem: was the obedience due to the Lord compatible with the obedience required by the various organs which the state authorizes?* For Israel this problem did not in theory exist at all; the theocratic constitution of Israel gave to this people one sovereign only, namely God, who exercised His authority through Moses and other officers on whom was incumbent the duty of explaining and applying the law. But as soon as

---

* Same preoccupations in 1 Tim. 2: 1, 2; Tit. 3: 1; 1 Pet. 2: 13-17.

the law lost its traditional function, the problem emerged. It was moreover so much the more pressing because the very wide dispersal of Christians made impossible the formation of a common tacit opinion or "custom" which could dictate the attitude to be adopted towards the civil authority and thus counterbalance the inevitable pressures of the latter. The church in the capital of the empire must have been more preoccupied than any other with this problem. There is no positive indication, however, that Paul is replying to a Roman problem of which he had been informed from other sources.*

The discussion of the state authority is moreover closely linked with the preceding passages of thought. The break between chs. 12 and 13 is only apparent; Paul was led to broach the matter by the very movement of his own ideas. Not to render evil for evil, to suffer injustice, to give to the evildoer proofs of the kind sentiments one entertains towards him, are after all problematic attitudes. From one point of view they are in practice dangerous because they might have a result contrary to what was intended and favour the triumph of evil. Further, are they not theologically debatable? Faith is not temerity; on the pretext of trust in God, may we not be making use of God in a spirit of imprudence or lack of foresight? The attitude of the believer described in 12: 14–21 can hardly be put forward as the way to be followed by all men. Similarly, should it be generalized as applicable to all the cases with which the believer may find himself confronted? Thus for every reason there arises the question as to what one should think of the civil institutions whose task it is to control and repress evil actions. Are they contrary to the will of God?

In a sense vv. 1 to 7 of this chapter form a parenthesis; we should note the characteristic fact that the Christian rule of *agape* inspires and informs the considerations which form a framework to these seven verses dealing with the question of state authority.† Now in the course of the latter, Paul makes

* It has been supposed that in Rome certain who prided themselves on their "spirituality" praised some form or other of anarchy. No trace of polemic in ch. 13 permits us to confirm this opinion.

† It is a question of love towards one's neighbour at the end of ch. 12 and again from 13: 8.

no allusions to the fundamental theme of Christian ethics; so far from doing so, he speaks of the sword which we must tremble to see in the hands of the magistrate! Paul does not evade the problem by falsifying its basic data; he does not claim that the public authorities are ancillary to the Kingdom of God; there is no attempt to make of these men angelic powers; there is no suggestion of enjoining the magistrate to bring his methods into line with those of Christ even by alluding to the whip which Christ once handled. There is no common measure between the whip and the sword. With the whip in its hands the civil authority will not be sufficiently dreaded to command obedience. Paul is thoroughly a realist. Thus there arises in all its tension the conflict between "civil justice" and the "righteousness of the Kingdom", between compulsion and love. But this conflict is of a special kind; it is not formulated in terms of antitheses but in terms of things that are complementary. This is a point which we must grasp in order to understand why it is that a parenthesis of this sort has its appropriate place between passages that are devoted to Christian *agape*.

The essential feature of Paul's attitude in fact is the positive character of its position regarding public authority, and the reason given for this. These civil authorities serve the "good". If we do not forget the richness of meaning associated with this latter term, and which makes it a synonym of *agape*, we realize that for Paul the mission of the state is quite compatible with the practical requirements of faith. The civil power is a stranger to the love revealed in Jesus Christ, but its special task is not outside the control of God's providential will in Jesus Christ. The Christian will adopt a positive attitude towards it in the belief that his obedience will contribute to the realization of God's plan through the magistracy considered as a particular instrument of the divine mercy.

It is such considerations which justify the Christian's attitude of obedience towards the magistrate. The basis of the Christian's obligation in this respect lies in the fact that the magistrate is subjected to the claims implied in his function. If the latter departs from the good in order to serve the purposes of evil, the Christian ceases to have the same reasons for submission to his authority. He then has grounds for criticizing the state authority and enlightening it with regard to its true tasks, warning it of its mistakes and helping it to correct its ways. The manner in which the apostle establishes the principle of obedience excludes all servility. Obedience is due only for reasons of conscience. Thus obedience is not in itself a virtue. As soon as it ceases to be critical, this positive attitude towards state authority forgets the real justification of the latter which lies in the service of God; hence when it ceases to be conscientious it becomes idolatrous. In order to remain conscientious, obedience always includes the possibility of resistance, and even, at the extreme limit, of disobedience.

Positive and critical, the Christian's attitude to state authority has yet another characteristic qualification. Here is its third feature whose importance is not less. Paul speaks of obedience but not of collaboration. He asks us to entertain with regard to state authorities feelings of respect and fear; but he takes care not to speak of the Christian's attachment or affection for the state, still less of love for it. Of course the Roman state was not a republic; those sectors of public life in which one could feel political obligations were extremely limited; the voting rights did not allow any citizen whatsoever to exercise civic responsibilities. Such circumstances did not favour the development of a doctrine of active participation in the life of the city. Attention has also been called, in explanation of the apostle's attitude, to the expectation of the end of the age, to which we see an allusion in v. 11. Thus, according to this view, the attitude of Paul is one of ironical resignation towards a power whose essential nothingness would soon be manifested at the *parousia* of the Lord. But if these had been the implicit convictions of Paul he would not have troubled to expound such a well-developed doctrine, nor in particular one which reposed on such solid foundations. Nor would he have failed to tell us that the puppet show of state authority belonged to the transience of this world. His argument would have had a different ring about it: "Let us bend our backs for the time being; very soon the Lord will bring us deliverance." The apostle does not say this. Moreover, while doubts about some concrete political action might modify practical deductions, they could not

324

influence the theory itself which considered state authority to be rooted in the will of God, whatever the forms its exercise assumed. In fact, Paul's reserve with regard to this authority is so much the more striking, seeing that its basis is divine.

In order to explain this reserve, we must remember the realism of the apostle. The civil power has both motives and methods of action which are not inspired by faith. Its aim is to organize society for the good of man, and it is all to the good that it acts with this end in view; but this end does not constitute the ultimate good of man. Faith understands that there can be no truly good society of which the Lord is not Christ; and that the means of attaining such a society have nothing to do with political, economic, or social organization but are a matter of converting the human heart to the Lord of all mankind. The magistrate is obliged to ignore this ultimate end and this central means. Hence his endeavours can only disregard what should be their essential core. In consequence the attitude of believers towards the civil power will be positive but marked with a strong note of reserve. Far from despising the magistrate, they will obey him and if need be will try to promote his understanding of his mission. But they will not forget the limits that are placed, and should be placed, on the functioning of such authority whose competence extends only to outward matters, and cannot intrude on the heart of which the Lord alone is master. Believers know that it is a good thing to organize the life of the world, but that the only necessary and truly good thing is to change it.

(1) Every person* should be subject to the governing authorities, whose exercise, to be efficacious, should extend to all. Submission to established authority was very widely taught by Judaism; its tradition on this point went back to Daniel (2: 21, 37, 38; 4: 14, 26). Even after the destruction of the temple by the Romans, the authority of the latter was still considered to be of divine origin. The prince will be required to render an account of the exercise of his authority

---

* ψυχή: person, individual, inasmuch as he has a soul and is alive. Πᾶσα ψυχή: whoever (Epict. I, 28, 4; Lev. 7: 27, etc.; Acts 2: 43; 3: 23; Rom. 2: 9; Rev. 16: 3).

to God from whom he holds it in trust, and this consideration justifies exhorting him to practise wisdom in the name of the Most High.* Since God's sovereignty over history extends to foreign princes, Jeremiah can urge the exiles to pray for Babylon (Jer. 29: 7).† Such a theology of authority provoked some burning problems, if taught without qualification or reserve. It is understandable that some Israelites were fiercely hostile to it; the zealots were the spearhead of this movement of resistance, especially in Palestine where they stirred up much serious trouble, but they were active too in Rome and Alexandria.

State authority is manifested in authorities (ἐξουσίαι), in officials whose legitimate task it is to exercise that authority. Authority (ἐξουσία) is in the first place the effectual power of accomplishing something and secondly the right to exercise such power. Finally it is political power in general considered as a synthesis of lawful right and executive ability. This synthesis is characteristic; government is able to declare what is the right and this is its legislative power; and also to execute or put in operation that right, which is its executive power. The state is essentially the organ which promulgates law and enforces it.‡ These two aspects constitute the structure of power in the eyes of Paul, who refers to the legislative aspect when he describes its essential aim as the "good" and to the executive when he speaks of its operative instrument, the "sword".

The attitude to be adopted towards constituted authority is indicated by the verb ὑποτάσσεσθαι, to submit.§ The term does not by any means imply servility. Paul uses the word in regard to the mutual respect and submission of brothers (1 Cor. 16: 16) in the fear of Christ (Eph. 5: 21).‖ Similarly the church is submitted to Christ and the wife to the husband (Eph. 5: 24). In all these relationships agape plays a decisive part and inspires a submission "as is fitting in the Lord".

* Wis. 6: 1–11; cf. Strack-Billerbeck, III, p. 303 and 45.

† Cf. also Jer. 27: 5, 6; Is. 45: 1, 2. Orientals and Greeks shared the opinion that the prince is invested with divine authority.

‡ Οἱ ὑπερέχοντες are those who effectively exercise power, in Wis. 6: 5. Cf. οἱ ἐν ὑπεροχῇ ὄντες, 1 Tim. 2: 2.

§ D G it read: πάσαις ἐξουσίαις ὑπερεχούσαις ὑποτάσσεσθε.

‖ Cf. 1 Pet. 5: 5 in the Koiné.

More generally speaking, submission is a dovetailing of the parts of an organic whole, with the aim of preventing disorder and furthering peace and unity; this is the point which Paul brings out when he speaks of the submission of the spirits of the prophets (1 Cor. 14: 32) or when he is discussing the untimely interventions of women in the Christian assemblies (1 Cor. 14: 34). Such submission then implies a positive obedience to common need, incumbent on an individual in view of the position he occupies in a collective whole whose good he is obliged to promote.

This requirement applicable to all will not be felt as a bad thing, a piece of coercion, which it might be legitimate or even advisable to shake off. The validity of authorities flows from the authority of God who has conferred on His creation a hierarchical structure. The fact is that all things are not interchangeable and reversible. To each one his responsibilities, the correct and due fulfilment of which manifests the providential government of God and His presiding plan. God is pre-eminently the subject of all valid authority;* in Him right and executive power are perfect. He is the source of every historic manifestation of the dual functioning of right and power. He is both the source and the legitimation of right and its enforcement. It is divine authority which is being exercised when the civil authorities exercise their authority in the service of the "good" which is soon afterwards to be the theme of Paul's discourse.

Having thus laid down the principle of ideal authority, Paul passes to the concrete case; existing and contemporary (αἱ δὲ οὖσαι) authorities are established by God. We have here a judgment on the Roman government, for which Paul marks his esteem. It should not be forgotten that from A.D. 54 to 62 the administration was in the hands of Seneca, who had noble aims. Before him, influence belonged to Narcissus who probably had Christians in his household (cf. 16: 11; Lagrange). In any event we must abstain from extrapolating.

* The two most remarkable analogies for God in the Bible are taken from earthly realities in which is manifested most commonly and in most exemplary fashion the principle of authority: the king and his kingdom; the father and the family (brethren). As for Christ, He is Head of His body, the church.

327

Just because Paul passes a judgment on a particular state, he does not invite us to extend that judgment to all other states. In many ways the modern state cannot be identified with that which was known to Paul. Criticism begins in making such distinctions, which must turn on the question of what is involved in the "good". For Paul the Roman state satisfied the basic requirements of authority, as is clear from his appeal to Caesar's tribunal; in so doing he was asking Nero to defend the church from arbitrary action. We are still obeying authority when we oblige it to assume its proper responsibilities, and, eventually, to unmask its intentions.*

* The plural αἱ ἐξουσίαι is not without currency in Greek (cf. Foerster, *Th.Wb.NT*, II, pp. 557ff.). In order to explain it, it is not necessary to equate the political authorities with those demonic "authorities" of which Paul makes mention several times in connexion with other principalities and powers (ἀρχαί, δυνάμεις, κυριότητες, θρόνοι; 1 Cor. 15: 24; Col. 1: 16; 2: 10, 15; Eph. 3: 10; 6: 12). The comparison of the political ἐξουσίαι with the demonic has found decided partisans in G. Dehn, K. L. Schmidt, K. Barth, O. Cullmann. It cannot be denied that in the view of Paul public authorities may be inspired by demonic agencies; this was evidently so in the case of the crucifixion of Christ (1 Cor. 2: 8). To what extent however can we take this connexion of the two orders of authority? Is their junction constant and necessary, or is it occasional? Several points prevent us from affirming a close solidarity such as would make of political authorities a manifestation of those demonic powers mentioned elsewhere. The "state" as an entity does not exist in the thought of the apostle, who is aware of authorities, that is, men, and realizes the authority they wield; when he speaks of what is historically established as authority, he does so in the plural, because he has in mind not the abstract notion of the state, but the concrete fact of an order of functionaries, magistrates, and princes. The action of demonic agencies cannot be exercised on the body politic except in so far as it is exercised on men. It is not denied that Paul affirmed the reality of such influences over man the sinner, and consequently over magistrates. (Perhaps we find an indication of this view in 1 Cor. 2: 8; though it should be noted that here what is in question is not the ἐξουσίαι but the ἄρχοντες; the assimilation with Rom. 13 may not be taken for granted. Oepke, *Th.L.Z.*, 1952, no. 8, p. 458 observes in this connexion that the ἄρχοντες of 1 Cor. 2 are very unlikely to denote demonic powers, since these rulers are accused of not having recognized the "wisdom of God", which it was not the business of demonic powers to do.) It is difficult to see in what way or where the demonic powers might exercise any other influence than that which they wield over the magistrates in so far as the latter are sinners, so that there is no reason to affirm that there exists a special relation between them and the state. Secondly,

(2) The consequence which flows from this is that resistance to public authority is contrary to the intentions of God, since it overthrows the order which God has appointed (διαταγή). Anarchy must be prevented, and powers of repression are necessary to the exercise of governmental authority.*

(3) Paul has thus given a formal definition of political authority such as justifies the Christian in adopting a positive attitude towards it and lays a theological basis for his obedience. This definition implies also the duty of the state to be

these demonic powers are always presented by the apostle as evil and maleficent. Christ has fought against them and conquered them: He has not placed them in His service, but has rendered them powerless to harm the elect who in spite of everything have still to struggle against them with the strength which Christ the Victor supplies. How can we conceive of these powers as being converted and becoming servants of the good? How could believers be exhorted to obey powers which they have still to fight against? How could Paul himself, who has just mentioned (ch. 8) the powers which seek to separate the believer from his Lord, regard these same powers as the basis of a useful authority worthy of conscientious obedience on the part of the believer? It has been thought that, by the channel of these powers, it might be possible to explain the coincidence, evident in ch. 13, between the moral judgment of the pagan state and the Christian judgment: these powers having been created in Christ, hence also for Christ, and being subject to Christ. Now, were it necessary in this case to have recourse to the demonic powers, we should likewise have to have recourse to them in order to explain the more general fact that pagans themselves occasionally accomplish the will of God. Paul however has given a more direct and simple explanation of this fact: God has not left His creatures without any knowledge of the good; "the requirement of the law" is written in the heart of the heathen (2: 15). The knowledge of the good which the magistrates have springs from the same cause; man was created in the image of God, he has by nature that knowledge of the right which the facts evidently oblige us to admit, and which Paul took good care not to deny him. We should not confuse this doctrine of creation with the murky classical theories about natural law, to envelop both things in the same scepticism and comprise both in the same condemnation. Cf. the most recent exposition of the thesis which we here reject in O. Cullmann, *Dieu et César*, 1956, pp. 97–120. (E.T. *The State in the New Testament*.)

* Michel interprets 2b as referring to divine sanctions and not the punitive reactions of the state; he thinks Paul is making an eschatological judgment. This is improbable, since the idea is immediately resumed in connexion with the use of the sword.

the instrument of divine government on the level of human societies. This is the condition for its becoming effectively what it is in principle. In practice the positive side of the magistrate's task is not always clearly apparent, for the initiative in social life springs in the first place from the members of the social body, so that the interventions of the civil authority are often restrictive of liberty since their aim is to secure for society the balance necessary between divergent and sometimes conflicting spontaneities.

Paul has in view the situation of the citizen in face of this responsibility which is incumbent on the magistrate and civil authority. The citizen encounters authority primarily in the restrictions which it imposes on the free manifestation of the individual's spontaneous inclinations. Submission to rules which limit freedom must be understood as a positive necessity, not as an ill to be endured but as a real good. The "magistrates"* whose function it is to secure order and peace to the body of society must see to it that each one has his due place and plays his distinctive part. The citizen whose intention it is to live in his sphere and to play his part, without trespassing on the rights of his neighbour, is acting in the same sense as state authority and has nothing to fear from the latter;† he is performing a good work for which he will be praised by the authority of the state.

"The power of the state does not mean simply the policeman who pursues crime, but it is concerned furthermore with promoting good," says Lagrange, who adds; "Usually however it is only by means of flattering words and honorific titles, etc." Is such a cynical remark in place here? Can we suppose Paul to have been ironically mocking the mania for decorations? Not everyone is French! It would be far more appropriate in this connexion to think of the ancient custom of public inscriptions in praise of benefactors (Michel); this fits in better with Paul's theme. Doubtless the apostle's thought goes still further. If we remember that civil authority represents to each individual the mind of his neighbours, because the magistrate gives shape and effect to the will of

* Οἱ ἄρχοντες: those who effectively exercise authority, i.e. the subordinate magistrates, with whom people have active dealings.

† Φόβος: object of fear; cf. Is. 8: 13.

the citizens as a whole whose feeling is expressed through his words and who act through his decisions, then we shall understand that the praise which flows from authority has real weight and value. Authority does in the name of all what many individuals cannot do; its praise should be precious not because it is official and flattering, but because it expresses universal recognition and the approval of God (cf. Rom. 2: 7, 10). Hence civil authority has the task not only of repressing evil, but also of furthering the good.

(4) By acting thus, the magistrate shows himself to be the "servant of God". He helps to co-ordinate the activity of each with that of all, he facilitates the individual's choice of socially good actions. In fact, one of the chief difficulties confronting the citizen in his action is that of foreseeing distant repercussions, in time and space, of an initiative which in its intention may be entirely praiseworthy. Ignorance of the real conditions prevailing in collective life may lead well-intentioned people into undertakings whose ultimate effect is contrary to the end pursued. The individual cannot have at his disposal the necessary information or experience which would enable him to adapt his excellent intentions to the concrete circumstances governing their execution. The isolated individual is again at a disadvantage because of his limited information, in the question of understanding the degree of urgency attaching to certain actions which are to be undertaken for the good of the social body or certain of its members. In both cases the state authority proves itself to be in the service of God, since it is equipped to discover what is for the good of all, and to concentrate and direct individual energies towards that common good.

This good ($\tau\grave{o}$ $\dot{a}\gamma a\theta\acute{o}\nu$) does not consist in personal comfort or advantage, or derivable selfish profit;* the word must be

---

* Lagrange understands $\sigma o\grave{\iota}$ $\epsilon\grave{\iota}s$ $\tau\grave{o}$ $\dot{a}\gamma a\theta\acute{o}\nu$ as follows: "authority is exercised in the interest of each one, $\sigma o\acute{\iota}$". Likewise Calvin, Godet, etc. This egocentric interpretation is contrary to the general trend of thought in the passage. We should understand: authority is exercised as a service of God, a ministry for you, inasmuch as it leads you ($\epsilon\grave{\iota}s$) to the good. The antithesis with $\tau\grave{o}$ $\kappa a\kappa\acute{o}\nu$ confirms that it is a question of social good and evil, since there cannot be a reference to the harm which the citizen might do himself.

understood in a wide social significance; the good is that communal life which tends to secure for each those conditions of life in which his creaturely vocation will find the framework most suitable to its fulfilment. It is impossible to state with precision what in concrete fact these conditions are, since they constantly depend on ever-changing factors; neither socialism nor capitalism, neither a republican nor a monarchical system of government, nor any other economic nor political system, can claim *a priori* to harmonize better with the demands of that good of which the apostle speaks. Every system of government is worth what the men who handle it are worth, or the degree to which they are able to embody their theoretical principles. This remark is not meant to be conducive to indifference, for in the given circumstances we must choose (positive attitude) and choose what seems to us the best formula (critical attitude). Paul did not shrink from judging matters of fact when he gave his approbation to the Roman authority (v. 1c). But if we think on these lines we shall be careful not to confound the particular and ever changing forms of political life with the end which is immutably assigned to all forms and which must ultimately judge them. It may be useful to complete what Paul says here about the "good" of which the state is the minister, by recollecting his indications in 12: 18. If Christians must try to establish peaceful relations with all men, the task of the magistrate too is certainly to secure peace among men; but such peace is not the immobility or restraint imposed by the rule of the strongest; for peace, as understood both in Hebraic and New Testament thought, provides a healthy normal situation which harmonizes with God's will for men.*

If the restraint imposed by the strongest (whether an individual, a party, or a class) cannot be compatible with the pursuit of the "good" of society as a whole, since it implies the exclusive pursuit of sectional interests; then public authority must use compulsion in order to check, for the good of all, the one-sided and devious aims of some. Social disorder like disorder in the church† has always arisen from the pre-

* Cf. Foerster, *Th.Wb.NT*, II, p. 410.
† Paul reminds us that God is a God of peace and not of chaos (1 Cor. 14: 33) in connexion with the troubles caused in the church assemblies

dominance of particular over general interests. The authority of the state must enable the common will to express and impose itself whenever it is threatened by sectional interests. This coercive power is in concrete fact manifested, in extremes, by the right to use the sword. By this is meant the sword of the magistrate (*jus gladii*),* not the sword of the soldier. What is in question is the exercise of social justice and constraint, not war. Paul's argument envisages the police acting in the service of the right, not the army as an instrument of power.

In his capacity as bearer of the sword, the magistrate is still a minister of God. This second aspect of his ministry is the reverse side of the first; he must prevent evil deeds and, if need be, punish them, thus implementing the right of society to defend itself against anyone who acts harmfully to the interests of all. The magistrate's condemnation, eventually enforced, echoes the judgment of God Himself (cf. Rom. 2: 8, 9).† It is part and parcel of the prerogatives of authority, since the evil-doer impedes the action contributory to the public good which God Himself has entrusted to the state.‡

by those prophets who are so preoccupied with their own charismatic gift that they do not give other prophets the scope due to them.

* Cf. bibliography in Michel, p. 285, n. 9.

† Ἔκδικος: he who invokes the law and executes justice. Εἰς ὀργήν: to manifest the anger of God . . . the word recalls 12: 19 which already conveyed the idea of the anger of God. D G it omit εἰς ὀργήν.

‡ This is the point at which to refer to the passivist interpretation of Nygren: submission to authority in all events. This interpretation imposes on Paul's thought a characteristic distortion. On the one hand, Nygren insists that authority is the servant of God, but forgets to explain that this is so εἰς τὸ ἀγαθόν: the alternative of good and evil, so clear in the text, plays no part in his scheme; hardly is it mentioned. In such conditions authority cannot but have a gloomy look. And in fact the second characteristic of Nygren's exegesis is that it identifies Paul's definition of authority with what he says (cf. 4c) about the reaction of authority to him who does evil! As soon as one eliminates εἰς τὸ ἀγαθόν the predominant feature in the scheme of authority will be inevitably the aspect of wrath: "The civil magistracy is God's servant in the aeon of wrath" (italicized in the text), p. 305; "a power which executes God's work here in this world, mostly of course God's offensive work, the judgment of His anger . . .", p. 306. In fact as soon as one confounds civil justice with the wrath of God, there is no alternative but to submit with-

We must remove from the framework of this text any possibility of allusion to war—a problem which Paul did not visualize and in the elucidation of which he does not help us except in so far as it is reflected in the functions of the police; for what he says about authority is applicable to every stage of social life, culminating in the supra-national stage.* Paul makes no allusion whatever to the ideas of country or nation and he does not seek from that source any contribution to his definition of the good. Authority, inasmuch as it is the servant of God, could not consider as a good for its own subjects what would be harmful to other children of God. The grouping of God's children into nations—the rightness of which we have not to discuss here—nevertheless sets a problem bearing on the question of authority as treated by Paul; for to the extent to which all particular social groupings are in solidarity with each other, no one of such particular authorities can exercise a mandate for the "good" without having the consent and collaboration of the others. The solidarity of mankind and of particular societies with each other (states and nations, etc.)—a solidarity required by that pursuit of the good which is the special responsibility of all authority—implies then that above these particular authorities a supreme authority should exist in which are vested the prerogatives assigned by the apostle to ἐξουσία. To judge by contemporary facts, the delays and the ineffectiveness of international law makes such ideas almost fantastic.

The fact that the magistrate bears the sword and that he does not bear it in vain, implies that the penalties inflicted by the state may even go so far as capital punishment. It would seem, however, that Paul wished to avoid an express admission that the state may freely dispose of the lives of its citizens. It is not the same thing to say: "the magistrate has the right of life and death" and to say: "the magistrate bears the

out reserve. It belongs to the historians to decide whether or not the exegesis of the Lutheran bishop is attributable to Luther.

* It will be noted that the Roman army had to fulfil in part the functions of the police; and in fact of an international police, in an empire which combined so many various nations. The situation known to Paul was very different from the diversity of national groups with which we are familiar, and our present distinction between the police and the army.

334

sword and does not bear it in vain". Capital punishment is an extreme case and perhaps we should say that the sword represents a threat rather than a right. We must always bear in mind that the evildoer who is punished by it has himself put into motion a machinery which can be dangerous to his life.

(5) Since a creative purpose is assigned to state authority, the obedience which we owe to it is not a resigned submission inspired by fear of the police. It must rather feel justified by the approbation which conscience gives to the ends to which state authority is dedicated. It is only such conscientious approbation which will make of our obedience a vital participation in the mission with which the civil authority is entrusted. Συνείδησις, *conscience*, suggests this deliberate participation of the subject in civil life as organized and controlled by official authority: obedience actuated by such motives becomes self-committal. It is significant that Paul has brought out in this connexion the positive character of obedience, because such a point of view at the same time implies the limits of obedience. If obedience is a matter of conscience, then it is no longer servile; when conscience is introduced as the motive of obedience, the latter can no longer be counted on! It becomes possible to object to authority on the grounds of conscience.

(6) The mention of taxes is not justified by psychological considerations: it has been asserted that this is the point where Christians were most sorely tempted or worried by scruples. What proportion of the wealth which might be used for charitable purposes should be given to Caesar? Paul does not discuss this point. He wishes to emphasize the conscientious duty of which he has just been speaking: and precisely in the matter of taxation, because this is the most general and permanent form of contribution to the life of the social group. The word "dues" expresses the matter very well. The work of the individual does not bear fruit to his sole advantage. Each one contracts a debt towards all, for he cannot live without their help. It is his conscientious duty to contribute his share to the common work and weal, and to hand on the patrimony which he has received and which has

335

enabled him to live in an improved condition. The extreme mobility of money enables this aid to be effectually felt wherever each one by his work is obliged to promote the good of all. Paul does not say to the Christian taxpayer: "Allow yourself to be fleeced!" but he does say: "Contribute for reasons of conscience to the common good!"*

Hence the treasury officials are also servants of God. This is the meaning of λειτουργὸς Θεοῦ which is parallel to Θεοῦ διάκονος applied to the magistrates. The choice of this word may seem surprising, but there is nothing unusual about its use here if we take secular usage as a guide, for there it implies ideas of public service and pecuniary contribution.† Paul uses the word in 15: 16 in order to describe the cultic aspect of his apostolic ministry; but the word has not necessarily such a meaning and it will not do to force its sense here.‡ The office of him who levies taxes is not presented as a sacred function, nor is it suggested that taxes are a sacred offering. The thought of Paul is always marked by the same note of sobriety. It is enough for him to suggest that the fiscal official, like the magistrate, is the servant of God.

(7) Obedience to authority freely given, in the way suggested, on conscientious grounds is therefore a due which each one owes to society as a whole. The debt is not merely a question of opening the purse strings; it is something that requires inner spiritual consent. We shall pay the fiscal authorities the tax contribution§ they demand while entertaining for them feelings of respectful fear and consideration, because of the functions which God has entrusted to them

* Τελεῖτε may be either indicative or imperative.

† In the Greek cities *liturgies* were the prestations imposed on certain citizens, according to the degree of their wealth. By means of these extraordinary levies the insufficiency of the normal taxation was supplemented and the rich were thus made to bear the expenses of certain public services such as sports, choreography and, in time of war, the equipment of the fleet or cavalry. The ambitious found in the *liturgies* an opportunity of flattering the people. On the general use of the word, cf. Strathmann, *Th.Wb.NT*, IV, p. 236.

‡ In the LXX λειτουργός is applied to the priest (Is. 61: 6; Sir. 7: 30), but also to any kind of servants (2 Kgs. 12: 20, etc.).

§ Φόρος: direct taxation. Τέλος: indirect taxation. Ἀπόδοτε reminds us at once of the answer of Jesus, Mk. 12: 17.

for the wholesome providential government of society.*

⁸Owe no one anything, except to love one another; for he who loves his neighbour has fulfilled the law. ⁹The commandments, "You shall not commit adultery, You shall not kill, You shall not steal, You shall not covet," and any other commandment, are summed up in this sentence, "You shall love your neighbour as yourself." ¹⁰Love does no wrong to a neighbour; therefore love is the fulfilling of the law.

¹¹Besides this you know what hour it is, how it is full time now for you to wake from sleep. For salvation is nearer to us now than when we first believed; ¹²the night is far gone, the day is at hand. Let us then cast off the works of darkness and put on the armour of light; ¹³let us conduct ourselves becomingly as in the day, not in revelling and drunkenness, not in debauchery and licentiousness, not in quarrelling and jealousy. ¹⁴But put on the Lord Jesus Christ, and make no provision for the flesh, to gratify its desires.

(8–10) The apostle has just expounded a political theology in which for the Gentile Christian there was a rich store of thought to be treasured. But for the Jewish Christian such a doctrine suggested serious scruples. Theocracy had come to grief in the political disasters which had overtaken the elect people, yet the authority of the law of Moses persisted; it remained as the permanent expression of the will of God. Once a theological significance was assigned to civil law by this Pauline doctrine the problem arose as to whether the two laws were mutually exclusive.† Paul declares that there

* Awe is not the same as fear; it is the reaction of man in the face of what transcends him; it implies a confession of weakness imbued with reverence; the OT makes this the ground feeling of the believer in the face of God. "Honour" is the manifestation of the respect entertained towards him who is worthy of the confidence placed in him.

† Most commentators note a break between vv. 7 and 8 and in vv. 8–10 see only "an excursus having no close connexion with what precedes" (Michel). It may be pointed out however that $\mu\eta\delta\epsilon\nu\acute{\iota}$ corresponds to $\pi\hat{a}\sigma\iota\nu$ (v. 7) and $\dot{o}\phi\epsilon\acute{\iota}\lambda\epsilon\tau\epsilon$ to $\dot{o}\phi\epsilon\iota\lambda\alpha\acute{\iota}$ (v. 7). If we break the connexion with the preceding passage, we are inclined to construct thus verse 8: "he who loves his neighbour has fulfilled the law". The use of $\ddot{\epsilon}\tau\epsilon\rho os$ does not make this exegesis inevitable (cf. Willi Marxsen, "Der $\ddot{\epsilon}\tau\epsilon\rho os$ $\nu\acute{o}\mu os$ Röm. 13: 8" Th.Z., 1955, p. 234). A coherent view of the text as a whole would weigh against it. Hence the translation will be: "he who loves has fulfilled the other law".

is no contradiction between the civil law and the law of Moses which he at once goes on to cite. There is no contradiction because the law of Moses is after all summed up in the one embracing commandment of loving each other: "You who have been brought up in the Mosaic law owe no man anything except brotherly love."* He who loves fulfils the whole law. He has at least fulfilled the law as understood by Paul,† for his thought does not include the ritual prescriptions which could hardly be fitted into this argument.‡ The whole of Moses' law-giving insights is summed up§ in the commandment of Lev. 19: 18. Now the love of one's neighbour has a direct connexion with the requirement of the civil law; he who practises such love will do nothing to bring him into conflict with the latter, besides which the imagination of the heart inspired by love supplements the clumsy techniques of the administrative routine. Paul then concludes with a play on words, taking πλήρωμα νόμου in the double meaning of fulfilling the law of God and fulfilling the civil law.

(11) Vv. 11 to 14 round off chs. 12 and 13 by reminding readers of the eschatological basis of Christian conduct such as had already been suggested in 12: 2. When it is realized that the time in which one lives is marked by a special character, then one does not live like everyone else, like those who do not know this; one conforms one's conduct to this special character.‖ Not to conform to it is equivalent to

* We realize the apparent contradiction: "give to all their dues" (v. 7) and: "you owe no man anything" (v. 8) if we admit that these sentences are not spoken from the same point of view.

† Paul quotes in the order given also by B to Deut. 5: 17. Similarly P. Nash, LXX, etc.

‡ The remark "and any other commandment" must refer to commandments of the same character as the second table of the Decalogue, or perhaps the complete text of these commandments, which are only summarized here.

§ 'Ανακεφαλαιοῦν: to bring under the same heading, give a summary (κεφάλαιον). Cf. Schlier, Th.Wb.NT, III, p. 681. On this idea in Judaism, cf. Strack-Billerbeck, I, pp. 357–359; III, p. 306. 'Εν τῷ is lacking in B G, and only repeats ἐν τῷ λόγῳ τούτῳ.

‖ Καὶ τοῦτο; ποιεῖτε should be understood; do this, do it so much the more because . . . Καιρός (cf. 8: 18): the suitable moment, the oppor-

closing one's eyes as if in sleep; in that case the Christian fails to seize opportunities and lets the time slip by, behaving as though it were still night. Now, says Paul, the time to wake up has struck; we must become aware of the new situation, for it is now different. In fact, "now"* salvation has drawn nearer to us (or else, our salvation is nearer) than when we first believed. The soberness with which Paul expresses himself at this point is significant. He shares with his brethren the conviction that the inauguration of the reign of God through the final glorious manifestation of his Lord is to be realized in a relatively short space of time;† but he refrains from any calculation or prediction because he is not interested in the chronological aspect of the event but in the event itself, in which he hails in advance the disclosure of God's love and sovereignty in the created universe.‡

The certainty that salvation is nearer must not then be understood with pedantic rigour. Paul did not claim to know the day and the hour any more than his Lord. He wishes merely to stress the urgency of this νῦν, now. Each passing hour counts in the time scheme of God because each hour as it strikes marks the moment for man's ultimate decision, the occasion (καιρός) for the affirmation of faith. Easeful ignorance, like slumber, is now a thing of the past; now every moment counts, we must watch and be ever vigilant.

(12) The character of the present time is further illustrated by the image of day succeeding night. Nothing could bring out

tunity. Cf. Delling, *Th.Wb.NT*, III, pp. 456–465. The best MSS. read ὑμᾶς; P 46 D G: ἡμᾶς.

* Cf. the νῦν of 3:26; 5:9, 11; 7:6; 8:1, 18, 22; 11:5, 30, 31; 16:26.
† Cf. 1 Th. 4:15.
‡ If primitive Christianity could note, without its faith being shaken thereby, that "the end" did not come within the calculated times, that is just because the chronological framework of its hope was a secondary matter. The latter could be given up, and yet the essence of the hope retained, by refraining from canalizing this hope in rash previsions of the time and mode of realization, the secret of which was left to God as indeed it rightly belongs to Him (cf. Mk. 12:24; Matt. 22:29; and Mk. 13:32; Matt. 24:36). It must be remembered that, for a true eschatological mentality, the unrolling of time periods is above all relative to the *quality* of time; chronological and quantitative succession symbolizes the development of time in view of the realization of divine purposes.

more clearly the contrast between a period of time which is undetermined, useless, without particular potentiality, and a time that is propitious and pregnant with fateful decisions. At night nothing can be done except works that are evil (Jn. 9: 4; 11: 9, 10). This reflects common experience, for man has everywhere felt the ambiguous character of the night time.* In the Jewish tradition the sect of Qumran illustrates the struggle between the children of light and the children of darkness.† 1 Th. 5: 5–8 should be read in order that we may realize the full scope of the image in Paul's thought.‡ Its current use may explain the fact that Paul has had recourse to it, but he certainly has given a much deeper significance to the phenomenon of the transition from darkness to light. Not only did Old Testament tradition connect the idea of Yahweh with the appearance of light, as in fact is true of many religions,§ but further the advent of the Messianic age in Christian thought was regarded as marking the dawn of an age of light (Lk. 1: 79, an allusion to Is. 9: 2; Lk. 2: 32, cf. Is. 42: 6; 49: 6; Jn. 1: 9; Lk. 17: 24; Matt. 17: 2). For Paul in particular, the glory of Christ, the image of the Father, irradiates His divine countenance and sheds its resplendent light on those who by the grace of faith can contemplate Him with their faces unveiled (2 Cor. 3: 18; 4: 4). Thus the apostle likens accession to life in Christ to an effulgence of divine light flooding the darkness which enfolds the old Adam—an event comparable to the original creation of light; the knowledge of Christ spells illumination (2 Cor. 4: 6; cf. Eph. 1: 18).‖

If then the darkness is progressively dispelled as it gives

* All peoples have thought that the night was the time when demons and sorcerers prefer to do their work.

† The mention of the "sons of light", up to now reserved to the NT, is to be found in the manual of discipline and the fragments relating to this struggle.

‡ Cf. Eph. 5: 8, 9, 14; 6: 13–18. Similarly the expressions in Col. 1: 13 (ἐξουσία τοῦ σκότους) and Eph. 6: 12 (κοσμοκράτωρ τοῦ σκότους τούτου).

§ On Hellenism in particular, cf. Oepke, *Th.Wb.NT*, IV, p. 18.

‖ This text does not allude simply to the conversion of Paul; for every "new creature", the creative powers are at work. It is still the same struggle of God against darkness which is continued and completed in the work of redemption.

place to the light, that is because the inner light which Christ sheds illuminates the believer's soul, for believers are sons of the light (1 Th. 5: 5). It is not the solar system which regulates the life of the Christian. He who sleeps in broad daylight is acting wrongly; he is not in fact what he is essentially; he is out of harmony with his objective and true situation. In order to get rid of this contradiction, we must work out our salvation with fear and trembling (Phil. 2: 12); that is, both put on the armour of light which God alone can give, and fight by the power of this armour which transforms the weakness of the combatant into triumphant strength.* Paul contrasts the "works of darkness" with the "armour of light"; the choice of words is doubtless deliberate, for in Gal. 5: 19 and 22 he contrasts in a similar way the "works of the flesh" with the "fruit of the Spirit" (cf. Eph. 5: 9; the "fruit of light").† The flesh or darkness engender works characteristic of the source from which they spring. He who lives under the control of the Spirit bears the fruit of good works because a sap flows within him which causes him to bear such fruit, or because the armour which he has put on imparts to his obedience the power of the One who has forged that armour. It is not the zeal of the combatant which secures victory, just as the zeal of the Jew failed to enable him to attain righteousness (cf. 10: 2); good arms are needed for victory and it is God alone who can supply them.

(13f.) In the thought of Paul the exhortation to put on the armour of light had a tremendous reverberation, as also had the injunction to cast off the works of darkness. For there is a close relation between these two exhortations and the affirmations of ch. 6: 1–14 and 7: 4–6 or Gal. 2: 19. The faithful Christian is exhorted to consider that his carnal life has been crucified with Christ, that he has died unto sin and that a new life is offered to him in Christ. The image of the new garment is explicitly connected with the rite of baptism:

* It was fairly common for religions to picture their deities as armed; the faithful receive arms from the tutelary gods. Yahweh is a valiant warrior (Ex. 15: 3).

† A D etc. deplorably replace τὰ ὅπλα by τὰ ἔργα. P 46 D* G read ἀποβαλώμεθα instead of ἀποθώμεθα.

"For as many of you as were baptized into Christ have put on Christ" (Gal. 3: 27). The contrast between darkness and light suggested equally forcefully the transition from the old to the new state of life, of which baptism is the sacramental sign. The faithful has submitted to a death which has buried his body. The situation thus created may be understood, according to 2 Cor. 5: 1–3, as a state of nudity comparable with that brought about by the destruction of the "earthly tent" through death. In writing εὐσχημόνως, Paul is perhaps making an allusion to this nudity: it is indecent in fact to appear naked in broad daylight. If so, the image is very striking. It is a matter of urgency to put on the Lord Jesus, since, stripped bare of the flesh and its desires by baptism, you are now quite naked. It will be recalled that the thought of clothing sometimes evokes the reality of the inmost being. It is not a question of changing externals merely. In this connexion "the habit makes the monk", because the garment alluded to is being itself considered in its status and decisive orientation.

If a man asks Christ to deliver him from his sinful state by allowing him to share in Christ's own death and then to clothe him with the armour of light, he is asking to be henceforth Christ's soldier, to serve under His command, and to receive from Him the reward of life which He offers to those who serve Him. It is the function which creates the instrument just as the habit makes the monk.* The parenetic use of the image of clothing which we find in these verses offers no difficulty. For example, a man is fit to fight when he has been equipped with the proper clothing and weapons, and

* The verb "put on" receives variable meanings in Paul: to put on Jesus Christ (Gal. 3: 27; Rom. 13: 14); to put on the armour of light (Rom. 13: 12): the perishable nature puts on the imperishable and the immortal (1 Cor. 15: 53, 54); to put on the new man (Col. 3: 10); to put on bowels of mercy (Col. 3: 12); to put on the heavenly dwelling (2 Cor. 5: 3). In Eph. 4: 24; 6: 12, 14 similar uses. Faced by this wide and flexible use of an expression which common life supplies to almost anyone, there is surely no need, to explain its presence in Pauline writings, to have recourse to the myth of the *Urmensch*, the primal original pattern of humanity which fallen souls have to put on in order to attain salvation (W. Bousset, Murmelstein, Käsemann, Schlier, etc.). Both the Greeks and the Latins used the word in a metaphorical sense already (Latin: *induere*), (cf. Wettstein and Zahn *ad loc.*)

he is then not fit to undertake agricultural work; the honourable citizen who has put on his evening dress will not go and clean dirty drains. In putting on a particular type of dress, one commits oneself and decides. Similarly the faithful who have put on the Lord Jesus can no longer go and take part in the dark orgies which are practised under the cover of night.‡

‡ A high degree of licentiousness prevailed among the Romans and in fact they devoted their nights to licentious practices. Paul no doubt is referring to real facts. But it is difficult to understand his choice of vices known and practised at Rome. The point may be elucidated if we re-collect what according to the first letter to the Corinthians are the types of behaviour most contrary to the Christian state, those excluded by union with Christ. Three themes are treated in this letter: the meetings of the church for the supper of the Lord, the control of the body, *agape*. Now, in 13b Paul says: "abstain from those feasts where drunkenness leads to blasphemy, from those debaucheries where the worst turpitude is displayed, from those quarrellings where people rend each other. All that must be particularly abhorrent to you; you share in the table of the Lord and take part in meetings where the Spirit inspires prophecy and glossolaly; your body is the temple of the Spirit; love neither says nor suspects evil." Well then! to put on the Lord means to hold such things in horror and just for that reason. It will be remembered that Paul is in Corinth at the moment of writing his letter.

CHAPTER

14

¹As for the man who is weak in faith, welcome him, but not for disputes over opinions. ²One believes he may eat anything, while the weak man eats only vegetables. ³Let not him who eats despise him who abstains, and let not him who abstains pass judgment on him who eats; for God has welcomed him. ⁴Who are you to pass judgment on the servant of another? It is before his own master that he stands or falls. And he will be upheld, for the Master is able to make him stand.

⁵One man esteems one day as better than another, while another man esteems all days alike. Let every one be fully convinced in his own mind. ⁶He who observes the day, observes it in honour of the Lord. He also who eats, eats in honour of the Lord, since he gives thanks to God; while he who abstains, abstains in honour of the Lord and gives thanks to God. ⁷None of us lives to himself, and none of us dies to himself. ⁸If we live, we live to the Lord, and if we die, we die to the Lord; so then, whether we live or whether we die, we are the Lord's. ⁹For to this end Christ died and lived again, that he might be Lord both of the dead and of the living.

¹⁰Why do you pass judgment on your brother? Or you, why do you despise your brother? For we shall all stand before the judgment seat of God; ¹¹for it is written,

"As I live, says the Lord, every knee shall bow to me,
and every tongue shall give praise to God."

¹²So each of us shall give account of himself to God.

THE TWO CHAPTERS to which we now come have caused considerable perplexity to commentators. Paul is addressing a community which not only has he not personally founded, but which he does not even know by direct acquaintance. In these chapters we see him concerning himself with concrete problems raised by the existence of two tendencies in the church which are not very charitable towards each other.

How does Paul know what is going on in Rome, and what is his authority for intervening in the dispute? This is all very surprising to us, and rightly so. If only we could gain a precise understanding of the Roman situation! But again we are astonished at the lofty and serene tone of the passage and at the somewhat vague expressions used by this censurer to depict the evil. Will it be said that he does not know the community and wishes to spare its feelings? In that case what necessity was there to intervene at all? If the situation was serious, the style and the expressions used would inevitably be ineffective; while if it was a mild affair, why did the apostle discuss it at such length? Our perplexity is increased when we come to the conclusion in 15:14 where our censurer begins to flatter the correspondents whom he has been criticizing: "I myself am satisfied about you, my brethren, that you yourselves are full of goodness, filled with all knowledge and able to instruct one another." If that be so, what need was there to have broached the subject at all? Lietzmann is right to point out that this verse rings false in the context of what has preceded.

Some explanation of these curious features must be found. One is suggested in fact by the literary form. Here and there Paul does use the second person plural, but in the section as a whole, from 14:1 to 15:13, we find the first person plural or the third person singular. It is clear from this that Paul is not really addressing a particular group of people, whose concrete circumstances he is considering while pointing out their errors. Everything is explained if we are prepared to admit that in spite of certain appearances Paul is not here concerned to remonstrate with Christians at Rome, whom he does not know any more than he knows their special problems. But there is one generally felt problem which Paul knows all about, and he is writing in Corinth where this problem was a burning issue not so long before.* Wherever, in a Christian community, Christians of Jewish and Gentile origin exist side by side the problem emerges in a more or less

* Taken as a whole, the arguments in chapters 14 and 15 directly recall those of 1 Cor. 8: 1–13; it is to be noted that terms such as "knowledge" and "conscience" play a great part in 1 Cor. 8, but are absent from Rom. where the word "faith" occupies the central place.

acute form. Jewish Christians have "scruples" while Gentile Christians have none, or not enough, at least from the point of view of their brethren.

This is a question of education and diversity of tradition, but it is one in which faith is involved. It is very probable that problems of this nature were felt at Rome. But it is clear from the way in which Paul discusses the matter that he does not write about it with the local situation in view. If he touches on the theme, it is because he is driven to do so by the very logic of the problem which underlies the whole letter. The young church which is developing in the west must try to resolve by peaceable coexistence the difficulties arising from the confrontation of divergent mentalities. The problem which the apostle is treating is theoretical rather than practical, or perhaps we should say that it is a practical problem which he is treating theoretically and abstractly. His experience has shown him the importance of the issue in the developing life of the church; facts show that the unity of the church is at stake also in this local and practical sphere. Hence the subject could not be avoided. But the conditions in which the apostle speaks of it explain the way in which he speaks of it. He is not aiming at correcting a particular situation, nor is he assuming pastoral responsibilities.

(1) The matter is approached without any transitional link. Addressing doubtless the majority, Paul enjoins them not to hold the "weak" Christian at a distance so as not to compromise the unity of the brethren. "Welcome" is a particularly strong expression in the light of 15: 7; what Christ has done is an example and even more: it is the basis of what there is reason to do, and also renders this possible. The man who has tasted of the mercy of Christ is constrained to show something of it. *Benedictus benedicat.* Receive then the "weak" into the communion of the church, do not hold anyone at arm's length because of his weakness.* The weak brother is not in difficulties with regard to his faith; his weakness arises from the fact that he has not thought out sufficiently nor with sufficient illumination the implications

* It is exaggerating the situation to suppose, as does Michel, that there is here an allusion to a legalistic measure.

of the faith in such a way as to enable it to inspire the whole of conduct and to sweep aside all hesitations. The "weak" brother is one who feels the pressure of the unconscious and is paralysed by prejudices and inhibitions springing from the unconscious; he is a scrupulous, inhibited, over-conscientious type of person.*

The "weak" brother must be welcomed and not judged so that he may not be led to do things which he could not inwardly and freely approve of; he should not be disturbed or forced by the pressure of debates which only upset without convincing those who are not sufficiently mature to understand their scope, and who only go away with the undeserved feeling of being inferior and perhaps faithless Christians. The outcome of such debates is that we lose confidence in ourselves and our brethren; we begin to suspect our own faith and that of others; all is shaken, both inwardly and outwardly. And yet Christ had made us one!†

(2f.) It is not that all opinions are equally valid, but we must be discriminating. For example, if it is a question of whether to eat meat or not,‡ we should recognize that the matter does not concern the essential elements of the faith. Hence an attitude of charity becomes obligatory, as is fitting among brethren. He who has the inner liberty§ to make no distinction between various foods is inclined to despise the

---

* His συνείδησις is too weak and sensitive; cf. 1 Cor. 8: 7-12.

† Verse 1b has been variously interpreted: (1) "Do not enter into discussion on controversial matters" (many ancients, Zahn, Lagrange); διάκρισις from διακρινεῖν in the meaning of "dispute with". (2) "Do not disturb consciences" (Luther, Bengel); διάκρισις from διακρινεῖν in the meaning of doubt, hesitate. (3) "Do not judge opinions with the pretension of distinguishing the true from the false" (Augustine, Oltramare, Lietzmann, Gaugler, Michel); διάκρισις as in 1 Cor. 12: 10. These three meanings are only to a certain extent incompatible: the presence of all of them is felt in the text.

‡ P 46 D G lat Ephrem read ἐσθιέτω.

§ Πιστεύει φαγεῖν: a curious expression which may mean: he has the faith to eat. "His faith is strong enough to enable him to eat (such things)" (Godet); or else: "he believes he may eat" (Lagrange). In this chapter, the psychological and theological points of view do not seem to be mutually exclusive; faith is here envisaged in its relation to practical decisions, which are the fruit of faith (in this sense, Lietzmann, Bauer).

scrupulous; while the latter for their part are inclined to judge the former with severity. For the weak can be as severe as and often more severe than the strong; they feel themselves threatened and defend themselves by condemning (μὴ κρινέτω) those whom they suppose to scorn them. These are subjective emotional reactions which a believer should sternly control by sane theological reflection. Each lives by the same divine grace as those who live differently from himself; God has welcomed into His covenant and His church both us and them. It is to this ultimate basic reality that we must look, since each of us depends on it and appeals to it. If we are agreed to invoke that authority only, our differences can no longer be deep and divisive.

(4) In fact what defines a man is not what other men think of him, but what God thinks of him. That is why no one should judge—that is catalogue, and enclose within a fixed definition. Men are in the same situation as servants who depend on their master;* whether they fall or not is their master's affair and it is to him alone that they have to render an account.† Hence the "weak" should not trouble themselves about the risks incurred by those who use a liberty which they themselves feel to be dangerous. This does not mean that recklessness should be encouraged (cf. 1 Cor. 10: 12) but that we should trust the Master of the "strong" to keep within the hold of His grace those whom He has once welcomed into His covenant: to each one the Lord will give according to his needs.‡

(5) What precisely is at issue in all this? Some make distinctions between the days.§ Since nothing suggests that we

* Οἰκέτης: domestic slave, servant, more familiar in tone than δοῦλος.

† "Whether he stands or falls, it is to the advantage or disadvantage of his master (τῷ ἰδίῳ κυρίῳ, dat. commodi): it concerns only the latter" (Lagrange).

‡ Σταθήσεται may be understood as a passive (he will be upheld) or as a middle voice (he will stand upright) (cf. Matt. 12: 25). The second meaning is preferable. Slight variants: P 46 C D etc. read δυνατὸς γάρ. D G etc. add ὁ Θεός.

§ Κρίνειν: to separate, to single out. Some attribute to certain days a special importance, others consider each day to be of equal importance (Büchsel, Th.Wb.NT, III, p. 922).

have here to do with Judaizers, we shall not regard this as an allusion to the Sabbath but to practices of abstinence and fasting on regular fixed dates.* What such practices were we do not know, and it is a pity, since great interest attaches to the apostle's estimate of them. The rise of such customs shows that each has come to a personal decision; he has committed himself and his inner being ($\nu o \hat{\upsilon} s$); he is inwardly convinced. Sharp differences of opinion in this field are not excluded by the renewing of the mind through the Spirit (12: 2). To entertain different opinions is not a bad thing, but what *is* bad is to dispute acrimoniously and divisively, for then we are arrogating to ourselves the right to judge our brother and are usurping the place of the Lord (cf. v. 4). A conviction with regard to such practices is to be respected if it is fully matured and commits the mind and heart, because then it flows from a real desire to obey the Lord. What would be inacceptable would be a practice arising not from full conviction but from inadequate or trivial motives, as for example when a man wishes to do as everyone else does, or adopts a certain practice ostentatiously. Diversity in such matters demands that each should test his own conviction and exercise charity with regard to those who do not share it.

(6) Again, this does not mean that sincerity is all-sufficient. Sincerity cannot accredit in the church any opinion whatsoever. V. 5 might have given the impression that Paul favoured complete laxity. This is not possible, for the Christian is no longer free to think whatever he likes; it is not enough for a conviction to be sincere to be true. The Christian is not free because he thinks in honour of the Lord ($K\upsilon\rho i\omega$).† The Lord is the centre of his liberty of thought. He is free certainly, but only in his capacity of *servant* ($o \grave{\iota} \kappa \acute{\epsilon} \tau \eta s$) of the Lord. This is the very guarantee of his freedom, for conscience is free in face of other men because it is

* $\Gamma \acute{\alpha} \rho$ is doubtful; it is absent from B sah Dgr Ggr, etc., and its meaning is problematical. It is usually taken as a simple connecting particle.

† As does a servant who is anxious for the honour of his master, desirous of pleasing him and attentive to his interests. Same construction as in v. 4.

bound to the Lord to whom it belongs. In order to stress this common inner attitude in face of the same Lord, among believers who differ as regards opinions and practices, Paul says of all of them that they give thanks, they rejoice, the scrupulous no less than the others.* They are all united in the presence of the same Lord, they all have the same basis of life, and are at one moreover in the act of adoration which consists in recognizing that all is of grace (cf. 1 : 21).

(7–9) The apostle here generalizes. The whole life of the Christian is under the guidance and control of his Lord, and so is his death, as is the case with the slave whose life and death are ordered in the interests of his master. There is, however, one big difference: the Master of Christians has earned this right of life and death at the cost of His own self-sacrifice (2 Cor. 5: 14–15; 1 Cor. 6: 20; 7: 23) and since His exaltation to the right hand of God, He exercises the right of a sovereign (cf. Phil. 2: 9–10).†

(10–12) Since the Master alone has the right to judge, no one of us may authoritatively judge another, neither the "strong" who despises the "weak" nor the "weak" who condemns the "strong". All of us must be judged, and this thought puts us in our true place and faces us with our real concern. In spite of the arrogance with which some judge their brethren, they will all have to appear before the judgment seat and bow the knee, which is not indeed the posture of a judge! Each will have to give account of himself, the

* In the concrete case envisaged by the apostle, it is a question of an act of thanksgiving made at the time of taking a meal. If we think more precisely of meals taken in common, the argument emphasizes still more strongly the unity of those who in other respects differ, e.g. in their choice of food.

† Νεκρῶν καὶ ζώντων: the order is surprising. It is to be explained perhaps by 2 Cor. 5: 14 and Rom. 6: 11: one may say, first, that believers are dead, since Christ died for them and they have died with Him; then they find with Him a new life under His Lordship. Antiquity likewise condemned the idea of living for oneself (Terence, *Adelphae*, V, 4, 9: "*ille suam semper egit vitam, in otio, in conviviis . . . sibi vixit, sibi sumptum fecit.*" Plut. *v. Cleom.* 31: αἰσχρὸν γὰρ ζῆν μόνοις ἑαυτοῖς καὶ ἀποθνήσκειν). The tradition of v. 9 is very fluctuating, but the variants are of no interest for exegesis.

"strong" of their liberty, and the "weak" of their scruples. And this means too that we shall not have to give account of what we consider to be the errors of others.*

¹³Then let us no more pass judgment on one another, but rather decide never to put a stumbling-block or hindrance in the way of a brother. ¹⁴I know and am persuaded in the Lord Jesus that nothing is unclean in itself; but it is unclean for any one who thinks it unclean. ¹⁵If your brother is being injured by what you eat, you are no longer walking in love. Do not let what you eat cause the ruin of one for whom Christ died. ¹⁶So do not let what is good to you be spoken of as evil. ¹⁷For the kingdom of God does not mean food and drink but righteousness and peace and joy in the Holy Spirit; ¹⁸he who thus serves Christ is acceptable to God and approved by men. ¹⁹Let us then pursue what makes for peace and for mutual upbuilding. ²⁰Do not, for the sake of food, destroy the work of God. Everything is indeed clean, but it is wrong for any one to make others fall by what he eats; ²¹it is right not to eat meat or drink wine or do anything that makes your brother stumble. ²²The faith that you have, keep between yourself and God; happy is he who has no reason to judge himself for what he approves. ²³But he who has doubts is condemned, if he eats, because he does not act from faith; for whatever does not proceed from faith is sin.

(13) From v. 13 the exhortation is addressed particularly to the "strong". They have a special responsibility, for their example may induce certain brothers to imitate them but without any rooted conviction. Such copying is a weakness inspired by the desire to do as other people do, or to be conveniently released from certain constraints, or the pride of ostentation, etc. Thus the conduct of the "strong" can become an occasion of falling.†

* Some MSS. read: $\tau\hat{\omega}$ $\beta\acute{\eta}\mu\alpha\tau\iota$ $\tauο\hat{\upsilon}$ $X\rhoι\sigma\tauο\hat{\upsilon}$ according to 2 Cor. 5: 10. The quotation of v. 11 combines Is. 49: 18 and 45: 23 cited probably from memory. In Phil 2: 11 Paul quotes Is. 45: 23; there, $\dot{\varepsilon}\xi\omega\mu o\lambda o\gamma\varepsilon\hat{\iota}\sigma\theta\alpha\iota$ means: to acknowledge and praise God for. . . . In our verse, the word may be given the sense of praise (Lietzmann, Bauer—cf. the literature he quotes—Michel). But such praise is always imbued with the feelings of humility and gratitude. In the article in *Th.Wb.NT*, V, p. 251, Michel gives to this verb the meaning of "confess one's sins at the last judgment" (*eschatologisches Sündenbekenntnis*).

† $K\rhoί\nu\varepsilonι\nu$ is understood in two different senses, and there is certainly

351

(14) The warning addressed to the "strong" not to become the occasion of a grave lapse in others is now given a doctrinal basis. It is quite true that all things are pure and that nothing obliges us to make a distinction between the various foods or the various days.* But it would be a grave error in this matter to consider only the objective facts without any reference to the persons concerned. Customs are always to be referred to persons as the expression of their sentiments and dispositions; they have not their value in themselves; they are good or bad according to the heart that has inspired them. But as such they acquire real value, for they reflect the reality of conscience. This interiorization of outward practices is the object of explicit teaching on the part of Jesus (Matt. 15: 11, 16–19; 23: 25).† What sullies a man resides in the inner chambers of the heart, not in the external objects which his ritual customs treat as unclean. If the heart is pure, everything is pure, and in consequence everything is permitted; man is then free to use the works of God in conscience, and it is a matter of no importance whether he abstains or not from such or such a thing.

This teaching of Jesus drew men's attention away from the act itself and fixed it on the dispositions of the heart which the action reveals. The polemic of Jesus was aimed at the hypocrisy expressed in certain practices rather than at those a play on words: "do not exercise your critical faculty to form an opinion on others, but rather to form an opinion on the means of not putting any obstacle in the spiritual path on which God is leading your weaker brethren". Πρόσκομμα suggests the stone in the road which causes one to stumble; σκάνδαλον the trap which ensnares and holds. The one is met with by chance; the other is the result of an intention. The former creates a less serious situation than the latter. Paul seems to be thinking of the words of Jesus, Matt. 7: 1–5; 17: 27; 18: 6–9 and par. Same theme in I Cor. 8: 9–13. Perhaps πρόσκομμα borrowed from v. 20 and I Cor. 8: 9 should be omitted as B does (Sanday and Headlam, p. 390).

* Δι᾽ ἑαυτοῦ is attested by S B C while A D G Koiné read δι᾽ αὐτοῦ, which would imply that nothing is impure in consequence of the Lord Jesus because He abrogated such distinctions.

† The tone of this verse is somewhat solemn: "I know and am persuaded in the Lord Jesus. . . ." It may be thought that this style is due to the fact that Paul intends to be understood as referring to a teaching of Jesus. This is confirmed by the mention of the name of Jesus itself, for everywhere else he speaks of the Lord only.

practices themselves. The principle which states that only those acts in which the heart is expressed have value, also requires us to recognize, conversely, that every act has value if the heart finds expression in it; such an act will have the value which the heart imprints on it. What matters is the will to obey, rather than the forms which on occasion this will assumes; but those forms should be respected for the sake of the respect which we owe to consciences whose concrete decisions are thus manifested. Although nothing is intrinsically impure, if anyone is convinced that God forbids him to partake of such and such a food he would disobey God by touching it; as far as he is concerned, this food is really impure.

(15) Hence one should respect a custom because of the significance which it has for the person who practises it, and not merely, on the plane of a cold and more or less rationalist objectivity, in virtue of its intrinsic value as estimated by a detached onlooker. And in consequence* we must be careful not to injure a brother† because of some practice the value of which we ourselves do not understand. By failing to place ourselves in the position of this brother we are failing in love, for it is the very mark of love thus to take the point of view of another and to act towards him with imaginative sympathy, in short to love him "as oneself". Does Paul wish us to refrain only from harmful attitudes or speech, or does he wish us to go so far as to renounce, out of consideration for the weak, the liberty which in other circumstances we might legitimately claim? He seems to require the latter. Compared with the distress caused to consciences, of what importance is it whether we eat or not such or such food? Here is a soul for which Christ has died, that it might have life; and would you

---

* Γάρ is difficult. V. 15 is generally connected with v. 13 and v. 14 is considered to expound the general idea apart from any concrete situation.

† Λυπέω: to grieve, distress; but also inconvenience, embarrass, harm (cf. Bauer, s.v.). If we keep to the idea of grieving, we shall understand the meaning to be the sadness which produces an inner feeling of collapse (cf. 2 Cor. 7: 10) because one has a bad conscience through having disobeyed God, and deliberately decided against Him with a full knowledge of all the facts.

tear it away from the Master who has bought it so dearly and for the pleasure of using your legitimate liberty be prepared to ruin it?*

(16) How is this possible? The fact is that the "scorn" betrayed by the attitude of the "strong" prevents their brothers from understanding, and the contention of the "strong", however legitimate in itself, eventually induces the weaker brethren to blaspheme and to attribute to Satan what is of God (as in the episode of Mark 3: 23–30). In order to defend truth, it is necessary to imbue it with love; in order to teach one must love, for he who feels that he is loved is in a better position to understand.†

(17) Once again, what lasting importance attaches to these foods which give rise to such difficulties and because of which the spiritual integrity of the brethren is threatened? Compared with the manifestation of the glory of God in the establishment of His Kingdom, the problems of this life undergo a revaluation, or rather become deeply devalued. One is neither enriched nor impoverished as far as the true riches of the Kingdom are concerned, because one eats or drinks in a particular way (cf. 1 Cor. 8: 8). Righteousness, peace, and joy are gifts of God which do not depend on culinary practices (cf. 15: 13).‡ The righteousness which God bestows

* In 1 Cor. 8: 11, same use of ἀπόλλυμι. Héring (ad loc.) translates: "That is how your brother who is weak will be drawn into evil as a result of your gnosis." Ἀπόλλυμι means, in the physical sense: to cause to perish, die: figuratively; to corrupt, lead astray. Here the fact of causing someone to act against his conscience implies leading him astray and bringing about his spiritual ruin.

† This verse may be understood quite differently if we suppose that Paul is addressing the strong and the weak together. He would then be thinking of the scandal which their disputes and divisions cause to people outside the church (cf. v. 18); the latter would be thus inclined to blaspheme against the Christian faith (ὑμῶν τὸ ἀγαθόν); this would explain the plural after the singular of the preceding verse. In this case, vv. 16–19 would seem to be a parenthesis between two exhortations addressed to the strong; a fact which would regrettably interrupt the sequence and flow of the passage.

‡ Here we should not oppose an eschatological (futurist) interpretation of the Kingdom and its values, to a spiritual ("realized") interpreta-

places the believer under the sign of God's forgiveness and takes from him any right to judge his brother. Peace with God engenders a new and creative relationship with the brethren. Joy expresses the believer's gratitude in the presence of God and unseals his heart towards his brother.

(18) It would be useless to claim to be pleasing to the Lord while at the same time behaving in such a way as to break the bruised reed or quench the dimly burning wick (cf. Matt. 12: 20 and Is. 42: 1–4).* The commandment to love one's neighbour is inseparable from the commandment to love God. It is impossible to render to God authentic worship while despising the weakness of the brethren.†

(19) Hence everything must be done to promote peace, which is the structure of life in harmony with God's plan, and the state of things which God wills His people to realize; such is the normal condition of relations in the church,‡ that which favours spiritual expansion and development and the growth of each member in Christ through the edification of the whole body of Christ. Each is responsible for the edifica-

tion. The Kingdom of righteousness, peace and joy is anticipated by the gift of the Holy Spirit, and thus here and now, in a partial way, some of the graces of the Kingdom are realized in the life of the church. Generally the mention of the Holy Spirit is specially connected with joy (cf. 1 Th. 1: 6). In v. 19 peace is a present grace of the church.

* Ἐν τούτῳ may mean: "to be *in this* Spirit the servant of Christ"—or else: "to be *in this way* the servant of Christ". The reading is in itself an interpretation.

† Δόκιμος: tested and tried; hence authentic and valid. The believer will be "authentic" in the eyes of his brethren if he is a true brother. Perhaps τοῖς ἀνθρώποις includes even people outside the church, who are appreciative of the Christian "virtues" because they are in such a high degree human. But the context concerns only the Christian community.

‡ The indicative is much better attested than the subjunctive (διώκωμεν in C D E lat). But the context seems to require an exhortation. Is it possible that the indicative may be used to insinuate that peace and edification are the "natural consequence" of obedience to Christ (Michel)? Exegetes are not in agreement; Foerster considers the indicative "impossible" (*Th.Wb.NT*, II, p. 414), and Lagrange sets aside the subjunctive as a "commonplace correction".

355

tion of all, and all are responsible for the edification of each.*

(20) If it is so important to remove obstacles and to strive to attain mutual edification in a common order of peace, that is because God calls every Christian to be His fellow worker (cf. 1 Cor. 3: 9) in the task of effecting the salvation of others which is precisely God's own task: you are the house of God, said Paul to the Corinthians. Hence, Paul repeats, since all is pure, it is not the question of the ritual cleanness attaching to objects which determines what is good or bad in the sight of God. Nevertheless, it is clear that love does nothing which can be harmful to one's neighbour (cf. 13: 10) or which might imperil the work that God is pursuing. Now, the "strong" are in danger of subordinating what love requires to the prerogatives of their liberty; on the pretext of understanding the truth, they are in danger of failing in truth because they lack charity. For by their fault, what is intrinsically pure becomes an occasion of scandal, and gives distress, thus causing others to stumble.†

(21) The "strong" will therefore bear in mind that in the light of the demands of love they should abstain from certain practices. This will be "right". In opposition to κακόν, wrong, of the preceding verse (cf. also 13: 10) this word καλόν suggests what has a good influence on one's neighbour. Hence we must not exaggerate its scope. What is in question

* Let us seek what will contribute to the edification which we owe to each other. There should be no personal edification which is not integrated with the edification of all; each is a member of the body and all are members one of another. No spiritual profit is valuable if it does not serve to help all. Neither individualistic piety nor delegated piety. P. Bonnard, *Jésus-Christ édifiant son église*, 1948, pp. 38, 44 is inclined to weaken too much the role of the individual. "It is not a question of edifying the community in a general sense, but of edifying the community through individual help given to individuals" (Gaugler, II, p. 353). What is in question here is being harmful or helpful to the faith of the brethren, considered as individuals.

† Διὰ προσκόμματος may be understood in two ways. As applied to the strong: "It is a bad thing to eat and cause thereby a scandal." As applied to the weak: "It is a bad thing to eat and feel scandalized, if when you are eating you feel that you are falling from grace." In the context, Paul has in view the conduct of the strong.

is a good relative to a given situation; Paul does not mean to say that it is always good to abstain. He has sufficiently affirmed that "everything is indeed clean"; no misunderstanding is possible and in theory the "strong" are in the right. We may wonder whether the attitude required by the apostle may not risk concealing the truth; to make so many concessions to the weakness of some, does not that in itself imply weakness and almost a betrayal of truth? Love is never cowardly as sentimentality is; but it never professes truth without a passionate concern to persuade others; it becomes a slave to all men so as to win more (1 Cor. 9: 19). Jesus had paid tribute "so as not to give offence", though after telling Simon that "the sons are free" (Matt. 17: 24–27). There is no reason to speak of the "nobility" of the attitude enjoined by the apostle (as Lagrange does). The brother who abstains is not competing for a prize in virtue; he is simply walking humbly before his God and by the side of his brothers.

(22f.) No hesitation is possible with regard to the essence of the matter; Paul in conclusion repeats his lesson. Let each one retain his own personal conviction, but let it be a matter between himself and God; not with the idea of flattering himself that he alone possesses the key to truth, but rather as a persuasion which springs from his faith and fulfils his duty of obedience.* He should not make a display of his opinions before men (κατὰ σεαυτόν). Let him search his heart so as to cleanse his belief from anything which might not flow from the true demands of God (ἐνώπιον τοῦ Θεοῦ).† By this dual reference both to one's neighbour and to God, we forestall the danger of being right in conflict with a brother; it is not

* Faith consists essentially in an inner decision taken in response to the call of God, challenging one to become obedient. Hence it includes both a theoretical aspect: to accept as true what God (or the preaching) proclaims; and a practical aspect: the decision to open one's heart to this truth and to welcome it by inner assimilation. This ambivalence explains why the word πίστις can assume here a more psychological character, in which the element of conviction and obedience is more emphasized than the element of adhesion and confession.

† *Ην is lacking in the Western text. In that case the translation must be: "*You* have a certain faith (or conviction); then keep it between yourself and God" (Godet, Gaugler). Lietzmann considers it impossible to decide about the authenticity of this reading.

enough to be orthodox; love is even more important than correctness of confession (Gaugler). Without this dual reference, we condemn ourselves even though we are actually in the right!

So much for the "strong". As for the "weak", let him unhesitatingly resist the temptations and the snares which arise for him from the opinions and attitudes of the "strong". Doubtless it is not easy to refute the latter, but one ought not for that reason to be shaken in one's own belief, unless it be that a full and integral conviction brings about a change of attitude. For in such situations the wrong does not lie in eating or abstaining; since everything is indeed clean there is no objective reason for qualifying attitudes as good or bad in this matter. The wrong lies in not obeying one's own sincere conviction, in a divided personality which agrees to act in contradiction to an inner persuasion.* People are thus influenced by human and social considerations, instead of following consistently the true tendencies of the deepest self. We are thus subjugated by the suggestions of others, for reasons of vanity, instead of freely obeying God. We are then obeying others instead of obeying God; we are acting contrary to the demands of our own faith. When this situation arises, we grow confused at heart; we doubt ourselves and God; we are inwardly divided and become reticent towards God.† Here lies the essence of sin, which consists not so much

* Paul is perhaps alluding to Prov. 11: 25 (LXX): ψυχὴ εὐλογουμένη πᾶσα ἁπλῆ. V. 22b may be understood in various ways. "Happy is he who has no need to put to himself any questions of conscience . . ."; κρίνειν: to investigate one's conduct (Godet); it is the happiness of the strong to be conscientiously certain of the path he is following, writes Gaugler. "Happy is he who does not condemn himself . . ."; but this interpretation may be understood both of the strong and the weak. In the first case, happy are the strong if they can eat anything without fearing to scandalize the weak; but let them pay heed to what the urgent exhortations of the apostle mean for them; as in the present circumstances they cannot avoid causing scandal, to speak to them thus is to bring them to give up their dangerous liberty—dangerous for their brothers (Michel). If this interpretation is applied to the weak: happy are they if, eating foods which they claim to be impure, they can do so with an undivided heart, and without feeling that they are yielding to the pressure of a bad motive.

† Διακρίνομαι: to doubt, to hesitate. Cf. Rom. 4: 20; Matt. 21: 21; Mk. 11: 23; Lk. 11: 38 D; Acts 10: 20; James 1: 6; 2: 4.

in doing this or that as in doing it while knowing that we are not obeying God.*

Vv. 22 and 23 should give both groups something to think about. But it is clear that the greater responsibility lies with the "strong", since they threaten to become an occasion for the fall of others. Paul is not suggesting that they should hypocritically pretend to abandon their real opinions. He is asking them to profess those opinions as is proper in the church among members who live in the solidarity of love. Let them humble instead of exalting themselves; knowledge makes conceited, the "orthodox" are people who often know too much not to presume on their knowledge. We should trust the inspiring *agape* to build up the church in love (1 Cor. 8: 1). *Agape* serves truth better than the pride of those who know the truth without having the patience which love inspires. If we meet the weaker brethren, not with a condescension which ill conceals contempt, but with the true fervour of love, they will recognize this as a grace. Nothing can better enlighten them with regard to the truth, than a conviction which is manifested with charity. Often in the history of the church the "weak" would have made more progress in the understanding of truth, if the "strong" had more often given to truth its true manifestation which is that of love (cf. Gaugler).†

---

* It has been concluded from v. 23b that pagan virtues, not proceeding from Christian faith, were only "splendid vices" (Augustine, *C. Jul.*, IV, 32). That this exegesis is absolutely arbitrary is quite clear. Not only is Paul not speaking of pagans, but the faith to which he here alludes is not the Christian faith in its generality and objectivity (*quae creditur*) but subjective faith, the inner disposition of the believer inasmuch as he believes (*qua creditur*), and in particular what he believes with regard to the specific problem of abstinence.

† On the question of the doxology which certain MSS. place here, see on 16: 25.

¹We who are strong ought to bear with the failings of the weak, and not to please ourselves; ²let each of us please his neighbour for his good, to edify him. ³For Christ did not please himself; but, as it is written, "The reproaches of those who reproached thee fell on me." ⁴For whatever was written in former days was written for our instruction, that by steadfastness and by the encouragement of the scriptures we might have hope. ⁵May the God of steadfastness and encouragement grant you to live in such harmony with one another, in accord with Christ Jesus, ⁶that together you may with one voice glorify the God and Father of our Lord Jesus Christ.

⁷Welcome one another, therefore, as Christ has welcomed you for the glory of God. ⁸For I tell you that Christ became a servant to the circumcised to show God's truthfulness, in order to confirm the promises given to the patriarchs, ⁹and in order that the Gentiles might glorify God for his mercy. As it is written,

"Therefore I will praise thee among the Gentiles,
and sing to thy name";
¹⁰and again it is said,
"Rejoice, O Gentiles, with his people";
¹¹and again,
"Praise the Lord, all Gentiles,
and let all the peoples praise him";
¹²and further Isaiah says,
"The root of Jesse shall come,
he who rises to rule the Gentiles;
in him shall the Gentiles hope."

¹³ May the God of hope fill you with all joy and peace in believing, so that by the power of the Holy Spirit you may abound in hope.

(1) HAVING CLEARED UP the doctrinal aspect of the issue, Paul comes to more personal considerations; he now brings

himself into the argument by classing himself with the "strong" and he addresses himself to the Christian conscience of those whom up to now he has theoretically approved as right. He uses the expression οἱ δυνατοί to make those whom it designates more fully aware of their responsibilities. So far he has spoken only of the "weak" (14: 1–2). The antithesis "strong—weak" is probably borrowed from the language of the "strong". This is an additional reason for reminding those who like to style themselves as the "strong" what is implied in the title they claim. It is their duty to bear the failings of the weak;* they owe them that, their very strength makes them debtors of the weak. It is for the strong to carry the burden of the weak, not the reverse. Strong-minded people who are in high positions, well provided for, powerful, are apt to be very complacent about their advantages, while their inferiors endeavour to please them, sometimes stooping to grovel. The Christian attitude requires the very reverse. The "strong" must try to please† the "weak". Love renders possible this reversal because love gives birth to humility.‡

(2f.) When we try to please someone, we work for his advantage and best interests. There is no greater good we can procure for our brother than to edify him (cf. 14: 19 on edification). But, after all, why should we try to please our neighbour, and why choose above all to edify him? The basic reason for both lies in the sacrifice of Christ; Paul takes up again the idea of 14: 15 to apply it positively. Your brother

* Βαστάζειν does not mean simply: to endure, passively to submit to, but rather to undertake the charge of, as a responsibility. Cf. Gal. 6: 2, 5 where Paul connects the meaning of βαστάζειν with the teaching and example of Christ, as in our text. Is. 53: 4 (cf. Matt. 8: 17) is not perhaps absent from his mind.

† Ἀρέσκειν occurs three times in these lines. It is from v. 3 that it receives its full significance. We may connect with the idea of "pleasing oneself" that expressed by Paul in 14: 7: "live to oneself" (Luther; cf. Michel, p. 318, n. 2).

‡ The originality of Christianity is here brilliantly manifested. The Greek sage aimed at an ideal of autarchy; the voice of conscience was sufficient for him and he despised the opinion of others. The Christian submits to a heteronomy which breaks the circle of the ego; we have to seek the good of our neighbour. Cf. J. Dupont, "Syneidesis aux origines de la notion chrétienne de conscience morale", Studia hellenistica, 5, 1948.

361

is a man for whom Christ died; the reason why you should try to please him is that Christ loved him with that supreme love which sacrifices itself for the beloved; the way to please him, and the good which you can do for him, is to collaborate with God in the work of his salvation. Paul does not here explicitly mention the imitation of Christ, although the idea is not foreign to him;* but because of what Christ has done, we must in fact do as He did, for He has created a situation which allows us to imitate Him; we have not to make our own way, but to follow in His footsteps. Christ lived, but not for Himself; He has thus shown how the true servant of God lives, on the lines of Ps. 69: 9.†

(4) Has Paul the feeling that this psalm, evoking (as it does) insults patiently endured, is hardly applicable to the circumstances? In any event, he makes a short digression to clarify his thought, so that the "strong" may be sure to profit from the quotation. In a certain way they are tried by the scruples of the "weak"; they do indeed need an exhortation to be patient so that they may bear with the slowness and timidity of the "weak". Similarly the psalmist suffering outrage endured patiently the most violent opposition. His example, if applied to the present situation, shows how scripture helps to guide the church into the way of patience and consolation which foster hopefulness.‡ Scripture is full of useful teaching for the present generation;§ it provides an anticipatory commentary, written in advance, enabling us to understand all the implications of the fact of Christ; in a sense it expounds all the underlying factors in the decision of God which Jesus Christ incarnates. In particular, it teaches patience and con-

* Cf. 1 Th. 1: 6; 2: 14; 1 Cor. 11: 1; 4: 6; Eph. 5: 1; especially in relation to the self-abasement of Christ (Phil. 2) as is also the case here. Cf. 1 Pet. 2: 21; Jn. 13: 15.

† Ps. 69 applies only indirectly to the Messiah. It describes the righteous Israelite suffering for God's cause. Jesus Christ was the righteous Israelite *par excellence*; He bore the uttermost opprobrium because His zeal for the house of God was supreme. This psalm has several times been applied to Jesus Christ (Rom. 11: 9, 10; Acts 1: 20; Jn. 2: 17; 15: 25; Lk. 12: 50; Mk. 15: 36).

‡ Zahn applies patience to the strong and consolation to the weak.

§ Cf. Rom. 4: 23; 1 Cor. 9: 10; 10: 11; 2 Cor. 3.

solation because it concerns that people of God which is constituted by God's promise, called to bear persecutions, but consoled by the help of God which has maintained in its mind the hope of seeing the realization of the promise—which in fact came to pass with Jesus Christ. Thus the "strong" will learn the nature of a patience which is not resigned but is consoled, if we may so say, because it clings to faith in the promise. The case of the "weak" should not appear desperate to them, and in consequence they should avoid having recourse to desperate remedies which are always violent and lacking in love.

(5f.) On the contrary, let them turn to God, as scripture already invites them to do, to ask, as does the apostle in his letter, that they may receive from Him the patience and consolation which they need. May God's promise that all will be one in Christ be the object of their hope. Striving towards the fulfilment of this promise, they will experience the grace of being patient and comforted. Seeing that Paul did not condemn the position of the "weak" although he classed himself with the "strong", differences will continue, at least for a time. Two interpretations, differing but little, are possible here. Paul enjoins them to pray, either that all may have the same opinion on the matter of abstinences, or else that all may have the same sense of their fraternity in Christ, differences of opinion remaining but being submerged and overcome by unanimity on the fundamental points of the faith. In either case the church's prayer is essentially a petition that praise to God may be uttered by all with one voice.* No divergences should compromise this unity in worship, and, on the other hand, the unity in worship should deprive of their sting any differences which still persist.

(7f.) The spectre of divisions, so disastrous for the life of the community, has reared its ugly head before Paul's imagination. Hence he hammers at his point. There is no positive indication that parties had already emerged in the life of the Roman community. Nevertheless these lines presuppose that

* The formula used seems to be liturgical (2 Cor. 1: 3; 11: 31: Eph. 1: 3; 1 Pet. 1: 3).

a situation existed in which the brethren did not show an equal cordiality towards all, since Paul exhorts believers to welcome each other as Christ has already welcomed them all. The example of Christ, once again invoked, is not, strictly speaking, to be imitated. But here again they are to consider the situation created by the ministry of Christ, and on that basis to behave in the same spirit, in harmony with their pattern (cf. above). Now Christ had but one thought, which was to disclose the glory of God to men; and He wished to show forth the divine glory by gathering all men together into one single family of brothers. Nothing glorifies God so much as the unity of His children, which alone is in harmony with His essential will of love. That is why Christ welcomed you* all without distinction (cf. 10: 12; Gal. 3: 28; 1 Cor. 12: 13; Col. 3: 11). "That is what I mean", explains the apostle, who has reason to suppose that his readers do not yet grasp in what sense he is speaking about Christ's welcoming love extended to all men.

With regard to the difficulties which he has been discussing, Paul is well aware that the "weak" are believers influenced by the rules of conduct which they have inherited from their Israelite past; the "strong" are rather believers of pagan origin who have not had to undergo that treatment of disintoxication from Judaism which their brothers have found so difficult. The discussions arising on the subject are an echo from this historic past which in a sense they perpetuate, whereas Christ abolished it for ever. Consider, then, Christ your pattern, says Paul to both groups. What else did He do but "please" by bringing to each what he most needed, by adapting Himself to the situation of each in order to give a like welcome to all? For the people of Israel, He confirmed in His ministry and accomplished ($\beta\epsilon\beta\alpha\iota o\hat{v}\nu$) the promises made to their forefathers. This special ministry of Christ to the elect people is suggested in the words: "Christ became a servant to the circumcised to show God's truthfulness". Jesus devoted His ministry to the people of the circumcision alone; this temporary exclusiveness in the dealings of God mani-

* The witness of the texts is in favour of $\dot{v}\mu\hat{a}s$ S A C bo sa, etc. For $\dot{\eta}\mu\hat{a}s$ B D* P. The change of person would make the final exhortation more urgent, whilst $\dot{\eta}\mu\hat{a}s$ is more doxological.

fested "God's truthfulness", that is, His veracity, His fidelity to the promises originally made to this people (cf. 3: 4–7).

(9–12) Just as He led to its end and crown the way of the ancient promise, so Christ opened up to the pagan world the way of divine mercy,* to bring them too in their turn to glorify God. David was the first to celebrate the pagans' praise of God (Ps. 18: 49; 2 Sam. 22: 50). Scripture invites pagans as a whole to praise God (Deut. 32: 43; Ps. 117: 1), as it proclaims also the One who will be their best hope (Is. 11: 10).† Thus Christ, according to the witness of scripture and the ways chosen by God (promise and mercy) has welcomed both groups and especially those who were the weakest, the most underprivileged, the most remote. The inspiring example is divine. In the church, the strongest are not those who show their superiority, but those who hide it out of love for the weak, and in order to give them a more assured welcome.

(13) The exhortation finishes on a note of intercession. The obedient believer is thus committed to the grace of God. Nothing can better help the faithful Christians of Rome to judge in its proper perspective the "vegetarian controversy" which agitates their minds than to view the question within the framework of the great hope in which all share. Instead of remaining with your attention confined to the graces already granted, open your minds to the vision of the graces promised for the future; do not be fettered by the past, go forward in faith to meet the future which God will open out before you. This is the very essence of faith.‡ He who looks ever backward to what he has been, can draw from his contemplation of the past only regret and inner disturbance; he who realizes that the God who bestows forgiveness wipes out the past and makes all things new, looks forward, and his faith, rooted in God, engenders in his mind joy and peace (cf. Rom. 14: 17; Gal. 5: 22). Thus troubled hearts will be freed from the dead

* Ὑπὲρ ἐλέους: mercy is the characteristic of God's attitude towards pagans: Rom. 9: 15, 16, 23; 11: 30, 31, 32.

† On the problems raised by these quotations, cf. Lagrange, *ad loc.*

‡ Ἐν τῷ πιστεύειν is wanting in D G it.

weight of their natural inertia and will attain abundance of hope. No one can really hope unless by faith he turns away from the past, that is, from himself, to offer himself to God who is the Creator and Dispenser of the world to come. Here lies the secret work of the Holy Spirit, who scatters in the present moment of time the seeds of the future (Rom. 8: 16, 23; 2 Cor. 1: 21–22). Thus God opens up to man possibilities of life which are inaccessible to natural energies; the Holy Spirit is triumphant energy and power, the Giver of new life, the Grace which renews the old world. In order to overcome their differences of opinion, the Romans will join with the apostle in asking God to open their eyes by the inspiration of the Holy Spirit to the vision of the things promised to obedience and faith.

> [14]I myself am satisfied about you, my brethren, that you yourselves are full of goodness, filled with all knowledge, and able to instruct one another. [15]But on some points I have written to you very boldly by way of reminder, because of the grace given me by God [16]to be a minister of Christ Jesus to the Gentiles in the priestly service of the gospel of God, so that the offering of the Gentiles may be acceptable, sanctified by the Holy Spirit. [17]In Christ Jesus, then, I have reason to be proud of my work for God. [18]For I will not venture to speak of anything except what Christ has wrought through me to win obedience from the Gentiles, by word and deed, [19]by the power of signs and wonders, by the power of the Holy Spirit, so that from Jerusalem and as far round as Illyricum I have fully preached the gospel of Christ, [20]thus making it my ambition to preach the gospel, not where Christ has already been named, lest I build on another man's foundation, [21]but as it is written,
>
> "They shall see who have never been told of him,
>   and they shall understand who have never heard of him."

(14) Thus we come to the end of the letter. We must emphasize (with Michel) that its essential notes correspond to those struck in the introduction (1: 8–17); plans for a journey to Rome, apostolic mission, the bonds of intercession, fellowship in divine grace.* Coming from the pen of the apostle,

* 1: 10=15: 22–24, 28, 29, 32; 1: 5, 14, 15=15: 15, 16; 1: 9, 10= 15: 30, 33; 1: 11–13=15: 29.

the note of praise in this verse concerning the spiritual condition of the community is astonishing. "If we were to take this verse seriously, ch. 12 to 15: 13 would be useless," writes Lietzmann. Let us then suppose that these lines are addressed to the church as a whole; the attitude of certain of its members did not commit everyone; the fact that the church is not seriously threatened is shown by the lack of any note of great severity in the preceding exhortations. Paul is convinced that his remarks will find readers of good will.* In fact they are "filled with all knowledge" and so capable of working to their mutual edification and encouragement.

(15f.) Paul recognizes that he has shown some boldness in writing as he has done. Doubtless not because he has been too severe† but because he has been addressing a church which he does not know and so seems to be concerning himself with matters which do not fall within his province. But how could this be the subject of complaint? He has said nothing which was not already known at Rome; as for the contents, he has limited himself to reminding his readers of undisputed traditional teaching. As for the liberty he has taken in writing thus, it is not on personal grounds that he claims it; it is on the grounds of his apostleship. He obeys the mission imposed on him by the grace which has made of him the priestly servant of Christ among the Gentiles.‡

Λειτουργός does not of itself imply a sacerdotal function; we have seen this in regard to 13: 6. But here the context makes this meaning§ irresistible; however, it must still be understood in terms of the author's thought. The apostle is a liturgical minister because he exercises a priestly function (ἱερουργοῦντα) through the preaching of the gospel, thus

* Ἀγαθωσύνη: the word is found only in the LXX, the *corpus paulinum* and the ecclesiastical writers (cf. Rom. 15: 14; Gal. 5: 22; Eph. 5: 9; 2 Th. 1: 11). G lat replace it by ἀγάπης.

† Ἀπὸ μέρους (in part) has been connected with ἔγραψα: "there are parts of my letter which are somewhat bold"; or with τολμηροτέρως: "I have written to you with rather considerable boldness"; or with ἐπαναμιμνήσκων: "to remind you to some extent of these matters".

‡ Instead of ἀπὸ Θεοῦ we read ὑπὸ τοῦ Θεοῦ (by the will of God) in P 46 A C D G etc.

§ As in Hebr. 8: 2.

offering to God a sacrifice that is well pleasing; namely, the converted Gentiles who are sanctified by the Holy Spirit. The priest whose function culminated in the offering of sacrifice was part of a divine institution, the object of which was to restore the relations between God and His people menaced and even broken off by sin. In the new economy which God has established in Jesus Christ, the gospel proclaimed by the apostle is the new way by which the sinner is reconciled to God: it brings the sinner to the obedience flowing from faith in Christ, the sacrificial victim who replaces every other. But the sacrifice of Christ includes and implies the sacrifice of every believer who is united to the Crucified by faith and baptism (cf. 6: 2–3). Through this union the sinner becomes with Christ an offering that is living, holy and well-pleasing to God (cf. 12: 1). Hence the preacher of the gospel assumes a sacerdotal function, as formerly did the priest of the temple who offered animal victims. Exactly as the priest, the apostle is entrusted with the mission of preparing the way for the return of men to God by the medium of the offering of a victim. Truths like these are fundamental: henceforth the priesthood is assumed by the apostle not because he sacrifices at a new altar to offer a new sacrifice, but because he proclaims the gospel and becomes the instrument by which the Holy Spirit associates believers with the sacrifice of the cross. If ancient sacrifices and the priesthood which was ordained to accomplish them are henceforth superseded, it is because the end pursued by this institution is now attained in a superior way by the apostolate which Christ has instituted.

Paul is now looking towards the horizons of that new world to which he has already announced his intention of going. He is about to offer on the altar (the cross of Christ) those Gentiles whom he will soon reach through his preaching.¶ Will it not be an offering well-pleasing to God? Certainly, and because of the sanctifying grace of the Holy Spirit which will be shed on it. Only pure victims were brought to the altar. All uncleanness has been removed from the Gentiles

¶ Ἡ προσφορὰ τῶν ἐθνῶν, gen. appos.: the offering constituted by the Gentiles. Cf. Is. 66: 20. Cf. K. Weiss, "Paulus Priester", Th.L.Z., 1954.

by their communion with the crucified and risen Christ, who has abolished their old state of life and bestowed upon them the sanctifying presence of the Holy Spirit (Rom. 7: 5–6; 1 Cor. 6: 11; Rom. 6: 22; see also 12: 1).

(17–19a) Just as the priest at the altar merely obeyed the prescriptions of Moses, so that his individuality was effaced behind the divine institution which alone gave to his actions their value, so the sacerdotal ministry of the apostle does not give rise to any personal vanity (cf. 1 Cor. 15: 10–31; 2 Cor. 10: 13).* It is Christ who is the unseen actor and who imparts to this ministry its astonishing fecundity (cf. 2 Cor. 3: 5; 4: 7; 13: 3). He has instituted the ministry of gospel preaching and He continues to accomplish through the apostle the task which He had in view in instituting the apostolic order. According to the synoptics† this was a double task—it was to proclaim the Kingdom and heal the sick; *word* and *action*, two complementary manifestations of that Gospel which is the "power of God" (1: 16). This was in fact the very structure of Christ's own ministry, which His disciples were to assume in His name and place, as veritable apostles, which is to say representatives (see on 1: 1) so that it is He, the Sender, who is still efficaciously acting through them to bring the Gentiles to the obedience of faith (cf. 1: 5; 6: 17; 16: 26). Their ministry has the same structure as His own (λόγῳ καὶ ἔργῳ). The double mention of δύναμις, *power*, emphasizes the efficacity of the abiding action of Christ in the apostolate; it is Christ who is the hidden Author of the "signs and wonders"‡ and it is Christ who gives the Holy Spirit by whose power testimony is given to the Lord.§

* There is no article before καύχησιν in P 46 S A etc. The meaning will be: "I have indeed reason to congratulate myself in Christ, for. . . ." With the article: "such (i.e. my ministry) is the glory that I have in Christ, and, in fact. . . ."
† Cf. Mk. 3: 14; Matt. 10: 1; Lk. 9: 2.
‡ Cf. 2 Cor. 12: 12. Similar formulae are frequent in the OT already.
§ Cf. Matt. 10: 20; Lk. 12: 12. In spite of the inverted order, it is probable that the first ἐν δυνάμει qualifies ἔργῳ, the second λόγῳ. After Πνεύματος A C D G etc. read ʽΑγίου and P 46 S L P Θεοῦ.

(19b) If such then is the nature of the apostolic mission, we can see why Paul might well consider himself justified in addressing the Christians at Rome as he has done. We may add that the fruits prove the goodness of the tree. The results achieved by this mission are the very seal of the Lord Himself, the proof that Christ Himself is here at work (1 Cor. 9: 2; 2 Cor. 3: 2). Travelling by roads which radiated from one centre,* Paul has pushed his activities as far as Illyria.† This indication suggests a triumphal march of the gospel from east to west, and the feeling that everything lying eastwards from Rome has already been evangelized. The success of Paul's apostolic mission consists then both in the power which it has displayed (v. 18) and the extension it has assumed (v. 19). The gospel has been endowed with the twofold richness of having been both very effective and universally recognized (the use of the perfect in πεπληρωκέναι suggests that all this is an accomplished fact). Paul can say that he has "fully preached" the Gospel, the word εὐαγγέλιον denoting here the Gospel both as preached and also in its power to save; it is the Gospel of the missionary.‡

(20f.) It may be considered that Paul gives too optimistic a view of his missionary activity. For after all, he has not reached every region around the eastern basin of the Mediterranean; for example, he did not touch Egypt; and even

---

* Κύκλῳ may mean: either the various journeys which Paul made in a limited circuit from Jerusalem or else his activity "around Jerusalem".

† A certain lack of precision in the use of the name Illyria by ancient authors makes it impossible to know exactly what territory is covered by the term (cf. Paulys, *Real Enc.*, 9, 1, 1087). Equally we must wonder whether Paul comprised Jerusalem and Illyria in his fields of activity, or whether he mentions them here as outer limits. The Book of Acts does not mention Illyria, and the special responsibilities which fell to Paul's apostolate would not lead us to believe that he worked in Jerusalem. Finally it is possible that the mention of Jerusalem expresses a theological intention, since Jerusalem was the holy city of the elect people and the sphere in which the mother church was situated.

‡ This text has also been interpreted of the activity of the preacher of the gospel which has reached complete fulfilment (Delling, *Th.Wb.NT*, VI, p. 296). Or again "of the event which fulfils prophecy" (Lyonnet). Cf. Col. 1: 25: "to accomplish the Word of God, i.e. to reveal its full meaning and efficacity" (Masson).

where he did go, he preached only in a few towns. Even so, he feels that his task is completed in that part of the *oikoumene* and that he must direct his efforts elsewhere if he does not want to be content with preaching to people who have already heard the gospel.* It may be that Paul's missionary work was more intense than appears from the Book of Acts, which from every point of view is incomplete and would not exclude such a hypothesis. Paul too may have expected that the faith would spread from the communities which he did found. Let us remember also that here too as in chs. 9–11 he has probably been thinking in terms of collectivities; there was no need to ensure that all the towns and all the individuals of any particular area had heard the gospel to feel justified in asserting that it had been evangelized.†

However that may be, the apostle now requires for his further activity virgin territory. His apostolic zeal and honour‡ were staked on the point of not touching regions where others had worked. Not because he feared the competition of authorities,§ but because the general task was so pressing. Did he not even exclude from his understanding of his apostolic mission the widespread practice of baptism (1 Cor. 1: 17)? doubtless because he himself was concerned only to lay the foundations, leaving to others (1 Cor. 3: 10) the much longer discipline of instruction which culminated in baptism. Paul is in a hurry not from motives appertaining to ecclesiastical politics, but out of fidelity to his vocation: the Gentile world is waiting. Prophecy itself, that is, the plan

* "Where Christ has not been named", i.e. invoked, solemnly called upon. Cf. 2 Tim. 2: 19; Is. 26: 13; Amos 6: 10.

† Cf. Munck, pp. 45, 272 who speaks of a "representative acceptance of the Gospel".

‡ S A C: φιλοτιμούμενον. P 46 B D* G P: φιλοτιμοῦμαι. Cf. 1 Th. 4: 11; 2 Cor. 5: 9 ("we make it our aim", Allo, *ad loc.*).

§ Critics have generally tracked down in this verse an allusion to the difficulties which Paul had with the Judaizers. In our view the motivation should be theological rather than personal. The same applies to φιλοτιμούμενον concerning the apostle's honour, but not the honour of the man, what one might call (*mutatis mutandis*) professional conscience, but not vanity, self-esteem; we should avoid giving an interpretation which, in the phrase of Munck, p. 45, *secularizes* Paul.

of God revealed to the prophets, shows this to be his pro-gramme.*

[22]This is the reason why I have so often been hindered from coming to you. [23]But now, since I no longer have any room for work in these regions, and since I have longed for many years to come to you, [24]I hope to see you in passing as I go to Spain, and to be sped on my journey there by you, once I have enjoyed your company for a little. [25]At present, however, I am going to Jerusalem with the aid for the saints. [26]For Macedonia and Achaia have been pleased to make some contribution for the poor among the saints at Jerusalem; [27]they were pleased to do it, and indeed they are in debt to them, for if the Gentiles have come to share in their spiritual blessings, they ought also to be of service to them in material blessings. [28]When therefore I have completed this, and have delivered to them what has been raised, I shall go on by way of you to Spain; [29]and I know that when I come to you I shall come in the fullness of the blessing of Christ.

[30]I appeal to you, brethren, by our Lord Jesus Christ and by the love of the Spirit, to strive together with me in your prayers to God on my behalf, [31]that I may be delivered from the unbelievers in Judea, and that my service for Jerusalem may be acceptable to the saints, [32]so that by God's will I may come to you with joy and be refreshed in your company. [33]The God of peace be with you all. Amen.

(22-24a) The labours with which he has been occupied up to the present, and doubtless also the difficulties he has had to surmount, have hitherto always† deprived Paul of the necessary time, opportunity and perhaps freedom of mind for a journey to Rome, in spite of the hopes which he had fostered about this. Certainly his sweeping vision of apostolic tasks embraced the "confines of the inhabited world".‡

* The use of Is. 52: 15 may be understood in two ways in this context. Either: "the heathen wait and it was necessary for me to go to them". Or else: "Were I to go to them who already know the name of Christ, I should be evading the command of the prophet." Paul cites Is. 52 be-cause he finds in it the programme of the apostolic ministry; but he does not compare Christ with the Servant of Yahweh (Gaugler).

† P 46 S D G have πολλάκις, which is less emphatic.

‡ Spain was far from being considered an unknown land. Constant commercial relations connected it with the East. Indeed it seems to have been even a tourist centre. Jewry appears to have been fairly important there (cf. Michel, p. 332, n. 2).

Hence with his work in the eastern regions of the empire now completed and sufficiently consolidated, he can revive and carry out his old plan.*

In going to Rome, Paul does not feel that he is breaking with the principle which has regulated his conduct so far (v. 20). No doubt he visualizes working not so much in Rome itself as in the regions through which he will pass (cf. πρὸς ὑμᾶς): and especially it should be remembered that he will only pass through Rome and Italy (vv. 24-32); his real aim is Spain.

(24b) And yet he keenly looks forward to his passing through Rome. In the first place, in order to make the acquaintance of the community, and to bring them the comfort which the members of the church both receive and give when in mutual edification they testify to each other of the graces which they have been granted (cf. 1:13).† Then, with the hope of finding there the support he needs for his work in Spain (letters of recommendation, material equipment, and perhaps guides or travelling companions).‡

(25-27) But this burning hope cannot be realized at once. He must first go to Jerusalem with aid for the saints, i.e. the members of the mother church; this designation inherited from ancient Israel, while not exactly reserved to the Jerusalem Christians, seems to have been applied to them as being specially appropriate.§ The service of the apostle con-

---

* The sentence remains incomplete: perhaps under the stress of emotion?

† Ἐμπίμπλημι: to fill, and: satiate. Here, to enjoy fully and to the point of satiety the personalities and the spiritual riches of the believers in Rome. The word connotes the ideas of joy, comfort, relief (Delling, Th.Wb.NT, VI, p. 131).

‡ On προπέμπω cf. 1 Cor. 16: 6, 11; 2 Cor. 1: 16; Acts 15: 3; Tit. 3: 13; 3 Jn. 6. Cf. Acts 20: 38; 21: 5. Sanday and Headlam, p. 411, only see in it the fact of speeding someone on his journey by the accompaniment of prayers and good wishes.

§ Cf. Lietzmann, ad loc., Procksch, Th.Wb.NT, I, pp. 107-109. Paul denotes thus not only the church of Jerusalem (Rom. 15: 25, 26; 1 Cor. 16: 1, 15; 2 Cor. 8: 4, etc.) but Christianity as a whole (Rom. 1: 7; 1 Cor. 1: 2, etc.). "In principle there is no difference between the ἅγιοι of the mother church and those of the missionary churches" (Procksch,

sisted in bringing them the funds which he had collected for them from the Gentile churches* in Macedonia and Achaia. Paul has devoted much care and attention to this matter. He saw in it much more than a simple undertaking for mutual help. To be sure, such economic solidarity was an inevitable form of brotherly love, in face of the difficult situation of the Jerusalem community or some at least of its members.† But the poverty of these brothers is only an occasion; the Christians of Macedonia and Achaia‡ are not strictly speaking being generous, they are acquitting a debt; they owe (the root ὀφειλ is used twice) this material help to those who have been the means of procuring for them a far more precious wealth. Hence the money collected has been very willingly and gladly given, it has not been wrenched from them (ηὐδόκησαν, *they have been pleased to*, is repeated!). This is no imposition but an exchange of goods; he who has received is happy to return the gift in another form;§ it is a κοινωνία, a reciprocity of services (the radical κοιν is no less than twice used).

Paul dwells on this matter more than was necessary, it appears. Did he wish to suggest to the Romans that they should associate themselves with the undertaking, without daring to ask them directly? Did he hope to prepare them in this way to be equally generous towards himself, by helping him in his future work with their gifts? The possibility may explain the fact that he makes no mention of his own efforts to procure the gift and presents it as if it were an entirely spontaneous gesture on the part of the churches. In any case, the collection is a manifest sign of the unity of the church. It

ibid. p. 108). Cf. also L. Cerfaux, *La Théol. de l'Église suivant saint Paul,* 2nd ed., 1948, pp. 89–110.

* Cf. Gal. 2: 10; 1 Cor. 16: 1–4; 2 Cor. 8–9; Acts 24: 17.

† Τῶν ἁγίων: partitive genitive.

‡ We should add those of Galatia and Asia Minor according to 1 Cor. 16: 1; Acts 20: 4.

§ Cf. the formula borrowed from business language which qualifies ἐκοινώνησεν in Phil. 4: 15; εἰς λόγον δόσεως καὶ λήμψεως, a debit and credit account. Similarly Gal. 6: 6; the Christians of Greece have been instructed as the pupil by the master; the pupil must share with his master the material wealth which he has at his disposal.

374

shows in concrete fashion that the young shoots are firmly linked to the old trunk.*

(28f.) Paul will have completed the task when he will have handed over to the Jerusalem saints what he calls "this fruit", perhaps to suggest that this is the harvest that they are gathering as a result of having sown the seeds of the gospel.† The sense of σφραγισάμενος presents some difficulty. Since the seal serves as a certificate of authentication, it has been thought that Paul meant to say: "when I have handed over this sum to those for whom it is intended in a way which removes any dispute about its administration"; for suspicions had arisen earlier (2 Cor. 8: 20–21; 12: 16). But it seems unlikely that Paul would refer to these difficulties in writing to the Romans. Or did he wish to assure them of the true import and value of this gift? "When I have assured them that this is the fruit of their spiritual seed, and that it has been sent out of gratitude for the spiritual wealth which they first lavished." The seal is also the mark of the completion of an undertaking; the goods which are about to be delivered are sealed. Did Paul mean: "When I have presented this fruit bearing the seal of a well-completed task, i.e. after doing all that could be done to see that the work was well done"? In that case the seal would be the guarantee of integrity and fine quality. Between these various interpretations the choice is open.‡

The declared intention of the apostle was not to settle at Rome, which he would merely pass through on his way to Spain. Short, however, as this visit would be, Paul is certain that he will not be only a debtor to the Romans. He now completes what he said in v. 24 where he referred to the spiritual good which he hoped would accrue to his hosts (cf.

* J. Munck, p. 299, thinks that Paul hopes, by giving this witness to the faith of the Gentiles, to help on the conversion of the Jews who would be moved to jealousy. The text of the letter does not suggest this interesting interpretation.

† The image is familiar to Paul: 1 Cor. 9: 11; Phil. 4: 17.

‡ L. Cerfaux connects the idea of the seal with the contract to which the church of Jerusalem has agreed: the handing over of the contribution will constitute the seal ratifying that the Gentiles are conclusively admitted to communion with the mother church (*op. cit.* p. 102).

1: 11). He will come, in point of fact, "in the fullness of the blessing of Christ". This should be understood in a dual sense: the blessing of Christ rests fully on his plans of travel in pursuit of his mission: hence as a result the blessing of Christ will be communicated to those who receive and help him. His passing through will be the occasion of a veritable κοινωνία (Michel).

(30–33) But the heart of the apostle was oppressed by the contrast between the joy which his proposed visit to Rome caused him and the anxiety aroused by his journey to Jerusalem—an anxiety which was only too well founded. The Book of Acts (ch. 20) confirms that Jewish circles were becoming increasingly opposed to the apostle. The latter was fully aware of the situation and had suffered from it many times already. Yet he will not retreat in spite of the warnings which his friends multiply for his sake. In his resolution, the prayers of his brothers at Rome will provide him with precious help. For he will have to confront hostile powers which can be dealt with only by faith armed with prayer. Already the apostle has begun to fight with the weapon of prayer, and he begs his readers to take part (cf. Col. 4: 12). They are in a way his allies, since they have a common Lord and both he and they are united in the same love which is shed abroad by the Holy Spirit.

They too must ask on behalf of the apostle what he himself asks, namely that he should not be ensnared by the nets which the Jews who have rejected Jesus the Messiah have laid for him.* But he also asks for their prayers in order that his journey may fulfil its essential aim, namely, that the gift† should be acceptable to the saints. Hence Paul has enemies at the heart of the church who will no doubt find some pretext for attacking him personally in connexion with his behaviour concerning the gift. Even if the worst is spared him the apostle is afraid lest discussions provoked at Jerusalem may delay and perhaps prevent the realization of his missionary schemes. This implies that he does not want to make a decisive break with the Jerusalem community; he does not

* Οἱ ἀπειθοῦντες is certainly polemical; cf. 2: 8; 10: 21; 11: 30, 31.
† Instead of διακονία B D* F G read δωροφορία.

propose to proceed on his way to Rome unless he can do so with the joy of having found a kind welcome at Jerusalem.* Only on those conditions will he have the certainty of going to Rome† in harmony with the will of God;‡ and inner peace of mind will then enable him to be refreshed§ in the company of those brethren.‖

* The second ἵνα depends on the first.
† P 46 B: ἔλθω instead of ἔλθων. B: κυρίου Ἰησοῦ instead of Θεοῦ.
‡ "By the will of God" may also be linked with ἀναπαύσωμαι. Grammatically better, this construction, which is adopted by Lietzmann, gives a less satisfactory meaning.
§ Συναναπαύεσθαι is found only here and in Is. 11: 6.
‖ In place of ἀμήν P 46 gives the vv. 16: 25–27.

CHAPTER

16

¹I commend to you our sister Phoebe, a deaconess of the church at Cenchreae, ²that you may receive her in the Lord as befits the saints, and help her in whatever she may require from you, for she has been a helper of many and of myself as well.

³Greet Prisca and Aquila, my fellow workers in Christ Jesus, ⁴who risked their necks for my life, to whom not only I but also all the churches of the Gentiles give thanks; ⁵greet also the church in their house. Greet my beloved Epaenetus, who was the first convert in Asia for Christ. ⁶Greet Mary, who has worked hard among you. ⁷Greet Andronicus and Junias, my kinsmen and my fellow prisoners; they are men of note among the apostles, and they were in Christ before me. ⁸Greet Ampliatus, my beloved in the Lord. ⁹Greet Urbanus, our fellow worker in Christ, and my beloved Stachys. ¹⁰Greet Apelles, who is approved in Christ. Greet those who belong to the family of Aristobulus. ¹¹Greet my kinsman Herodion. Greet those in the Lord who belong to the family of Narcissus. ¹²Greet those workers in the Lord, Tryphaena and Tryphosa. Greet the beloved Persis, who has worked hard in the Lord. ¹³Greet Rufus, eminent in the Lord, also his mother and mine. ¹⁴Greet Asyncritus, Phlegon, Hermes, Patrobas, Hermas, and the brethren who are with them. ¹⁵Greet Philologus, Julia, Nereus and his sister, and Olympas, and all the saints who are with them. ¹⁶Greet one another with a holy kiss. All the churches of Christ greet you.

IN THOSE LETTERS which Paul addressed to communities he knew personally, he did not include long individual greetings. Addressing himself to all, he did not greet anyone in particular. It is surprising therefore that in writing to Rome which he has never visited he should know so many members of the church and should name them in concluding his letter.

378

No doubt this peculiarity may be explained by supposing that Paul knew several Christians at Rome; the empire maintained constant relations with the capital and many converts whom Paul vividly remembered may have settled in the capital. Nevertheless a problem remains, the other factors in which will be seen from our introduction.

(1f.) The first name to be mentioned is that of Phoebe, doubtless because she is the bearer of the letter, for her arrival is not announced as a later event and it is not suggested that she should be greeted but received. This "sister", whose name is of pagan and even mythological origin, is a "deaconess" in the church at Cenchreae.* What exactly her task consisted of we do not know (visits to the sick and to strangers?) but it seems that this office was familiar to the Romans.† They are to receive Phoebe "in the Lord" (the frequency with which this expression occurs in the chapter should be noted), that is, "as befits the saints", as should be done among brothers and members of the same body. Some material assistance which will probably be necessary is also included.

Phoebe is described as προστάτις. This word denoted the legal representative of strangers and their protector, for as aliens they were deprived of civil rights. Since a woman is in question, the official meaning of the term is excluded. It should be understood figuratively: Phoebe has had occasion to intervene on behalf of Christians, and at times before authority, perhaps simply from an exceptional degree of devotion. She had earned a considerable claim to the gratitude of the brethren; those of Rome are informed of this so that they may treat her accordingly.

(3–5a) The greetings begin at v. 3 with the mention of Prisca,‡ who is named before her husband Aquila. This

* As it is very problematic that in 1 Tim. 3: 11 women are in question, our text here constitutes the only mention of the fact that a woman exercised the function of the diaconate.

† It is admitted that διάκονος designates here an office, an established function, having οὖσαν as a participle and τῆς ἐκκλησίας as its genitive (Michel, p. 340).

‡ Priscilla is the diminutive of Prisca, used in Acts 18: 2, 18, 26 and, by some MSS., in 1 Cor. 16: 19.

379

couple had fled from Rome in consequence of the edict of Claudius. Paul had met them at Corinth where they had taken refuge (Acts 18: 2). They must have been drawn together by similarity of trade and perhaps Paul found work with them. We do not know how they were led to the faith, but they followed Paul to Ephesus (Acts 18: 18, 19, 26) where they worked for the Lord. Paul mentions them specially and adds the church which meets in their house (1 Cor. 16: 19).* Prisca is named first, probably because she had played a preponderant part in co-operating in the apostolic work. The devotion of this couple to the apostle must have been proved in a quite moving way on a certain occasion, perhaps at Ephesus itself (cf. 1 Cor. 15: 32; Acts 19: 23)†.

(5b-6) Epaenetus, who is unknown to us, bears a Greek name. He must have been of Gentile origin. We do not know why Paul shows a special regard for him. Was he one of Paul's converts, which might explain the attachment? The expression "first fruits for Christ"‡ may mean that Epaenetus was not only converted in Asia but that he was set aside for special dedication to the work of Christ.

Mary is probably a name of Jewish origin§ though it is found also as the feminine of Marius in Latin inscriptions. Paul does not remind his readers of this woman's great efforts on their behalf in order to refresh their memory as to facts which they know better than he, but to associate himself with their regard for her.‖

* For this expression cf. Acts 12: 12; Col. 4: 15; Philemon 2. Zahn thinks that the personages mentioned in vv. 5–13 are members of the church which meets at the home of Prisca and Aquila.

† One cannot fail to notice the mention of these two women, Phoebe and Prisca, who played a pre-eminent part in the life of the first church, and to contrast with that fact the pettily bourgeois theology, which, in our day, shows a "masculine" boldness in silencing women in church (cf. Gaugler, II, p. 397).

‡ Cf. the household of Stephanas, the first converts in Achaia, 1 Cor. 16: 15.

§ Μαρίαμ in P 46 S Koiné D G.

‖ If we read εἰς ὑμᾶς with L. Chrys. etc., we shall notice that Paul alludes to the intercourse he has had with those whom he greets.

380

(7) Andronicus and Junias are two Israelites. Some authors suppose that Junias is the wife of Andronicus (Lagrange, Lyonnet*). In what sense does Paul call them συγγενεῖς μου? Compatriots or kinsmen? It is difficult to say. Why is it that the other Jews mentioned are not qualified in the same way? But again, since the word recurs in vv. 11 and 21, it is surprising that Paul has so many kinsmen in so remote a community (Sanday and Headlam, and Michel, take the word in the first sense; Lagrange in the second).

Andronicus and Junias have suffered imprisonment like Paul (2 Cor. 11:23) but not necessarily with him; we do not know where or when. Above all they are "eminent apostles", who were won for the Christian faith before Paul himself. Two interesting notes. We should not weaken the significance of the first expression by saying that these persons "have a great reputation among the apostles" (Zahn)! The term ἀπόστολος, apostle, was not reserved to the Twelve; our text is one of those which prove this,† and it is not legitimate to distort the sense in order to save the dogmatic idea of a closed apostolate limited in time and space; Andronicus and Junias belong to the very first generation of Christians, since "they were in Christ" before Paul. This is an additional claim to the esteem of Christians at Rome.

(8) Ampliatus, a fairly common slave's name which is found in an inscription of the catacomb of Domitilla (perhaps first century). Is it the name of the Christian whom Paul is greeting?

(9) Urbanus is just as frequent a name. This Urbanus is called "our fellow worker in Christ". We do not know with whom he has worked. Stachys is a Greek name, often given to slaves; a slave of that name is known to have been in Caesar's household.

(10) Apelles, a fairly common Greek name, but borne

* Some witnesses have read here the name of a woman: 'Ιουλίαν (P 46 bo aeth Vulg. Cf. Jer. Amb.).
† Cf. Acts 14:4, 14; Gal. 1:19; 1 Cor. 15:7. Cf. Rengstorf, Th.Wb.NT, I, p. 422. E. Lohse, "Ursprung und Prägung des christlichen Apostolates", Th.Z., 1953, pp. 259–275.

equally by Jews. The person bearing it is described by Paul as an approved Christian ("approved in Christ"). But we do not know how or when he was tested and tried.

Those of the house of Aristobulus are his slaves or freedmen. Aristobulus is a Greek name, borne by Jews in high places; more than one is found in the family of Herod. The one named here may have been the brother of Agrippa I. Paul does not greet him directly; is he dead or a stranger to the faith?

(11) The name Herodian is unknown, but it must denote a freedman of Herod. If Aristobulus belongs to the family of Herod, Herodian might have belonged to the same household. The mention of this name just here might confirm that Aristobulus was a kinsman of Herod. Narcissus is a Greek name but it was widespread among the Latins and given to both free men and slaves. A freedman of this name was a minister of Claudius; he perished in 54 before Paul wrote to the Romans but his household (Narcissiani, CIL III 3973; VI 15640) may have persisted.

(12) Tryphaena and Tryphosa are Greek names but known at Rome. Names from the same root, they were perhaps those of two sisters. Persis is the name of a slave, but it is uncommon.

(13) Rufus, a Latin name, was frequently given to slaves or freedmen. Paul must have known well this man and his mother, whom he also calls his own mother according to the custom of orientals who speak thus of an older woman (Lagrange). Mark 15: 21 mentions a Rufus as the son of Simon of Cyrene; it is generally thought proper to identify the two personages, especially as the Gospel of Mark was probably written in Rome. Rufus might have been called ἐκλεκτὸς ἐν Κυρίῳ, *elected in the Lord*, on account of his occupying an eminent position among Christians.*

* *Distinguished for his special excellence* (Sanday and Headlam). Cf. 2 Jn. 1; 1 Pet. 2: 6. Schrenk, rather peevishly: "Should the actual excellence of Rufus be canonized in just this way, ἐν Κυρίῳ?" (*Th.Wb.NT*, VI, p. 195, n. 22).

(14) Asyncritus is very rare; it was the name of a freedman of Augustus. Phlegon, the name of a dog (Xen. *Cyn.* VII, 5) and also of a slave or freedman, is sometimes found. Hermes is very common and was often given to slaves, like the names of gods in general. Hermas is a special form of Hermes and is frequently met with as the name of a slave. These five names form one group to which the apostle adds the mention of certain brethren who are united with them by very special bonds. Were they all slaves or freedmen of the same person?

(15) Philologus is a Greek name borne by freedmen. Julia, a very common Latin name in Rome; perhaps the wife of Philologus. Nereus, a mythological name, given to slaves. Olympas, an abbreviation of Olympiodora, likewise a name given to slaves. These again perhaps formed one family group and the "saints who are with them" may be the church which gathered together in their house.

(16) The custom of greeting with a "holy kiss" was already widespread in the churches (cf. 1 Th. 5: 26; 1 Cor. 16: 20; 2 Cor. 13: 12; 1 Pet. 5: 14). It has been supposed that the letter was read during the celebration of the Eucharist, a holy kiss being given at the end of the reading.* The liturgical act expressed the bond of brotherhood which united all the believers in Christ their Master.

Finally, in the name of all the churches of Christ, Paul greets the Christians of Rome. Had he a special mandate to do so? He may have communicated to the churches which he had just visited his intention of going to Rome and have been charged to convey their good wishes to the church of the capital. Or again he may be speaking thus on his own initiative, but in the name of all the churches which he knows well enough to be certain of expressing their mind. Should we go so far as to suppose that he manifests thus his apostolic authority, and that he is of right the mouthpiece of all these communities? Nothing really suggests or justifies this. There

* "It would have as it were a sacramental value, to seal the unity of the brethren among themselves and their common bond with him whose letter had been read, and at whose bidding the holy kiss was given and received" (cf. Windisch, *Th.Wb.NT*, I, p. 499).

is nothing odd about his greeting the believers in Rome on behalf of all the churches, at a moment when he has just finished a long series of greetings addressed to various persons, several of whom have recalled to his mind the diverse communities from which they sprang. And from all these churches, Paul is pleased to give his readers a brotherly message which is a sign of Christian unity. It is not at all clear why this salutation should reveal that "the church of Rome was for all other churches the object of a quite special veneration".* Paul takes a comprehensive survey of the eastern basin of the Mediterranean where he has for a long time worked, and from the many churches of which he is to a large extent the apostle he sends a brotherly greeting to the distant church at Rome.

> [17]I appeal to you, brethren, to take note of those who create dissensions and difficulties, in opposition to the doctrine which you have been taught; avoid them. [18]For such persons do not serve our Lord Christ, but their own appetites, and by fair and flattering words they deceive the hearts of the simple-minded. [19]For while your obedience is known to all, so that I rejoice over you, I would have you wise as to what is good and guileless as to what is evil; [20]then the God of peace will soon crush Satan under your feet. The grace of our Lord Jesus Christ be with you.
>
> [21]Timothy, my fellow worker, greets you; so do Lucius and Jason and Sosipater, my kinsmen.
>
> [22]I Tertius, the writer of this letter, greet you in the Lord.
>
> [23]Gaius, who is host to me and to the whole church, greets you. Erastus, the city treasurer, and our brother Quartus, greet you.
>
> [[24]The grace of our Lord Jesus Christ be with you all. Amen. in R.S.V. margin.]

(17f.) Quite abruptly the reader is pulled up here by some sharply penned lines which the apostle has added to his

---

* Lagrange and, already, Hort, according to Sanday and Headlam. The verb "greet" which has just been used thirteen times, immediately before, does not in itself suggest any special sentiments of veneration. These remarks would be superfluous if we were to consider v. 16b as inauthentic (D G it). Note however that D* G it add to v. 21: καὶ αἱ ἐκκλησίαι πᾶσαι τοῦ Χριστοῦ.

384

greetings, according to a habit of composition which is found again in Gal. 6: 11–16; 1 Cor. 16: 22. Are these words the personal signature of the author? They sound a jarring note in the flow of this eirenical writing.

The community is threatened; it is necessary to be very vigilant* with regard to certain people who apparently have not yet been admitted into its midst, but who are watching for an opportunity of making this flourishing church their prey.† Paul writes as a man who has confidence in his readers, who knows that one and the same faith unites him with them, and who feels he can count on a sane reaction on their part. Not only will they take their stand on received doctrines in order to condemn erroneous teaching, but they will avoid the presence of these fomenters of dissensions and scandals.‡ He does not say that they should be driven out, but that they should be prevented from exercising their injurious influence. The "holiness" of the people of God has always required a certain rigour of government, and corporate discipline. One cannot afford to play with fire nor tamper with deadly poisons.

Who are these people?§ Paul does not define them clearly by saying that instead of serving Christ they serve their own appetites.|| This very brief note could designate both judaizers and gnostics; the former would be sarcastically stigmatized as servants of their stomachs, of which their stupid food laws oblige them to be constantly thinking.¶ The latter would be appropriately condemned as libertines enslaved to the delights of the flesh. Moreover these same people skilfully use their gift of eloquence to attract simple

* D G it write even ἀσφαλῶς σκοπεῖτε.

† We cannot equate the persons alluded to in these verses with the weak of chapters 14 and 15.

‡ Cf. 2 Th. 3: 6; Tit. 3: 10; Matt. 18: 17.

§ Τοιοῦτοι: people of this kind. . . .

|| Cf. Phil. 3: 19.

¶ This is an ancient exegesis (Theod. Mops., Ambr. Pel.: cf. Behm, Th.Wb.NT, III, p. 788). Origen sees in κοιλία the seat of cupidity: Michel makes it synonymous with σάρξ (cf. Phil. 3: 19). Citing the Assumption of Moses (7: 4–7) Lagrange considers these Judeo-Christian agitators to be avaricious people who amass money in order to enjoy it comfortably later. Not epicureans, but self-interested people (Sanday and Headlam).

and inexperienced minds who do not suspect the evil of doctrines which they no doubt interpret too favourably and generously.

(19) This is no doubt the reason for the severity of Paul's warning to the Romans: Christianity holds the church at Rome in great esteem* and the apostle rejoices in the realization of its fundamental sanity of outlook (cf. ὑπακοή). It owed both to itself and to other churches the duty of removing the contamination of these authors of erroneous doctrines so that it may abide in the obedience of the faith (cf. 1:5; 15:18; 16:26). He hopes that it will prove its wisdom in seeking what is good, i.e. what is in conformity with the will of God in Christ, and that it will remain impervious to all pernicious influences.†

(20) To conclude, Paul makes a solemn declaration of prophetic character which he is convinced will be fulfilled: for the prophet does not speak in vain. Soon,‡ he says, God, who is the God of peace (that is, of good order) will crush Satan under their feet, for Satan is indeed the source of all the dangers against which the church needs to be warned. The allusion to Gen. 3:15 is obvious. Paul is certainly making use at this point of an apocalyptic tradition (Test. Levi 18:12).§ The normal concluding formula is here found before the greetings of Paul's companions; this unexpected situation has led some copyists to place it after v. 23 (D G it) even after v. 27 (*Peshitta*).

In passing, let us note that these exhortations to remain

* The esteem due to the good reputation of the Roman church, widely enjoyed (1:8), is not the same thing as the veneration which people claim to be able to detect in the apostle's attitude to a church occupying an eminent position, and already wielding a singular fascination and an almost exceptional authority (cf. also the introduction).

† Σοφοί-ἀκέραιοι recalls φρόνιμοι-ἀκέραιοι of Matt. 10:16. Michel thinks it likely that Paul is here in touch with a tradition going back to Jesus.

‡ The victory is in sight; but it is not an allusion to the *parousia*.

§ In making these remarks, Michel emphasizes that Paul shows himself to be less hellenized than has sometimes been thought, and much more penetrated with the essence of the traditions of Palestinian Judaism. The whole letter confirms this observation.

386

faithful to the traditional confession (v. 17) in the fight against the contingency of heresy make no allusion whatever to any help which might be forthcoming from the special privileges imparted to the apostle Peter, who is nowhere named either as the founder or as the head of the Church of Rome.

(21–23) In the style of a postscript Paul adds greetings from his companions. Timothy is the first named. On other occasions Paul mentions him in the opening address;* the situation here seems to imply that Timothy has joined Paul after the composition of the letter. Lucius is a Roman name (cf. Acts 13: 1); Jason and Sosipater are Greek names.† It may be conjectured that the two latter have joined Paul to take him the gifts from the churches of Macedonia. They are Jews (συγγενεῖς, unless this word is meant to suggest that they are kinsmen of the apostle; cf. 16: 7). Tertius, who acts as a secretary to Paul, personally adds his greetings, contrary to what is usual, and for a reason which escapes us: was he known to the Romans? is he somewhat proud (legitimately?) to have been associated with the composition of so long and important a letter? Let us note the unexpected detail that he has written this letter "in the Lord"; what exactly did he mean by that? Gaius, certainly the one named in 1 Cor. 1: 14, who showed generous hospitality to Paul and the whole church at Corinth by receiving the church assemblies and offering shelter and food to Christians who were passing through. Erastus, the town treasurer,‡ who will not be confused with Paul's companion (Acts 19: 22; 2 Tim. 4: 20). Of Quartus we know nothing.

²⁵Now to him who is able to strengthen you according to my gospel and the preaching of Jesus Christ, according to the revelation of the mystery which was kept secret for long ages ²⁶but is now disclosed and through the prophetic writings is made known to all nations, according to the command of the eternal God, to bring about obedience to the faith—²⁷to the only wise God be glory for evermore through Jesus Christ! Amen.

* 2 Cor. 1: 1; Phil. 1: 1; Col. 1: 1; 1 Th. 1: 1; 2 Th. 1: 1: Philemon 1.
† Cf. Acts 17: 5, 7, 9; 20: 4.
‡ Οἰκονόμος; district treasurer.

387

(25–27) The final doxology has a beautiful solemnity. It confirms the message of the whole letter by summing it up in a liturgical form. Recurring to the idea of ch. 1: 11 the apostle* praises God because He is able to strengthen the Romans in their faith, both by causing them to advance in the knowledge of the truth and by enabling them to avoid errors which would undermine that faith; a purpose which Paul himself has striven to realize in the writing of the letter he now concludes. In fact it is to the message which this letter contains that Paul is alluding when he speaks of his gospel; an expression which certainly denotes his teaching, but not his preaching in Rome itself since he has not yet been there. And if he adds to the mention of his gospel the phrase "the preaching of Jesus Christ" it is to remind his readers that his gospel is nothing other than the preaching of Jesus Christ as he interprets this, with the characteristic emphasis required by his special task as apostle to the Gentiles. The special theme of the Pauline gospel, the proclamation of the good news to the Gentile world, is already implied in the faith in Jesus as Messiah.

But the apostle feels the need of a more complete expression of his thought. The good news which he has just expounded to the Romans presupposes a general understanding of the development of history, such as would permit the Roman Christians to understand the character of the present time and its special significance in the story of God's dealings with men. The gospel which Paul proclaims is a "revelation of the mystery" which up to now has been hidden. The "mystery" means the plan of God (cf. Col. 1: 25–29; Eph. 3: 9–10) which the gospel discloses by presenting Jesus Christ as the centre and justification of human history from the point of view of the Jews as well as that of the Gentiles.† Hitherto‡ God has maintained silence concerning His plan, but now He has spoken through His Son whose word it is the apostle's mission to proclaim, that the gospel may come to full fruition (Col. 1: 25).

* If Paul is the author of this doxology. On the problems raised by these vv., cf. the introduction.

† Cf. 1 Cor. 2: 6, 7, 10; Eph. 3: 5, 6; Tit. 1: 2, 3; 2 Tim. 1: 9, 10.

‡ Χρόνοις αἰωνίοις may mean "eternal ages", the eternity of God, or the time which lapsed until the coming of revelation.

The νῦν, now, of v. 25 should be heard in its full resonance; it expresses the eschatological character of the present moment, a drama in which the action of God is embodied in man's history in order that he may be directed towards his true end. As the apostle has emphasized at great length, both the law and the prophets have prophetically foreshadowed the plan of God now realized in Jesus Christ (ch. 1: 1–2; 3: 21; 9 to 11 and the argument of ch. 4 on the faith of Abraham). Thus, after the disclosure of the mystery in Jesus Christ, God has willed that preachers of the gospel of His Son, on the basis of the prophetic and preparatory witness of the scriptures, should make known to the pagan world this Saviour. The *motif* of the opening reappears at the close (1: 5). Paul indirectly refers to his own ministry which has been specially dedicated to the task of bringing pagans into the obedience of faith, and thus shows it to be an integral moment in the unfolding of the divine plans which are now disclosed to believers.*

God is wise in that He has conceived a plan appropriate to His eternal will (the "mystery") and inasmuch as He fulfils it perfectly in Jesus Christ and the institution of the preaching of the gospel to the Gentiles. The two terms μόνῳ and σοφῷ may be understood in separation (to the one God and the wise God) or conjointly (the only wise God). The relative ᾧ should be related not to Jesus Christ but to God, according to the normal style of doxologies which are always addressed to God.† In any case the sentence remains somewhat broken though the underlying anacolouthon is softened.‡

* On Θεὸς αἰώνιος cf. Michel, p. 354, n. 2. "As a predicate of God, αἰώνιος implies not only the idea of limitless time, without beginning or end, but also the idea of an eternity which transcends time" (Sasse, *Th.Wb.NT*, I, p. 208).

† Ὅι is not found in B pesh., no doubt in order to facilitate the reading. Unless we think that these MSS. have the right reading, and admit that Tertius the secretary added the pronoun from habit, which is a plausible supposition, for it is found again in several doxologies, Gal. 1: 5; 2 Tim. 4: 18; Hebr. 13: 21. Other considerations in Sanday and Headlam and J. Dupont, *ΜΟΝΩΙ ΣΟΦΩΙ ΘΕΩΙ* (Rom. 16: 27), 1946, and "Pour l'histoire de la doxologie finale de l'Épître aux Romains", *Revue bénédictine*, 1948.

‡ P 46 B C L etc. omit τῶν αἰώνων, perhaps in accordance with 11: 36.

389